ZAGAT
2014

America's Top Restaurants

EDITOR
Josh Rogers

Published and distributed by
Zagat Survey, LLC
76 Ninth Avenue
New York, NY 10011
E: feedback@zagat.com
www.zagat.com

ACKNOWLEDGMENTS

We're grateful to our local editors, Claudia Alarcon, Alicia Arter, Olga Boikess, Nikki Buchanan, Chris Chamberlain, Suzi Forbes Chase, Bill Citara, Jeanette Foster, Mary Ann Castronovo Fusco, Rona Gindin, Meesha Halm, Lynn Hazlewood, Valerie Jarvie, Elizabeth Keyser, Michael Klein, Rochelle Koff, Naomi Kooker, Gretchen Kurz, Mary Sue Lawrence, Sharon Litwin, Lori Midson, David Nelson, Jan Norris, Laura Reiley, Mike Riccetti, Heidi Knapp Rinella, Julia Rosenfeld, Shelley Skiles Sawyer, Helen Schwab, Merrill Shindler, Kelly Stewart, Pat Tanner, Martha Thomas, John Turiano, Alice Van Housen and Carla Waldemar. We also sincerely thank the thousands of people who participated in this survey – this guide is really "theirs."

We also thank the following members of our staff: Danielle Borovoy (editor), Aynsley Karps (editor), Brian Albert, Sean Beachell, Maryanne Bertollo, Reni Chin, Larry Cohn, Bill Corsello, John Deiner, Nicole Diaz, Carol Diuguid, Kelly Dobkin, Jeff Freier, Alison Gainor, Curt Gathje, Michelle Golden, Randi Gollin, Justin Hartung, Marc Henson, Anna Hyclak, Ryutaro Ishikane, Cynthia Kilian, Mike Liao, Vivian Ma, Caitlin Miehl, Molly Moker, James Mulcahy, Polina Paley, Emil Ross, Emily Rothschild, Josh Siegel, Albry Smither, Amanda Spurlock, Chris Walsh, Jacqueline Wasilczyk, Art Yagci, Yoji Yamaguchi, Sharon Yates, Anna Zappia and Kyle Zolner.

ABOUT ZAGAT

In 1979, we asked friends to rate and review restaurants purely for fun. The term "user-generated content" had yet to be coined. That hobby grew into Zagat Survey; 35 years later, we have loyal surveyors around the globe and our content now includes nightlife, shopping, tourist attractions, golf and more. Along the way, we evolved from being a print publisher to a digital content provider. We also produce marketing tools for a wide range of corporate clients, and you can find us on Google+ and just about any other social media network.

The reviews in this guide are based on public opinion surveys. The ratings reflect the average scores given by the survey participants who voted on each establishment, while the text is based on quotes from, or paraphrasings of, the surveyors' comments. Phone numbers, addresses and other factual data were correct to the best of our knowledge when published in this guide.

JOIN IN

To improve our guides, we solicit your comments – positive or negative; it's vital that we hear your opinions. Just contact us at **nina-tim@zagat.com.**

Contents

Ratings & Symbols

Name | **Symbols** | **Cuisine** | **Zagat Ratings**

FOOD | DECOR | SERVICE | COST

Area, Address & Contact

Tim & Nina's ◑ *American*

Chelsea | 76 Ninth Ave. (bet. 15th & 16th Sts.) | 212-977-6000 | www.zagat.com

▽ 23 | 9 | 13 | $15

Review, surveyor comments in quotes

"T&N take sustainability to exciting new heights" at their "tasty", "costly" Chelsea rooftop New American where "they grow all the produce" and "raise chickens too"; but respondents wonder "why is the staff so sanctimonious?" – and "couldn't they have covered up the air-conditioning units?"

Ratings

Food, Decor & **Service** are rated on a 30-point scale.

26 – 30 extraordinary to perfection

21 – 25 very good to excellent

16 – 20 good to very good

11 – 15 fair to good

0 – 10 poor to fair

▽ low response | less reliable

Cost

The price of dinner with a drink and tip; lunch is usually 25% to 30% less. For unrated **newcomers,** the price range is as follows:

I $25 and below

E $41 to $65

M $26 to $40

VE $66 or above

Symbols

◑ serves after 11 PM

Ⓢ closed on Sunday

Ⓜ closed on Monday

⊘ cash only

About This Survey

TOP FOOD SAMPLER: Le Bernardin (New York), **Asanebo** (Los Angeles), **Gary Danko** (San Francisco), **Katsu** (Chicago), **Neptune Oyster** (Boston), **Rasika** (Washington, DC)

SURVEY STATS:

- 1,478 restaurants covered
- Over 224,000 surveyors
- In our recent National Dining Trends Survey, respondents reported eating 2.3 dinners out per week, spending an average of $40.53 per person. New Yorkers spend the most ($48.56), while Dallas/Ft. Worth diners spend the least ($31.87).
- The reported average tip is 19%. San Franciscans leave the least (18.4%), while the Denver area is home to the biggest tippers (19.6%).
- When presented with a list of dining irritants, surveyors chose noise as the most annoying, with 73% saying they avoid restaurants that are too loud.
- Fifty-two percent of surveyors typically make reservations online, and 48% won't wait longer than 30 minutes at places that don't take reservations.
- Fifty-six percent say that taking photos of food in a restaurant is ok in moderation. And most are not opposed to children using tablets and mobile devices in restaurants (46% say ok in moderation; 19% find it perfectly acceptable). However, 57% say it's rude and inappropriate to text, e-mail, tweet or talk on mobile phones at the table.

BIG NAMES: Star chefs and restaurateurs continue to expand empires. Witness Marc Forgione's **American Cut** (Atlantic City), Rich Torrisi and Mario Carbone's **Carbone** (NYC), Michael Chiarello's **Coqueta** (San Francisco), Kevin Rathbun's **KR SteakBar** (Atlanta), Stephen Starr's **Serpico** (Philadelphia), Stephan Pyles' **Stampede 66** (Dallas) and Ludo Lefebvre, Jon Shook and Vinny Dotolo's **Trois Mec** (LA).

CAMPFIRE SCENT: Wood-grilled food is smoking hot at **CopperFish** (Tampa/Sarasota), **Hinoki & The Bird** (LA), **Husk Nasville** (a new outpost of the Charleston original), **Ox** (Portland, OR), **The Whale Wins** (Seattle) and **Woodshed Smokehouse** (Dallas/Ft. Worth).

SOURCE MATERIAL: The farm-to-table movement is still growing, with local food coming from a variety of sources such as a kitchen garden (Long Island's **Topping Rose House**); a chef-owned farm (Baltimore's **Fleet Street Kitchen**); foraging (Chicago's **Elizabeth**); and sustainable catch (Connecticut's **The Whelk**).

DOWN THE HATCH: Mixology is a key ingredient at many newcomers, like **Grace** (Chicago), **The Optimist** (Atlanta), **The Populist** (Denver), **Range** (Washington, DC) and **Rolf & Daughters** (Nashville). Places that specialize in a particular spirit include Houston's **Latin Bites Cafe** (pisco); Denver's **Uncle** (sake); LA's **Bar Amá** (tequila); and Seattle's **Radiator Whiskey** (whiskey, of course).

New York, NY
October 14, 2013

Nina and Tim

Nina and Tim Zagat

Top Food Rankings by Area

ATLANTA

29 Bacchanalia
28 Antico Pizza
Aria
Bone's Restaurant
Valenza

ATLANTIC CITY

27 Chef Vola's
26 Amada
Old Homestead
25 Buddakan
Il Mulino New York

AUSTIN & HILL COUNTRY

29 Uchi
Louie Mueller BBQ
28 Barley Swine
Snow's BBQ
Carillon
Franklin Barbecue*

BALTIMORE/ANNAPOLIS

29 Charleston
28 Di Pasquale's
Samos
Vin 909
Bartlett Pear Inn

BOSTON

28 Neptune Oyster
Island Creek Oyster
Oleana
Craigie on Main
Lumière

CHARLESTON

29 Peninsula Grill
Bertha's Kitchen
28 Dell'z Deli
Langdon's
Two Boroughs Larder

CHARLOTTE

28 McNinch House
Barrington's
27 Fig Tree
Fiamma
Passion8 Bistro

CHICAGO

29 Katsu Japanese
Next
Alinea
28 Ruxbin
Schwa
EL Ideas
Les Nomades
Riccardo Trattoria
Topolobampo
Takashi

CONNECTICUT

28 Le Petit Cafe
Thomas Henkelmann
Golden Lamb Buttery
Altnaveigh
27 Mill at 2T

DALLAS/FT. WORTH

29 Saint-Emilion
Lucia
28 French Room
Bijoux
Pappas Bros. Steakhouse

DENVER AREA

29 Carlos' Bistro
Junz
Splendido at the Chateau
28 Penrose Room
Fruition

FT. LAUDERDALE

28 La Brochette
27 Canyon
Casa D'Angelo
Eduardo de San Angel
Valentino's

HONOLULU

29 La Mer
Mitch's Sushi Restaurant
28 Alan Wong's
Sushi Sasabune
27 Chef Mavro

HOUSTON

29 Da Marco
28 Chez Nous
Mark's American Cuisine
Pappas Bros. Steakhouse
27 Nino's

---

* Indicates a tie with restaurant above

Visit zagat.com

LAS VEGAS

29 Joël Robuchon
Michael's
28 L'Atelier de Joël Robuchon
Raku
Picasso

LONG ISLAND

28 North Fork Table & Inn
27 Onsen Sushi
Stone Creek Inn
Lake House
Mosaic

LOS ANGELES

29 Asanebo
28 Sushi Zo
Hamasaku
Mélisse
Matsuhisa
Providence
Angelini Osteria
Urasawa
27 Gjelina Take Away
Michael's on Naples

MIAMI

29 Naoe
28 Palme d'Or
Zuma
Palm
27 Il Gabbiano

MINNEAPOLIS/ST. PAUL

29 Travail
Alma
La Belle Vie
28 Lake Elmo Inn
Lucia's

NASHVILLE

28 Etch Restaurant
Mitchell Delicatessen
Miel
Margot Cafe & Bar
Silly Goose*

NEW JERSEY

28 Nicholas
Lorena's
27 CulinAriane
De Lorenzo's Tomato Pies
Shumi

NEW ORLEANS

28 Cochon Butcher
Clancy's
La Provence
Brigtsen's
GW Fins

NEW YORK CITY

29 Le Bernardin
Bouley
28 Per Se
Daniel
Eleven Madison
Jean Georges
Sasabune
Sushi Yasuda
La Grenouille
Gramercy Tavern

ORANGE COUNTY

29 Bluefin
Marché Moderne
28 Basilic
Blake's Place
Gabbi's Mexican

ORLANDO

29 Cress
Victoria & Albert's
28 Nagoya Sushi
Chatham's Place
Norman's*

PALM BEACH

28 Marcello's La Sirena
Chez Jean-Pierre
27 11 Maple Street
Captain Charlie's
Café L'Europe

PHILADELPHIA

29 Fountain
Vetri
Birchrunville Store
Bibou
28 Sycamore

PHOENIX/SCOTTSDALE

29 Binkley's
Kai
28 Pane Bianco
Mastro's City Hall Steakhouse
Dick's Hideaway

PORTLAND

- 29 Painted Lady
- 28 Le Pigeon
- Genoa
- Evoe
- Cabezon

SAN ANTONIO

- 28 Bistro Vatel
- 27 Sorrento
- Bohanan's
- Dough
- Silo

SAN DIEGO

- 29 Sushi Ota
- 28 Tao
- Market Restaurant
- Tapenade
- 27 Pamplemousse

SAN FRANCISCO AREA

- 29 Gary Danko
- 28 Erna's Elderberry
- French Laundry
- Sierra Mar
- Acquerello
- Cafe Gibraltar
- Kiss Seafood
- Evvia
- Kokkari Estiatorio
- 27 Chez Panisse

SEATTLE

- 29 Nishino
- Staple & Fancy Mercantile*
- Il Terrazzo Carmine
- 28 Herbfarm
- Paseo

TAMPA/SARASOTA

- 29 Beach Bistro
- 28 Restaurant BT
- 27 Cafe Ponte
- Maison Blanche
- SideBern's

WASHINGTON, DC, METRO

- 28 Rasika
- L'Auberge Chez François
- Komi
- Marcel's
- Prime Rib

WESTCHESTER/ HUDSON VALLEY

- 28 Sushi Nanase
- Xaviars at Piermont
- Il Cenàcolo
- Freelance Cafe & Wine Bar
- 27 Restaurant X & Bully Boy Bar

Most Popular by Area

ATLANTA
1. Bacchanalia
2. Bone's Restaurant
3. Antico Pizza
4. Canoe
5. Atlanta Fish Market

ATLANTIC CITY
1. Chef Vola's
2. Bobby Flay Steak
3. Buddakan
4. Angelo's Fairmount Tavern
5. Old Homestead

AUSTIN & HILL COUNTRY
1. Eddie V's
2. Uchi*
3. Salt Lick
4. Uchiko
5. Wink

BALTIMORE/ANNAPOLIS
1. Woodberry Kitchen
2. Double T Diner
3. Prime Rib
4. Charleston
5. G&M

BOSTON
1. Abe & Louie's
2. Border Cafe
3. Chateau
4. 224 Boston Street
5. L'Espalier

CHARLESTON
1. Charleston Grill
2. FIG
3. 82 Queen
4. Peninsula Grill
5. 39 Rue de Jean

CHARLOTTE
1. Barrington's
2. Del Frisco's
3. Good Food on Montford
4. Cowfish
5. Carpe Diem

CHICAGO
1. Alinea
2. Gibsons
3. Frontera Grill
4. Girl & The Goat
5. Topolobampo*

CONNECTICUT
1. Frank Pepe
2. Barcelona Restaurant
3. Tarry Lodge
4. Plan B Burger Bar
5. Morton's

DALLAS/FT. WORTH
1. Abacus
2. Fearing's
3. Al Biernat's
4. Stephan Pyles
5. Del Frisco's

DENVER AREA
1. Beau Jo's
2. Rio Grande
3. Elway's
4. 240 Union
5. Snooze

FT. LAUDERDALE
1. Blue Moon
2. Casa D'Angelo
3. Greek Islands
4. Anthony's
5. Bonefish Grill*

HONOLULU
1. Alan Wong's
2. Assaggio
3. Big City Diner
4. Sansei
5. 3660 on the Rise

HOUSTON
1. Da Marco
2. Brennan's
3. Mark's American Cuisine
4. Carrabba's
5. Pappas Bros. Steakhouse

LAS VEGAS
1. Bouchon
2. Feast Buffet
3. Mon Ami Gabi
4. Joe's Stone Crab
5. Aureole

LONG ISLAND
1. Peter Luger Steak House
2. 1 North Steak House
3. Besito
4. Kotobuki
5. 1770 House Restaurant

LOS ANGELES

1. Sugarfish
2. Angelini Osteria
3. Mélisse
4. Bazaar by José Andrés
5. Spago

MIAMI

1. Joe's Stone Crab
2. Michael's Genuine
3. Prime One Twelve
4. Michy's
5. Il Gabbiano

MINNEAPOLIS/ST. PAUL

1. 5-8 Club
2. Big Bowl
3. Kincaid's
4. Axel's
5. Doolittle's

NASHVILLE

1. Amerigo
2. Loveless Cafe
3. Pancake Pantry
4. Blackstone Restaurant
5. Puckett's Grocery

NEW JERSEY

1. Nicholas
2. Ninety Acres at Natirar
3. CulinAriane
4. Amanda's
5. Cafe Panache

NEW ORLEANS

1. Commander's Palace
2. Acme Oyster House
3. Café Du Monde
4. Galatoire's
5. August

NEW YORK CITY

1. Le Bernardin
2. Gramercy Tavern
3. Peter Luger
4. Daniel
5. Bouley

ORANGE COUNTY

1. Marché Moderne
2. Anaheim White House
3. 21 Oceanfront
4. 3-Thirty-3 Waterfront
5. 230 Forest Avenue

ORLANDO

1. Bahama Breeze
2. 4 Rivers Smokehouse
3. Cheesecake Factory
4. Seasons 52
5. Charley's

PALM BEACH

1. Café Boulud
2. Abe & Louie's
3. Kee Grill
4. Seasons 52
5. Bonefish Grill

PHILADELPHIA

1. Buddakan
2. Amada
3. Iron Hill Brewery
4. Zahav
5. Vetri

PHOENIX/SCOTTSDALE

1. P.F. Chang's
2. Fleming's Prime
3. Grimaldi's Pizzeria
4. Chompie's
5. Capital Grille

PORTLAND

1. Gustav's
2. Andina
3. Flying Pie
4. Higgins
5. Jake's Famous Crawfish

SAN ANTONIO

1. Biga on the Banks
2. Boudro's
3. Bohanan's
4. Dough
5. Rudy's

SAN DIEGO

1. Anthony's Fish
2. Brigantine Seafood
3. Phil's BBQ
4. George's Cal. Modern/Ocean
5. 94th Aero Squadron

SAN FRANCISCO AREA

1. Gary Danko
2. Kokkari Estiatorio
3. Boulevard
4. French Laundry
5. Slanted Door

SEATTLE

1. 13 Coins
2. Dick's Drive-In
3. Canlis
4. Wild Ginger
5. Blue C Sushi

TAMPA/SARASOTA

1. Bern's Steak House
2. Beach Bistro
3. Michael's On East
4. Columbia
5. Euphemia Haye

WASHINGTON, DC, METRO

1. Clyde's
2. 2 Amy's
3. Zaytinya
4. Rasika
5. 1789

WESTCHESTER/ HUDSON VALLEY

1. X2O Xaviars on the Hudson
2. Blue Hill at Stone Barns
3. Crabtree's Kittle House
4. Tarry Lodge
5. Xaviars at Piermont

RESTAURANT DIRECTORY

Atlanta

Antico Pizza ⊠ *Pizza* | 28 | 17 | 19 | $19 |
Westside | 1093 Hemphill Ave. (Northside Dr.) | 404-724-2333 | www.anticoatl.com

"Real-deal" ovens and "genuine Italian ingredients" make for "other-worldly" pizzas at this "family-run" Westside joint near Georgia Tech, where "heavenly" Neapolitan pies with "perfect crusts" have earned a "cult following"; "blaring" acoustics, "limited" communal seating and "hectic" weekend scenes come with the territory, but in return there's "opera on the speakers", "soccer on the telly" and a money-saving BYO policy.

Aria ⊠ *American* | 28 | 26 | 26 | $60 |
Buckhead | 490 E. Paces Ferry Rd. NE (Maple Dr.) | 404-233-7673 | www.aria-atl.com

Dubbed *the* place for "special occasions", this "longtime favorite" in Buckhead via chef-owner Gerry Klaskala "continues to impress" with "masterful" New American fare abetted by a "phenomenal wine list" and "Kathryn King's fabulous desserts"; the "elegant", "contemporary art"–adorned digs work for both "business" and "romance" and service is "attentive", so the "expensive" tabs are deemed "worth the money", given the overall "impeccable" experience; P.S. there's a tiny "table in the wine cellar" that doubles as a "den of iniquity."

Atlanta Fish Market *Seafood* | 24 | 21 | 23 | $41 |
Buckhead | 265 Pharr Rd. NE (bet. Fulton Dr. & Peachtree Rd.) | 404-262-3165 | www.buckheadrestaurants.com

The "only thing missing is the ocean view" at this "steady" Buckhead seafood "mecca" that offers "anything that swims" – "except Michael Phelps" – and serves it, "still flapping", in a lofty setting with a "bus-tling", "big-city" feel; "loud" decibels, "long waits" and "crowded" conditions are par for the course, but the pricing is "decent", the service "tight" and the specials "truly special."

Babette's Cafe Ⓜ *European* | 26 | 22 | 25 | $39 |
Poncey-Highland | 573 N. Highland Ave. (Freedom Pkwy.) | 404-523-9121 | www.babettescafe.com

Chef-owner Marla Adams "continues to please" at this "unassuming bistro" in Poncey-Highland, where the "labor-of-love" European cooking shows "attention to detail" and is a match for the "quaint" setting; a "dedicated local following" touts the "easygoing" mood, "charming back porch" and "valet parking", while "reasonable pricing" makes it a "best value" for "food of this caliber."

Bacchanalia ⊠ *American* | 29 | 26 | 28 | $111 |
Westside | Westside Mktpl. | 1198 Howell Mill Rd. NW (Huff Rd.) | 404-365-0410 | www.starprovisions.com

Holding fast as the "pinnacle of refined dining" (voted No. 1 for Food and Popularity in Atlanta), this near-"flawless" Westside New American "keeps it fresh year after year" with "absolutely outstanding" fare, served in a five-course, prix fixe menu that can be paired with an "impeccable" wine list for a "feast befitting its name"; the "well-trained" staff works with "panache", the setting is done up in "chic retro-industrial" style and there's a definite "sense of occasion" in the air, leaving the "extraordinary" cost as the only sticking point;

P.S. à la carte ordering is available at the bar and allowed, if not en-couraged, in the dining room.

Bishoku ⓈⓂ *Japanese*   26 | 21 | 24 | $33

Sandy Springs | Parkside Shopping Ctr. | 5920 Roswell Rd. (I-285) | 404-252-7998 | www.bishokusushi.com
Purists rate this "authentic Japanese" in Sandy Springs as one of "Atlanta's best-kept secrets", thanks to "super-fresh" sushi, "inno-vative" small plates and "gracious" owner Jackie Fukuya-Merkel, who "makes you feel like a member of the family"; "beautiful" de-cor and "cozy" vibrations embellish its "intimate" appeal, and help explain why it's "often busy" – "not what you'd expect in a half-empty strip mall in suburbia."

BLT Steak *Steak*   26 | 23 | 23 | $62

Downtown | W Atlanta-Downtown | 45 Ivan Allen Jr. Blvd. NW (Spring St.) | 404-577-7601 | www.bltsteak.com
In a city with "a lot of great steakhouses", this "NYC transplant" in Downtown's W Hotel stands out for its "fantastic" chops and "to-die-for" popovers that are "worthy of a visit alone"; despite "noisy" acoustics and "not-cheap" tabs suited for the "expense-account" crowd, payoffs include "classy" quarters, a "trendy" mood and "on-top-of-everything" service – when it comes to "splurge" dining, this one's pretty "unforgettable."

Bone's Restaurant *Steak*   28 | 24 | 28 | $66

Buckhead | 3130 Piedmont Rd. NE (Peachtree Rd.) | 404-237-2663 | www.bonesrestaurant.com
"Hobnob" with the "who's who" of Buckhead at this "old-school" "ca-thedral of steak" renowned for "phenomenal" chops "cooked to per-fection" and served by a team so "stellar" that it's been voted No. 1 for Service in Atlanta; "manly", "power-broker" decor, a "private-club" feel and an "epic wine list" ("presented on an iPad", no less) make the "platinum-card" prices easier to digest.

Cakes & Ale ⓈⓂ *American*   27 | 23 | 26 | $42

Decatur | Decatur Square | 155 Sycamore St. (Church St.) | 404-377-7994
Cafe at Cakes & Ale ⓈⓂ *Bakery*
Decatur | Decatur Square | 151 Sycamore St. (Church St.) | 404-377-7960 www.cakesandalerestaurant.com
Occupying a "comfortable", airy space in a historic Decatur Square building, this "assured" American "celebration" spot via "virtuoso" chef Billy Allin features "imaginatively prepared", "farm-fresh" dishes composed from "seasonal ingredients" and served by a staff versed in "attention to detail"; a "fab" adjacent bakery stocked with "tasty treats" makes the scene even more "happening", so be prepared for "a little noise" along with a true "community feel."

Canoe *American*   27 | 27 | 27 | $50

Vinings | Vinings on the River | 4199 Paces Ferry Rd. SE (Woodland Brook Dr.) | 770-432-2663 | www.canoeatl.com
"Beautiful scenery" meets "exceptional" food at this Vinings "superstar", nestled in a "picturesque" setting overlooking the Chattahoochee River with "breathtaking gardens" that are a "gorgeous complement" to the "farm-to-table" New American cooking of "brilliant" chef Carvel

Grant Gould; "seamless" service and a "romantic" ambiance enhance the overall "sensational experience" that's so "well above the watermark", it's "easy to overlook" the "upscale" pricing.

Chops Lobster Bar *Seafood/Steak*   27 | 25 | 27 | $66

Buckhead | Buckhead Plaza | 70 W. Paces Ferry Rd. (Peachtree Rd.) | 404-262-2675 | www.buckheadrestaurants.com

"Still thriving after all these years", this "powerhouse" Buckhead Life Group surf 'n' turfer is "always packed" with "socialites", "businessmen" and "good ol' boys" with a hankering for "delectable" "man food" served by a "congenial", "old-school" team; upstairs, "dark wood and red leather" lend a "corporate-boardroom" feel, while downstairs, the tiled arched ceilings recall "Grand Central Station's Oyster Bar", but wherever you sit you can expect a "loud", "happening" scene and "wildly expensive" tabs.

di Paolo Ⓜ *Italian*   27 | 21 | 25 | $42

Alpharetta | Rivermont Sq. | 8560 Holcomb Bridge Rd. (Nesbit Ferry Rd.) | 770-587-1051 | www.dipaolorestaurant.com

"Wow" is the word for this Alpharetta Northern Italian via chef Darin Hiebel, whose "excellent" cooking is so "superb" it's the kind of "food you'd expect to get in Buckhead" (the menu "changes with the season" and even includes "half portions for lighter eaters"); an "intimate" setting, "outstanding wine list" and "helpful", "first-name-basis" service offset the "high noise levels" and "depressing" strip-mall location.

Ecco *European*   26 | 25 | 25 | $42

Midtown | 40 Seventh St. NE (Cypress St.) | 404-347-9555 | www.ecco-atlanta.com

"Gorgeous patrons" frequent this "lively" Midtown European "crowd-pleaser" where the "modern", "ever-changing menu" includes "stunning small plates", "excellent" charcuterie and "higher-end entrees", all served in "beautiful", "fashionable" environs; granted, it's "not cheap" and some find it "more trendy than substantive", but the "good buzz" and staffers showing "pride in what they are doing" lead fans to say this one only "gets better with age."

Flip Burger Boutique *Burgers*   23 | 21 | 19 | $22

Westside | 1587 Howell Mill Rd. (Chattahoochee Ave.) | 404-352-3547
Buckhead | 3655 Roswell Rd. NE (Piedmont Ave.) | 404-549-3298
www.flipburgerboutique.com

Explore the "new burger frontier" at these "trendy" twins via *Top Chef* winner Richard Blais, who thinks "outside the bun" with "flippin' great", "nontraditional" patties washed down with "smoking milkshakes" made with liquid nitrogen; devotees don't mind the "lines out the door" or "bumping elbows" at communal tables in the "witty", ultra-"modern" digs, but the "overly loud music" and "lackluster service" are another story.

Floataway Cafe Ⓢ Ⓜ *American*   26 | 24 | 25 | $48

Emory | Floataway Bldg. | 1123 Zonolite Rd. NE (bet. Briarcliff & Johnson Rds.) | 404-892-1414 | www.starprovisions.com

"Seasonally" minded types seeking "creative" food paired with "superb wine" cite this "innovative" New American near Emory, a Bacchanalia sibling with "all the flavor of the mother ship" – "without the cost or pretense"; a "knowledgeable staff" oversees the "soothing" contemporary dining room, and though it's in a "funky", "industrial-wasteland" location, many say it's "worth finding" for those with "romance" in mind.

4th & Swift *American*   26 | 24 | 25 | $47

Old Fourth Ward District | 621 North Ave. NE (Glen Iris Dr.) | 678-904-0160 | www.4thandswift.com

Quite the "foodie oasis" in the "up-and-coming" Old Fourth Ward District, this "progressive" New American via chef-owner Jay Swift offers a "seasonal", locally sourced menu paired with "awesome" cocktails that "meet at the corner of creative and delicious"; carved out of a "former dairy space", the "cavernous", "warehouse-chic" setting can be "louder than optimal" and a bit "hard to find", but appropriately "swift" service and "honest-value" pricing compensate; indeed, admirers say it's simply "perfect for every occasion."

Holeman & Finch Public House ● *American* 27 | 23 | 24 | $36

South Buckhead | 2277 Peachtree Rd. NE (Peachtree Memorial Dr.) | 404-948-1175 | www.holeman-finch.com

Ok, it looks like a "packed college bar", but this "cutting-edge" South Buckhead gastropub adjacent to sibling Restaurant Eugene puts forth a "smart", "meat-heavy" American menu built around the "whole-animal concept" (it also offers a "pretty special" burger sold in "limited" quantities after 10 PM and all day Sunday); even though the dimensions are "tight" and the seating "cramped", the scene is "chic" and it "can be as expensive as you want."

Iberian Pig *Spanish*   26 | 24 | 24 | $37

Decatur | 121 Sycamore St. (Church St.) | 404-371-8800 | www.iberianpigatl.com

An "homage to the wonderfulness of pork", this ultra-"popular" Decatur Spaniard serves "everything but the squeal" via "mouthwatering" tapas as well as a slate of "exquisite" non-porcine plates, all washed down with "crazy good" cocktails and a "terrific wine list"; the "dark", "modern industrial" setting has a "lively", "cool vibe", the price is "great" and the hospitality "exceptional", so it's no surprise that this one works for everything from a "romantic" date to a "night with friends."

JCT. Kitchen & Bar *Southern*   25 | 23 | 23 | $35

Westside | Westside Urban Mkt. | 1198 Howell Mill Rd. (Huff Rd.) | 404-355-2252 | www.jctkitchen.com

"Down-home gourmet" cooking is "no contradiction" at chef Ford Fry's "trendy" Southerner on the "hip Westside", where the "updated" eats include "heavenly shrimp and grits" and "delightful 'angry' mussels"; the interior exudes "Zen"-like charm, but when the "dining room volume" is comparable to the "Georgia Dome at kickoff", insiders escape to the "magical upstairs bar" and its view of the skyline; P.S. the Sunday Supper prix fixe is a "fabulous deal."

Kevin Rathbun Steak ⓩ *Steak*   27 | 26 | 26 | $59

Inman Park | 154 Krog St. NE (Lake Ave.) | 404-524-5600 | www.kevinrathbunsteak.com

"King of meat" Kevin Rathbun delivers "definitive" steaks and "modern twists on traditional sides" at this "contemporary" exercise in chophouse "perfection" in Inman Park; service is "unbeatable", the price tags "splurge"-worthy and the "dimly lit", "converted-warehouse" setting has a "cool atmosphere", and overall most feel this one "really exceeds the hype"; P.S. those with "romance" in mind head for the "secluded tables downstairs."

KR SteakBar *Italian/Steak*

| - | - | - | E |

South Buckhead | ADAC West | 349 Peachtree Hills Ave. (Lindbergh Dr.) | 404-841-8820 | www.krsteakbar.com

Superstar Kevin Rathbun (Rathbun's et al.) beefs up his edible empire with this boisterous, upscale South Buckhead retreat boasting Italian small plates and steaks; fans, neighbors and Design District mavens mill about the cozy bar's communal table in the modern wood-centric digs that also feature an open kitchen and curtained semi-private dining.

Kyma *Greek/Seafood*

| 26 | 24 | 25 | $50 |

Buckhead | 3085 Piedmont Rd. NE (Paces Ferry Rd.) | 404-262-0702 | www.buckheadrestaurants.com

"Like a vacation escape", this "haute Greek" seafooder from the Buckhead Life Group offers "classically prepared" fish along with an "extensive selection" of Hellenic wine in a "sophisticated", "white palace"-like setting that's simply "transporting"; granted, the "exorbitant" pricing is "just slightly less than a round-trip ticket to Athens", but in return you get "impeccable" service and "quiet" acoustics – and Sunday's "magnificent meze" specials are an "exceptional value."

La Grotta 🗷 *Italian*

| 26 | 23 | 27 | $56 |

Buckhead | 2637 Peachtree Rd. NE (bet. Lindbergh Dr. & Wesley Rd.) | 404-231-1368

La Grotta Ravinia 🗷 *Italian*

Dunwoody | Crowne Plaza Ravinia Hotel | 4355 Ashford Dunwoody Rd. NE (Hammond Dr.) | 770-395-9925
www.lagrottaatlanta.com

"Sophisticated" and "elegant", this "old-money" Buckhead "tradition" is "still going strong", offering "beautifully prepared" Northern Italian cuisine and "wonderful" wines in a "mature", white-tablecloth setting that's got "special occasion" written all over it (there's also a "transporting" patio "straight out of *Rear Window*"); a "quiet", "relaxing" atmosphere and "read-your-mind" service make the "upscale" tabs easier to digest, while the equally "memorable" OTP Dunwoody satellite is a "welcome independent in a sea of chains."

Local Three *American*

| 25 | 24 | 24 | $39 |

Buckhead | The Forum | 3290 Northside Pkwy. NW (Howell Mill Rd.) | 404-968-2700 | www.localthree.com

"Down-to-earth" despite its location in a luxury Buckhead complex, this "something-different" enterprise via chef Chris Hall and his Muss & Turner's partners "lives up to the hype", purveying an "honest" New American menu with "locavore" leanings paired with "unique cocktails" and a "great" wine list; the "food fits the mood" of the "noisy", "energetic" space with a "warm, witty" design, "handcrafted" wooden furniture and "laid-back" "hipster waiters" – in sum, it's "upscale without uppityness" and, best of all, comes at "un-Buckhead prices."

	FOOD	DECOR	SERVICE	COST

LPC 🅂 Italian
27 | 21 | 25 | $48

(fka La Pietra Cucina)

Midtown | 1 Peachtree Pointe | 1545 NW Peachtree St. (Spring St.) |
404-888-8709 | www.lapietracucina.com

This "super" Midtown trattoria offers a contemporary Italian menu
that includes "outstanding pasta" and "incredible" black spaghetti
with rock shrimp; the "office-building" location on "busy" Peachtree
Pointe can be "difficult to find", but payoffs include "polished" service and an "artistic setting" that's "perfect for pre-theater" or a
"romantic" date; granted, the tabs are decidedly "high-end", but
"worth every penny."

Miller Union 🅂 American
24 | 23 | 24 | $47

Westside | 999 Brady Ave. (10th St.) | 678-733-8550 |
www.millerunion.com

"Hidden away" in an "off-the-beaten-track" Westside address, this
"hip" New American set in a "cool" space lures "farm-fresh" fans
thanks to the "brilliant" work of chef Steven Satterfield, whose
"thoughtful", Southern-accented cooking is highlighted by a "memorable" monthly harvest dinner; "debonair" co-owner Neal McCarthy
oversees the "well-informed" staff, and even though critics cite a
"smug" attitude and "pricey" tabs, most affirm it's "as good as they
say"; P.S. lunchtime ice cream sandwiches enjoy a lot of "hype."

Nan Thai Fine Dining Thai
27 | 28 | 26 | $51

Midtown | 1350 Spring St. NW (17th St.) | 404-870-9933 |
www.nanfinedining.com

"Bring your camera" urge aesthetes "completely impressed" by this
"classy" Midtown Thai, voted No. 1 for Decor, with its "superb interior
design", "awesome bathrooms" and relaxing, "Zen-like ambiance";
the "beautifully presented", "top-drawer" cooking is on par with the
scenery and "gracious service" adds to the "winning formula", but
there are "no deals here", so be prepared for dining that's "quite expensive" for the genre.

New York Prime Steak
26 | 24 | 25 | $62

Buckhead | Monarch Tower | 3424 Peachtree Rd. NE (Lenox Rd.) |
404-846-0644 | www.newyorkprime.com

At this "upscale" Buckhead protein palace, "killer steaks" that you
can "hear across the room, sizzling with butter", are presented by
an "unmatched" team in a white-tablecloth, "dress up"–appropriate
setting; too bad about the "expensive" tabs, cigar "smoking at the
bar" and "loud, NYC-style" acoustics, but at least the scene is "active" and the "people-watching" (think "young girls on the arms of old
businessmen") is choice.

No. 246 Italian
24 | 24 | 23 | $36

Decatur | 129 E. Ponce De Leon Ave. (Church St.) | 678-399-8246 |
www.no246.com

This "hot-spot" collaboration between chefs Ford Fry (JCT. Kitchen)
and Drew Belline (ex Floataway Cafe) "hits high notes" with "inspired"
Italian plates prepared in a wood-fired oven; the "hip" crowd, "feel-at-
home" ambiance and "place-to-be" outdoor patio lead some to label
it "Decatur's first destination restaurant."

The Optimist *Seafood*

| - | - | - | M |

Westside | 914 Howell Mill Rd. (9th St.) | 404-477-6260 |
www.theoptimistrestaurant.com

This Westside seafooder from owner Ford Fry (his JCT. Kitchen & Bar
is just a clam's throw away) baits crowds with a range of raw to
roasted fin fare and beachy cocktails that match the toes-in-the-sand
mood; the lofty space (it's in a former ham-curing factory) charts a
breezy course with nautically inspired trappings, and the moderate
prices won't leave wallets in knots.

Quinones Room at Bacchanalia 🗷🅜 *American*

| 28 | 27 | 29 | $163 |

Westside | Courtyard of Bacchanalia | 1198 Howell Mill Rd. (Huff Rd.) |
404-365-0410 | www.starprovisions.com

"Fine dining at its best" is alive and well at this "super-duper fancy"
Westside sibling of Bacchanalia, where "exquisite", "multicourse"
New American meals backed up with "choreographed", "personalized" service add up to "memory-making experiences"; granted, this
"three-hour event" doesn't come cheap (it's prix fixe only, starting at
$125) and is open Saturday nights only, but when it comes to "over-
the-top" dining, this one's "in a league of its own."

Rathbun's 🗷 *American*

| 27 | 24 | 25 | $51 |

Inman Park | StoveWorks | 112 Krog St. NE (bet. Edgewood Ave. &
Irwin St.) | 404-524-8280 | www.rathbunsrestaurant.com

Chef-owner Kevin Rathbun's flagship property, this "innovative"
Inman Park American is "always spot-on" for "brilliant" dining,
"whether you get a few large plates or a million small ones"; the "cool"
warehouse setting and "outstanding" service lure a "lively" crowd of
"celebrities" and "influential Atlanta natives", and if it gets too "loud",
the patio is a "quieter" alternative; wherever you sit, however, the tabs
are "quite pricey."

Restaurant Eugene *American*

| 27 | 25 | 27 | $66 |

South Buckhead | The Aramore | 2277 Peachtree Rd. NE
(Peachtree Memorial Dr.) | 404-355-0321 |
www.restauranteugene.com

"Everything's just right" at this "spectacular" New American in South
Buckhead, an "adult" exercise in "quiet sophistication" that's touted
for chef Linton Hopkins' "rewarding" farm-to table menu and "superlative wine pairings"; granted, it's "costly" and what's "intimate" to
some is too "staid" for others, but ultimately the "soft lights", "elegant" furnishings and "impeccable" service make for the "most consistent fine dining in Atlanta."

Seed *American*

| - | - | - | M |

Marietta | Merchant's Walk Shopping Ctr. | 1311 Johnson Ferry Rd.
(Roswell Rd.) | 678-214-6888 | www.eatatseed.com

Boosters vie for a seat at this OTP spot from chef-owner Doug Turbush
that brings affordable modern American eats with Asian and Latin accents to Marietta; the sleek, ai3-designed digs include a tucked-away
patio and a bustling bar where carefully cultivated cocktails lure shop-
pers on breaks from Merchant's Walk; P.S. reserve ahead or you may
be sprout of luck.

Sotto Sotto   *Italian*

27 | 22 | 25 | $46

Inman Park | 313 N. Highland Ave. NE (Elizabeth St.) | 404-523-6678 | www.sottosottorestaurant.com

This "heavenly", "intimate" Northern Italian in Inman Park via chef-owner Riccardo Ullio "just gets better with age", dispatching "superb pasta" and "memorable risotto" paired with a "well-thought-out wine list"; "special-occasion" pricing and "tables packed on top of each other" to the contrary, this is the "kind of place you dream about" thanks to its "charming" mien and "precision" service "beyond compare."

Star Provisions 🅂 *Deli*

27 | 20 | 21 | $21

Westside | Westside Mktpl. | 1198 Howell Mill Rd. NW (Huff Rd.) | 404-365-0410 | www.starprovisions.com

Atlanta foodies "can find anything they want" at this Westside "gourmet-to-go" deli (basically sibling "Bacchanalia's grocery store") offering a "spectacular" variety of goodies – think meats, cheeses, baked goods – along with "brilliant lunch fare" that can be consumed on-site at tables scattered throughout; the "mega-rich" price tags "make Whole Foods look like Food Lion", but for such "top-notch" noshing, it's "worth it."

Table & Main 🅼 *Southern*

- | - | - | M

Roswell | 1028 Canton St. (bet. Norcross & Woodstock Sts.) | 678-869-5178 | www.tableandmain.com

In a pristinely restored cottage, chef Ted Lahey lures Roswell residents with grown-up riffs on classic Southern comfort fare (think Velveeta bechamel mac 'n' cheese) washed down with small-batch bourbons; local art adorns the walls, and there's a relaxing patio overlooking the historic district's main drag.

Taka 🅂 *Japanese*

27 | 16 | 23 | $40

Buckhead | 385 Pharr Rd. NE (Grandview Ave.) | 404-869-2802 | www.takasushiatlanta.com

"Real sushi lovers" eschew "trendy" joints in favor of this "tiny" neighborhood Japanese in Buckhead where the eponymous chef's "artful presentation" and "huge flavors" keep things "honest and real", "without the glitz"; adherents ignore the "nondescript" decor and "small" dimensions, and "sit at the bar to get the whole experience."

Tomo 🅂 *Japanese*

▽ 28 | 20 | 23 | $49

Buckhead | 3630 Peachtree Rd. NE (Peachtree Dunwoody Rd.) | 404-835-2708 | www.tomorestaurant.com

"Seriously sensational sushi" from chef-owner Tomohiro Naito is the hallmark of this beloved Japanese in a "luxury" residential building in Buckhead; add in "impeccable" service, a "premium sake" list and "expensive" tabs, and followers say it's "like going to Nobu" but "without the NYC hassles."

Valenza *Italian*

28 | 24 | 25 | $39

Brookhaven | 1441 Dresden Dr. (bet. Appalachee & Camille Drs.) | 404-969-3233 | www.valenzarestaurant.com

Brookhaven diners dig this "delightful" Northern Italian "neighborhood place" where chef Matt Swickerath offers "fine pastas" and other "super-fresh" food in "large portions" paired with a "well-chosen" wine list; "prompt" service, "value" pricing and a "familial" setting with Venetian plastered walls add to the overall "pleasant" experience.

Woodfire Grill ☒Ⓜ *American*

| 27 | 22 | 26 | $58 |

Cheshire Bridge | 1782 Cheshire Bridge Rd. (Piedmont Rd.) | 404-347-9055 | www.woodfiregrill.com

Foodies swoon over this "stunning" Cheshire Bridge "splurge" known for its "phenomenal" American "farm-to-table" fare from the "tantalizing" eponymous grill (though a post-Survey chef change puts the Food rating in question); servers make guests "feel beyond welcome" in the "unpretentious" setting, and though a few lament "micro portions" at "macro prices", overall this "not-to-be-missed" experience is "well worth it."

Atlantic City

TOP FOOD RANKING

	Restaurant	Cuisine
27	Chef Vola's	Italian
26	Amada	Spanish
	Old Homestead	Steak
25	Buddakan	Asian
	Il Mulino New York	Italian
	Fin	Seafood
	Dock's Oyster House	Seafood
	Bobby Flay Steak	Steak
	Ruth's Chris Steak House	Steak
	Morton's The Steakhouse	Steak

OTHER NOTEWORTHY PLACES

American Cut	Steak
Angelo's Fairmount Tavern	Italian
Cafe 2825	Italian
Continental	Eclectic
Knife & Fork Inn	American
Luke Palladino	Italian
Palm	Steak
P.F. Chang's China Bistro	Chinese
White House	Sandwiches
Wolfgang Puck American Grille	American

Amada *Spanish*   26 | 26 | 26 | $58

Atlantic City | Revel | 500 Boardwalk (bet. Metropolitan & New Jersey Aves.) | 609-225-9900 | www.revelresorts.com
Jose Garces hits the jackpot in Atlantic City's Revel Resort where "amazing presentations" of his "sublime" Spanish tapas and "spectacular" ocean views shine in "elegant", "modern" surroundings; "extremely helpful" service completes the "excellent experience", which fans concede is "expensive", but "worth every dollar."

American Cut *Steak*   24 | 25 | 24 | $81

Atlantic City | Revel | 500 Boardwalk (bet. Metropolitan & New Jersey Aves.) | 609-225-9860 | www.americancutsteakhouse.com
Iron Chef Marc Forgione "does wonders" at this "beautiful", "special-occasion" steakhouse at AC's Revel Resort, where carnivore classics get a "welcome twist" by way of à la carte sauces and sides, plus seafood such as chili lobster and hiramasa; "efficient" service is another plus, and if both the prices and the "noise level" trend high (with "Led Zeppelin playing in the background"), fans insist "you get your money's worth."

Angelo's Fairmount Tavern *Italian*   21 | 18 | 21 | $33

Atlantic City | 2300 Fairmount Ave. (Mississippi Ave.) | 609-344-2439 | www.angelosfairmounttavern.com
A "reasonably priced" "reprieve" from Atlantic City "casino food", this "old-style family Italian" delivers "huge portions" of "terrific red-

sauce dishes" with "homemade wine" to wash it all down; despite the "slightly dated" decor, it has a "friendly", "neighborhood feeling" that suits fans who've "been going for years" and are "prepared to wait" for an "authentic" experience that "still delivers."

Bobby Flay Steak Ⓜ *Steak*

| 25 | 25 | 24 | $69 |

Atlantic City | Borgata Hotel Casino & Spa | 1 Borgata Way (Renaissance Point Blvd.) | 609-317-1000 | www.bobbyflaysteak.com

Bobby Flay "nails it" with "inventive takes on standard steakhouse items" at his "top-notch" "carnivore's paradise" in AC's Borgata Hotel; granted, the David Rockwell–designed dining room can get "noisy" and tabs are "expensive", but service is "excellent" and most agree "you get what you pay for."

Buddakan *Asian*

| 25 | 26 | 24 | $55 |

Atlantic City | The Pier Shops at Caesars | 1 Atlantic Ocean (Arkansas Ave.) | 609-674-0100 | www.buddakanac.com

"As good as the original in Philly" and its NYC sib, this "high-end Stephen Starr creation" in the Pier at Caesars combines "interesting", "well-presented" Pan-Asian fare with "delightful" service that's fit for a "special occasion"; add in "beautiful", "modern" decor, with an enormous gilded Buddha overlooking the dramatic communal tables, and it's "like dining on a Hollywood set."

Cafe 2825 Ⓜ *Italian*

| 24 | 21 | 23 | $47 |

Atlantic City | 2825 Atlantic Ave. (Brighton Ave.) | 609-344-6913 | www.cafe2825.com

Those seeking an "alternative to the casino joints" don't go wrong at this "high-end" Atlantic City Italian where "consistently good" fare and a staff that "makes you feel at home" ensure a "relaxing" dine; it's small, with only a dozen tables alongside a "beautiful bar", but fans say it's just right for "taking out someone special."

Chef Vola's Ⓜ⊘ *Italian*

| 27 | 16 | 25 | $52 |

Atlantic City | 111 S. Albion Pl. (Pacific Ave.) | 609-345-2022 | www.chefvolas.com

"Those in the know" "plan well in advance" to score a "tough reservation" at this "off-the-beaten-trail" Atlantic City BYO where a "congenial" staff serves "excellent, authentic" Italian "home cooking" amid an "old-school" atmosphere that "feels like a secret club"; "don't expect fancy" in the "noisy" basement space (you'll be "jammed in like sardines"), but do bring cash to cover the "expensive" tabs for an all-around "delicious experience."

Continental *Eclectic*

| 23 | 22 | 22 | $37 |

Atlantic City | The Pier Shops at Caesars | 1 Atlantic Ocean (Arkansas Ave.) | 609-674-8300 | www.continentalac.com

Everything comes with a "twist" at Stephen Starr's "nuevo retro" Eclectic at Atlantic City's Pier Shops at Caesars, from "inventive" tapas bites (cheesesteak eggrolls, Korean tacos) to "fun" martinis ("Tang in an alcoholic drink" = "genius"); diners dig the "*Jetsons*-like atmosphere" with seating both inside and on a faux-outdoor patio with fire pit, and considering the shared-plate eating style, tabs are "reasonable."

	FOOD	DECOR	SERVICE	COST

Dock's Oyster House *Seafood*   25 | 21 | 24 | $54

Atlantic City | 2405 Atlantic Ave. (Georgia Ave.) | 609-345-0092 | www.docksoysterhouse.com

A "venerable establishment" since 1897, this "pricey" AC seafooder scores high with "outstanding", "classic" fin fare served by an "on-point" staff in a simple room so "tight" that you might "rub elbows" with your neighbors; nightly piano music, plus a wine list and mixed drink selection, "keep the place abuzz", though some find it merely "noisy" – still, for most it's a "memorable" experience.

Fin ⓜ *Seafood*   25 | 24 | 24 | $51

Atlantic City | Tropicana Casino & Resort | 2831 Boardwalk (Iowa Ave.) | 800-345-8767 | www.tropicana.net

The "sophisticated" menu showcases "super-fresh seafood, prepared simply", plus "fantastic" prime steaks at this "comfortable" fine-dining spot inside AC's Tropicana Hotel; though the "lively" setting can get "loud", soothing ocean views and a beachy color scheme make it "feel like summer", and given the accommodating service, fans say it's "worth every penny."

Il Mulino New York *Italian*   25 | 22 | 24 | $73

Atlantic City | Trump Taj Mahal | 1000 Boardwalk (Virginia Ave.) | 609-449-6006 | www.ilmulino.com

"Top-notch" cuisine wins high praise at this "exclusive" Trump Taj Mahal outpost of the famed NYC Italian, where the "lovely", "formal" decor matches "white-glove" service from a staff that "aims to please"; most justify the "pricey" tabs for a "special-occasion" dining experience that's "not to be missed."

Knife & Fork Inn ❶ *American*   24 | 23 | 24 | $54

Atlantic City | 29 S. Albany Ave. (Pacific Ave.) | 609-344-1133 | www.knifeandforkinn.com

This "wonderful" 1912 American "landmark" in an "oddly elegant building" may be an AC "institution", but its "menu has kept pace with the times", featuring "outstanding" "steaks and chops" along with "always fresh" seafood; an "excellent wine selection" and "efficient, friendly" service help ease the sting of "pricey" tabs.

Luke Palladino *Italian*   24 | 22 | 24 | $52

Atlantic City | Harrah's Resort Atlantic City | 777 Harrah's Blvd. (Renaissance Point Blvd.) | 609-441-5576 | www.harrahsresort.com

"Old-world peasant" meets "upscale" "foodie" at this "imaginative" Italian at Harrah's Atlantic City, where "well-sourced" seasonal ingredients and homemade pastas anchor an "unpretentious" menu; an open kitchen showcases chef Palladino and company, and reservations are a "must."

Morton's The Steakhouse ❶ *Steak*   25 | 23 | 24 | $67

Atlantic City | Caesars Atlantic City Hotel & Casino | 2100 Pacific Ave. (Missouri Ave.) | 609-449-1044 | www.mortons.com

A steakhouse "standard-bearer", this "big-ticket" chain link in AC offers "excellently prepared" cuts of beef and "grand sides" "served professionally" amid an "ambiance of wealth and class"; some find it a bit "staid" and could do without the "high" wine pricing, but overall it's considered among "the best."

	FOOD	DECOR	SERVICE	COST

Old Homestead ⧈ *Steak* — 26 | 25 | 25 | $72

Atlantic City | Borgata Hotel Casino & Spa | 1 Borgata Way (Renaissance Point Blvd.) | 609-317-1000 | www.theoldhomesteadsteakhouse.com
"Stellar" steaks and a wine list "worth reading" draw "high rollers" to this "upscale" spin-off of the NYC original in AC's Borgata; the "Jersey-chic" space is sometimes "loud", but the servers are "polished professionals", and meat eaters insist it's "worth the visit" and the expense.

The Palm *Steak* — 24 | 21 | 23 | $64

Atlantic City | The Quarter at the Tropicana | 2801 Pacific Ave. (Iowa Ave.) | 609-344-7256 | www.thepalm.com
Fans say this "upbeat", upscale steakhouse chain link in the Tropicana "comes up aces" with steaks "like butter", "knowledgeable" service and a "great bar scene"; critics cite "jackhammer-loud" acoustics, but others tout it as a worthwhile splurge "if you just won the jackpot."

P.F. Chang's China Bistro *Chinese* — 21 | 21 | 20 | $31

Atlantic City | The Quarter at the Tropicana | 2801 Pacific Ave. (bet. Brighton & Iowa Aves.) | 609-348-4600 | www.pfchangs.com
"Upscale Americanized Chinese" is the draw at this "consistently comforting" chain link in The Quarter at the Tropicana where signature specialties like "wonderful" lettuce wraps and "trendy" cocktails are "served efficiently at a reasonable cost"; while some gripe about the "noise level", others think the "busy" vibe makes it "fun."

Ruth's Chris Steak House *Steak* — 25 | 23 | 24 | $64

Atlantic City | The Walk | 2020 Atlantic Ave. (bet. Arkansas & Michigan Aves.) | 609-344-5833 | www.ruthschris.com
Carnivores love this chain chophouse in an Atlantic City open-air mall for "tender", "fail-safe" steaks on signature "sizzling plates", and there's plenty for seafood lovers too (e.g. "spectacular" crab cakes); the ambiance is "classy", service is "attentive" and, sure, an "expense account" would help, but loyalists deem the experience "worth every cent."

White House ⧎ *Sandwiches* — 25 | 13 | 17 | $15

Atlantic City | Trump Taj Mahal | 1000 Boardwalk (Virginia Ave.) | 609-345-7827
Atlantic City | 2301 Arctic Ave. (Mississippi Ave.) | 609-345-8599
www.whitehousesubshop.net
The "legendary" submarine sandwiches at this Atlantic City "staple" are so "delicious", fans of the original cash-only Arctic Avenue location have put up with "brusque" service, lines and "divey" digs for years; those in the know say the "cheap", "enormous" hoagies made with "fresh" fillings and "scrumptious", locally baked bread are "just as wonderful" at the newer Trump Taj Mahal locale – plus you can pay with plastic.

Wolfgang Puck American Grille *American* — 25 | 22 | 23 | $59

Atlantic City | Borgata Hotel Casino & Spa | 1 Borgata Way (Huron Ave.) | 609-317-1000 | www.theborgata.com
"Wolfgang is one of the best" say fans of chef Puck's "classy, tasty" New American in AC's Borgata Hotel where the "middle-of-the-casino" locale may be "exposed", but the "comfortable" setting is still "elegant"; the staff is "attentive", and though "expensive" tabs in the dining room mean it "helps to be a high roller", some say eating in the tavern area is "more fun" – plus it "won't break the bank."

Austin & The Hill Country

TOP FOOD RANKING

	Restaurant	Cuisine
29	Uchi	Japanese
	Louie Mueller BBQ	BBQ
28	Barley Swine	American
	Snow's BBQ	BBQ
	Carillon	American
	Franklin Barbecue*	BBQ
	Congress	American
	Uchiko*	Japanese
27	Smitty's Market	BBQ
	Hudson's on the Bend	American

OTHER NOTEWORTHY PLACES

Eddie V's	Seafood/Steak
Fonda San Miguel	Mexican
La Condesa	Mexican
Lenoir	Eclectic
Olivia	French/Italian
Salt Lick	BBQ
Second Bar + Kitchen	American
Swift's Attic	Eclectic
Vespaio	Italian
Wink	American

Barley Swine ⊠ *American* | 28 | 19 | 25 | $47 |

South Lamar | 2024 S. Lamar Blvd. (Hether St.) | 512-394-8150 |
www.barleyswine.com

One of the "hottest" places in town, this "amazing" "locavore" American in South Lamar from chef Bryce Gilmore provides "truly memorable" small plates made for sharing and enjoying alongside an impressive list of beers; it's "foodie central", but the space is "hopelessly small" and doesn't take reservations, so "arrive early or be prepared to wait for an eternity."

The Carillon *American* | 28 | 25 | 26 | $55 |

Campus | AT&T Executive Education & Conference Ctr. |
1900 University Ave. (Martin Luther King Blvd.) | 512-404-3655 |
www.thecarillonrestaurant.com

"Top-drawer for Austin", this "beautiful", "special-occasion" New American venue in the AT&T Executive Education and Conference Center is where chef Josh Watkins "moves Texas-native materials into haute cuisine territory", yielding "exceptional" dishes; considering such "superior" quality and service, many find the prices quite "reasonable"; P.S. the lounge features a separate bar menu with small plates.

---

* Indicates a tie with restaurant above

Congress ☒Ⓜ *American* | 28 | 28 | 27 | $98 |

Downtown | The Austonian | 200 Congress Ave. (2nd St.) | 512-827-2760 | www.congressaustin.com

"Hands down" among the "best" in town proclaim fans of this "up-scale" Downtown restaurant spotlighting chef David Bull's "over-the-top", "no-holds-barred" New American creations served in prix fixe feasts "fit for a foodie"; "wonderful wines", "fantastic" service (ranked No. 1 in Austin) and a "sophisticated" setting make it "worth every penny for a special occasion" – go for the "full-monty chef's tasting" "if you can afford it"; P.S. the adjacent Bar Congress has its own menu of cocktails and small bites.

Eddie V's Prime Seafood *Seafood/Steak* | 26 | 26 | 25 | $55 |

Arboretum | 9400 Arboretum Blvd. (Capital of Texas Hwy.) | 512-342-2642
Downtown | 301 E. Fifth St. (San Jacinto Blvd.) | 512-472-1860
www.eddiev.com

This "vibrant" chophouse chainlet – tied for Most Popular in Austin – "stands out" with "super" steaks and "excellent" "seafood without gimmicks" ("oysters as fresh as if you'd gotten them off the boat"), plus "exemplary" service and "elegant", "well-appointed" surroundings attracting a "high-rolling" crowd of "wealthy lobby-ists and dealmakers"; "you pay dearly" for it all, so many seek out the reduced-price app deals during happy hour, not to mention a "hopping" bar scene.

Fonda San Miguel *Mexican* | 25 | 27 | 23 | $42 |

Highland Park | 2330 North Loop Blvd. W. (Hancock Dr.) | 512-459-4121 | www.fondasanmiguel.com

"Colorful and full of beautiful pottery", this Highland Park haci-enda has long been "a treat for the eyes as well as the taste buds", with "impeccable" interior Mexican fare in a "casually elegant" setting tended by a "knowledgeable" crew; especially "memora-ble" is Sunday's bountiful buffet brunch – a long-standing "tradition" and quite the "event."

Franklin Barbecue Ⓜ *BBQ* | 28 | 11 | 19 | $17 |

East Austin | 900 E. 11th St. (Branch St.) | 512-653-1187 | www.franklinbarbecue.com

Originally a trailer, this brick-and-mortar BBQ joint in East Austin is "giving the big names a run for their money" with some of the "finest brisket in the entire state", plus pulled pork and other "exceptional", "simple smoked meats"; the modest space opens at 11 AM and closes whenever the eats run out, which is usually early.

Hudson's on the Bend *American* | 27 | 24 | 26 | $60 |

Lakeway | 3509 Ranch Rd. 620 N. (Hudson Bend Rd.) | 512-266-1369 | www.hudsonsonthebend.com

"Rattlesnake cakes, anyone?" – this "true Texas ranch house" in Lakeway spotlights Jeff Blank's "memorable" New American menu highlighting "exotic" game served by a "savvy", "pleasant" staff in a "romantic" setting; yes, it's "expensive", but it's truly a "unique experience" that makes any meal "feel like a special occasion"; P.S. reservations recommended.

FOOD | DECOR | SERVICE | COST

La Condesa *Mexican* | 23 | 26 | 22 | $38

Second Street District | 400 W. Second St. (Guadalupe St.) |
512-499-0300 | www.lacondesaaustin.com

"Fabulous, bold" takes on Mexican street food and "wonderful margaritas" await at this Second Street District destination set in "stunning",
"sophisticated" digs with a patio; just know the "lively" atmosphere
can be "a little too loud for conversation", and it's not exactly cheap,
unless you "go at happy hour for deals on appetizers and drinks."

Lenoir 🗷Ⓜ *Eclectic* | – | – | – | M

Bouldin Creek | 1807 S. First St. (Annie St.) | 512-215-9778 |
www.lenoirrestaurant.com

Chef Todd Duplechan (ex Trio) takes inspiration from an Eclectic array
of 'hot-climate' cuisines (Indian, Mediterranean, etc.) at this midpriced
Bouldin Creek boîte; sporting a romantic, serene blue-and-white mo-
tif, the tiny digs are bedecked with reclaimed furnishings, vintage cro-
chet curtains and an old drugstore-style bar doling out craft beers and
wines; P.S. check out the tree-shaded wine garden.

Louie Mueller BBQ 🗷 *BBQ* | 29 | 16 | 21 | $21

Taylor | 206 W. Second St. (Talbot St.) | 512-352-6206 |
www.louiemuellerbarbecue.com

The dining room itself is "charred with years of accumulating
smoke" at this "real-deal", circa-1949 Taylor BBQer declared "one
of the best in Texas" thanks to its "simply divine", "thickly crusted",
"flavorful" brisket that "passes the doesn't-need-sauce test"; service is "cafeteria-style" and "neon beer signs" are the only decor,
but it's "well worth the drive"; P.S. it "closes when they run out of
food", so "get there early."

Olivia *French/Italian* | 25 | 22 | 24 | $42

South Lamar | 2043 S. Lamar Blvd. (Oltorf St.) | 512-804-2700 |
www.olivia-austin.com

A "lovely" modern space with "good buzz", this South Lamar spot
boasts an "innovative" French-Italian menu that may "change your
mind about sweetbreads, lamb tongue and other oddities"; an "attentive and knowledgeable" staff and "thoughtful" wine list "filled with
gems" help take the sting off somewhat pricey tabs, adding up to a
"nice night out."

Salt Lick *BBQ* | 25 | 19 | 20 | $24

Round Rock | 3350 E. Palm Valley Blvd. (Harrell Pkwy.) | 512-386-1044
Southeast Austin | Austin-Bergstrom Int'l Airport | 3600 Presidential Blvd.
(Bastrop Hwy.) | no phone 🗷
Driftwood | 18300 FM 1826 (FM 967) | 512-858-4959 🗷
www.saltlickbbq.com

"Bring your appetite" to these "true Texas" BBQers for a "first-class
orgy of meat" via "piles" of pit-smoked, "fork-tender brisket", "spicy
sausage" and "fall-off-the-bone ribs" served "family-style" in a "rustic" atmosphere with "great" live music on weekends; it's cash only
with "looong waits" at Driftwood and Southeast Austin, and although
it's BYO beer, you can also pick up a bottle of wine from their tasting
room to open at the picnic tables; P.S. "buy a whole brisket at the airport to carry home and your friends will love you."

FOOD | DECOR | SERVICE | COST

Second Bar + Kitchen ● *American* 25 | 24 | 22 | $43

Downtown | The Austonian | 200 Congress Ave. (2nd St.) | 512-827-2750 |
www.congressaustin.com

This casual offshoot of chef David Bull's Congress specializes in
"superb", "farm-to-table" New American fare served all day along
with "awesome" cocktails and wines; the "cool", modern-industrial
Downtown space sports a wraparound bar for dining or drinks with max-
imum "people-watching", so the only downside is the lack of happy hour.

Smitty's Market ⇗ *BBQ* 27 | 14 | 15 | $18

Lockhart | 208 S. Commerce St. (bet. Market & Prairie Lea Sts.) |
512-398-9344 | www.smittysmarket.com

A "mecca" for "BBQ aficionados", this Lockhart butcher shop set in
the original site of the Kreuz Market is cherished for its "superb" brisket, "thick pork chops" that "rock your socks" and links "to die for"
(a good thing since "your arteries may never recover"); all comes
straight from the pit in an "old-time, fire-seared" setting abetted by a
friendly staff and cold beer.

Snow's BBQ ☒Ⓜ *BBQ* 28 | 15 | 22 | $18

Lexington | 516 Main St. (bet. 2nd & 3rd Sts.) | 979-773-4640 |
www.snowsbbq.com

It's "only open on Saturday mornings", so diehards "show up at dawn
and stand in line" for "melt-in-your-mouth" brisket and "tender" ribs
at this Lexington smokehouse called "as close to heaven as meat eaters can get"; its "no-pretensions", "far-off-the-path" locale "down a
back alley in a forgotten town" is definitely "part of the charm", and so
is the "friendly" hospitality.

Swift's Attic *Eclectic* - | - | - | M

Downtown | Swift Bldg. | 315 Congress Ave. (bet. 3rd & 4th Sts.) |
512-482-8842 | www.swiftsattic.com

This Downtown Eclectic features a playful, midpriced menu of small and
large plates from chef Mat Clouser that feature a range of international influences and include some not-your-usual meats (e.g. quail,
goat, antelope); set on the second floor of the historic Swift Building,
the space is done up in a retro-modern style with a long bar.

Uchi *Japanese* 29 | 25 | 27 | $56

Zilker | 801 S. Lamar Blvd. (Juliet St.) | 512-916-4808 | www.uchiaustin.com

"Heaven" for sushiphiles, this Zilker jewel box presents the "finest in
forward-thinking Japanese" cuisine via chef Tyson Cole – from "delish" raw fare and the signature deep-fried shag roll to "incredible" fusion plates that "make you cry tears of joy" – earning it Austin's No. 1
Food rating and tying it for Most Popular; a "sophisticated" vibe, "outstanding" service and a "great-looking clientele" mean it "surpasses
expectations" for most, just "take another hit of sake before you look
at the bill."

Uchiko *Japanese* 28 | 26 | 27 | $59

Rosedale | 4200 N. Lamar Blvd. (42nd St.) | 512-916-4808 |
www.uchikoaustin.com

"Simply brilliant", this "whimsical" Rosedale sib to Uchi features Tyson
Cole's "wildly creative" Japanese fare in "beautiful" presentations
capped by "dynamic" wines and "mind-blowing desserts"; service is

FOOD | DECOR | SERVICE | COST

"professional" and the space is modern, and while tabs are steep, that hasn't deterred the crowds.

Vespaio *Italian*
26 | 21 | 24 | $43

SoCo | 1610 S. Congress Ave. (Monroe St.) | 512-441-6100 | www.austinvespaio.com

"Long waits" are par for the course at this midpriced SoCo Italian, "hands down one of the best in Austin" thanks to its "superb" cooking, "wonderful wines" and a warm setting that's "one of the best places to spot a movie star or politician"; an "eager" staff is "helpful" with suggestions, but it's "noisy, noisy, noisy" at prime times.

Wink ☒ *American*
27 | 21 | 25 | $64

Old West Austin | 1014 N. Lamar Blvd. (11th St.) | 512-482-8868 | www.winkrestaurant.com

On the scene for over a decade and still utterly "original", this Old West Austin New American delivers "highly creative", "locavore"-driven fare with a tasting menu that will "blow you away"; service is "wonderful" too, so fans only "wish the space were a little hipper", and perhaps that the check were a bit lower, but at least "happy hour in the wine bar is a steal."

Baltimore/Annapolis

TOP FOOD RANKING

Restaurant	Cuisine
__29__ Charleston	American
__28__ Di Pasquale's	Italian
Samos	Greek
Vin 909	American
Bartlett Pear Inn	American
Prime Rib	Steak
Tersiguel's	French
Out of the Fire	American/Eclectic
Sushi King	Japanese
Milton Inn	American

OTHER NOTEWORTHY PLACES

B&O American Brasserie	American
Cheesecake Factory	American
Chesapeake	American
Double T Diner	Diner
Fleet Street Kitchen	American
Food Market	American
G&M	Seafood
Gertrude's	Chesapeake
Pabu	Japanese
Woodberry Kitchen	American

B&O American Brasserie *American*   **23** | **24** | **22** | **$43**

Downtown | Hotel Monaco | 2 N. Charles St. (bet. Baltimore St. & Wilkes Ln.) | Baltimore | 443-692-6172 | www.bandorestaurant.com
At the Hotel Monaco's "historic" beaux arts digs Downtown, this "lively" American turns out "innovative", seasonal small plates, brick-oven items and mains; the space is "very *Mad Men*", with a "chic" crowd downing "creative" drinks in the lounge and, overlooking the action from the mezzanine, a "swanky" dining room.

Bartlett Pear Inn Restaurant *American*   **28** | **25** | **27** | **$58**

Easton | Bartlett Pear Inn | 28 S. Harrison St. (bet. South Ln. & South St.) | 410-770-3300 | www.bartlettpearinn.com
"Extraordinary doesn't begin to describe this culinary temple" rave pear-amours of the "beautifully prepared" New American dishes presented by a "superb" staff at this "charming" and "gorgeous" Easton inn; prices place it "high on the romance and special-occasion scale", though the chef's tasting menu is a "relative bargain", and the bar offers a more casual approach; P.S. closed Monday and Tuesday.

Charleston ⌧ *American*   **29** | **28** | **28** | **$99**

Harbor East | 1000 Lancaster St. (Exeter St.) | Baltimore | 410-332-7373 | www.charlestonrestaurant.com
Cindy Wolf remains "at the top of her game", applying "world-class technique" to "Lowcountry" cuisine to create "phenomenal" New

American masterpieces at her Harbor East "destination", which ranks as "Baltimore's best restaurant" with its No. 1 ratings for Food, Decor and Service; "no detail goes unnoticed" by the "superlative" staffers, who "spoil" guests with selections from co-owner Tony Foreman's "epic" wine list in a "stunningly beautiful" space; just "be prepared" for the multicourse menu's "sticker shock" – for many, it's a "once-every-few-years kind of place."

Cheesecake Factory *American* | 24 | 22 | 22 | $30 |

Inner Harbor | Harborplace Pratt Street Pavilion | 201 E. Pratt St. (Light St.) | Baltimore | 410-234-3990
Hanover | Arundel Mills | 7002 Arundel Mills Circle (Arundel Mills Blvd.) | 410-579-5867 ◗
Columbia | Mall in Columbia | 10300 Little Patuxent Pkwy. (Wincopin Circle) | 410-997-9311
Towson | Towson Town Ctr. | 825 Dulaney Valley Rd. (Fairmount Ave.) | 410-337-7411
Annapolis | Annapolis Mall | 1872 Annapolis Mall Rd. (Jennifer Rd.) | 410-224-0565
www.thecheesecakefactory.com

"Folks need 15 minutes" just to "pore over" the "book"-length menu at this "perennial favorite" (indeed, it's ranked the Most Popular chain in Baltimore) that has lots of fans thanks to "scrumptious", midpriced American eats in "insanely large" portion sizes, including the "sinfully rich" signature cheesecakes; service is "prompt and courteous", and the "loud", "brassy", glitzy setting makes for a "lively" meal, though tables are tightly packed, and "eternal" waits "require patience."

The Chesapeake *American* | - | - | - | E |

Downtown North | 1701 N. Charles St. (Lanvale St.) | Baltimore | 410-547-2760 | www.thechesapeakebaltimore.com

One of Baltimore's landmark restaurants has been reborn after decades lying fallow, as new owners have dusted off this grand old Downtown North space and completely updated it with leather banquettes, a large marble bar and other elegant touches; the upscale American offerings include cheese and charcuterie boards and raw bar items in addition to heartier entrees.

Di Pasquale's Marketplace 🗷 *Italian* | 28 | 15 | 22 | $16 |

East Baltimore | 3700 Gough St. (Dean St.) | Baltimore | 410-276-6787 | www.dipasquales.com

"Bring your appetite" to this "old-fashioned" East Baltimore specialty store where Europhiles shop for "Italian staples" or sit in the cafe area for a quick meal of "homemade" soups and "big, fat" sandwiches heaped with "made-fresh-daily" mozzarella; staffers "make you feel at home", and though there is "no decor" to speak of, the "wonderful aromas" provide ambiance; P.S. closes at 6 PM.

Double T Diner *Diner* | 20 | 16 | 21 | $18 |

Bel Air | 543 Market Place Dr. (Veterans Memorial Hwy.) | 410-836-5591
White Marsh | 10741 Pulaski Hwy. (Ebenezer Rd.) | 410-344-1020 ◗
Catonsville | 6300 Baltimore National Pike (Rolling Rd.) | 410-744-4151 ◗
Ellicott City | 10055 Baltimore National Pike (Centennial Ln.) | 410-750-3300
Perry Hall | Joppa Corners | 4140 E. Joppa Rd. (Belair Rd.) | 410-248-0160 ◗
Pasadena | 1 Mountain Rd. (Ritchie Hwy.) | 410-766-9669 ◗

(continued)

Double T Diner

Annapolis | 12 Defense St. (Cedar Ave.) | 410-571-9070 ●
www.doubletdiner.com

For "sinful" breakfasts or "a quick bite anytime", eaters of "all ages" flock to this "always busy", "subtly Greek", retro-looking Maryland diner chain; the menu is "novel"-length, and the "tasty" grub and "phenomenal" desserts – served "lickety-split" by "courteous" staffers – are a "great value for the money"; P.S. some locations are open 24/7.

Fleet Street Kitchen ⊠ *American*

| – | – | – | E |

Harbor East | 1012 Fleet St. (Central Ave.) | Baltimore | 410-244-5830 |
www.fleetstreetkitchen.com

The team behind Bagby Pizza and Ten Ten also helms this Harbor East New American that makes use of seasonal, local ingredients – including some from the owner's Baltimore County farm; the bi-level interior is elegant (white linens, high ceilings) yet warm (exposed bricks, wrought iron), and though the prices may augur special occasions, a burger and a glass of wine at the bar is an affordable treat.

Food Market ● *American*

| – | – | – | M |

Hampden | 1017 W. 36th St. (Roland Ave.) | Baltimore | 410-366-0606 |
www.thefoodmarketbaltimore.com

From the open kitchen of a former Hampden grocery store made famous in John Waters' film *Pecker,* Chad Gauss dishes up traditional Americana with a twist; the sleek interior with rustic overtones, plus a bar pouring cool cocktails until late, make it a favorite on the 'Avenue.'

G&M *Seafood*

| 24 | 16 | 20 | $29 |

Linthicum | 804 N. Hammonds Ferry Rd. (Nursery Rd.) | 410-636-1777 |
www.gandmcrabcakes.com

"Bigger-than-your-head" crab cakes with "lots of lump meat" are the reason travelers "take cabs from BWI" during layovers to visit this "affordable" Linthicum "mecca", where the lengthy menu has Italian and Greek eats, but the crustacean creations are the "real star"; the simple, white-tablecloth setting is "pleasant" enough, and service is "old-school", but really, it's all about "one thing" here.

Gertrude's Ⓜ *Chesapeake*

| 22 | 25 | 23 | $37 |

Charles Village | Baltimore Museum of Art | 10 Art Museum Dr.
(bet. Charles St. & Wyman Park Dr.) | Baltimore | 410-889-3399 |
www.gertrudesbaltimore.com

"Manet and Cezanne would have stopped painting" to enjoy an alfresco meal "at the edge of the sculpture garden" or inside this "oasis" within the Baltimore Museum of Art say admirers of John Shields' "sassy, Southern", "Chesapeake Bay–oriented" menu presented by "knowledgeable" servers; prices are moderate, and $12 entrees on Tuesdays are "a great touch."

Milton Inn *American*

| 28 | 26 | 26 | $59 |

Sparks | 14833 York Rd. (Quaker Bottom Rd.) | 410-771-4366 |
www.miltoninn.com

Dripping with "ambiance", this circa-1740 fieldstone inn is an "enduring treasure" in Sparks, with "cozy fireplaces, oil paintings and white tablecloths" spread over multiple rooms that provide suitably "elegant" backdrops for its "sophisticated" American cuisine; service is "impeccable", and while a typical experience is "pricey", the lounge menu offers "lesser-priced" options.

Out of the Fire ☒Ⓜ *American/Eclectic* | 28 | 24 | 26 | $42 |

Easton | 22 Goldsborough St. (Washington St.) | 410-770-4777 | www.outofthefire.com

"Sit at the bar and watch the action" in the kitchen at this "superb" Easton American-Eclectic where "amazing chefs" who really "get the magic of fresh, local ingredients" "artfully plate" "great things" cooked via the showpiece open hearth; it's not cheap for such an "informal" vibe, but service is "attentive" and the space is "inviting" with a "warm" "Tuscan" palette.

Pabu *Japanese* | - | - | - | E |

Harbor East | Four Seasons Baltimore | 200 International Dr. (Aliceanna St.) | Baltimore | 410-223-1460 | www.michaelmina.net

Celebrity chef Michael Mina takes on Japanese cuisine (with partner Ken Tominaga) at this high-end izakaya in Harbor East's Four Seasons (but accessed via a separate entrance on Aliceanna Street) that serves classic dishes from a robata grill and a sushi bar, washed down with a world-class sake selection; the rough-wood tables, bamboo ceiling and privacy panels keep it casual even though there's a sleek sheen to everything.

Prime Rib *Steak* | 28 | 26 | 28 | $71 |

Mt. Vernon | 1101 N. Calvert St. (Chase St.) | Baltimore | 410-539-1804

Hanover | Maryland Live! Casino | 7002 Arundel Mills Circle (Arundel Mills Blvd.) | 443-445-2970
www.theprimerib.com

Do as they do in *Mad Men* – "dress up and have a martini" – at this "classic" Mt. Vernon steakhouse (with a branch at Maryland Live! Casino) that's operating at the "top of its game", delivering "fantastic" "slabs of meat" and "masterful seafood"; from the "1940s supper-club vibe" to the "sublime" tuxedoed service, it's a "perfect evening out"; P.S. business-casual dress is recommended.

Samos ☒⊅ *Greek* | 28 | 16 | 24 | $21 |

Greektown | 600 Oldham St. (Fleet St.) | Baltimore | 410-675-5292 | www.samosrestaurant.com

"As close to the real thing as you can get" say ardent admirers of the "phenomenal" food "like *yia-yia* used to make" at this Greektown elder statesman where even the "salad dressing has a huge following"; the wait is often "long" since there are no reservations and only "limited seating" in the "underwhelming", mural-bedecked space, but it's "stupidly cheap" and "so very worth it"; P.S. it's cash only and BYO.

Sushi King ☒ *Japanese* | 28 | 20 | 24 | $32 |

Columbia | 6490 Dobbin Rd. (Rte. 175) | 410-997-1269 | www.sushikingmd.com

An "insiders' jewel", this "decently" priced Columbia Japanese "hidden" near the MVA "isn't flashy" but "completely rocks" for "consistently terrific" sushi "masterpieces" created by veritable "artists" and delivered by "courteous" servers in "traditional garb"; "seating is packed", so regulars suggest calling ahead, "even on weekdays."

Tersiguel's *French* | 28 | 25 | 28 | $59

Ellicott City | 8293 Main St. (Forrest St.) | 410-465-4004 | www.tersiguels.com

"Exquisite" French country "creations" comprised of "prime ingredients", including produce from the family farm, plus a "refined but not stuffy" "white-napkin" ambiance and "attentive, unobtrusive" service have Ellicott City diners calling this "romantic" special-occasioner "a favorite for years"; it's "expensive", *oui*, but "a great treat when you want to play grown-up" (and prix fixe menus "help with the cost").

Vin 909 Ⓜ *American* | 28 | 25 | 26 | $32

Eastport | 909 Bay Ridge Ave. (Chesapeake Ave.) | 410-990-1846 | www.vin909.com

"Off the beaten path" in Eastport, this vin-centric venue appeals to locals and visitors alike with its "great-value" offering of "fabulous", "refined" New American fare and an "outstanding" wine selection; "exceptional" service and an "intimate", contemporary "cottage" setting create a "calming" backdrop "suitable for quiet conversation."

Woodberry Kitchen *American* | 27 | 26 | 25 | $49

Clipper Mill | 2010 Clipper Park Rd. (Clipper Mill Rd.) | Baltimore | 410-464-8000 | www.woodberrykitchen.com

"A smash" since it opened and still "wildly popular" (in fact, it's Baltimore's Most Popular restaurant), this Clipper Mill New American in a "rebuilt old factory" hosts a "hip", "boisterous" crowd happily devouring the "complex" farm-to-table "amazingness" ferried by "friendly, smart" servers who "aim to please"; some find it "a bit pricey", but its huge fan base deems it "worth the trip many times over" – which is why it's "oh so hard to get into" ("reserve way in advance").

Boston

TOP FOOD RANKING

	Restaurant	Cuisine
28	Neptune Oyster	Seafood
	Island Creek Oyster	Seafood
	Oleana	Mediterranean
	Craigie on Main	French
	Lumière	French
	Life Alive	Vegan/Vegetarian
	Menton*	French/Italian
	No. 9 Park	French/Italian
	Hamersley's Bistro	French
	Il Capriccio	Italian
	Sorellina	Italian
	Toro	Spanish
	Mistral	French/Mediterranean
	Coppa	Italian
	Oishii	Japanese
	L'Espalier	French/New England
27	Bistro 5	Italian
	Clio	French
	Morton's	Steak
	Del Frisco's	Steak

OTHER NOTEWORTHY PLACES

Restaurant	Cuisine
Abe & Louie's	Steak
B&G Oysters	Seafood
Bergamot	American
Bondir	American
Border Cafe	Cajun/Tex-Mex
Ceia Kitchen & Bar	European
Chateau	Italian
Cheesecake Factory	American
Deuxave	French
Flora	American
Harvest	New England
Hungry Mother	Southern
Journeyman	American
Myers + Chang	Asian
Rino's Place	Italian
Strip-T's	American
Sweet Cheeks Q	BBQ
Ten Tables	American/European
Toscano	Italian
224 Boston Street	American

* Indicates a tie with restaurant above

Visit zagat.com

Abe & Louie's *Steak*

27 | 25 | 26 | $61

Back Bay | 793 Boylston St. (bet. Exeter & Fairfield Sts.) | 617-536-6300 | www.abeandlouies.com

Meat lovers who want "top-shelf" fare "count on" this "traditional" Back Bay "carni-nirvana" – ranked Boston's Most Popular – for "succulent steaks", "mouthwatering sides" and "terrific" wines ferried by "exceptional" servers in "beautiful, bustling" confines complete with a "noisy" scene at the bar; tabs are "expensive", but try the "splendid brunch" (or lunch) for a slightly "more affordable experience."

B&G Oysters *Seafood*

27 | 22 | 24 | $47

South End | 550 Tremont St. (Waltham St.) | 617-423-0550 | www.bandgoysters.com

"Barbara Lynch delivers fabulous bivalves" at this "hip" South End "classic", but her "lobsta rolls" and other "classy" seafood picks are "fantastic" too – plus they come "served with a smile and some sass"; it's "pricey" and "you need to be willing to cozy up" in "tight", "crowded" digs (or on the "nice little" patio), but even those who "wish it were bigger" are willing to shell out for such an "absolute must."

Bergamot ◗ *American*

27 | 23 | 26 | $51

Somerville | 118 Beacon St. (Kirkland St.) | 617-576-7700 | www.bergamotrestaurant.com

"Every course is equally delightful" at this "upscale" "jewel of a find" in Somerville, each highlighting "inspired" farm-to-table New American fare and matched with wines from the "thoughtful" list by an "exceptional" staff; while "expensive", it's a "tremendous value for the quality", plus early arrivals can opt for three-course prix fixe deals.

Bistro 5 ⌧Ⓜ *Italian*

27 | 25 | 27 | $46

West Medford | 5 Playstead Rd. (bet. High & Irving Sts.) | 781-395-7464 | www.bistro5.com

"You might not expect to find it" in "out-of-the-way" West Medford, but this "intimate" Italian bistro is "worth the trip" to have chef-owner Vittorio Ettore "work his magic" with "delicious", "creatively prepared" seasonal fare, which is "perfectly matched" with international wines; "phenomenal" staffers oversee the "charming", artwork-lined space, which "fills up fast" thanks in part to serious "value."

Bondir *American*

27 | 24 | 25 | $58

Central Square | 279 Broadway (bet. Columbia & Elm Sts.) | Cambridge | 617-661-0009 | www.bondircambridge.com

You'll "relish every morsel" of "genius" chef-owner Jason Bond's "inspiring combinations" of "elegant", daily changing farm-to-table fare at this expensive Central Square New American; "impeccable" staffers oversee a "cute" space filled with "warmth and buzz", and while the "intimate" size means "reservations are a must", it's "well worth the trouble."

Border Cafe *Cajun/Tex-Mex*

23 | 21 | 21 | $18

Harvard Square | 32 Church St. (Palmer St.) | Cambridge | 617-864-6100 ◗
Burlington | 128 Middlesex Tpke. (2nd Ave.) | 781-505-2500
Saugus | 356 Broadway (Walnut St.) | 781-233-5308
www.bordercafe.com

"Filling" chow for "cheap" is the formula at this "family-friendly" trio, a "must-go" for "tasty" Cajun–Tex-Mex eats served up "extremely fast" with "bottomless chips" and salsa and "giant margaritas"; some find it "not super-authentic" and the setting "clichéd", but "still, they come in droves", so peak hours are a "total zoo."

Ceia Kitchen & Bar *European*

| - | - | - | M |

Newburyport | 38 State St. (bet. Essex & Middle Sts.) | 978-358-8112 | www.ceiakitchenbar.com

This "upscale" but moderately priced Newburyport spot specializing in European coastal cuisine pays special attention to Portuguese (the owner's heritage) dishes created by chef Patrick Soucy, a die-hard locavore; a new location in a historic three-story brownstone offers more seating than the old one down the block (as well as a communal chef's table, two bars and an extensive wine list), all while maintaining an "intimate" vibe with lots of candlelight and exposed brick.

The Chateau *Italian*

| 21 | 18 | 22 | $21 |

Braintree | 535 John Mahar Hwy. (bet. Pearl & Plain Sts.) | 781-380-8770
Waltham | 195 School St. (Exchange St.) | 781-894-3339
Burlington | Middlesex Commons Shopping Ctr. | 43 Middlesex Tpke. (Old Concord Rd.) | 781-202-3570
Norwood | 404 Providence Hwy. (Pleasant St.) | 781-762-5335
www.chateaurestaurant.com

Its name "may sound French", but this "red-sauce" chain is "100%" Italian, offering up "huge orders" of "crave"-worthy "classics" for "affordable prices"; the "congenial, homey atmosphere" is the result of "friendly, efficient" staffers and "comfortable", "old-school" environs scattered with "pictures from days gone by."

Cheesecake Factory *American*

| 23 | 23 | 22 | $24 |

Back Bay | The Shops at Prudential Ctr. | 115 Huntington Ave. (Belvidere St.) | 617-399-7777 ●
East Cambridge | CambridgeSide Galleria | 100 CambridgeSide Pl. (bet. Commercial Ave. & 1st St.) | Cambridge | 617-252-3810
Braintree | South Shore Plaza | 250 Granite St. (Shore Plaza Rd.) | 781-849-1001
Burlington | Burlington Mall | 75 Middlesex Tpke. (Burlington Mall Rd.) | 781-273-0060
Peabody | Northshore Mall | 210 Andover St. (Cross St.) | 978-538-7599
Natick | Natick Collection | 1245 Worcester St. (Speen St.) | 508-653-0011
www.thecheesecakefactory.com

"Everyone from the kids to granny will find something" on the "mammoth" menu at this "well-known" franchise, which ranks as Boston's Most Popular chain and is known for delivering "your money's worth", with "gigantic portions" of "enjoyable" American grub ("leave room" for "addictive" cheesecakes "galore"); most find the "ornate" settings "appealing" and "comfortable" and the service "efficient", even with such "crowds" and "waits" at "high-volume" times.

Clio 🗷 *French*

| 27 | 26 | 26 | $86 |

Back Bay | Eliot Hotel | 370 Commonwealth Ave. (Massachusetts Ave.) | 617-536-7200 | www.cliorestaurant.com

Savor "fine dining at its height" at this "world-class" "treat" in the Back Bay's Eliot Hotel, where chef Ken Oringer "stretches your imagination" with "exquisite" "layers of flavor" in his modern French cuisine, "presented elegantly" and matched with "terrific service" for a crowd that includes "famous" faces; the wine selection and "mixology" are also "quite special", so while you'll have to lay down "big bucks", it's "worth every penny", especially when "you want to impress."

Coppa *Italian*　　　28 | 21 | 24 | $40

South End | 253 Shawmut Ave. (Milford St.) | 617-391-0902 | www.coppaboston.com

"A knockout every time", this "spectacular" South End enoteca from Ken Oringer and Jamie Bissonnette specializes in "ambrosial" Italian small plates and charcuterie (think "pig parts" and other "bold" offerings) of "uncompromising quality" that are "worth lingering over", as long as you "bring the dollars"; "engaged service" earns praise, but as the "small", "funky" space is eternally "jammed" with a "lively crowd", it can be "hard to get a table."

Craigie on Main Ⓜ *French*　　28 | 24 | 26 | $72

Central Square | 853 Main St. (Bishop Allen Dr.) | Cambridge | 617-497-5511 | www.craigieonmain.com

"Always on its A-game", this "high-end" Central Square French earns "high accolades" for its "consistently stunning", "artistic", locavore-leaning cuisine from "meticulous" "genius" (and "snout-to-tail" "pioneer") Tony Maws; an "informed, passionate" staff works the "bustling" scene, and while "it'll cost you dearly", it's worth all your "bank account will permit."

Del Frisco's Double Eagle　　27 | 26 | 25 | $79
Steak House Ⓧ *Steak*

Seaport District | Liberty Wharf | 250 Northern Ave. (D St.) | 617-951-1368 | www.delfriscos.com

Carnivores get "serious" at this "first-class" Seaport branch of the Lone Star–based steakhouse chain where a "phenomenal" team presents "mouthwatering" beef paired with a "superior wine list" in "dynamic" upstairs environs flaunting "incredible views" of the harbor through a wall of windows; "you pay for" the quality, but "ignore the prices" – it's a "meal you'll not soon forget."

Deuxave ❶ *French*　　　26 | 25 | 25 | $62

Back Bay | 371 Commonwealth Ave. (Massachusetts Ave.) | 617-517-5915 | www.deuxave.com

"Savor the experience as well as the food" at this "memorable" Back Bay "occasion restaurant" where Chris Coombs' (Dbar, Boston Chops) "exquisite", nouvelle French–inflected cuisine to "linger over" is "beautifully served" in a "sexy" space with a "cool bar"; it runs "expensive", but "your date will be very impressed", so most consider it "worth the money."

Flora *American*　　　27 | 26 | 25 | $41

Arlington | 190 Massachusetts Ave. (Chandler St.) | 781-641-1664 | www.florarestaurant.com

For "fine dining without the pretense", this Arlington "go-to" is a "cut above" thanks to chef-owner Bob Sargent, who "uses local food in interesting ways" to create "exquisite" New American dishes that "change with the seasons"; staffers who are "attentive without being overbearing" and a setting in a "lovely" converted old bank complete what "never fails" to be a "fantastic" experience.

Hamersley's Bistro *French*
28 | 25 | 27 | $59

South End | 553 Tremont St. (Clarendon St.) | 617-423-2700 |
www.hamersleysbistro.com
"Gracious chef-owner" Gordon Hamersley is "on the line" almost every
night at his "consistently superb" South End bistro, cooking up "spectacular" French fare that's both "inventive" and – as with the "astonishing" signature roast chicken – "classic"; a "loyal", "knowledgeable"
staff presides over the "chic", "casually elegant" space, monitoring a
"gold-standard" experience that's commensurately "expensive" – and
"worth every penny."

Harvest *New England*
25 | 24 | 23 | $49

Harvard Square | 44 Brattle St. (Church St.) | Cambridge | 617-868-2255 |
www.harvestcambridge.com
"Forget the trendy places", this "longtime" Harvard Square "standard"-
bearer has been putting out "vibrant, seasonal, flavorful" New England
fare from its "reliably outstanding" kitchen for more than three decades; the "excellent" staff patrols the "lovely", "intimate" interior and
"beautiful courtyard", imparting an air of "class" to help ease the
minds of the "price-conscious."

Hungry Mother Ⓜ *Southern*
27 | 23 | 25 | $46

Kendall Square | 233 Cardinal Medeiros Ave. (Bristol St.) | Cambridge |
617-499-0090 | www.hungrymothercambridge.com
Chef Barry Maiden "adds an elegant flourish to down-home" but "incredible" Virginian cooking at this "ah-mazing", "pricey" American in
Kendall Square; if you can get in (it's "always super-booked"), "well-
versed" staffers "make you feel at home" in the "charming", "cozy"
space while proffering a "wonderful" selection of "fun" tipples.

Il Capriccio Ⓩ *Italian*
28 | 24 | 28 | $59

Waltham | 888 Main St. (Prospect St.) | 781-894-2234 |
www.ilcapricciowaltham.com
With "consistently superb, interesting" Northern Italian fare paired
with a "noteworthy" wine selection and served by an "outstanding"
staff in "comfy", "old-world" environs, this three-decade-old Waltham
"gem" is "not to be missed"; it gives even "upscale" Downtown eateries a "run for their money" – if you've got the "big bucks."

Island Creek Oyster Bar ❶ *Seafood*
28 | 26 | 26 | $49

Kenmore Square | 500 Commonwealth Ave. (Kenmore St.) |
617-532-5300 | www.islandcreekoysterbar.com
"Experienced restaurateur, oyster farmer" and co-owner Skip Bennett
offers "outstanding" bivalves from his own beds and other "fresh-as-
can-be", "delicious" seafood at this "hip" "must-eat" destination in
Kenmore Square; the "slick", "snappy" digs harbor "superb" staffers
with "expert" knowledge plus "thirtysomethings" knocking back
"amazing" drinks and – "pricey" tabs notwithstanding – having "the
time of their lives."

Journeyman *American*
27 | 23 | 25 | $90

Somerville | 9 Sanborn Ct. (Washington St.) | 617-718-2333 |
www.journeymanrestaurant.com
As "imaginative" and "playful" as "a Lewis Carroll story", this Somerville
"experience" pairs its "exciting", local, seasonal New American menu

with "geographically diverse" wines and "inventive cocktails"; "simple" decor and "attentive" service keep the focus on the "culinary adventure", which, while "on the pricey side", offers a "surprising amount of value."

L'Espalier *French/New England*

28 | 27 | 27 | $97

Back Bay | 774 Boylston St. (Ring Rd.) | 617-262-3023 | www.lespalier.com
Chef-owner Frank McClelland "continues to excel" at this "magical" Back Bay "foodie's dream", where "modern" twists on the "classics" result in New French–New English prix fixe dinners so "superb", you'll "want to lick the plate"; with "top-drawer" wines to sip and "impeccable" service from a "gracious" staff, "you could spend hours" in the "elegant", "romantic" environs – but prepare to pay "special-splurge" prices for the privilege; P.S. lunch has à la carte options in addition to tasting menus.

Life Alive *Vegan/Vegetarian*

28 | 23 | 21 | $14

Central Square | 765 Massachusetts Ave. (Inman St.) | Cambridge | 617-354-5433
Salem | 281 Essex St. (Sewall St.) | 978-594-4644
www.lifealive.com
"Health-conscious palates" are "in heaven" at this value-priced vegan/vegetarian outlet serving "outstanding", "nutritious" organic fare and "oh-so-good" smoothies; waits "till eternity" lead to complaints it's "outgrown" its "casual", "earth-friendly" space in Central Square, but "funky" staffers "happy to cater to whims" help ease the angst, plus the Salem outpost is an alternative.

Lumière *French*

28 | 24 | 27 | $57

Newton | 1293 Washington St. (Waltham St.) | 617-244-9199 | www.lumiererestaurant.com
Reflecting a seasonal, "local emphasis", the menu at Michael Leviton's Newton New French "always changes", but the "quality and inventiveness" of the "gorgeous" fare is "remarkably consistent"; a "knowledgeable, efficient" staff and "beautiful, cozy" setting help put it on the "short list" for a "fancy", "memorable" – and "pricey" – occasion.

Menton *French/Italian*

28 | 27 | 29 | $141

Seaport District | 354 Congress St. (A St.) | 617-737-0099 | www.mentonboston.com
Barbara Lynch "outdoes herself" at this "beautiful", "intimate", "white-tablecloth" Seaport District destination that ranks No. 1 in Service in Boston thanks to a "phenomenal" crew that's "always available but never intrusive" in stewarding the "exquisite" French-Italian prix fixe-only dinners ("every morsel will dance on your tongue") and "elegant" wines; while many agree you'll pay "in spades", "if you have the expendable income", it's "dining perfection" "worth every penny."

Mistral *French/Mediterranean*

28 | 27 | 26 | $66

South End | 223 Columbus Ave. (Clarendon St.) | 617-867-9300 | www.mistralbistro.com
Still "magnificent", Jamie Mammano's South End "special-occasion spot" "never disappoints", delivering "heavenly", "haute gourmet" French-Med plates with "excellent" wines in an "elegant, warm" space with a "lively buzz" and a "comfortable", less-formal bar scene; it also in-

FOOD DECOR SERVICE COST

cludes a "superb" crew that does an "impeccable" job, making sure your meal is "well worth it" – "if you don't mind spending money."

Morton's The Steakhouse Steak
27 | 25 | 26 | $64

Seaport District | World Trade Center E. | 2 Seaport Ln. (bet. Congress St. & Seaport Blvd.) | 617-526-0410 | www.mortons.com

A "high-end" Seaport District "treat", this "stupendous", contemporary chain chophouse pairs "huge" hunks of "cooked-to-perfection" meat with "fantastic", "traditional" sides and an "extensive" list of wines; "gracious" servers add to the experience, reinforcing the impression that it's hard to "ever go wrong" here.

Myers + Chang Asian
25 | 21 | 23 | $34

South End | 1145 Washington St. (Berkeley St.) | 617-542-5200 | www.myersandchang.com

"Creative", "beautifully prepared" small plates fuse the "essence of home-cooked Chinese" with "unique" Southeast Asian "flair" at Joanne Chang and Christopher Myers' "funky" South End "go-to"; the "cozy diner"-like digs are usually "hopping", but "slick" customer service keeps things moving, and if family-style eating means rates can "really add up", you also get to "sample a lot", so "bring your appetite."

Neptune Oyster Seafood
28 | 23 | 24 | $43

North End | 63 Salem St. (bet. Morton & Stillman Sts.) | 617-742-3474 | www.neptuneoyster.com

Although it's a "mecca for oyster lovers", this "fabulous" North End "seafood place you always dreamed of" earns Boston's No. 1 ranking for Food because "every single thing on the menu" is "unbelievable", from the "warm, butter-smothered" lobster rolls "worth dying for" to johnnycakes "wisely touted by insiders"; "if you can get in the door" (with no reservations, lines "form shortly after it opens"), expect "expensive" tabs – but also count on an "intimate" ambiance, with "professional" staffers catering to a "jovial crowd."

No. 9 Park French/Italian
28 | 26 | 27 | $79

Beacon Hill | 9 Park St. (Beacon St.) | 617-742-9991 | www.no9park.com

"Genius" chef Barbara Lynch "sets a high bar" at her "chic", "polished" Beacon Hill flagship, where "innovative" twists and "subtle" "depth of flavor" distinguish "impeccably prepared" French-Italian fare that's paired with "fantastic" wines and cocktails by "sublime" servers who "really know their stuff"; no, "it ain't cheap", but "smitten" foodies don't mind "breaking the bank" for such a "spectacular" experience.

Oishii Ⓜ Japanese
28 | 21 | 23 | $47

Chestnut Hill | 612 Hammond St. (Sheafe St.) | 617-277-7888 | www.oishiiboston.com

Sudbury | Mill Village Shopping Ctr. | 365 Boston Post Rd. (Concord Rd.) | 978-440-8300 | www.oishiitoo.com

Oishii Boston ◖Ⓜ Japanese

South End | 1166 Washington St. (bet. Berkeley & Perry Sts.) | 617-482-8868 | www.oishiiboston.com

"Creativity knows no bounds" at these Japanese "jewels" where the "heavenly" sushi prepared by "master" chefs is both "art" and an "adventure"; the Chestnut Hill original and Sudbury branch are both "tiny" and "packed", while there's more room at the "infamous" South

End "hot spot", but wherever you wind up, expect "extravagant prices" – "well worth" it for the "world-class" experience.

Oleana   *Mediterranean*

FOOD	DECOR	SERVICE	COST
28	24	26	$55

Inman Square | 134 Hampshire St. (bet. Elm & Norfolk Sts.) | Cambridge | 617-661-0505 | www.oleanarestaurant.com

Chef Ana Sortun continues to "expand dining horizons" by embedding "complex", "memorable spice combinations" in every "taste bud-tantalizing" Mediterranean dish (including vegetarian and vegan ones) at her "pricey-but-worth-it" Inman Square "treasure"; just "plan ahead" to score reservations from the "warm" staff, since the "inviting" interior fills up with "beautiful people" – or arrive early to wait for a table on the "delightful", leafy patio, which doesn't accept bookings.

Rino's Place   🅱 *Italian*

FOOD	DECOR	SERVICE	COST
29	17	22	$28

East Boston | 258 Saratoga St. (Putnam St.) | 617-567-7412 | www.rinosplace.com

"Wonderful" homemade pasta and other "absolutely spectacular" specialties based on the "best ingredients" "rival those found in Italy" at this Eastie "fave"; it's relatively "cheap" too, which can keep the "loud", "old-school" dining room "impossible to get into" and the staff "so busy" – though the "long lines" are "worth the wait."

Sorellina   *Italian*

FOOD	DECOR	SERVICE	COST
28	28	28	$71

Back Bay | 1 Huntington Ave. (Blagden St.) | 617-412-4600 | www.sorellinaboston.com

Voted Boston's No. 1 for Decor, this "special place for special occasions" in the Back Bay has a "sexy", "almost NYC feel" to its "breathtaking" "black-and-white setting", and Jamie Mammano's "elegant" Italian cuisine is equally "sensational"; "exceptional service" is another aspect that makes for a "memorable" experience that admirers say warrants "return visits" – "once your bank account recovers."

Strip-T's   🅱 *American*

FOOD	DECOR	SERVICE	COST
26	15	24	$29

Watertown | 93 School St. (bet. Cypress & Laurel Sts.) | 617-923-4330 | www.stripts.com

Pay no mind to the "deceiving" name and "bare-bones", "hand-me-down style" at this "good-value" Watertown "dive" – the "panoply" of "unique" flavors in chef Tim Maslow's "inventive, challenging" American eats "will surprise and delight you"; it does get "crammed" sometimes, but service remains "friendly and fast."

Sweet Cheeks Q   *BBQ*

FOOD	DECOR	SERVICE	COST
25	22	23	$29

Fenway | 1381 Boylston St. (bet. Kilmarnock St. & Park Dr.) | 617-266-1300 | www.sweetcheeksq.com

"Former *Top Chef* contestant–turned–BBQer extraordinaire" Tiffani Faison dishes out "scrumptious", "smoky" meats and "tempting" sides ("you can't not try" the "heavenly" biscuits) from this "down-to-earth, casual eatery" in Fenway; even though it's "not cheap" comparatively, it's "always packed" with folks dining at the "family-style tables" made from repurposed church doors and bowling-alley lanes.

Ten Tables   *American/European*

FOOD	DECOR	SERVICE	COST
27	23	24	$48

Jamaica Plain | 597 Centre St. (bet. Goodrich Rd. & Pond St.) | 617-524-8810

(continued)

(continued)

Ten Tables

Harvard Square | 5 Craigie Circle (Craigie St.) | Cambridge | 617-576-5444
www.tentables.net

"Small but mighty" is the motto of this "delightful" pair in Harvard Square and Jamaica Plain, where the "fabulous" seasonal European-New American menu "isn't large", same as the "tiny", "warm" digs (yes, the original on Centre Street has only 10 tables, and "everyone is a bit squished in, but in a friendly way"); with "solid service" and relatively "reasonable prices" thrown into the mix, you're sure to "impress your date", be they a "Boston foodie or grandma."

Toro *Spanish*

28 | 24 | 23 | $43

South End | 1704 Washington St. (Springfield St.) | 617-536-4300 |
www.toro-restaurant.com

You might have to "fight for a seat" at this no-reservations, "packed-to-the-gills" South End "mob scene" from Ken Oringer (of Clio), but "go, go, go": the "phenomenal" Spanish tapas, including the "amazing" signature grilled corn, are "arguably the best in town"; though it can "add up quickly" pricewise, it's "completely worth it", especially with such a "cool" setting – raw wood, exposed brick – and such "nice" servers.

Toscano *Italian*

26 | 25 | 24 | $47

Beacon Hill | 47 Charles St. (bet. Chestnut & Mt. Vernon Sts.) |
617-723-4090
Harvard Square | 52 Brattle St. (Story St.) | Cambridge | 617-354-5250
www.toscanoboston.com

"After all these years", this "elegant" 1983 Beacon Hill "treat" "still surprises" with "rich, deeply satisfying (and filling)" Tuscan plates that are "worth" their "pricey" costs, which may be why it decided to expand its operation with a Harvard Square sibling; there's a "clubhouse" vibe to the "attractive" surroundings thanks to a "packed" room of locals, students, the occasional "Hollywood stars" and "knowledgeable" servers who "think of every need."

224 Boston Street *American*

25 | 23 | 24 | $29

Dorchester | 224 Boston St. (St Margaret St.) | 617-265-1217 |
www.224bostonstreet.com

"A gem that's withstood the test of time", this "welcoming" two-decade-plus Dorchester New American is a "reliable" stop for "exciting" seasonal dishes and "excellent service"; fair prices help lure "big crowds" that spill from the "quaint" quarters with "tons of character" into an outdoor area "surrounded by beautiful trees and plants."

Charleston

TOP FOOD RANKING

Restaurant	Cuisine
29 Peninsula Grill	Southern
Bertha's Kitchen	Soul Food
28 Dell'z Deli	Health Food/Sandwiches
Langdon's	American
Two Boroughs Larder	Eclectic
Charleston Grill	Southern
FIG	Southern
Tristan	American
Trattoria Lucca	Italian
Halls	Steak

OTHER NOTEWORTHY PLACES

Bessinger's	BBQ
Cypress Lowcountry	American
82 Queen	Southern
Hominy Grill	Southern
Husk	Southern
MacIntosh	American
Magnolia's	Southern
McCrady's	American
Ordinary	Seafood
39 Rue de Jean	French

Bertha's Kitchen ⊠ *Soul Food*   29 | 17 | 25 | $11

Downtown | 2332 Meeting St. (Echo Ave.) | 843-554-6519
The "authentic" soul food satisfies like your mama's cooking "on ste-roids" at this friendly Downtown counter-service "staple" where "never-disappointed" patrons expect "nothing fancy", just that the folks in the kitchen "can really cook"; it's so "affordable" you "could eat here every day" – the "downside is it's only open [till 7 PM]" on weekdays (closed weekends).

Bessinger's *BBQ*   25 | 20 | 22 | $15

West Ashley | 1602 Savannah Hwy. (White Oak Dr.) | 843-556-1354 | www.bessingersbbq.com
A "Charleston icon" for its "Carolina-style" barbecue that's a "true taste of the South" (and onion rings that "just might steal your heart"), this West Ashley spot hosts a weekend "all-you-care-to-eat" buffet and a daily counter-serve sandwich shop; if service is minimal and the decor deemed "perfect for a BBQ joint", "waddling out the door after a full meal" will "leave you counting down till your next visit"; P.S. hours vary.

Charleston Grill *Southern*   28 | 27 | 27 | $64

Downtown | Charleston Place Hotel | 224 King St. (Market St.) | 843-577-4522 | www.charlestongrill.com
A "gold standard" for "decadent dining", this "upscale Southern kitchen" in Downtown's Charleston Place Hotel "delivers on the de-

tails", from chef Michelle Weaver's "beautifully presented", "divine" dishes to an "incredible wine program" to "helpful (and abundant)" staffers led by the "incomparable" GM Mickey Bakst; the "warm", "romantic" setting has windows "overlooking the courtyard", and often gets a boost from "soothing" live jazz, but since "you pay" for it all, you might want to save it for "important occasions."

Cypress Lowcountry Grille *American*   26 | 27 | 26 | $52

Downtown | 167 E. Bay St. (Queen St.) | 843-727-0111 | www.magnolias-blossom-cypress.com

"Fusing Southern ingredients with French and Asian touches", the "creative regional cuisine" makes "your idle taste buds think" at this "pricey", "upscale" Downtown American, part of the Hospitality Management Group; the "modern", "big-city" setting (including an open kitchen and "great upstairs bar") and "meticulous", "top-notch" service cap a "consistently superior" experience.

Dell'z Deli ☒ *Health Food/Sandwiches*   28 | 18 | 24 | $12

Downtown | 1A Cannon St. (King St.) | 843-722-5376

"Mama Dell makes every wrap with love" at this Downtown "favorite" that "packs a huge punch" with "unbeatable", "healthy" sandwiches at "great-value" prices; it has limited hours (11 AM to 7 PM weekdays, 11 AM to 5 PM Saturday) and there are just a handful of seats in the "tiny", "hole-in-the-wall" space, but "super-friendly" counter service and a "cool vibe" help make it "the bomb"; P.S. spin-offs include Dell'z Uptown, a vegetarian/vegan cafe, and Dell'z Vibez, a smoothie bar.

82 Queen *Southern*   25 | 25 | 25 | $41

Downtown | 82 Queen St. (bet. King & Meeting Sts.) | 843-723-7591 | www.82queen.com

Oozing "classic Charleston charm" from its "dreamy", "intimate" courtyard to the "super-swanky" bar, this "romantic" Downtown venue earns plaudits for its "delectable" Southern cooking "with a twist" and "professional" service; it can get "pricey", for sure, but insiders insist it's "worth the money" for a "true Lowcountry experience" that "stands the test of time."

FIG ☒ *Southern*   28 | 23 | 26 | $52

Downtown | 232 Meeting St. (Hasell St.) | 843-805-5900 | www.eatatfig.com

"Local before local was cool", this "fabulous" "foodie haven" Downtown features "elegant", "innovative" Southern fare by "inspired chef" Mike Lata, complemented by "interesting" cocktails; "knowledge-able", "easygoing" service and "well-designed" digs further boost its appeal, and while it may be "pricey", admirers insist it's "one of Charleston's finest."

Halls *Steak*   28 | 26 | 26 | $61

Downtown | 434 King St. (John St.) | 843-727-0090 | www.hallschophouse.com

"The place to go if you want to be pampered", this "old-school" Downtown steakhouse features "tremendous" cuts of beef and "awesome sides" proffered by an almost "overly attentive" staff; "expense-account" pricing and "noisy" acoustics are downsides, but most still find it "fabulous for a special occasion"; P.S. don't miss the "superb" Sunday gospel brunch.

	FOOD	DECOR	SERVICE	COST

Hominy Grill *Southern*

| 26 | 20 | 23 | $23 |

Downtown | 207 Rutledge Ave. (Cannon St.) | 843-937-0930 |
www.hominygrill.com

"A favorite" for breakfast and brunch, this "Lowcountry gem" slings "creative" Southern "comfort dishes" in a "cute" Downtown space with a "small-town feel" and a patio; despite its popularity, most are willing "to wait in line" for the "phenomenal shrimp and grits", "amazing" Big Nasty biscuit sandwich and other "reasonably priced", "down-home" eats.

Husk *Southern*

| 23 | 25 | 24 | $51 |

Downtown | 76 Queen St. (King St.) | 843-577-2500 |
www.huskrestaurant.com

"The farm-to-table theme prevails" at this Downtown "must", where "well-tattooed chef" Sean Brock's "ever-changing" menu offers "amazing" "spins on classic" Southern dishes featuring "local ingredients with interesting twists" (and plenty of pork); the setting's a "beautifully restored historic house" overseen by "knowledgeable and efficient" staffers, and if some find prices "high", so is its popularity – "make reservations early."

Langdon's ☒ *American*

| 28 | 24 | 26 | $46 |

Mount Pleasant | 778 S. Shelmore Blvd. (Frontage Rd.) | 843-388-9200 |
www.langdonsrestaurant.com

"The chef is at the top of his game" at this Mount Pleasant American, where the "top-tier" fare and "excellent wine list" are "presented with care" and "rival any Downtown" eatery; maybe it "doesn't look like much on the outside", but once indoors "a beautiful bar and romantic dining room" await – and if it's "pricey", devotees declare it's a "worth-it" "treat."

The MacIntosh *American*

| 27 | 26 | 27 | $44 |

Downtown | 479 King St. (Radcliffe St.) | 843-789-4299 |
www.themacintoshcharleston.com

"You won't be disappointed" promise partisans of chef Jeremiah Bacon's "delightful", "creative" American fare, including his "crazy good" bone-marrow bread pudding, at this "bustling" Downtowner; "awesome" servers oversee a space that's "industrial but still warm", and the "superb" Sunday brunch is "not to be missed."

Magnolia's *Southern*

| 26 | 25 | 26 | $45 |

Downtown | 185 E. Bay St. (Lodge Alley) | 843-577-7771 |
www.magnolias-blossom-cypress.com

For a "classic Southern culinary experience", diners descend upon this Downtown "pioneer" serving up a "perfect mix of homestyle cooking and big-city flair" that's "consistently a pleasure" (including a "phenomenal fried chicken dinner"); a "polished", "knowledgeable" staff adds further panache to the "elegant", "warm" environs, and despite tabs that run "a little high", insiders insist it's a "must-visit, whether it's your first time in town or your 50th."

McCrady's ☒ *American*

| 28 | 28 | 27 | $60 |

Downtown | 2 Unity Alley (Bay St.) | 843-577-0025 |
www.mccradysrestaurant.com

Always creating "something surprising and wonderful", chef Sean Brock "displays his passion" for the "new new thing" (and "local ingre-

FOOD   DECOR   SERVICE   COST

dients") at this "outstanding-in-every-way" Downtowner, where his "adventurous" American menu is complemented by "outstanding wine pairings"; an "exceptional" staff "pampers" diners in the "intimate", "historic" space, and though it's "pricey", supporters say "it's absolutely worth it" since it's "one of the best in town" – just "go hungry and go all the way."

The Ordinary Ⓜ *Seafood*   — | — | — | E

Downtown | 544 King St. (bet. Spring & Woolfe Sts.) | 843-414-7060 | www.eattheordinary.com

Oysters harvested from local waters star at this seafooder from celebrated chef Mike Lata of FIG, situated in a soaring, circa-1927 former bank Downtown with 25-ft. ceilings and Palladian windows; the rest of the somewhat pricey menu features plenty of cooked seafood, and it's all ferried to table by white-jacketed servers.

Peninsula Grill *Southern*   29 | 28 | 29 | $67

Downtown | Planters Inn | 112 N. Market St. (Meeting St.) | 843-723-0700 | www.peninsulagrill.com

Rated No. 1 for Food in Charleston, this "classic dining room" in Downtown's "historic" Planters Inn offers "gastronomic bliss" in the form of "sublime" "interpretations of Lowcountry classics" presented with "flair" in an atmosphere with "loads of Southern charm"; diners are "lavished with attention" from servers who are "amazingly in sync, yet never obtrusive" as they work the "elegant" but "not over-stuffy" velvet-walled space, and if it's in the "special-occasion price category", all agree it's "an experience to remember."

39 Rue de Jean *French*   25 | 24 | 24 | $35

Downtown | 39 John St. (King St.) | 843-722-8881 | www.39ruedejean.com

The "*magnifique* mussels" get special attention at this "Parisian-like" Downtown bistro offering a "well-priced" menu that'll "satisfy anyone's taste buds" – from "French food with flair" to one of the "best burgers in town" to "amazing sushi" ("shut up, you'll love it!"); service is "friendly and experienced", and the "terrific bar scene" within the "bustling", brick-walled setting is the "original place to see and be seen."

Trattoria Lucca Ⓢ *Italian*   28 | 22 | 25 | $44

Downtown | 41A Bogard St. (Ashe St.) | 843-973-3323 | www.luccacharleston.com

"Absolutely divine" Northern Italian fare distinguishes this "higher-end" Downtowner, "a real treat" where star chef-owner Ken Vedrinski "makes magic" with his "unusually creative" renderings of "obviously very fresh" ingredients; the staff likewise "performs at the highest level", so despite acoustics that aren't for "the faint of heart" and pricing that'll "lighten your wallet", admirers advise it's "worth it"; P.S. a set-price, family-style dinner is offered on Mondays.

Tristan *American*   28 | 26 | 27 | $58

Downtown | 10 Linguard St. (State St.) | 843-534-2155 | www.tristandining.com

"Retreat from the hoi polloi" at this "upscale" Downtown American that'll "delight any foodie" with a menu that takes "innovative cuisine" to the level of "perfection"; "sleek, modern" yet "restful" environs and "top-notch" service ("expected for this price point") round out a "special-occasion place" that's also a "fave for quiet business meals."

Two Boroughs Larder ⊠Ⓜ *Eclectic*

28 | 26 | 25 | $34

Downtown | 186 Coming St. (Morris St.) | 843-637-3722 | www.twoboroughslarder.com

Dining "can be an adventure" at this Downtown Eclectic "treat" thanks to a "wildly diverse" and "constantly changing" all-day midpriced menu that "challenges the eater" with "out-of-this-world" fare; "friendly" service reflects the "low-key, informal atmosphere", and if a few quibble that the small room can get "crowded", most agree it's a "total home run"; P.S. an attached shop purveys boutique food items and tableware.

Charlotte

TOP FOOD RANKING

	Restaurant	Cuisine
28	McNinch House	Continental
	Barrington's	American
27	Fig Tree	Continental
	Fiamma	Italian
	Passion8 Bistro	European
	Capital Grille	Steak
26	Soul Gastrolounge	Eclectic
	Good Food on Montford	American
	Bonterra Dining & Wine Room	American
	Carpe Diem	American

OTHER NOTEWORTHY PLACES

Amélie's	Bakery
Bistro La Bon	European
Copper	Indian
Cowfish	American/Japanese
Del Frisco's	Steak
Luce	Italian
Rooster's	Southern
Toscana	Italian
Upstream	Seafood
Zebra Restaurant	French

Amélie's ● *Bakery*   25 | 23 | 21 | $13
NoDa | 2424 N. Davidson St. (28th St.) | 704-376-1781
Amélie's Petite *French*
Uptown | 330 S. Tryon St. (Martin Luther King Jr. Blvd.) | 704-376-1782
www.ameliesfrenchbakery.com
Open 24 hours a day – "and packed for all of them" – this French-inspired NoDa bakery (its smaller Uptown branch has more limited hours) attracts "hipsters" and other folks who "bring in laptops and camp out" while enjoying the "addictive" salted caramel brownies and "to-die-for" pastries, plus light fare like sandwiches and soups; the "bohemian" "houselike" setting is also perfect for "people-watching" while relaxing with a cuppa.

Barrington's 🗷 *American*   28 | 23 | 27 | $54
SouthPark | Foxcroft East Shopping Ctr. | 7822 Fairview Rd.
(bet. Simsbury Rd. & Valencia Terr.) | 704-364-5755 |
www.barringtonsrestaurant.com
Voted Charlotte's Most Popular restaurant, this SouthPark New American provides "magic on a nightly basis" thanks to chef-owner Bruce Moffett, who employs a "farm-to-fork strategy" in his "excellent" seasonal creations; the traditional-looking dining room is quite "small" but "cozy", service is "top-notch" and the menu "changes just enough" for frequent visitors, so even those who find it "pricey" declare it's "worth every penny" – just "book well in advance."

	FOOD	DECOR	SERVICE	COST

Bistro La Bon *European*   25 | 20 | 22 | $29

Plaza Midwood | 1322 Central Ave. (Clement Ave.) | 704-333-4646 | www.bistrolabon.com

A "delightful surprise" awaits for those who get past this Plaza Midwood bistro's "odd" strip-mall location to find a "rustic" old-world eatery with an "upscale feel" serving "amazing" European fare with some "interesting" Swedish specialties; solid service and an "enjoyable" Sunday brunch smorgasbord also help make it "highly recommended."

Bonterra Dining & Wine Room *American*   26 | 27 | 26 | $51

Dilworth | 1829 Cleveland Ave. (Worthington Ave.) | 704-333-9463 | www.bonterradining.com

An "incredible wine selection" (notably the extensive "by-the-glass list") lifts the spirits of diners who also appreciate the "excellent" locally sourced American fare at this "upscale" eatery/wine bar in a "charming old church building" in Dilworth; the faithful sing the praises of the "knowledgeable" and "attentive" servers, and the whole package works for an evening of "fine dining or wine and appetizers."

The Capital Grille *Steak*   27 | 25 | 27 | $60

Uptown | IJL Financial Ctr. | 201 N. Tryon St. (5th St.) | 704-348-1400 | www.thecapitalgrille.com

"Incredible", "skillfully" prepared cuts of beef are the draw at this clubby Uptown chain steakhouse that's "outstanding in every way"; service is "impeccable" and the bar provides a "great place to mix and mingle" – "but pack the plastic, you'll need it."

Carpe Diem ☒ *American*   26 | 25 | 26 | $44

Elizabeth | 1535 Elizabeth Ave. (Travis Ave.) | 704-377-7976 | www.carpediemrestaurant.com

"Excellent", eminently "reliable" New American fare and an "outstanding" staff have made this elegant Elizabeth dining destination "a long-term winner"; its "beautiful" art nouveau decor, featuring ornate woodwork, is "great for a romantic dinner", but it's also an "anytime favorite" because you "don't [have] to mortgage the house on dinner."

Copper *Indian*   26 | 23 | 23 | $35

Dilworth | 311 East Blvd. (Cleveland Ave.) | 704-333-0063 | www.copperrestaurant.com

"Terrific", "inventive" subcontinental dishes enhanced by "great presentation" plus a setting in an "old Victorian" house in Dilworth signal that this is "not your run-of-the-mill Indian" spot; prices may be a "splurge" for the genre, but they're "worth" it, and though a few cite service "inconsistencies", most feel that "Copper is gold."

Cowfish *American/Japanese*   25 | 23 | 23 | $27

SouthPark | 4310 Sharon Rd. (Morrison Blvd.) | 704-365-1922 | www.thecowfish.com

"Not-to-be-missed 'burgushi'" (sushi that uses burger ingredients and vice versa) joins other "delicious, creative spins" on those dishes at this SouthPark American-Japanese mash-up that ensures "something on the menu for everyone"; the bold red, white and black space is "often crowded, with long waits", but once seated by the "friendly" staff, it's a "lively and fun" experience, abetted by a strong "bar scene."

Del Frisco's Double Eagle Steak House *Steak*

26 | 23 | 25 | $60

SouthPark | 4725 Piedmont Row Dr. S. (Fairview Rd.) | 704-552-5502 | www.delfriscos.com

"Always excellent" cuts of beef and a first-rate "bar scene" make this SouthPark steakhouse a popular dining option; "exceptional" service and an elegant, wood-paneled setting work as well for "business dinners" as "special occasions" – just "bring the Brink's truck."

Fiamma *Italian*

27 | 19 | 24 | $36

Dilworth | Park Square Shopping Ctr. | 2418 Park Rd. (Ordermore Ave.) | 704-333-3062 | www.fiamma-restaurant.com

Its strip-mall location "doesn't prepare [diners] for the level of cuisine and service" provided at this Dilworth spot, which wows patrons with its "outstanding" Northern Italian cooking, including "great homemade pastas", and "friendly" staff; the simple, yellow-hued digs are "homey", in keeping with its "good-value" prices.

Fig Tree *Continental*

27 | 27 | 27 | $53

Elizabeth | 1601 E. Seventh St. (Louise Ave.) | 704-332-3322 | www.charlottefigtree.com

"Take time to find" this Elizabeth Continental tucked into a "romantic" 1913 Craftsman-style house, where an "excellent" wine list supports fare that's "adventurous" yet "comforting at the same time"; tabs may be "high", but the staff is sure to "make your special occasion very special."

Good Food on Montford 🗷 *American*

26 | 22 | 24 | $38

SouthPark | 1701 Montford Dr. (Park Rd.) | 704-525-0881 | www.goodfoodonmontford.com

This "hip and stylish" SouthPark American small-platery from Barrington's Bruce Moffett and his brother, Kerry, provides "inventive" fare and "reasonable" wines that help keep the atmosphere "buzzing" (read: "noisy"); a few folks sigh about the "no-reservations" policy, which means you can "wait and wait" at busy times, but even so it's "not to be missed."

Luce 🗷 *Italian*

26 | 24 | 24 | $47

Uptown | Hearst Plaza | 214 N. Tryon St. (bet. 5th & 6th Sts.) | 704-344-9222 | www.conterestaurantgroup.com

The "elegantly served" *molto buono* Italian cuisine shines at restaurateur Augusto Conte's "small" but "beautiful" columned dining room in the Hearst Plaza Uptown; it's not cheap, but it's "very well run" and in a "wonderful location" for those headed to the Blumenthal Performing Arts Center.

McNinch House 🗷🗹 *Continental*

28 | 27 | 29 | $104

Uptown | 511 N. Church St. (bet. 8th & 9th Sts.) | 704-332-6159 | www.mcninchhouserestaurant.com

"The consummate special-occasion spot", this Uptown Queen Anne–style house is "the perfect backdrop for a romantic evening" lingering over multicourse flights of "flawless" Continental dishes that earn it Charlotte's No. 1 rating for Food; the "gracious" service (also voted tops in the city) is "marvelous", though the tabs are "equally special"; P.S. jackets required.

	FOOD	DECOR	SERVICE	COST

Passion8 Bistro 🌱Ⓜ *European* | 27 | 20 | 26 | $48 |

Fort Mill | 3415 Hwy. 51 N. (Rte. 21) | 803-802-7455 |
www.passion8bistro.com

Set in an "out-of-the-way" former brothel, this "delightful" Fort Mill "gem" is "small" but boasts "huge flavor", along with Italianate leanings, in its locally sourced European fare; prices are robust, but with "great" service and a romantic vibe, it's considered a "date-night" destination.

Rooster's *Southern* | 24 | 23 | 24 | $33 |

SouthPark | 6601 Morrison Blvd. (Sharon Rd.) | 704-366-8688
Uptown | 150 N. College St. (bet. 5th & Trade Sts.) | 704-370-7667
www.roosterskitchen.com

Fans of this Southern "favorite" with SouthPark and Uptown branches advise you to "come with a crew" so you can "try a lot" of the small plates that "really pop", from "great" roasted chicken to "outstanding" mac 'n' cheese; moderate tabs, "accommodating" service and a "rustic" feel add up to a "casual" experience, while a creative cocktail program and an open kitchen lend a "vibrant" atmosphere.

Soul Gastrolounge ❶ *Eclectic* | 26 | 24 | 21 | $29 |

Plaza Midwood | 1500 Central Ave. (Pecan Ave.) | 704-348-1848 |
www.soulgastrolounge.com

Part Eclectic "tapas bar", part "nightclub", this resto-lounge in the heart of Plaza Midwood pleases a late-night crowd with its "clever" collection of small plates soundtracked by "great music"; a "friendly" staff adds to the overall "good value", making it a smart choice "for a date" or for groups relaxing in the cozy, denlike setting.

Toscana 🌱 *Italian* | 26 | 22 | 24 | $44 |

SouthPark | Specialty Shops on the Park | 6401 Morrison Blvd.
(bet. Coca-Cola Plaza & Roxborough Rd.) | 704-367-1808 |
www.conterestaurantgroup.com

Even "Italy does not get much better" than this SouthPark Italian stalwart from Augusto Conte, a restaurateur "who cares", which is evident in everything from the "fabulous", "authentic" fare to the "excellent" service; it's not cheap, but fans say it's "always a pleasure", whether seated in the "comfortable", cheerful dining room or on the "lovely" patio complete with a fountain.

Upstream *Seafood* | 25 | 25 | 24 | $50 |

SouthPark | Phillips Pl. | 6902 Phillips Place Ct. (Cameron Valley Pkwy.) |
704-556-7730 | www.upstreamit.com

You "can't go wrong with anything" here say fans of this SouthPark seafooder with "incredibly fresh" cooked fish preparations plus "great" sushi and "top-quality" oysters – and "save room for dessert"; though regular dinner prices aren't cheap, the "beautiful" maritime-themed space also hosts an "awesome", more affordable Sunday brunch.

Zebra Restaurant 🌱 *French* | 26 | 24 | 25 | $56 |

SouthPark | 4521 Sharon Rd. (bet. Coltsgate Rd. & Morrison Blvd.) |
704-442-9525 | www.zebrarestaurant.net

"Every bite is a 'wow'" at this "superb" New French dining room tucked into a SouthPark office building; it's "expensive", *bien sûr*, but a "wonderful" wood-paneled setting, exacting service and "a good wine cellar" help make it an "excellent special-occasion place."

Chicago

	FOOD	DECOR	SERVICE	COST

Acadia ☑ *American/Seafood*   27 | 25 | 24 | VE

South Loop | 1639 S. Wabash Ave. (bet. 16th & 18th Sts.) | 312-360-9500 | www.acadiachicago.com

A "special-occasion place", this seafood-focused South Loop New American impresses with Ryan McCaskey's "imaginative", "delicious" prix fixe meals presented "beautifully" in a "sleek, modern" space with "natural accents"; "helpful" staffers "genuinely care", and while "expensive" prices match the "fine-dining" cuisine, you can always "stop by the bar" for a more affordable "spur-of-the-moment" meal.

Alinea ☑ *American*   29 | 28 | 29 | $273

Lincoln Park | 1723 N. Halsted St. (bet. North Ave. & Willow St.) | 312-867-0110 | www.alinea-restaurant.com

"Expect to be wowed" at Grant Achatz's "unrivaled" Lincoln Park New American, a "culinary experience of a lifetime" (and Chicago's Most Popular restaurant) where "transcendent flavors", "unforgettable, artistic presentation" and "mind-blowing technique" highlight a multi-course tasting menu that's akin to "going on a food safari"; "über-modern" decor is enhanced by "interactive, accommodating" staffers, and while you may need to "bring the Brink's truck" to pay, well, that might be the cost of "foodie heaven."

Arami ☑ *Japanese*   27 | 22 | 23 | $47

West Town | 1829 W. Chicago Ave. (bet. Wolcott Ave. & Wood St.) | 312-243-1535 | www.aramichicago.com

A "favorite for sushi", this "hip, urban" West Town storefront delivers "fresh, imaginative" rolls alongside other highly rated Japanese dishes including small plates, noodles and robata grill items; service is "helpful" in the "relaxing" "spa"-like setting done up in bamboo and exposed brick, and prices are moderate.

Avec ◑ *Mediterranean*   28 | 23 | 24 | $48

West Loop | 615 W. Randolph St. (bet. Desplaines & Jefferson Sts.) | 312-377-2002 | www.avecrestaurant.com

"Small plates at their best" can be found at this "energetic" West Loop Mediterranean, Blackbird's more "casual", less expensive sibling that's "still going strong" with "delicious" "elevated comfort food" (including "mandatory" chorizo-stuffed dates) dispensed by a "friendly, helpful" crew; the "teeny" space has a "festive", "lively" vibe, and while "social" communal seats "may not be for everyone" and "no reservations can mean a wait", it's still one of the "most consistently great" choices in town; P.S. it now serves brunch.

Balena *Italian*   24 | 23 | 23 | $53

Lincoln Park | 1633 N. Halsted St. (bet. North Ave. & Willow St.) | 312-867-3888 | www.balenachicago.com

Between the "consistently impressive" pizzas, "must-have" pastas, "delicious" cocktails and "oustanding wine list", fans find lots to like at this Lincoln Park 'in' spot where chef Chris Pandel's "inventive" dishes offer an "original" take on Italian cuisine; the "sprawling", earth-toned space includes a brown leather and steel bar and can be a "bit of a scene", but service remains "helpful", and its location across from the Steppenwolf makes it an "excellent choice for pre-or post-theater dining."

	FOOD	DECOR	SERVICE	COST

Blackbird 🗄 *American* — 27 | 23 | 25 | $69

West Loop | 619 W. Randolph St. (bet. Desplaines & Jefferson Sts.) | 312-715-0708 | www.blackbirdrestaurant.com

"Interesting", "sophisticated" New American dishes are "beautifully presented" by "attentive" staffers at this "well-established" West Loop "classic" from Paul Kahan and crew; the "sleek, modern" space can get "a bit loud", and it's certainly not cheap, but many still consider it a "top" place to "impress" and just right for a "special occasion."

Brindille 🗄 *French* — - | - | - | E

River North | 534 N. Clark St. (bet. Grand Ave. & Ohio St.) | 312-595-1616 | www.brindille-chicago.com

French fine dining from Carrie Nahabedian and the Naha team regales River North at this luxury dinner-only destination with both à la carte and tasting menu options (and plenty of wine, champagne, craft cocktails, absinthe and fromage); the sophisticated, urban Paris-inspired setting is done in earth tones with soft lighting and forest murals that echo the name of the restaurant (translation: twig).

EL Ideas 🗄 Ⓜ *American* — 28 | 20 | 26 | $189

Pilsen | 2419 W. 14th St. (bet. 15th St. & Ogden Ave.) | 312-226-8144 | www.elideas.com

"Genius" chef Phillip Foss has "reinvented fine dining" at this Pilsen New American where he prepares an "original", "standout" tasting menu in "intimate" (read: tiny) digs with decor so simple it has a "kind of pop-up feel"; the open kitchen "allows you to interact with the chef", so "real foodies" shrug off big-ticket prices since it's "more like an experience" than a meal – just "bring some nice wine" as it's BYO.

Elizabeth 🗄 Ⓜ *American* — - | - | - | VE

Lincoln Square | 4835 N. Western Ave. (bet. Gunnison St. & Lawrence Ave.) | 773-681-0651 | www.elizabeth-restaurant.com

At this Lincoln Square New American, forager/underground chef Iliana Regan serves a fine-dining take on 'new gatherer cuisine' (farm-to-table, nose-to-tail and root-to-branch) in an "innovative" tasting menu reserved online through a ticketing system; the setting evokes a funky cottage with white, wood and metal surfaces, mismatched chairs and animal figurines, and though it's pricey, early adopters say it's one of "Chicago's most creative and artistic new restaurants."

Fat Rice 🗄 Ⓜ *Eclectic* — - | - | - | M

Logan Square | 2957 W. Diversey Ave. (Sacramento Ave.) | 773-661-9170 | www.eatfatrice.com

From the X-Marx supper club team comes this midpriced Logan Square Eclectic purveying "complexly" flavored comfort foods from China, India, Africa and the Caribbean accompanied by European wines, a handful of beers and crafty cocktails; the rustic-modern space has communal tables and a dining bar overlooking the open kitchen, and since it's tiny you might want to "get there early."

Frontera Grill 🗄 Ⓜ *Mexican* — 27 | 22 | 24 | $45

River North | 445 N. Clark St. (bet. Hubbard & Illinois Sts.) | 312-661-1434 | www.fronterakitchens.com

Still "hip", "always packed" and "innovative" after more than 25 years, Rick Bayless' "top-notch" River North Mexican draws 'em in with "per-

FOOD | DECOR | SERVICE | COST

fectly constructed" "gourmet" dishes elevated by "creative and novel" flavor combinations and further boosted by "powerful but refined" margaritas; "helpful" staffers work the colorful, art-enhanced digs, and even if reservations are tough to come by and "you could have a birthday waiting for a table", it remains a "perennial favorite" that fans say "belongs on eveyone's bucket list."

Gaetano's 🗷 *Italian* — 27 | 21 | 24 | $58

Forest Park | 7636 Madison St. (bet. Ashland & Lathrop Aves.) | 708-366-4010 | www.gaetanos.us

"Prepare for an experience" at this smallish Forest Park Italian, where the "talented" chef delivers "completely unexpected", praiseworthy dishes available à la carte or in "unbelievable" tasting menus; service earns strong marks too in the upscale-casual space, and while tabs aren't cheap, fans still consider it "affordable" given the quality.

Gibsons Bar & Steakhouse *Steak* — 26 | 22 | 25 | $67

Gold Coast | 1028 N. Rush St. (Bellevue Pl.) | 312-266-8999 ☻
Rosemont | Doubletree O'Hare | 5464 N. River Rd. (bet. Balmoral & Bryn Mawr Aves.) | 847-928-9900 ☻
Oak Brook | 2105 S. Spring Rd. (22nd St.) | 630-954-0000
www.gibsonssteakhouse.com

A "big-time steakhouse for big-time folks", this Gold Coast "staple" and its suburban spin-offs deliver "cooked-to-perfection" chops, equally "excellent" seafood and drinks and "absurdly large desserts"; "professional, accommodating" staffers lend more appeal, while an "energetic" atmosphere (especially at the flagship, which can get "crowded" and "noisy") means it's tops for "people-watching."

Girl & The Goat *American* — 27 | 24 | 25 | $58

West Loop | 809 W. Randolph St. (bet. Green & Halsted Sts.) | 312-492-6262 | www.girlandthegoat.com

"Believe the hype" say fans of this spendy West Loop "blockbuster" where "genius" Stephanie Izard takes diners on a New American "culinary adventure" courtesy of "mind blowingly interesting" small plates including "brilliant" nose-to-tail creations ("how is it possible for pig face to be so delicious?"); the "warm", "casual" digs have a "lively" (some say "noisy") buzz and service is "knowledgeable", so many are left with but "one wish" – to be able to "get in more often."

Goosefoot 🗷🅼 *American* — ▽ 29 | 24 | 26 | $126

Lincoln Square | 2656 W. Lawrence Ave. (Washtenaw Ave.) | 773-942-7547 | www.goosefoot.net

Dining is an "event" at this big-ticket New American in Lincoln Square where Chris Nugent's "finely thought out" tasting menus yield "creative, beautiful and delicious" plates in a simple, upscale-casual space; it's BYO, but the "helpful" staff will assist in "selecting the wine before coming" – just note the tiny surrounds mean scoring reservations can be "very difficult."

Grace *American* — ▽ 29 | 27 | 29 | $239

West Loop | 652 W. Randolph St. (Desplaines St.) | 312-234-9494 | www.grace-restaurant.com

Superlatives abound ("superb", "fabulous") at this "fine-dining" destination in the West Loop where chef-owner Curtis Duffy (ex Avenues,

Alinea) prepares two "unforgettable" contemporary American tasting menus (omnivore and vegetable-focused) featuring "complex yet pure flavors" and "stunning" presentations; the space has a "minimalist elegance" with soothing neutrals, plush leather chairs, abstract art and a see-and-be-scene cocktail lounge, and service is "impeccable", so "huge" bills aren't unexpected.

Green Zebra *Vegetarian*   27 | 23 | 24 | $49

Noble Square | 1460 W. Chicago Ave. (Greenview Ave.) | 312-243-7100 | www.greenzebrachicago.com

"Exciting" meat-free dishes impress "even confirmed carnivores" at this Noble Square destination, where Shawn McClain's "upscale", "inventive" small plates make it the "best vegetarian in town"; a "knowledgeable" staff elevates the sage-colored space, and notable cocktails plus "interesting" wines are further enticements.

Joe's Seafood, Prime Steak & Stone Crab *Seafood/Steak*   27 | 22 | 26 | $66

River North | 60 E. Grand Ave. (Rush St.) | 312-379-5637 | www.joes.net

"If you can't get to Miami Beach", fans recommend this River North echo of the famed Florida original, where steaks are "cooked just right" and the "high-quality" seafood includes "not-to-be-missed" stone crab; it's all served by "charming, unpretentious" staffers in "bustling" dark wood–accented digs, and if the "special-occasion" tabs make some "crabby", well you can always go when "someone else is paying."

Katsu Japanese Ⓜ *Japanese*   29 | 19 | 24 | $61

Northwest Side | 2651 W. Peterson Ave. (bet. Talman & Washtenaw Aves.) | 773-784-3383

"If you crave real Japanese sushi" (and "not Westernized maki rolls") fans say "don't miss" this Northwest Side stalwart where chef-owner Katsu Imamura makes use of "excellent-quality" ingredients in his "expertly prepared" fare ("one word: omakase"), earning it top Food honors in Chicago; "friendly" staffers work the minimalist space, and "expensive" tabs aren't a surprise given the highly rated offerings.

Les Nomades Ⓢ Ⓜ *French*   28 | 26 | 28 | $126

Streeterville | 222 E. Ontario St. (bet. Fairbanks Ct. & St. Clair St.) | 312-649-9010 | www.lesnomades.net

"One of the last classic French white-tablecloth occasion restaurants", this Streeterville destination set in an "elegant" townhouse dispenses chef Roland Liccioni's "perfectly executed" plates paired with an "amazing wine list"; maybe it "costs a fortune", but "impeccable" service helps, and anyway, devotees swear it's "as good as it is expensive"; P.S. jackets required.

Longman & Eagle ◑ *American*   27 | 21 | 23 | $42

Logan Square | 2657 N. Kedzie Ave. (Schubert Ave.) | 773-276-7110 | www.longmanandeagle.com

"Expect the hipsters" at this "in-demand" Logan Square New American where a "clear affection for niche ingredients" results in "exciting", "absolutely delicious" fare, including an "especially decadent" brunch; a "ridiculous" whiskey list and "killer" cocktails are other reasons to go, but "come early or plan on waiting" as it doesn't take reservations; P.S. if you overindulge, you can get a room upstairs and "sleep it off while your liver mends."

L2O *Seafood* | 26 | 28 | 27 | $182 |

Lincoln Park | The Belden-Stratford | 2300 N. Lincoln Park W. (Belden Ave.) | 773-868-0002 | www.l2orestaurant.com

"Imaginative, exquisitely executed" tasting menus evoke "oohs and aahs" at this "fine-dining" seafood specialist in Lincoln Park; the "classy", "calming" space is tended by an "attentive, knowledgeable" staff, so those deep-pocketed enough to weather "aftershocks of the bill" declare it "money well spent."

Mixteco Grill Ⓜ *Mexican* | 27 | 17 | 22 | $30 |

Lakeview | 1601 W. Montrose Ave. (Ashland Ave.) | 773-868-1601 | www.mixtecogrill.com

"Interesting, flavorful" fare, including "excellent moles", is what it's about at this midpriced Lakeview Mexican that pairs its "delicious" dishes with a BYO policy ("what could be better?"); the colorful modest space is decorated with framed art, and since it's small, it can get "crowded" fast.

MK *American* | 27 | 25 | 26 | $72 |

Near North | 868 N. Franklin St. (bet. Chestnut & Locust Sts.) | 312-482-9179 | www.mkchicago.com

Given the "inventive", "always changing" seasonal menu, "well-prepared" dishes and "excellent wine list", regulars insist you "won't go wrong" at Michael Kornick's Near North New American; "professional" staffers work the "high-energy" space that's "elegant without being stuffy", so all in all it's a "special-occasion" "go-to" – with "special-occasion" tabs to match.

Naha Ⓩ *American* | 26 | 23 | 25 | $74 |

River North | 500 N. Clark St. (Illinois St.) | 312-321-6242 | www.naha-chicago.com

Carrie Nahabedian has a "track record" of providing "consistently excellent", "high-quality" meals at this River North New American where many dishes feature "Mediterranean influences" and get a boost from "inventive" combinations of flavors; "top-line" service and "Zen-like decor" further justify the "pricey" tabs and also help cement its status as a "fine-dining favorite."

Next Ⓜ *Eclectic* | 29 | 26 | 29 | $175 |

West Loop | 953 W. Fulton Mkt. (bet. Morgan & Sangamon Sts.) | 312-226-0858 | www.nextrestaurant.com

Part "foodie dinner theater", part "culinary adventure", Grant Achatz's West Loop Eclectic venue presents a "simply mind-blowing", often-changing themed tasting menu prepared with an "unmatched" level of detail and "impeccably presented" by an "exemplary", "professional" staff that earns top Service honors in Chicago; the modern, high-style space provides a fitting backdrop, and given the "stunningly good" offerings, sky-high prices barely register – just note you'll need to score a "hard-to-get" online ticket in order to go.

	FOOD	DECOR	SERVICE	COST

NoMI Kitchen *American* | 26 | 27 | 26 | $72 |

Gold Coast | Park Hyatt Chicago | 800 N. Michigan Ave., 7th fl. (bet. Chicago Ave. & Pearson St.) | 312-239-4030 | www.parkchicago.hyatt.com

You can "relax and get away from the loudness of the city" at this "expensive" but "worth it" New American in the Gold Coast's Park Hyatt where local ingredients feature heavily on the "fantastic" menu, which includes "incredibly fresh" sushi too; the upscale-casual space with "beautiful views" overlooking Michigan Avenue and a "delightful" roof garden works well for "date night" or "business meetings", and an "excellent" staff adds to the appeal.

The Publican *American* | 26 | 23 | 23 | $50 |

West Loop | 837 W. Fulton Mkt. (Green St.) | 312-733-9555 | www.thepublicanrestaurant.com

"Try everything" say fans of Paul Kahan's "inspired" West Loop New American, where the pork-centric menu allows for a "superb pigtastic experience" and includes other "well-prepared, full-of-flavor" share plates plus oysters too; "lots of craft beers" and "stiff" cocktails up the "cool" factor and the "huge communal tables" add group appeal, so even if it's "loud" and the bill can "add up quickly", it's still considered "all the rage (and rightfully so)."

Pump Room ◑ *American* | 21 | 27 | 24 | $62 |

Gold Coast | Public Chicago | 1301 N. State Pkwy. (Goethe St.) | 312-229-6740 | www.pumproom.com

"As elegant" as the first "historic" iteration, but in a "new, edgy way", this high-end New American in the Gold Coast's Public Hotel offers "celebrated" chef Jean-Georges Vongerichten's "inventive", seasonally inspired fare lifted by a "robust wine list" and "thoughtful, precisely prepared" cocktails; sure, a few say it has "lost some charm" of the original, but most can still appreciate the "beautiful", "swanky" setting, where a "hoity-toity crowd" makes it a "favorite" for "people-watching."

Purple Pig ◑ *Mediterranean* | 26 | 21 | 21 | $42 |

River North | 500 N. Michigan Ave. (Illinois St.) | 312-464-1744 | www.thepurplepigchicago.com

It's "always packed" at Jimmy Bannos Jr.'s "intimate" River North gastropub where the "interesting" Med menu is a "foodie adventure", full of "delicious", "mind-blowing" small plates including "unusual" "comfort zone"–busting choices you "won't see anywhere else"; "terrific" wines, "dynamite beers" and "friendly" staffers help fuel a "lively" scene, and while it's "easy to rack up a bill", it has all the makings for a "memorable" meal – if you can outlast the "long" wait (no reservations), that is.

Riccardo Trattoria *Italian* | 28 | 21 | 25 | $49 |

Lincoln Park | 2119 N. Clark St. (bet. Dickens & Webster Aves.) | 773-549-0038 | www.riccardotrattoria.com

It's "just like being in Italy" at this "cozy" Lincoln Park Italian that's "still one of the best after all these years" thanks to its "delicate", "simply wonderful" fare; service is "helpful" and the "relaxed" atmosphere is "romantic" enough for a date, and while it's not inexpensive, it's still deemed "reasonable" "given the quality"; P.S. when it's "hard to get in" you can try its newer enoteca sister across the street.

Ruxbin ⓜ Eclectic

28 | 24 | 24 | $45

Noble Square | 851 N. Ashland Ave. (Pearson St.) | 312-624-8509 | www.ruxbinchicago.com

"Come early or be prepared to wait" at this Noble Square Eclectic, where Edward Kim puts together an "amazing" menu of "inventive", "high-end" "comfort food"; "small" digs lead to "crowded" conditions ("every inch of space is claimed"), and it doesn't accept reservations (except on Sundays), but service is "welcoming", and the BYO policy makes it an "incredible value"; P.S. don't forget to check out one of the "best bathrooms in the city."

Schwa ⓈⓂ American

28 | 15 | 23 | $143

Wicker Park | 1466 N. Ashland Ave. (Le Moyne St.) | 773-252-1466 | www.schwarestaurant.com

"Super high-end food without the attitude" describes Michael Carlson's "very small" Wicker Park BYO where a "hyper-creative", "well-executed" New American tasting menu is delivered by the chefs themselves; "less than minimalist" decor "fits the vibe", and it all adds up to a "singular dining experience", so even with spendy tabs, reservations are "nearly impossible to come by."

Shanghai Terrace Ⓢ Chinese

26 | 28 | 26 | $69

River North | Peninsula Chicago | 108 E. Superior St., 4th fl. (bet. Michigan Ave. & Rush St.) | 312-573-6744 | www.chicago.peninsula.com

You'll feel "transported into another era" at this dining room in River North's Peninsula Hotel, where "excellent", "upscale" Chinese fare is served in an "exquisite" 1930s-styled room that "makes you feel like you're in Shanghai" (and wins top Decor honors in Chicago); "genuine" service and a "romantically lit" terrace provide further enticements – just expect "premium" pricing.

Spacca Napoli Pizzeria ⓜ Pizza

27 | 19 | 22 | $25

Ravenswood | 1769 W. Sunnyside Ave. (bet. Hermitage & Ravenswood Aves.) | 773-878-2420 | www.spaccanapolipizzeria.com

You'll feel like you're "truly in Italy" at this affordable Ravenswood pizzeria where a "traditional, Naples-style" wood oven bakes "amazing" thin-crust Neopolitan pies; the casual space may lag a bit behind, but it's joined by a "wonderful" patio, and the staff is "friendly and efficient."

Spiaggia Italian

26 | 26 | 26 | $104

Gold Coast | One Magnificent Mile Bldg. | 980 N. Michigan Ave. (Oak St.) | 312-280-2750 | www.spiaggiarestaurant.com

"The place for a romantic evening" say fans of Tony Mantuano's Gold Coast Italian where "absolutely heavenly" fare is matched by an "elegant" dining room (jackets required) with a "nice view of the lake"; sure, it's "not for the faint of heart or light of wallet", but with "wonderful" service it has all the ingredients for a "special night."

Takashi ⓜ American/French

28 | 23 | 25 | $66

Bucktown | 1952 N. Damen Ave. (Armitage Ave.) | 773-772-6170 | www.takashichicago.com

Fans are "blown away" by "true master" Takashi Yagihashi's "inspired", "soulful" New American–New French dishes at this Bucktown destination, where the "beautifully" presented Japanese-tinged dishes are set down by a "courteous" crew; the "cozy" space has an "understated upscale" vibe, and "pricey" tabs go hand in hand with the "fine-dining" experience.

Topolobampo 🅂🅼 *Mexican*

28 | 24 | 26 | $70

River North | 445 N. Clark St. (Illinois St.) | 312-661-1434 | www.rickbayless.com

"Tops in its category", Rick Bayless' "world-class" River North destination ranks as a "magnificent experience", offering "wow"-worthy, "high-end" "nuevo" Mexican meals made up of "innovative", "flavorful" dishes plus "don't-miss" margaritas and "excellent" wines; its "upper-crust" atmosphere ("totally different from Frontera next door") further explains the "premium" prices, while "welcoming, passionate" staffers are another reason to "keep going back" (if you can "snag a table").

Tru 🅂 *French*

27 | 27 | 28 | $150

Streeterville | 676 N. St. Clair St. (bet. Erie & Huron Sts.) | 312-202-0001 | www.trurestaurant.com

When you want to "splurge and impress", fans suggest this Streeterville "fine-dining" destination that "hits all the high notes", from Anthony Martin's "artistic, creative and sublimely delicious" contemporary French tasting menus to the "thoughtfully paced flow of courses" overseen by a "personable" staff; the "elegant" art-filled dining room (jackets required) further ups the ante, and while the cost may make it a "once-in-a-lifetime" meal for some, at least it's a "truly special" one.

Vie *American*

29 | 25 | 28 | $69

Western Springs | 4471 Lawn Ave. (Burlington Ave.) | 708-246-2082 | www.vierestaurant.com

City dwellers say this Western Springs New American is "worth the travel" to the 'burbs for Paul Virant's "exceptional" New American cooking that showcases "the season's best" ingredients in "outstanding" "fine-dining" dishes; the space is "warm and inviting but still elegant", and "impeccable" service further justifies the spendy tabs.

Connecticut

TOP FOOD RANKING

	Restaurant	Cuisine
28	Le Petit Cafe	French
	Thomas Henkelmann	French
	Golden Lamb Buttery	American
	Altnaveigh	Continental
27	Mill at 2T	American
	Bar Bouchée	French
	Craftsteak	Steak
	Union League Cafe	French
26	Pasta Nostra	Italian
	Winvian	American
	Rebeccas	American
	La Tavola	Italian
	Mondo*	Italian
	Cavey's Restaurants	French/Italian
	Oyster Club	New England
	Cedars	Steak
	Great Taste	Chinese
	Community Table	American
25	Carbone's Ristorante	Italian
	Modern Apizza	Pizza

OTHER NOTEWORTHY PLACES

Artisan	American
Barcelona Restaurant & Wine Bar	Spanish
Bernard's	French
David Burke Prime	Steak
Firebox	American
Frank Pepe	Pizza
Ibiza	Spanish
Le Farm	American
Max Downtown	American/Steak
Métro Bis	American
Millwright's	New England
Morton's	Steak
Ondine	French
Plan B Burger Bar	Burgers
River Tavern	American
Schoolhouse at Cannondale	American
Tarry Lodge	Italian
Valbella	Italian
West Street Grill	American
Whelk	Seafood

* Indicates a tie with restaurant above

	FOOD	DECOR	SERVICE	COST

The Altnaveigh ⧈Ⓜ *Continental* | 28 | 24 | 24 | $42 |

Storrs | Altnaveigh Inn | 957 Storrs Rd. (bet. Beebe Ln. & Spring Hill Rd.) |
860-429-4490 | www.altnaveighinn.com

"Always wonderful" Continental cuisine is served up by a "superb"
staff at this "very quaint" Storrs eatery housed in a 1734 farmhouse-
turned-inn, whose "cozy" period dining rooms and fireplace make
you feel "as though you are stepping back in time"; it's a "wonderful
special-occasion" destination, and another plus: it's located "near
the UConn campus."

Artisan *American* | 25 | 28 | 23 | $64 |

Southport | Delamar Hotel Southport | 275 Old Post Rd. (Rennell Dr.) |
203-307-4222 | www.artisansouthport.com

Parisian chef Frederic Kieffer dreams up "wonderful" New England–
style cuisine spotlighting "sensational" seafood at this "easygoing"
but "elegant" Southport American in the Delamar Hotel, where the
menus in both the main dining room and the no-reservations tavern emphasize seasonal, "mostly local" ingredients; "unobtrusive"
servers navigate the "lively" scene amid "old-world", 18th-century
Swedish furniture, striking floral murals and contemporary copper
chandeliers, while dining on the "amazing" outdoor patio is "like
being on vacation."

Bar Bouchée *French* | 27 | 22 | 24 | $49 |

Madison | 8 Scotland Ave. (Boston Post Rd.) | 203-318-8004 |
www.barbouchee.com

"Step into Paris in Madison" at this "very French" bistro from the
owners of New Haven's Union League Cafe, serving "simple" but
"beautifully prepared" classics (like "excellent" cassoulet) in a
"charming" traditional Gallic setting with "attentive" service; it's a
"boisterous", "convivial" scene – in fact, plan on "rubbing elbows"
with other diners in the "tight" space and note that it's "hard to
get a reservation."

Barcelona Restaurant & Wine Bar ❶ *Spanish* | 20 | 18 | 18 | $42 |

New Haven | Omni New Haven Hotel | 155 Temple St. (bet. Chapel &
Crown Sts.) | 203-848-3000
New Haven | Merritt Parkway Motor Inn | 4180 Black Rock Tpke.
(Congress St.) | 203-255-0800
South Norwalk | 63 N. Main St. (bet. Ann & Marshall Sts.) |
203-899-0088
Stamford | 18 W. Putnam Ave. (bet. Benedict Pl. & Greenwich Ave.) |
203-983-6400
Stamford | 222 Summer St. (bet. Broad St. & Summer Pl.) |
203-348-4800
West Hartford | 971 Farmington Ave. (bet. Lasalle Rd. & Main St.) |
860-218-2100
www.barcelonawinebar.com

Whether you "go with girlfriends, a group of couples or on a date"
there's "something for everyone" at this "festive", "atmospheric"
Spanish chainlet that "never fails to please" with its "original" tapas
complemented by an "extensive" wine list; the "friendly" staff helps
diners "navigate" the myriad choices, but "beware" – you may "spend
a small fortune" if you "over-order" those little plates.

	FOOD	DECOR	SERVICE	COST

Bernard's Ⓜ *French*
| 25 | 24 | 23 | $70 |

Ridgefield | 20 West Ln. (bet. High Ridge Ave. & Main St.) | 203-438-8282 | www.bernardsridgefield.com

Chef-owner Bernard Bouissou's classic French cuisine is both "consistent and imaginative" and "worth the money for a special evening out" say fans of this "lovely" Ridgefield "gem"; service is "crisp and courteous" and live piano on weekends ups the "elegant" atmosphere; P.S. the "lively" Sarah's Wine Bar upstairs offers a separate bistro menu and "less sticker shock."

Carbone's Ristorante Ⓢ *Italian*
| 25 | 21 | 24 | $47 |

Hartford | 588 Franklin Ave. (bet. Goodrich & Hanmer Sts.) | 860-296-9646 | www.carboneshartford.com

Family-owned since 1938, this "old-fashioned" "Hartford standard" continues to "attract couples for date nights" as well as "area politicos" with its "top-notch" "classic" Northern Italian cuisine that "never disappoints"; devotees deem the clubby environs "pleasant" and "comfortable", noting everything is "outstanding from coat check to check."

Cavey's Restaurants Ⓜ *French/Italian*
| 26 | 22 | 24 | $55 |

Manchester | 45 E. Center St. (bet. Main & Summit Sts.) | 860-643-2751 | www.caveysrestaurant.com

An "elegant", "classy" French restaurant on the ground floor and a more casual, Tuscan-feel second floor serving "consistently delicious" Italian cuisine make this Manchester hybrid "an experience to treasure" for loyalists; if a few find the "old-fashioned" decor "outdated", most deem it "enchanting" and are also charmed by the "attentive" staff and "extensive wine list"; P.S. only the Italian space is open Sunday.

Cedars *Steak*
| 26 | 24 | 24 | $50 |

Ledyard | Foxwoods Resort Casino | 350 Trolley Line Blvd. (bet. Foxwoods Blvd. & Lantern Hill Rd.) | 860-312-4252 | www.foxwoods.com

The "fantastic" fare at this spacious steakhouse at Foxwoods wins over carnivores who also deem the atmosphere "perfect" given that "you're never too close to another table"; the lavish cherry-wood and leather decor matches the big-ticket prices – and if you don't have a good day at the tables, you can always enjoy a "hamburger in the attached lounge."

Community Table *American*
| 26 | 20 | 23 | $56 |

Washington | 223 Litchfield Tpke. (Wilbur Rd.) | 860-868-9354 | www.communitytablect.com

A "true farm-to-table locavore gem", this "terrific" Washington New American is home to seasonal dishes made with "extremely fresh" local ingredients and prepared with "creative flair" by "talented chef" Joel Viehland; loyalists appreciate the "Scandinavian sparseness" of the "simple", airy space, whose centerpiece is a black-walnut communal table; P.S. closed Tuesday and Wednesday, except during the summer, when it has expanded hours.

Craftsteak *Steak*
| 27 | 25 | 25 | $71 |

Ledyard | MGM Grand at Foxwoods | 240 MGM Grand Dr. (Norwich Westerly Rd.) | 860-312-7272 | www.foxwoods.com

"When you've had a good day" at the gaming tables at the Foxwoods Casino, duck into this sleek steakhouse from *Top Chef* Tom Colicchio

	FOOD	DECOR	SERVICE	COST

for an "enjoyable" "splurge"; attentive service and lavish decor complete with Brazilian walnut, bronze and leather accents make for a high-roller ambiance, suitable for indulging in some of the "best" beef around, "hands down."

David Burke Prime Steak

25	24	23	$66

Ledyard | Foxwoods Resort Casino | 350 Trolley Lane Blvd. (bet. Foxwoods Blvd. & Lantern Hill Rd.) | 860-312-8753 | www.davidburkeprime.com

"Outstanding" dry-aged steaks and other "inventive" fare by celeb chef David Burke bring famished gamblers to this "glitzy", "gorgeous" carnivore's den in the Foxwoods Resort Casino; the presentation is "phenomenal" and service is "attentive", as you'd expect given the cost.

Firebox M American

25	22	22	$46

Hartford | Billings Forge | 539 Broad St. (bet. Capitol Ave. & Russ St.) | 860-246-1222 | www.fireboxrestaurant.com

An "inventively prepared" menu of "outstanding farm-to-table" New American cuisine offers "something for everyone" at this "casual-yet-classy" destination in Downtown Hartford's renovated Billings Forge; a "beautiful", soaring brick-walled interior and a "nice" wine list plus live music on Wednesdays and Sundays make it an enjoyably "trendy" option for "a special evening with friends."

Frank Pepe Pizzeria Napoletana Pizza

22	11	15	$19

Danbury | 59 Federal Rd. (International Dr.) | 203-790-7373
Fairfield | 238 Commerce Dr. (Brentwood Ave.) | 203-333-7373
Manchester | 221 Buckland Hills Dr. (Buckland St.) | 860-644-7333
New Haven | 157 Wooster St. (Brown St.) | 203-865-5762
Uncasville | Mohegan Sun Casino | 1 Mohegan Sun Blvd. (Sandy Desert Rd.) | 860-862-8888 ●

Frank Pepe's The Spot M Pizza

New Haven | 163 Wooster St. (Brown St.) | 203-865-5762
www.pepespizzeria.com

"Cheesy, luscious" and "piping hot", the coal-fired brick-oven pizzas at this regional chainlet (ranked as Connecticut's Most Popular) are a "dream come true" attest admirers who tout the "thin, charred, crispy" crusts and the simply "amazing" "signature" white clam pie; if some feel that the outposts are "not as good as the original", at least you don't have to "wait in line" like at the New Haven "mother ship" at 157 Wooster Street – though die-hard fans say even that is "worth" it.

The Golden Lamb Buttery ⊠M American

28	25	27	$98

Brooklyn | 499 Wolf Den Rd. (Bush Hill Rd.) | 860-774-4423 | www.thegoldenlamb.com

The Booth family's "breathtaking" 1,000-acre sheep farm in Brooklyn is the "peaceful" backdrop to a truly "unique" dining experience: partaking of "exceptional" "home-cooked" American cuisine in an antiques-filled, circa-1856 barn; the four-course prix fixe dinner – served Friday and Saturday only by a staff voted No. 1 for Service in Connecticut – starts with cocktails and an optional hayride, and is "beyond compare" for a "special occasion" making it "worth every dime and the long drive"; P.S. jacket and tie suggested, and lunch, served Tuesday–Saturday, is à la carte.

Great Taste *Chinese*

26 | 21 | 25 | $23

New Britain | 597 W. Main St. (bet. Homestead Ave. & Westerly St.) | 860-827-8988 | www.greattaste.com

Devoted Sinophiles "come back over and over again" to sample "some of the best" Chinese cuisine around at this New Britain stalwart with "personable service" and a "pretty" white-tablecloth setting; the large menu boasts "many traditional items" at "excellent" prices – the "unbeatable" Peking duck is "highly recommended" or "just ask the owner what's good that day."

Ibiza Ⓢ *Spanish*

25 | 21 | 21 | $51

New Haven | 39 High St. (bet. Chapel & Crown Sts.) | 203-865-1933 | www.ibizanewhaven.com

Ibiza Tapas *Spanish*

Hamden | 1832 Dixwell Ave. (Robert St.) | 203-909-6512 | www.ibizatapaswinebar.com

Ibiza Tapas and Wine Bar *Spanish*

Danbury | 93 Mill Plain Rd. (bet. Aunt Hack Rd. & Westwood Dr.) | 203-616-5731 | www.ibizatapaswinebar.com

It would be hard to find more "exciting, flavorful" Spanish cuisine "without going to Spain itself" rave "real foodies" who "feel right at home" at this "outstanding" Downtown New Haven destination (with more casual, affordable tapas bar offspring in Danbury and Hamden); though it can get a "bit noisy" and "expensive", a "wonderful" wine list, fairly "seamless" service and a bright, "nicely decorated" contemporary space seal the deal.

La Tavola Ⓢ *Italian*

26 | 20 | 19 | $47

Waterbury | 702 Highland Ave. (Wilkenda Ave.) | 203-755-2211 | www.latavolaristorante.com

From the "top-notch" savory Italian dishes to the "outstanding" dessert, this "consistently excellent" Waterbury spot helmed by chef Nicola Mancini is a "delightful dining experience", even if it's on the "pricey" side; added perks are its "friendly" staff and rich dark-wood decor offset by a waterfall wall, plus there's live music on Wednesday nights.

Le Farm ⓈⓂ *American*

24 | 18 | 23 | $61

Westport | 256 Post Rd. E. (bet. Compo Rd. & Imperial Ave.) | 203-557-3701 | www.lefarmwestport.com

Making "meticulous use" of local, "in-season" ingredients, "brilliant" chef-owner Bill Taibe coaxes "big, bold flavors" out of the "innovative" New American cuisine on offer at his Westport "farm-to-table" spot; an "attentive" staff, "interesting" wines and a "cozy" space with a modern farmhouse look further explain why it's "popular."

Le Petit Cafe Ⓜ *French*

28 | 21 | 26 | $68

Branford | 225 Montowese St. (Main St.) | 203-483-9791 | www.lepetitcafe.net

"Make sure you book" well in advance advise admirers of this Branford Gallic bistro, voted No. 1 for Food in Connecticut and run by "passionate" chef-owner Roy Ip and his "polished staff"; each evening's four-course, prix fixe "gourmet extravanganza" consists of "absolutely scrumptious" classics served in a "cozy" "French-countryside" atmo-

	FOOD	DECOR	SERVICE	COST

sphere that makes for "fine dining without the pretense", and while tabs aren't *petit*, it's "very reasonably priced for the quality" of the fare; P.S. two seatings nightly.

Max Downtown   *American/Steak*

| 25 | 24 | 24 | $57 |

Hartford | City Pl. | 185 Asylum St. (Trumbull St.) | 860-522-2530 | www.maxrestaurantgroup.com

Perhaps the "classiest" of the Max restaurant group, this "sophisticated" New American steakhouse in Downtown Hartford impresses with "amazing" chops, "novel sides", a "superb" wine list and "local cheeses and desserts"; "top-shelf" service (the "bartenders know their cocktails") and a "wonderful" clubby atmosphere help attract a "business-dress" crowd, and while tabs are "expensive", it's "definitely worth it."

Métro Bis ⑤ *American*

| 25 | 20 | 24 | $48 |

Simsbury | Simsburytown Shops | 928 Hopmeadow St. (Massaco St.) | 860-651-1908 | www.metrobis.com

A Simsbury "old reliable", this New American boasts "high-end" bistro fare that's "imaginative" and "always well prepared" by chef Chris Prosperi, who, along with his wife and co-owner, Courtney Febbroriello, "make you feel at home"; add in "interesting specials and wine pairings" and a "French-country-house" ambiance and you have a "special-occasion" dining experience with plenty of "panache."

Mill at 2T ⑤Ⓜ *American*

| 27 | 23 | 24 | $64 |

Tariffville | 2 Tunxis Rd. (Hartford Ave.) | 860-658-7890 | www.themillat2T.com

"Reservations are a must" at this "intimate" New American in a converted mill in Tariffville where "welcoming" owners Kelleanne and (chef) Ryan Jones make you feel like you're "going to a friend's house for dinner"; the "always seasonal and inventive" dishes are complemented by a "small but terrific wine list", while the wood-beamed ceilings and brick walls create a "comfortable" atmosphere – in short, it's "fine dining at its best", "not rigid and stuffy", and "worth every penny"; P.S. closed Sunday–Tuesday.

Millwright's Ⓜ *New England*

| - | - | - | VE |

Simsbury | 77 West St. (Waterfall Way) | 860-651-5500 | www.millwrightsrestaurant.com

Chef-owner Tyler Anderson cooks sophisticated New England cuisine with an emphasis on local ingredients at this Simsbury destination in a former 17th-century mill; the skylit main dining room is modern and elegant, but also evokes the structure's past life via its rough-hewn wooden beams, plank ceiling and a wall of windows that overlook the waterfall that once powered it all; P.S. for a more casual (read: less expensive) meal, try the downstairs tavern.

Modern Apizza Ⓜ *Pizza*

| 25 | 13 | 17 | $19 |

New Haven | 874 State St. (Humphrey St.) | 203-776-5306 | www.modernapizza.com

"In a town full of famous pizza" spots, this "not-so-well-kept secret" (around since 1934) may have "less legend" attached than its rivals, but its "amazing" brick-oven, thin-crust pies "rank up there" as "some of the best" among New Haven's "outstanding" offerings; there are "lines on weekends" and the "family-friendly" digs equipped with "big booths" may "lack ambiance", but fans find that's "part of the charm" and swear "it's worth the wait."

Mondo *Italian*   26 | 17 | 17 | $19

Middletown | 10 Main St. (bet. Metro Sq. & Union St.) | 860-343-3300 | www.mondomiddletown.com

"Excellent" thin, "crispy-crust" New York–style pizza stars at this retro diner–style Middletown Italian that takes pie-making "to a new level", with "interesting", "delicious" "specialty" renditions like "oozy egg" and spicy sausage; rounding out the experience are "reasonable" tabs and "friendly" service.

Morton's The Steakhouse *Steak*   23 | 21 | 22 | $71

Hartford | 852 Main St. (Asylum St.) | 860-724-0044
Stamford | UBS Investment Bank | 377 N. State St. (Washington Blvd.) | 203-324-3939
www.mortons.com

"Dedicated carnivores" descend upon this über-"reliable" steakhouse chain for "tender", "perfectly prepared" cuts of beef and "excellent" sides presented in a "lovely, refined setting" that's a natural "for business meals or celebrations" and predictably "priced for the finance crowd"; factor in a "fantastic" wine list and "attentive" service from a "knowledgeable" crew, and it's "always an enjoyable experience."

Ondine Ⓜ *French*   25 | 23 | 23 | $68

Danbury | 69 Pembroke Rd. (bet. Wheeler Dr. & Woodridge Ln.) | 203-746-4900 | www.ondinerestaurant.com

"A must" if you crave "classic" French cuisine, this quiet Danbury long-timer set in a pink stone-and-stucco cottage offers "superb" dishes that satisfy fans "year after year", enhanced by "gorgeous views at sunset" overlooking Margerie Lake Reservoir; service is "excellent" and the "romantic" countrified ambiance adds to the "lovely" experience – plus the $62 dinner prix fixe and $39 Sunday dinner options help take the sting out of upscale pricing.

Oyster Club *New England*   26 | 21 | 23 | $49

Mystic | 13 Water St. (bet. Main St. & New London Rd.) | 860-415-9266 | www.oysterclubct.com

At this "outstanding" seafooder in historic Downtown Mystic, "brilliant" executive chef James Wayman delivers a daily changing menu of "creative" New England coastal cuisine based on ingredients that "come straight from the fisherman and the farmer" to your plate; add in attentive service, a contemporary clapboard setting and a "great selection of fresh oysters" from the raw bar, and fin fans say it's "always a pleasure"; P.S. check out the tree-shaded deck with a separate, more casual menu.

Pasta Nostra Ⓩ Ⓜ *Italian*   26 | 13 | 20 | $61

South Norwalk | 116 Washington St. (bet. Main & Water Sts.) | 203-854-9700 | www.pastanostra.com

From "incredible homemade pasta" to "superior" fish dishes, everything on Joe Bruno's frequently changing menu "sings" insist loyalists of this venerable SoNo Italian trattoria; if a few report "rushed" service, "cramped" seating and occasional "attitude", a "repeat crowd" insists that the "outstanding" fare made from "fresh ingredients" more than "makes up for it"; P.S. open Wednesday–Saturday for dinner only.

Plan B Burger Bar *Burgers*
21 | 18 | 17 | $24

Glastonbury | 120 Hebron Ave. (bet. Main St. & New London Tpke.) | 860-430-9737
Milford | 1638 Boston Post Rd. (Woodruff Rd.) | 203-713-8700 ●
Simsbury | 4 Railroad St. (bet. Phelps Ln. & Station St.) | 860-658-4477
Stamford | Stamford Town Ctr. | 230 Tresser Blvd. (bet. Edith Sherman Dr. & Greyrock Pl.) | 203-964-8353
West Hartford | 138 Park Rd. (bet. Beverly Rd. & Troy St.) | 860-231-1199
www.planbburger.com
"Burger heaven" proclaim partisans of this "lively" chainlet who "savor every bite" of the "gourmet" patties, "ground on premises" daily and smothered with "unique and traditional toppings"; it can be "loud", but "friendly" service and an "expansive" bourbon and beer selection "round out the experience", making it a "favorite" for most; P.S. the Simsbury branch is set in a retrofitted train station.

Rebeccas 🅱🅼 *American*
26 | 22 | 24 | $84

Greenwich | 265 Glenville Rd. (Riversville Rd.) | 203-532-9270 | www.rebeccasgreenwich.com
"Superb", "original" New American cuisine is complemented by a "nice wine list" and served by a "professional" staff, keeping this "place-to-be-seen" Greenwich "treat" from "creative" chef Reza Khorshidi and his "charming" co-owner wife, Rebecca, "packed at all times"; the "modern" industrial-chic decor is fairly "simple", but the -"Bentleys in the parking lot" are a hint you should "stop by a bank first"; P.S. "sit at the kitchen-view counter if you can."

River Tavern *American*
24 | 21 | 24 | $51

Chester | 23 Main St. (Rte. 148) | 860-526-9417 | www.rivertavernchester.net
"Tucked away" in the "charming" town of Chester overlooking the Pattaconk Brook, chef-owner Jonathan Rapp's "fantastic" New American turns out an "inventive", "ever-changing" menu "starring local seafood and produce" underscored by a "superb" wine list; add in "outstanding" service and "lovely" 19th-century digs enhanced with modern art, and it's no wonder this "delightful" experience can be a tough reservation; P.S. the signature date pudding is worth a try.

Schoolhouse at Cannondale 🅼 *American*
25 | 23 | 23 | $64

Wilton | 34 Cannon Rd. (Pimpewaug Rd.) | 203-834-9816 | www.theschoolhouseatcannondale.com
"It doesn't get much cozier" than this "charming" 19th-century Wilton schoolhouse where chef-owner Tim LaBant turns locally sourced ingredients into "exquisitely prepared", upscale New American fare; if a few grumble that the "close quarters" get a "bit noisy" when there's a "full house", most applaud the "romantic ambiance" and "excellent" staff, noting it's "perfect for special occasions"; P.S. in summer "sit on the patio" next to the Norwalk River.

Tarry Lodge *Italian*
22 | 19 | 18 | $52

Westport | 30 Charles St. (Franklin St.) | 203-571-1038 | www.tarrylodge.com
Mario Batali and Joe Bastianich are behind this "happening" Westport eatery dispensing "delicious Italian of every kind" from chef Andy

Nusser including "outstanding", "fresh-made" pasta and "gourmet" pizza; a "professional" crew tends the "attractive", if "a bit noisy", surroundings, which have a "NYC feel" – and the "big prices" and "hard-to-get reservations" to match.

Thomas Henkelmann *French*

28 | 27 | 26 | $91

Greenwich | Homestead Inn | 420 Field Point Rd. (I-95) | 203-869-7500 | www.thomashenkelmann.com

The "sublime" New French cuisine made from local and organic ingredients is "in a class by itself" at chef Thomas Henkelmann's "outstanding" "country-elegant" auberge set in a "lovely" Victorian mansion in Greenwich; service is "impeccable" too, making this "special-occasion champion" that's "reminiscent of fine dining in Europe" well "worth the splurge" (and the jacket required for dinner).

Union League Cafe ☒ *French*

27 | 27 | 25 | $64

New Haven | 1032 Chapel St. (bet. College & High Sts.) | 203-562-4299 | www.unionleaguecafe.com

The "quintessential special-occasion" restaurant, this New Haven "favorite" in a "historic" former men's club across from the Yale campus is "elegant without being stuffy", offering a "lovely" setting for enjoying the "divine" French cuisine from "perfect host" chef-owner Jean-Pierre Vuillermet; factor in an "excellent" wine list, "top-notch" service and a "graceful" beaux arts interior accented by "high ceilings" and "beautiful" woodwork, and the consensus is it's always "worth the splurge."

Valbella ☒ *Italian*

25 | 23 | 23 | $80

Riverside | 1309 E. Putnam Ave. (Sound Beach Ave.) | 203-637-1155 | www.valbellact.com

"You never know who will be dining next to you" at this Riverside mainstay that's been a gathering spot for "local celebrities" for many years, serving "exquisite" Italian cuisine and a "great wine list" in "elegant" Victorian-style digs surrounded by greenery; it's "expensive", but for most, the "atmosphere and food are worth it"; P.S. the candlelit wine cellar is "great for private groups."

West Street Grill *American*

22 | 19 | 20 | $54

Litchfield | 43 West St. (Meadow St.) | 860-567-3885 | www.weststreetgrill.com

"Still going strong", this Litchfield New American "manages to be a special-event place and a neighborhood" destination and "does both well", serving "really delicious" fare "prepared with elegance and imagination"; the owners are "welcoming" and service is "cheerful", and if a few find prices "staggering", for most it's "worth it", especially if you want to "bump into local celebrities."

The Whelk ☒ Ⓜ *Seafood*

25 | 20 | 22 | $56

Westport | 575 Riverside Ave. (Ketchum St.) | 203-557-0902 | www.thewhelkwestport.com

"Unique", "wonderfully presented" fish dishes made with local and sustainable species reel in a "crowd" to this "amazing" seafooder from chef-owner Bill Taibe (LeFarm) in Westport's Saugatuck section; the "tight digs" sport a commercial-maritime look, and though it can be "loud" (there's a "lively bar scene") and "hard to get a reservation", those who've signed on for the journey say this hot spot is "worth every penny."

Winvian Ⓜ *American* 26 | 26 | 26 | $124

Litchfield | Winvian Resort | 155 Alain White Rd. (bet. County & E. Shore Rds.) | 860-567-9600 | www.winvian.com

"Top-shelf" seasonal American cuisine with an emphasis on local ingredients makes for an "outstanding" prix fixe "dining experience" at this "seriously upscale" Relais & Châteaux resort on 113 lush acres in Litchfield, and it's further "enhanced by spending a night in one of the cottages"; the "staff couldn't be nicer", and the upscale-rustic decor is "fantastic" – just "be prepared to test the limits of your credit card"; P.S. lunch is à la carte.

Dallas/Ft. Worth

TOP FOOD RANKING

Restaurant	Cuisine
29 Saint-Emilion	French
Lucia	Italian
28 French Room	American/French
Bijoux	French
Pappas Bros. Steakhouse	Steak
Mercury	American
27 Abacus	Eclectic
Bonnell's	Southwestern
Stephan Pyles	Southwestern
Cacharel	French
Suze*	Mediterranean
Nick & Sam's	Seafood/Steak
Hattie's	American
Cavalli Pizza	Pizza
Sushi Sake	Japanese
Al Biernat's	Steak
Esperanza's	Mexican
Fearing's	Southwestern
Del Frisco's	Steak
Lanny's Alta Cocina	Eclectic
Lonesome Dove Western Bistro*	Southwestern
Nonna Tata*	Italian

OTHER NOTEWORTHY PLACES

Angelo's	BBQ
Bolsa	American
Cane Rosso	Pizza
Charlie Palmer	American
Five Sixty	American
FT33	American
Grace	American
Joe T. Garcia's	Tex-Mex
Komali	Mexican
Mansion	American
Mia's	Tex-Mex
Mi Cocina	Tex-Mex
Neighborhood Services	American
Nonna	Italian
Oak Restaurant	Eclectic
Salum	American
Smoke	BBQ
Stampede 66	Southwestern
Tei An	Japanese
Woodshed Smokehouse	Eclectic

* Indicates a tie with restaurant above

	FOOD	DECOR	SERVICE	COST

Abacus ⊠ *Eclectic*   27 | 25 | 27 | $69

Knox-Henderson | 4511 McKinney Ave. (Armstrong Ave.) | Dallas | 214-559-3111 | www.kentrathbun.com

Once again ranked Most Popular in the Dallas/Ft. Worth area, this Knox-Henderson Eclectic is "still tops" thanks to "superstar" chef Kent Rathbun's "sublime", "innovative" cuisine ("the lobster shooters are a must") and "sophisticated" "see-and-be-seen" surroundings where you feel equally "at home whether in jeans or dressed up"; service is "polished" too, so despite a few gripes about "noise", most are "blown away" – just "bring your sense of adventure" (and your platinum card).

Al Biernat's *Steak*   27 | 24 | 27 | $65

Oak Lawn | 4217 Oak Lawn Ave. (bet. Herschel & Wycliff Aves.) | Dallas | 214-219-2201 | www.albiernats.com

"A haven for star athletes and their fans who crave a good steak", this "loud", lively Oak Lawn "classic" "stands out" with "top-notch" fare and "supreme" service from Al himself, which "makes you feel important"; all this comes at a "high price", though many find it worthwhile given the "incredible ambiance for deal-making and celebrations."

Angelo's Barbecue ⊠ *BBQ*   25 | 15 | 17 | $16

Near West | 2533 White Settlement Rd. (bet. Henderson St. & University Dr.) | Ft. Worth | 817-332-0357 | www.angelosbbq.com

"Eat here to understand what brisket is in Texas" proclaim fans of this BBQ "standard" in Near West Ft. Worth where "exceptional" meat is chased with "frosty mugs of cold beer" in an atmosphere that's "a taxidermist's delight"; in sum, it's "a guaranteed good time for little coin."

Bijoux *French*   28 | 25 | 26 | $77

West Lovers Lane | Inwood Vill. | 5450 W. Lovers Ln. (Inwood Rd.) | Dallas | 214-350-6100 | www.bijouxrestaurant.com

"Lovely for a special occasion", this "classy, quiet" West Lovers Lane destination provides "superb" New French fare from chef Scott Gottlich offered in six-course tastings with à la carte options available too; though it's "expensive", many consider it among "Dallas' finest"; P.S. formality in the main dining area has been dialed back post-Survey with a more relaxed, contemporary look.

Bolsa *American*   25 | 21 | 21 | $35

Oak Cliff | 614 W. Davis St. (Cedar Hill Ave.) | Dallas | 214-367-9367 | www.bolsadallas.com

It can be a "mob scene" at this "foodie delight" in Oak Cliff cooking up an "exciting", ever-"changing" New American menu backed by "awesome drinks" crafted by some of the "best mixologists in Dallas"; look for an "energetic" vibe, "casual but attentive service" and a "fun" patio packed with "hipsters."

Bonnell's ⊠Ⓜ *Southwestern*   27 | 24 | 27 | $53

Southwest | 4259 Bryant Irvin Rd. (Southwest Blvd.) | Ft. Worth | 817-738-5489 | www.bonnellstexas.com

"Where else can you get elk, ostrich, bison, antelope and boar?" but at this Southwest Ft. Worth "treasure" specializing in Jon Bonnell's own brand of "unique" "upscale" "cowboy cuisine" that's "always a treat"; it's not inexpensive, but add in "top-notch" service and "casually elegant" surroundings and it's a "pleasure on every level."

	FOOD	DECOR	SERVICE	COST

Cacharel 🍽 *French* — 27 | 23 | 27 | $50

Arlington | Brookhollow Tower Two | 2221 E. Lamar Blvd., 9th fl. (Ballpark Way) | 817-640-9981 | www.cacharel.net

Set in an Arlington office tower "overlooking the Cowboys Stadium dome", this upscale entry delivers true "French fine dining" including "wonderful" Grand Marnier soufflés; it's "a little old-fashioned" and not inexpensive, but with "charming" service and a "spectacular view", it's "perfect" for a business lunch or "romantic dinner."

Cane Rosso *Pizza* — - | - | - | M

Deep Ellum | 2612 Commerce St. (Henry St.) | Dallas | 214-741-1188
Lakewood | 7328 Gaston Ave. (Garland Rd.) | Dallas | 214-660-3644
www.ilcanerosso.com

Certified-authentic Neapolitan pizza comes to Dallas via this parlor in Deep Ellum and Lakewood, the latter sporting a trellised patio; prices are moderate, there's beer and wine and the rustic-industrial setting boasts a large wood-burning oven imported from Italy that makes quite the centerpiece; P.S. a mobile oven makes the food truck rounds too.

Cavalli Pizza Napoletana *Pizza* — 27 | 16 | 22 | $15

McKinney | 6851 Virginia Pkwy. (Stonebridge Dr.) | 972-540-1449
Irving | 3601 Regent Blvd. (Belt Line Rd.) | 972-915-0001
www.cavallipizza.com

Some of the "best pizza" "outside of Rome" with "chewy crusts" and "interesting" toppings turns up at this Neapolitan twosome in Irving (quick-bite BYO) and McKinney (full service); "reasonable" prices keep it "crowded" but "worth the wait."

Charlie Palmer *American* — 25 | 26 | 25 | $68

Downtown Dallas | Joule Hotel | 1530 Main St. (bet. Akard & Ervay Sts.) | Dallas | 214-261-4600 | www.charliepalmer.com

A "jewel" in the "luxury" Joule Hotel Downtown, this glitzy showcase from celeb chef Charlie Palmer "pampers" guests with "excellent" New American fare, "impressive" wines and "gracious" service in an "elegant" room brimming with "business types"; "it's definitely a wow locale", even if a few find the fare "hit-or-miss" given the prices.

Del Frisco's Double Eagle Steak House *Steak* — 27 | 24 | 26 | $67

North Dallas | 5251 Spring Valley Rd. (Dallas N. Tollway) | Dallas | 972-490-9000
Downtown Ft. Worth | 812 Main St. (8th St.) | Ft. Worth | 817-877-3999
www.delfriscos.com

You might just "need two stomachs" for the "outrageous", "buttery" steaks "cooked to perfection" at this high-end chophouse chain catering to an "expense-account" clientele with its "extensive wine list", "fine" service and setting akin to a "chic Western saloon"; it's especially "great for a special occasion" "if money is no object."

Esperanza's Mexican Bakery & Cafe *Mexican* — 27 | 17 | 23 | $16

Hospital District | 1601 Park Place Ave. (8th Ave.) | Ft. Worth | 817-923-1992
North Side | 2122 N. Main St. (21st St.) | Ft. Worth | 817-626-5770
www.joets.com

The "wow factor" is high at this Ft. Worth Mexican duo from descendents of the Joe T. Garcia–Lancarte family serving "superb" takes on the classics in "homey" surroundings; expect long lines, especially for the "unbeatable" Sunday brunch; P.S. the on-site bakeries vending pan dulce are "not to be missed on the way out."

Fearing's *Southwestern*
27 | 28 | 27 | $75

Uptown | Ritz-Carlton Hotel | 2121 McKinney Ave. (Pearl St.) | Dallas | 214-922-4848 | www.fearingsrestaurant.com

Smitten fans say it "doesn't get any better" than Dean Fearing's "fine-dining" venue in Uptown's Ritz-Carlton Hotel featuring his "spectacu-lar", "sophisticated" Southwestern cooking that's "just plain awesome"; it follows through with "warm" service (Dean himself often "works the room") and a glitzy setting that's a total "scene", so even if some sniff "overrated", the "overall event" is "quite an experience."

Five Sixty Wolfgang Puck *American*
24 | 26 | 24 | $69

Downtown Dallas | Reunion Tower | 300 E. Reunion Blvd. (Houston St.) | Dallas | 214-741-5560 | www.wolfgangpuck.com

A "perfect spot to take out-of-town guests", this New American from celeb chef Wolfgang Puck offers "spectacular" 360-degree vistas from a revolving room atop Downtown's Reunion Tower, "fabulous" Asian-accented cuisine and "top-notch" service; some prefer to "stick with drinks and appetizers", because "you pay for the view" dearly.

French Room ⑤Ⓜ *American/French*
28 | 29 | 29 | $90

Downtown Dallas | Hotel Adolphus | 1321 Commerce St. (Field St.) | Dallas | 214-742-8200 | www.hoteladolphus.com

"For a splurge", fans tout this "top-flight" haute French inside the Hotel Adolphus, voted Dallas' No. 1 for Decor and Service thanks to its "breathtaking" "rococo" interior and "impeccable" hospitality; "cre-ative", "perfectly executed" fare and "marvelous wines" round out an ex-perience that's "memorable in every way"; P.S. jackets required.

FT33 ⑤Ⓜ *American*
- | - | - | E

Market Center | 1617 Hi Line Dr. (Oak Lawn Ave.) | Dallas | 214-741-2629 | www.ft33dallas.com

The name stands for one of the best seats in the house – Fire Table 33 – which faces the open kitchen in this Market Center New American, where chef-owner Matt McCallister whips up ultracreative dishes from a daily-changing menu; expect a laid-back, rustic setting with ex-posed beams and lots of wood, and prices that may scorch your wallet.

Grace ⑤ *American*
25 | 26 | 25 | $60

Downtown Ft. Worth | 777 Main St. (7th St.) | Ft. Worth | 817-877-3388 | www.gracefortworth.com

"Contemporary, chic" surroundings, "perfectly prepared" steaks and "imaginative" New American dishes, along with a wine list that's "worth a night's reading" and "stellar" service, are the reasons this Downtown eatery is considered one of the "best places for a special evening in Ft. Worth"; though some wince at "expense-account" prices, most concur it's "well worth it."

Hattie's *American*
27 | 25 | 24 | $39

Oak Cliff | 418 N. Bishop Ave. (8th St.) | Dallas | 214-942-7400 | www.hatties.com

"Charleston comes to Dallas" via this American "gem" in a "buzzy area" of Oak Cliff turning out "contemporary", "fancified" takes on

Lowcountry fare ("superb" shrimp and grits, chicken and waffles "to die for"), plus a standout Sunday brunch, in a "modern, civilized" setting; "impeccable" service, a "casual atmosphere" and moderate prices all "soothe the soul."

Joe T. Garcia's 🎫 *Tex-Mex* | 20 | 23 | 21 | $24 |

North Side | 2201 N. Commerce St. (22nd St.) | Ft. Worth | 817-626-4356 | www.joets.com

Devotees dub this "iconic" Ft. Worth "institution" on the North Side the "Holy Grail of Tex-Mex", offering a "solid", "no-surprises" menu in the "huge" dining room or on the "massive", "beautiful" patio with a poolside garden; some critics find the fare "routine" and contend its appeal is strictly the "scene" and the "fab" margaritas; P.S. cash only.

Komali *Mexican* | 24 | 26 | 24 | $40 |

Uptown | 4152 Cole Ave. (Fitzhugh Ave.) | Dallas | 214-252-0200 | www.komalirestaurant.com

A "bright, cheery", "modern" space with a long bar and a mosaic fireplace is the backdrop for chef Abraham Salum's "exciting" "interior Mexican" cuisine at this Uptown sibling (and next-door neighbor) of Salum; "fabulous" margs and a "good selection of mescals" help fuel a lively scene that "can redefine 'loud' on weekend nights."

Lanny's Alta Cocina Mexicana 🅂🅼 *Eclectic* | 27 | 23 | 25 | $52 |

Cultural District | 3405 W. Seventh St. (Boland St.) | Ft. Worth | 817-850-9996 | www.lannyskitchen.com

"A special-occasion place" that's "matured perfectly in sync with its chef", this upscale Eclectic in the Cultural District "shines" with an "excellent" "creative" menu of Mexican-inspired cuisine from chef-owner Lanny Lancarte (of the Joe T. Garcia's dynasty), backed by a "terrific selection of wines and beers"; the mood is "romantic" in the contemporary space, but some balk at the prices unless they can "dine on someone else's tab."

Lonesome Dove Western Bistro 🅂 *Southwestern* | 27 | 24 | 26 | $55 |

Stockyards | 2406 N. Main St. (24th St.) | Ft. Worth | 817-740-8810 | www.lonesomedovebistro.com

Celeb chef Tim Love's "signature cowboy cuisine" "shines" in a "Western-themed" setting "with a touch of elegance" at his flagship in the Ft. Worth Stockyards, where "innovative" takes on "game, pork and anything else you'd find on a ranch" are served by an "outstanding" staff amid a "cool", if "loud" scene; "extremely reasonable" lunch specials offset otherwise "high-end" prices.

Lucia 🅂🅼 *Italian* | 29 | 21 | 25 | $58 |

Oak Cliff | 408 W. Eighth St. (Bishop Ave.) | Dallas | 214-948-4998 | www.luciadallas.com

"It takes weeks to get in" to chef David Uygur's tiny Oak Cliff Italian, but his "awesomely creative" cuisine that's "executed to perfection" is "worth the effort"; led by the chef's wife and co-owner, Jennifer, the front-of-house staff "treats you like beloved family" in the rustic 36-seat space, which is housed in a historic building dating back to the '20s.

	FOOD	DECOR	SERVICE	COST

The Mansion *American*
26 | 28 | 27 | $89

Uptown | Rosewood Mansion on Turtle Creek | 2821 Turtle Creek Blvd. (Gillespie St.) | Dallas | 214-559-2100 | www.mansiononturtlecreek.com
"Divine as it's always been", this Uptown icon showcases chef Bruno Davaillon's "impeccable" French-influenced New American fare, served by a staff that "couldn't be kinder" in "elegant" environs in a historic hotel; while a few feel "it's not what it used to be", most "highly recommend" it when you want to "pamper yourself and a loved one", though all agree "it helps if the oil wells are still producing when the check arrives."

The Mercury ⌧ *American*
28 | 24 | 25 | $62

Preston Forest | Preston Forest Vill. | 11909 Preston Rd. (Forest Ln.) | Dallas | 972-960-7774 | www.themercurydallas.com
Chef Chris Ward "blends tastes like a harmonious work of art" in his "exceptional" French- and Mediterranean-influenced New American cuisine, served "without attitude" by an "attentive" staff at this upscale sophisticate in Preston Forest; "don't be fooled by the strip-mall location", for it's "beautiful inside", with a "cool, New Yorkish" ambiance and "lively" lounge scene, making it a "must-visit" for many, including former President George W. Bush.

Mia's *Tex-Mex*
23 | 13 | 19 | $22

Lemmon Avenue | 4322 Lemmon Ave. (Wycliff Ave.) | Dallas | 214-526-1020 | www.miastexmex.com
"Two words: brisket tacos" sum up much of the appeal of this Lemmon Avenue *cocina*, a "longtime favorite" for "wonderful", "no-fuss" Tex-Mex, as evidenced by the near-perpetual "lines" out front; no, there's "not much decor" nor "elbow room" either, but bargain prices compensate.

Mi Cocina *Tex-Mex*
21 | 19 | 20 | $25

Lake Highlands | 7215 Skillman St. (Walnut Hill Ln.) | Dallas | 214-503-6426
Park Cities | Highland Park Vill. | 77 Highland Park Vill. (Douglas Ave.) | Dallas | 214-521-6426
Preston Forest | Preston Forest Vill. | 11661 Preston Rd. (bet. Forest Ln. & Preston Haven Dr.) | Dallas | 214-265-7704
West Village | West Vill. | 3699 McKinney Ave. (bet. Blackburn St. & Lemmon Ave.) | Dallas | 469-533-5663
North Dallas | 18352 N. Dallas Pkwy. (Frankford Rd.) | Dallas | 972-250-6426
West Plano | Lakeside Mkt. | 4001 Preston Rd. (Lorimar Dr.) | Plano | 469-467-8655
West Plano | Shops at Legacy | 5760 Legacy Dr. (Bishop Rd.) | Plano | 972-473-8745
Las Colinas | 7750 N. MacArthur Blvd. (I-635) | Irving | 469-621-0451
Southwest | Chapel Hill Shopping Ctr. | 4601 West Frwy. (Hulen St.) | Ft. Worth | 817-569-1444
Sundance Square | Sundance Sq. | 509 Main St. (bet. 4th & 5th Sts.) | Ft. Worth | 817-877-3600
www.mcrowd.com
Additional locations throughout the Dallas/Ft. Worth area
It's "always a scene" at these "smartly designed" Tex-Mex cantinas favored by the "young and beautiful" for "well-prepared" "lighter alternatives" and "killer" Mambo Taxi 'ritas ("after two you'll want to mambo and need a taxi"); though a few critics find them "overrated" and "overpriced" for what they are with "spotty" service, defenders insist "these guys know how to run a restaurant."

	FOOD	DECOR	SERVICE	COST

Neighborhood Services 🗷 *American* | 25 | 22 | 23 | $41

West Lovers Lane | 5027 W. Lovers Ln. (Inwood Rd.) | Dallas | 214-350-5027

Neighborhood Services Bar & Grill 🗷 *American*

Preston Royal | 10720 Preston Rd. (Royal Ln.) | Dallas | 214-368-1101
www.neighborhoodservicesdallas.com

"Haute blue-plate specials" headline chef Nick Badovinus' "ingredient-driven" New American menu delivering "creative twists on home-style food" at these "hip" "favorites"; the servers are "impressive", and while some critics cite "extremely long waits", others take the opportunity for a little "social networking" at the "trendy bar", or "call ahead and get your name on the list."

Nick & Sam's Steakhouse *Seafood/Steak* | 27 | 25 | 25 | $75

Uptown | 3008 Maple Ave. (bet. Carlisle & Wolf Sts.) | Dallas | 214-871-7444 | www.nick-sams.com

Imagine, a "New York steakhouse in the middle of Texas" exclaim fans of this Uptown meatery, the "place to be seen" over "excellent" prime beef and seafood in "dark", "attractive" digs highlighted by a grand piano player in the kitchen; whether you're seated in the "gorgeous" dining room or "less-formal, action-packed bar", you'll find "eye candy", "top-notch" service and "Texas-size" tabs.

Nonna 🗷 *Italian* | 25 | 19 | 23 | $53

Lemmon Avenue | 4115 Lomo Alto Dr. (bet. Bowser & Lemmon Aves.) | Dallas | 214-521-1800 | www.nonnadallas.com

Chef Julian Barsotti's "sophisticated", "upscale" Northern Italian cuisine "reigns supreme" at this cozy "bit of heaven" off Lemmon Avenue; a wood-burning oven highlights the "small" contemporary space, and while some grouse about "terrible acoustics", many others insist "it's worth the wait", which may be unavoidable "even with reservations."

Nonna Tata 🗷 🅜 ⇗ *Italian* | 27 | 15 | 20 | $27

Hospital District | 1400 W. Magnolia Ave. (6th Ave.) | Ft. Worth | 817-332-0250

"Lines form quickly" at this BYO Italian "gem" in the Hospital District, where chef-owner Donatella Trotti creates "incredible" "Italian home cooking, done just right" at modest prices; while some deem the "tiny", "cafe"-style setting "not too comfortable" "unless you're able to eat outside", the "authentic" experience is a "bucket-list" item for many; P.S. cash only.

Oak Restaurant 🗷 *Eclectic* | - | - | - | E

Market Center | 1628 Oak Lawn Ave. (Hi Line Dr.) | Dallas | 214-712-9700 | www.oakdallas.com

Reservations are a hot ticket at this Design District stunner in Market Center featuring seasonal Eclectic fare served in posh neutral-toned digs; prices may be high, but that shouldn't be surprising considering the high-end ingredients and artful presentation.

Pappas Bros. Steakhouse 🗷 *Steak* | 28 | 25 | 27 | $71

Love Field | 10477 Lombardy Ln. (Stemmons Frwy.) | Dallas | 214-366-2000 | www.pappasbros.com

The "melt-in-your-mouth" steaks "blow the competition away" at this "classy" Love Field chophouse where the "excellent" cuts are matched with an "unbelievable" wine list ("a sommelier's dream"); yes, it's "pricey", but the "impeccable" service and "elegant, masculine" setting make it a "favorite for special occasions."

Saint-Emilion 🗷🅼 *French* | 29 | 26 | 28 | $57 |

Cultural District | 3617 W. Seventh St. (Montgomery St.) | Ft. Worth | 817-737-2781 | www.saint-emilionrestaurant.com

Bernard Tronche's *"fantastique"* "jewel" in the Cultural District is "always tops" proclaim fans who vote it No. 1 for Food in Dallas/Ft. Worth, a tribute to the daily blackboard menu of "exquisite" fare from the South of France complemented by a "fabulous" wine list; "impeccable" service and a "quaint-old-house" setting are more reasons why it's a "favorite destination" of many.

Salum 🗷 *American* | 26 | 24 | 25 | $54 |

Uptown | 4152 Cole Ave. (Fitzhugh Ave.) | Dallas | 214-252-9604 | www.salumrestaurant.com

Though it's hidden in an unassuming Uptown strip center, chef-owner Abraham Salum's upscale "culinary haven" "takes its rightful place in the upper echelon" of the Dallas dining scene thanks to his "superb", "eclectic" New American menu, which changes monthly and is served by a "caring" staff; the "simple", "elegant" venue is adjacent to sibling Komali.

Smoke *BBQ* | 24 | 20 | 21 | $35 |

Oak Cliff | Belmont Hotel | 901 Ft. Worth Ave. (Sylvan Blvd.) | Dallas | 214-393-4141 | www.smokerestaurant.com

So hot it's practically smoldering, this "quirky" American adjacent to the Belmont Hotel takes its inspiration from the smokehouses of yore, with oak floors, "comfortable" leather banquettes and a midpriced farm-to-fork menu that runs the gamut from grass-fed steaks to other "complex", "gourmet" dishes; there's also "amazing" 'cue galore.

Stampede 66 *Southwestern* | - | - | - | M |

Arts District | 1717 McKinney Ave. (Akard St.) | Dallas | 214-550-6966 | www.stampede66.com

Celeb chef Stephan Pyles provides Texas comfort food updates – think chicken-fried buffalo steak and 'faux' gras mousse with jalapeño jelly – washed down with margaritas and long necks at his Arts District Southwestern venue; moderate tabs befit the casual digs outfitted with eye-popping Western-inspired art like horse-head wall sculptures rendered in wire.

Stephan Pyles 🗷 *Southwestern* | 27 | 27 | 27 | $69 |

Arts District | 1807 Ross Ave. (St. Paul St.) | Dallas | 214-580-7000 | www.stephanpyles.com

The "master of New Texas cuisine", Stephan Pyles "reigns" at his "classy, modern" Arts District Southwestern where diners can watch the chef create his "amazing", "constantly evolving" globally influenced fare in the glass-enclosed display kitchen; with "outstanding" service and a "cosmopolitan vibe", it's the "perfect place to take out-of-towners" – "particularly if they're paying."

Sushi Sake 🗷 *Japanese* | 27 | 22 | 21 | $40 |

Richardson | 2150 N. Collins Blvd. (Campbell Rd.) | 972-470-0722 | www.sushi-sake.com

You feel like "you're in Japan" at this discreet, "authentic" Richardson hideaway serving "generous" portions of "amazing sushi" and plentiful sake choices; though critics say the "decor doesn't quite live up to the phenomenal fish" and grouse over "indifferent" service, "excellent" cuisine at "reasonable prices" makes up for most glitches.

Suze 🅂Ⓜ _Mediterranean_   27 | 20 | 25 | $53

Preston Hollow | Villages of Preston Hollow | 4345 W. Northwest Hwy. (Midway Rd.) | Dallas | 214-350-6135 | www.suzedallas.com

"Unpretentious and friendly", Gilbert Garza's "hidden gem" in Preston Hollow is a "high-end neighborhood place" offering "beautifully presented" Mediterranean fare, an "excellent wine list" and "perfect" service in an "intimate, quiet" setting; given its "reasonable prices", it's no surprise that it's "always booked."

Tei An Ⓜ _Japanese_   26 | 27 | 24 | $59

Arts District | One Arts Plaza | 1722 Routh St. (bet. Flora St. & Ross Ave.) | Dallas | 214-220-2828 | www.tei-an.com

Foodies "feel transported to Japan" by chef-owner Teiichi Sakurai's "brilliant" cuisine at this "cutting-edge" Japanese atelier in the Arts District showcasing "amazing" handmade soba, sushi and more "esoteric" specials, all "flawlessly served" in a "Zen-like" interior ("like a spa"); it's a splurge, yes, but the "price is right for the product"; P.S. there's also a rooftop cocktail bar available to those dining at the restaurant.

Woodshed Smokehouse _Eclectic_   - | - | - | M

Cultural District | 3201 Riverfront Dr. (University Ave.) | Ft. Worth | 817-877-4545 | www.woodshedsmokehouse.com

Set on the banks of the Trinity River in the Cultural District, celeb chef Tim Love's Eclectic tribute to a smokin' backyard party showcases a mix of wood-enhanced dishes in a menu so esoteric it comes with a glossary; an enthusiastic staff provides a warm welcome in the casual garage-chic space spilling out onto picnic benches on the patio.

Denver & Mountain Resorts

TOP FOOD RANKING

Restaurant	Cuisine
29 Carlos' Bistro	Eclectic
Junz	Asian
Splendido at the Chateau	American
28 Penrose Room	Continental
Fruition	American
Keystone Ranch	American
Masalaa	Indian/Vegetarian
Amu	Japanese
Matsuhisa	Japanese
Sweet Basil	American
Zucca	Italian
Sushi Sasa	Japanese
Walter's Bistro	American
Palace Arms	American
Saigon Landing	Vietnamese
Hearthstone Restaurant	American
Twelve	American
Ski Tip Lodge	American
Zamparelli's	Italian
Sushi Den	Japanese

OTHER NOTEWORTHY PLACES

Barolo Grill	Italian
Beau Jo's	Pizza
Cafe Brazil	S American
ChoLon	Asian
Elway's	Steak
Euclid Hall	Eclectic/Pub Food
Frasca	Italian
Kelly Liken	American
Luca d'Italia	Italian
Mizuna	American
Panzano	Italian
Populist	American
Restaurant Kevin Taylor	French
Rio Grande	Mexican
Rioja	Mediterranean
Snooze	American
Table 6	American
TAG	Eclectic
240 Union	American
Uncle	Asian

Amu *Japanese*

28 | 24 | 25 | $38

Boulder | 1221 Spruce St. (bet. Broadway & 13th St.) | 303-440-0807 | www.izakayaamu.com

"Just superb" say those who've gotten into this Boulder izakaya where a "highly professional chef and staff" "beautifully present" an "ever-changing" selection of "inspired" Japanese small plates alongside an "extensive sake list"; just come "willing to wait", as the "serene", "sparse" setting only has a few bar seats and tatami tables – and "be prepared to take off your shoes."

Barolo Grill ⓈⓂ *Italian*

27 | 24 | 26 | $56

Congress Park | 3030 E. Sixth Ave. (bet. Milwaukee & St. Paul Sts.) | Denver | 303-393-1040 | www.barologrilldenver.com

"One of the standard-bearers in Denver", this "flat-out wonderful" Congress Park venue presents "dreamy" Northern Italian creations for "premium prices" in a "beautiful" setting suited for "special occasions" and "romance"; what's more, the staff, which famously gets "flown to Italy every year for training", is as "scalpel sharp" as ever, while "the owner's passion for wine" shines on the "extensive", "impressive" list; just be sure to "make your reservations early", otherwise you might have to dine at the bar (though that's a "great experience" too).

Beau Jo's Pizza *Pizza*

25 | 20 | 22 | $21

Arvada | 7525 W. 53rd Ave. (Wadsworth Bypass) | 303-420-8376
Evergreen | 28186 Hwy. 74 (Co. Rd. 73) | 303-670-2744
South Denver | 2710 S. Colorado Blvd. (Yale Ave.) | Denver | 303-758-1519
Boulder | 2690 Baseline Rd. (27th Way) | 303-554-5312
Steamboat Springs | 704 Lincoln Ave. (7th St.) | 970-870-6401
www.beaujos.com

A "kitschy" "tradition", this "Colorado-themed" chain, voted Denver's Most Popular restaurant, slings "outrageous", "one-of-a-kind", "deep, deep-dish" pizzas with "plentiful toppings" and "honey for dipping" on the side, so essentially the "amazing crust does double duty as dessert"; the cost can seem either "reasonable" or "pricey" depending on how many people you have to feed, though the "decadent lunch buffet" is an undisputed "great deal", as is the "wonderful salad bar."

Cafe Brazil ⓈⓂ *S American*

27 | 22 | 25 | $32

Berkeley Park | 4408 Lowell Blvd. (44th Ave.) | Denver | 303-480-1877 | www.cafebrazildenver.com

"Amazing, authentic" Brazilian cuisine, including "brilliant seafood", and "spot-on caipirinhas" keep folks coming to this "festive" "tropical vacation" – complete with "laid-back" service – in Berkeley Park; it's all a bit "kitschy" and "pricey" for a few "meat-and-potatoes" types, but the "loyal" "crowds speak volumes."

Carlos' Bistro *Eclectic*

29 | 25 | 28 | $46

Colorado Springs | 1025 S. 21st St. (Cimarron St.) | 719-471-2905

"Phenomenal" "gastronomical pleasures" – voted tops for Food in Colorado's Restaurant Survey – are "worth" the "fairly high prices" at this Colorado Springs Eclectic with a "romantic" setting; "personalized service" comes from the "accommodating" staff and chef-owner

Carlos Echeandia himself, a real "character" who's "always out on the floor meeting and greeting his customers."

CholOn Modern Asian Bistro 🖼 *Asian*

| 27 | 25 | 24 | $41 |

LoDo | 1555 Blake St. (16th St.) | Denver | 303-353-5223 | www.cholon.com

LoDo is "lucky to have" chef Lon Symensma, whose "talent is on display" in every "exquisite" Southeast Asian morsel (including "brilliant" sweet onion and Gruyère soup dumplings) that this "sleek" spot sends out of its open kitchen; fetched by "knowledgeable, efficient" servers and accompanied by "fantastic cocktails", the "artistic" small plates are "made to share" – and you may as well, since the "earsplitting noise level" promotes getting close.

Elway's *Steak*

| 25 | 24 | 24 | $59 |

Airport | Denver Int'l Airport | 8500 Peña Blvd., Gate B Center Core (Jackson Gap St.) | Denver | 303-342-7777
Cherry Creek | 2500 E. First Ave. (University Blvd.) | Denver | 303-399-5353
Downtown Denver | Ritz-Carlton Denver | 1881 Curtis St. (19th St.) | Denver | 303-312-3107
Vail | 174 E. Gore Creek Dr. (Mill Creek Rd.) | 970-754-7818
www.elways.com

"Melt-in-your-mouth steaks" "score big" at the "posh" Cherry Creek flagship of the eponymous former pro quarterback's chophouse mini-chain, but the real "highlight" may be its "meat-market" bar scene, comprised of "big-spending" "cougars", "sugar daddies" and other "beautiful" folk who can afford the "Super Bowl prices" (though there's "value" to be found on the "bold wine list"); similar offerings, including "smooth" service, are found in the "glitzy, ritzy" Downtown branch sporting a "sushi bar that's the bomb" and the "bustling" Vail offshoot; P.S. there's also a branch in the airport's Concourse B for jet-setters.

Euclid Hall ❶ *Eclectic/Pub Food*

| 24 | 24 | 23 | $29 |

Larimer Square | 1317 14th St. (Larimer St.) | Denver | 303-595-4255 | www.euclidhall.com

"Gut-busting" "haute" Eclectic pub grub "won't break the bank" at this Larimer Square "necessity" (sibling of Rioja and Bistro Vendôme) with an "industrial"-"modern" "gastropub-chic" setting; though it's sometimes "loud", it remains an "awesome spot, especially late-night", thanks to the "well-curated beer list" that boasts brews you might have "never heard of before" ("don't be afraid to ask questions" – the servers "always have an answer").

Frasca Food & Wine 🖼 *Italian*

| 28 | 25 | 28 | $80 |

Boulder | 1738 Pearl St. (18th St.) | 303-442-6966 | www.frascafoodandwine.com

"Sublime in every way", this Boulder "must" "lives up to the hype" thanks to Lachlan Mackinnon-Patterson's "exceptional" Northern Italian prix fixe menu (à la carte also available), which is "perfectly paired" with "informed, articulate sommelier" Bobby Stuckey's "spectacular" wines; a staff that has "hospitality down to a science" and "minimalist modern" decor only add to its appeal, and though "long lead times for reservations" and "exorbitant prices" are part of the deal, most deem it "well worth the wait" and expense for such a "transformative experience."

Fruition *American*

28 | 23 | 26 | $56

Country Club | 1313 E. Sixth Ave. (bet. Lafayette & Marion Sts.) | Denver | 303-831-1962 | www.fruitionrestaurant.com

This Country Club "diamond" – ranked No. 1 for Food in Denver – has a menu that reads "like a foodie romance novel", which its author, farmer-chef Alex Seidel, brings to life with his "seductive" approach to "garden-to-table" New American cuisine, by turns "rustic" and "ethereal", "nuanced" and "startling" (matched by a "well-thought-out wine list"); meanwhile, the "deft" manner of the "astute" staff makes the "close quarters" seem "charming", and everything comes for "fair prices."

Hearthstone Restaurant *American*

28 | 26 | 27 | $45

Breckenridge | 130 S. Ridge St. (Washington Ave.) | 970-453-1148 | www.stormrestaurants.com

"Celebrate something" – anything – with the "delicious" local American cuisine at this "magical" old home where everything from the "high-end" Victorian-era decor and "gorgeous mountain views" to the "friendly staff" oozes "warmth and charm"; though "one of the fanciest restaurants in Breckenridge", with "pricey" tabs to match, it "often offers special menus that are a bargain for the quality."

Junz *Asian*

29 | 24 | 25 | $34

Parker | 11211 S. Dransfeldt Rd. (Twenty Mile Rd.) | 720-851-1005 | www.junzrestaurant.com

The "sushi is amazing", but devotees say the entire menu at this bright, cheerful Asian fusion "gem" in suburban Parker is "full of great (and sometimes unexpected) dishes", including "swell choices" for the raw-fish-phobic; affordable prices and solid service also mean it's as "wonderful" for colleagues on a lunch break as it is "for families" at dinner.

Kelly Liken *American*

26 | 25 | 25 | $81

Vail | Gateway Bldg. | 12 Vail Rd. (I-70 Frontage Rd.) | 970-479-0175 | www.kellyliken.com

Offering "exceptional" New American prix fixes and "gourmet cocktails" with service that "misses nothing" in an "elegant yet down-to-earth dining room", the eponymous chef-owner of this "total package" in Vail "would be a star anywhere"; critics crack that "you need a microscope to see the food" – "but not the huge bill" – so some recommend ordering fewer courses "for a reduced price."

Keystone Ranch 🗷Ⓜ *American*

28 | 28 | 28 | $73

Keystone | Keystone Ranch Golf Course | 1437 Summit County Rd. 150 (Keystone Ranch Rd.) | 970-496-4161 | www.keystoneresort.com

"Year in and year out", the "perfectly prepared", "inventive" New American "mountain fare" at this "old working ranch house" in Keystone remains worthy of its setting, a "wonderful" "hunting lodge" suitable for "cowboy duds or uptown threads"; it's "not a place for the budget conscious", but with the added attraction of "professional, friendly" service (which extends through "dessert and after-dinner drinks by the fireplace"), it offers a level of "satisfaction few restaurants" achieve; P.S. reservations required.

Luca d'Italia ⑤Ⓜ *Italian*

28 | 23 | 27 | $54

Capitol Hill | 711 Grant St. (7th Ave.) | Denver | 303-832-6600 | www.lucadenver.com

Chef-owner Frank Bonanno "puts his heart and soul" into the "phenomenal" Italian "plates of beauty" at this Capitol Hill "foodie destination", where the wines are equally "fab" and service is "impeccable"; it may be true that the "stylish" if "simple" decor "doesn't match" the "attention to culinary detail", but the prices sure do.

Masalaa *Indian/Vegetarian*

28 | 17 | 21 | $16

Aurora | 3140 S. Parker Rd. (Peoria St.) | 303-755-6272 | www.masalaausa.com

"Excellent curries and dosas" as well as "lots of vegan and gluten-free options" "could make a vegetarian" out of the strictest carnivore at this unadorned Aurora eatery providing bargain rates and one of the "best Indian buffets in town"; "quick", "courteous" service adds to the altogether "satisfying" experience.

Matsuhisa *Japanese*

28 | 25 | 24 | $77

Aspen | 303 E. Main St. (Monarch St.) | 970-544-6628 | www.matsuhisaaspen.com

Vail | Solaris Bldg. | 141 E. Meadow Dr. (Village Centre Dr.) | 970-476-6628 | www.matsuhisavail.com

"The holy grail" of sushi is found at these Nobu siblings whose "world-class" "haute Japanese" "feasts for the senses" are as "jaw-dropping" as the "astronomical prices"; the Aspen branch is a "hip", "crowded" basement, the Vail venue boasts "dramatic" scenery and a "Zen vibe", while both feature a "savvy" staff and "raucous" bar scenes.

Mizuna ⑤Ⓜ *American*

28 | 23 | 28 | $60

Capitol Hill | 225 E. Seventh Ave. (bet. Grant & Sherman Sts.) | Denver | 303-832-4778 | www.mizunadenver.com

"Culinary genius" Frank Bonanno's "polished" New American fare, "designed to let the beautiful tastes and colors" of the "outstanding ingredients" "shine", makes fans of this Capitol Hill "masterpiece" "dizzy with glee"; sure, its "prices aren't for the parsimonious" and the seating is "cheek by jowl" in its "intimate" confines, but with "impeccable" service and a "stunning" wine list, it'll still "sweep a first date off [their] feet."

Palace Arms ⑤Ⓜ *American*

28 | 27 | 28 | $60

Downtown Denver | Brown Palace Hotel & Spa | 321 17th St. (bet. B'way & Tremont Pl.) | Denver | 303-297-3111 | www.brownpalace.com

"A top choice for impressing out-of-towners" or for a "romantic anniversary dinner", this "impeccable" "grande dame" in Downtown's "elegant" Brown Palace Hotel presents "outstanding" New American creations both "classic" and "daring" in a "posh", "old-world" setting; "ouch, the price is high" warn wallet-watchers, but those wistful for "fine dining as it used to be" - complete with "superb" wines and "gracious service" - say it's "well worth the cost"; P.S. jackets and reservations suggested.

Panzano *Italian*

26 | 24 | 25 | $44

Downtown Denver | Hotel Monaco | 909 17th St. (Champa St.) | Denver | 303-296-3525 | www.panzano-denver.com

Chef Elise Wiggins "deserves all the praise heaped on her" fawn fans of the "scrumptious", "innovative" and "reasonably priced" Northern

Italian fare (featuring "superb" freshly baked breads) she whips up at this "casually elegant" Downtown "jewel" in the "trendy Hotel Monaco"; a "polite" staff "puts the meal over the top", and "not-to-be-missed" happy-hour "bargains" only add to the "pleasure."

Penrose Room ⑤Ⓜ *Continental* | 28 | 29 | 29 | $101 |

Colorado Springs | Broadmoor Hotel | 1 Lake Ave. (Lake Circle) | 719-577-5773 | www.broadmoordining.com

After half a century, the Broadmoor Hotel's signature "celebration" spot (maybe "the only place in Colorado Springs where you must wear a jacket") still offers one of "the most prestigious and posh dining experiences" around, with "heavenly" Continental prix fixes, an "extensive wine list" and a "fabulous" staff – rated No. 1 for Service in Colorado – whose "attention to detail" makes for a "fairy-tale evening"; an "amazing" penthouse view of the lake and mountains is another reason the "unforgettable experience" is "well worth" the "expensive" tabs.

The Populist ⑤Ⓜ *American* | - | - | - | M |

RiNo | 3163 Larimer St. (32nd St.) | Denver | 720-432-3163 | www.thepopulistdenver.com

Jonathan Power and Noah Price (Crema coffeehouse) are behind this New American hipster mecca in RiNo that composes small plates studded with seasonal ingredients; the airy interior harbors a carefully curated mishmash of thrift-store finds (a piano, old gym lockers, lots of cookbooks), and it buzzes with conversation fueled by accessibly priced wines plus craft cocktails mixed and muddled at the patchwork-copper bar.

Restaurant Kevin Taylor ⑤ *French* | 27 | 25 | 27 | $69 |

Downtown Denver | Hotel Teatro | 1106 14th St. (Arapahoe St.) | Denver | 303-820-2600 | www.ktrg.net

"Astounding flavors" and "thoughtful presentations" continue to set the "benchmark of excellence" at chef Kevin Taylor's French flagship in Downtown's Hotel Teatro, where the "formal" ambiance comes with commensurately "impeccable hospitality" and a "superior wine list"; a few find it "a bit too pricey", but it's "worth every penny" "if you lust for old-fashioned", "high-class" "magic."

Rio Grande Mexican Restaurant *Mexican* | 21 | 20 | 21 | $22 |

LoDo | 1525 Blake St. (bet. 15th & 16th Sts.) | Denver | 303-623-5432
Lone Tree | 9535 Park Meadows Dr. (Yosemite St.) | 303-799-4999
Boulder | 1101 Walnut St. (11th St.) | 303-444-3690
Fort Collins | 143 W. Mountain Ave. (College Ave.) | 970-224-5428
Greeley | 825 Ninth St. (9th Ave.) | 970-304-9292
Steamboat Springs | 628 Lincoln Ave. (Hiltop Pkwy.) | 970-871-6277
www.riograndemexican.com

You go for the "superlative", "crazy-strong margaritas" at this "vibrant", "festive" local Mexican chain, but you "stay for the quesadillas" and "to-die-for chiles rellenos", all delivered by a "cheerful" staff; most of its "young, noisy clients" find the costs "reasonable", though a couple of "more refined palates" deem them "overpriced"; P.S. the Boulder location boasts an "incredible rooftop deck."

Rioja *Mediterranean*
28 | 24 | 26 | $49

Larimer Square | 1431 Larimer St. (bet. 14th & 15th Sts.) | Denver | 303-820-2282 | www.riojadenver.com

Jennifer Jasinki's "creative hand is evident" in every "meticulously thought-out" Mediterranean-inspired dish, each "presented like art-work" alongside an "extraordinary wine list" at this "cosmopolitan" "Larimer Square gem" (sibling to Euclid Hall and Bistro Vendôme); the dining room with "Chihuly-esque blown-glass" fixtures gets "justifiably jam-packed", but "unobtrusive" service that "goes above and beyond" helps mitigate the "raucous echoes"; P.S. it's "expensive", but the "killer brunch" is more "reasonably priced."

Saigon Landing *Vietnamese*
28 | 25 | 25 | $23

Evergreen | 28080 Douglas Park Rd. (Bear Creek Rd.) | 303-674-5421
Greenwood Village | 6585 Greenwood Plaza Blvd. (Arapahoe Rd.) | 303-779-0028 🗷
www.saigonlanding.com

"Not a typical Vietnamese menu", but "unique" (and "outstanding") dishes are what you'll find at this "cute", "spacious" Greenwood Village and Evergreen pair "par excellence"; with "friendly" staffers on hand, it remains many a local's "happy place."

Ski Tip Lodge 🗷Ⓜ *American*
28 | 27 | 29 | $94

Keystone | 764 Montezuma Rd. (Independence Rd.) | 970-496-4950 | www.keystoneresort.com

Prepare to be "pampered" from the moment you "schuss" in from the mountain to "dessert in front of the fire" at this "rustic, romantic" former stagecoach stop in Keystone; in between, you'll savor "black-diamond" New American fare (at "splurge"-worthy prices) from a "limited" but "sublime" prix fixe menu complete with "wonderful wine pairings" – a "relaxing way to end a day on the slopes"; P.S. reservations required.

Snooze *American*
26 | 23 | 23 | $17

Ballpark | 2262 Larimer St. (Park Ave.) | Denver | 303-297-0700
Centennial | Southglenn Mall | 6781 S. York St. (bet. Arapahoe Rd. & Easter Ave.) | 303-734-9655
Park Hill | 700 N. Colorado Blvd. (7th Ave.) | Denver | 303-736-6200
Boulder | 1617 Pearl St. (17th St.) | 303-225-7344
Fort Collins | 144 W. Mountain Ave. (Mason St.) | 970-482-9253
www.snoozeeatery.com

"Imaginative", "grown-up" "breakfasts of champions", "excellent cof-fee" and "spicy Bloody Marys" are shuttled by "happy" staffers amid "retro space-age kitsch" at this American mini-chain; however, if you don't "wake up before the roosters", you'll have to brave "outrageously long" lines (to pay prices some feel are "slightly high"), but "there's a reason for the wait"; P.S. a pared-down lunch menu is also offered (no dinner).

Splendido at the Chateau Ⓜ *American*
29 | 29 | 28 | $85

Beaver Creek | Beaver Creek Resort | 17 Chateau Ln. (Scott Hill Rd.) | 970-845-8808 | www.splendidobeavercreek.com

"Living up to the name", the "first-class kitchen" at this Beaver Creek "special-occasion" "experience" offers nothing less than "splendid" New American fare, which is complemented by an "exceptional wine list" presented by an "impeccable" staff; "sure, it's expensive", but "as you relax by the fire" in the "gorgeous setting" ("what views!") to the strains of "live piano from the bar", you can only conclude that "life is good."

Sushi Den *Japanese*

28 | 25 | 24 | $48

Platt Park | 1487 S. Pearl St. (Florida Ave.) | Denver | 303-777-0826 | www.sushiden.net

Be prepared to "wait for a table" at this "hot spot" in Platt Park, known for its "delightfully presented", "incredibly high-quality" fish "flown in daily" from Japan, as well as lots of "people-watching" in the "packed" dining rooms ("ask to be seated" downstairs or at the sushi bar, because "the upstairs is a bit isolated"); though it can get a bit "spendy", most agree "it's always worth it."

Sushi Sasa *Japanese*

28 | 24 | 24 | $47

Highland | 2401 15th St. (Platte St.) | Denver | 303-433-7272 | www.sushisasadenver.com

The "exotic", "superb sushi" tastes so "fresh-off-the-boat", you'll think you're dining "by the ocean" and not in Highland at this "consistently outstanding" Japanese by "inventive" "rock star" chef-owner Wayne Conwell; "you'll certainly pay for the pleasure", but you're also getting an "artfully minimalist" environment and "excellent" staffers "at the top of their trade."

Sweet Basil *American*

28 | 25 | 26 | $65

Vail | 193 E. Gore Creek Dr. (Bridge St.) | 970-476-0125 | www.sweetbasil-vail.com

Still considered the "gold standard" in Vail, this "pioneer" of "forward-thinking" "luxury" presents "fab", "cutting-edge" New American cuisine and "pampering" service in an "energizing", "sexy" setting with "sparkling views" of Gore Creek through "picture windows"; "sky-high prices" are no issue for the "glitzy" "mountaineers" who frequent it – in fact, "the only downside is its popularity" (read: it's "achingly noisy").

Table 6 *American*

25 | 22 | 24 | $45

Capitol Hill | 609 Corona St. (bet. 6th & 7th Aves.) | Denver | 303-831-8800 | www.table6denver.com

A "decadent" "high-end–meets-lowbrow" "gourmet" New American menu that's "heavy with meat" is complemented by a "well-advised" wine and beer selection at this Capitol Hill "locavore" destination now helmed by longtime sous-chef Carrie Shores after the departure of Scott Parker (not reflected in the Food rating); with "decent" prices and "attentive", "informal service" to match the "rustic" dining room, it's no wonder "all the cool kids are eating here."

TAG *Eclectic*

26 | 23 | 23 | $49

Larimer Square | 1441 Larimer St. (14th St.) | Denver | 303-996-9985 | www.tag-restaurant.com

While "it's difficult to peg" "magician" Troy Guard's "unexpected", "unreal" Eclectic eats (Kampachi with Pop Rocks?) and "off-the-wall" drinks, this Larimer Square "hot spot" is proof his "star is on a Rocky Mountain high"; service is "super", and if a few bemoan that it's "kind of pricey" and the "brick interior with orange lights and upbeat pop music" is "noisier than a train station", well, that's the cost of "cool", so "dress hip" to fit in.

Twelve 🖂Ⓜ *American*   28 | 23 | 27 | $51

Ballpark | 2233 Larimer St. (bet. Park Ave. & 22nd Ave.) | Denver | 303-293-0287 | www.twelverestaurant.com

The "menu changes every month", but "astounding gourmet" chef Jeff Osaka's New American fare is always "sublime and refined" at his "tiny" Ballpark eatery whose setting brims with "old-world charm"; "spot-on service", "great wines by the glass" and a "classic oak bar" are more reasons why fans "want to return often."

240 Union *American*   26 | 23 | 25 | $40

Lakewood | 240 Union Blvd. (6th Ave.) | 303-989-3562 | www.240union.com

"Exceptional" New American fare, including "impressive" seafood and "to-die-for homemade bread", makes this "light, airy" "oasis of class" "off the beaten path" in a Lakewood strip center a "go-to" for the "meet-and-greet business crowd"; some say "the noise gets a little overbearing at times", but with "efficient" service and "fair prices" to bolster the mood, most find the total package "reliably agreeable."

Uncle 🖂 *Asian*   - | - | - | M

LoHi | 2215 W. 32nd Ave. (Vallejo St.) | Denver | 303-433-3263 | www.uncledenver.tumblr.com

This LoHi Asian fusion destination struts the talents of chef-owner Tommy Lee, whose sleek, modern blond-wood dining room is a magnet for locals and farther-flung foodies who dig into a seasonally driven, always-changing menu of small plates and ramen noodle bowls; tipplers stay lubricated with chilled sakes, Asian beer and wine.

Walter's Bistro ●🖂 *American*   28 | 25 | 27 | $46

Colorado Springs | 146 E. Cheyenne Mountain Blvd. (Vietnam Veterans Memorial Hwy.) | 719-630-0201 | www.waltersbistro.com

From the "famous lobster bisque" onward, the "splurges" to be had at this "classy" New American bistro in Colorado Springs are near "perfection"; the backdrop is fittingly "rich" yet "tasteful", and you're sure to "feel at home" thanks to the "gentlemanly" eponymous owner, who's often there overseeing his "knowledgeable" staff.

Zamparelli's Italian Bistro 🖂 *Italian*   28 | 21 | 26 | $28

Lafayette | 2770 Arapahoe Rd. (95th St.) | 303-664-1275 | www.zamparellis.com

For "amazing", "unusual wood-fired pizzas" with topping options like roasted poblanos and wine-poached pears, plus pastas and salads, this Italian bistro in Lafayette comes "strongly recommended"; add in some of the "friendliest service around", and locals say the simple dining room and bar area feel like their own *"Cheers."*

Zucca Italian Ristorante *Italian*   28 | 26 | 26 | $31

Louisville | 808 Main St. (Pine St.) | 303-666-6499 | www.zuccalouisville.com

"Some new ideas" in Italian cooking can be found on the "awesome" menu at this "heavenly" Louisville neighborhood spot whose fare is complemented by an "extensive wine list"; add in "terrific" service, a "snug", "warm" setting and "good prices", and it's no surprise that locals call it "a must-visit."

Ft. Lauderdale

TOP FOOD RANKING

	Restaurant	Cuisine
28	La Brochette	Mediterranean
27	Canyon	Southwestern
	Casa D'Angelo	Italian
	Eduardo de San Angel	Mexican
	Valentino's	Italian
	Kitchenetta	Italian
	Cafe Maxx	American/Eclectic
26	Thai Spice	Thai
	Sette Bello	Italian
	Market 17	American/Eclectic

OTHER NOTEWORTHY PLACES

Anthony's	Pizza
Asia Bay	Japanese/Thai
Blue Moon	Seafood
Bonefish Grill	Seafood
Capital Grille	Steak
Chima	Brazilian/Steak
Greek Islands	Greek
Grille 66	Seafood/Steak
Steak 954	Steak
3030 Ocean	American/Seafood

Anthony's Coal Fired Pizza *Pizza* — 22 | 16 | 20 | $23

Ft. Lauderdale | 2203 S. Federal Hwy. (22nd St.) | 954-462-5555
Pompano Beach | Pompano Mktpl. | 1203 S. Federal Hwy. (McNab Rd.) | 954-942-5550
Coral Springs | Magnolia Shoppes | 9521 Westview Dr. (University Dr.) | 954-340-2625
Pembroke Pines | Home Depot Shopping Ctr. | 11037 Pines Blvd. (Hiatus Rd.) | 954-443-6610
Weston | Weston Commons | 4527 Weston Rd. (Orange Dr.) | 954-358-2625
Plantation | Publix Plaza | 512 N. Pine Island Rd. (American Express Way) | 954-474-3311
www.anthonyscoalfiredpizza.com

"Deliciously scorched" thin-crust pies with "high-end toppings" – plus "killer" wings and "awesome" salads for two – have made this Florida-based chain "a hit" with "families" and other pizza partisans; its self-described "well-done" 'za strikes a few as simply "burned" and the "nothing-fancy", "fast-paced" settings can be "loud", but "prompt" service and "low costs" keep 'em "crowded."

Asia Bay *Japanese/Thai* — 25 | 21 | 22 | $40

Ft. Lauderdale | 1111 E. Las Olas Blvd. (bet. SE 10th Terr. & 12th Ave.) | 954-848-9900 | www.asiabayrestaurants.com

"Both sides of the menu are winners" at this "sleek" Ft. Lauderdale dual concept offering "authentic" Thai fare and a "large" Japanese selection that includes cooked dishes plus over 60 choices of sushi and sashimi; diners deem the moderate bills a "fair price for such wonderful food", especially if you "sit outside overlooking" the Tarpon River.

Blue Moon Fish Co. *Seafood* — 24 | 23 | 23 | $49

Lauderdale-by-the-Sea | 4405 W. Tradewinds Ave. (Commercial Blvd.) | 954-267-9888
Coral Springs | 10317 Royal Palm Blvd. (Coral Springs Dr.) | 954-755-0002 Ⓜ
www.bluemoonfishco.com

"Thoughtfully chosen and prepared" seafood and "gorgeous" views of the Intracoastal's "yacht parade" make this "upscale" Lauderdale-by-the-Sea fish house Broward's Most Popular eatery, whether "for a romantic dinner or just to show friends why you moved to South Florida"; there's "attentive" service plus "ambiance to spare" on the outdoor deck, though "steep" prices convince many to opt for the "doubly wonderful" two-for-one lunch "bargains"; P.S. Coral Springs is separately owned, sans view and cheaper.

Bonefish Grill *Seafood* — 22 | 19 | 21 | $36

Ft. Lauderdale | The Promenade Shopping Ctr. | 6200 N. Federal Hwy. (Bayview Dr.) | 954-492-3266
Coral Springs | 1455 N. University Dr. (bet. Shadow Wood Blvd. & 16th St.) | 954-509-0405
Davie | Weston Commons Shopping Ctr. | 4545 Weston Rd. (Griffin Rd.) | 954-389-9273
Plantation | 10197 W. Sunrise Blvd. (Nob Hill Rd.) | 954-472-3592
www.bonefishgrill.com

"Just-out-of-the-water fish in many forms" "draws droves" to these "delightful", "easygoing" seafooders ("hard to believe it's a chain"); "longish waits, even with a reservation" and "noise" are balanced by "prompt and courteous" service and "competitive prices"; P.S. the "Bang Bang shrimp is bang-on."

Cafe Maxx *American/Eclectic* — 27 | 19 | 24 | $57

Pompano Beach | 2601 E. Atlantic Blvd. (NE 26th Ave.) | 954-782-0606 | www.cafemaxx.com

Chef Oliver Saucy's "innovative" Eclectic–New American cuisine is "always prepared with a special touch" and complemented by co-owner Darrel Broek's "inspired" wine list and "pleasantly low-key" service at this "one-of-a-kind" "treasure" in Pompano Beach; it's "not cheap" and some gripe that the storefront setting "doesn't do [the experience] justice", but longtime loyalists plead "don't move – it's part of the charm."

Canyon *Southwestern* — 27 | 22 | 23 | $52

Ft. Lauderdale | 1818 E. Sunrise Blvd. (N. Federal Hwy.) | 954-765-1950 | www.canyonfl.com

It's "quite a scene" at this "popular" Ft. Lauderdale bistro offering an "imaginative", "pricey" menu of Southwestern and American "fusion" fare; "enormous portions", prickly pear margaritas that "wow" and "helpful" servers are the reward "once you are finally seated" after often long "waits", the result of a "small" space and a no-reserving policy that can be "a real drag."

The Capital Grille Steak

| 26 | 25 | 25 | $67 |

Ft. Lauderdale | 2430 E. Sunrise Blvd. (bet. Bayview & Seminole Drs.) | 954-446-2000 | www.thecapitalgrille.com

"Where the elite meet to eat meat" sums up this Ft. Lauderdale chop-house that's deemed a "cut above other national steak chains" – not just for its "perfect sear" but also for a staff that treats everyone "like a VIP"; a "solid wine list" and "clubby", "dark-wood" environs make for a "relaxing" time, so go ahead and "break the bank."

Casa D'Angelo Italian

| 27 | 22 | 24 | $61 |

Ft. Lauderdale | Sunrise Square Plaza | 1201 N. Federal Hwy. (bet. E. Sunrise Blvd. & NE 13th St.) | 954-564-1234 | www.casa-d-angelo.com

Chef-owner Angelo Elia's "outstanding" Northern Italian fare, including a "wide variety of homemade pasta", takes diners on a "delightful" "journey to Italy" without leaving Ft. Lauderdale; it's "expensive" (i.e. an excuse to "wear your Valentino") and tables are "a tad too cozy" in the "bustling" space, but "warm" service and a "wine room that has to be seen to be believed" help explain why it's "beloved" by many – reservations are highly recommended.

Chima Brazilian Steakhouse Brazilian/Steak

| 25 | 24 | 25 | $64 |

Ft. Lauderdale | 2400 E. Las Olas Blvd. (SE 25th Ave.) | 954-712-0580 | www.chimasteakhouse.com

"Come hungry" to this "upscale churrascaria" in Ft. Lauderdale where an "endless" variety of meat is carved tableside by "cute" skewer handlers in gaucho-style "black pants" until "belts rip" (yours, not theirs) – and that's aside from the "expansive" salad bar (included in the fee) and dessert (not included); a courtyard bar with an "old banyan" tree is the perfect place to enjoy an "authentic caipirinha."

Eduardo de San Angel ⚡ Mexican

| 27 | 22 | 26 | $59 |

Ft. Lauderdale | 2822 E. Commercial Blvd. (bet. Bayview Dr. & NE 28th Ave.) | 954-772-4731 | www.eduardodesanangel.com

This Ft. Lauderdale "favorite" is "not your typical" "neighborhood taco place" – rather, "under the artful eye" of chef-owner Eduardo Pria, it's a "scintillating" tribute to "refined" "haute Mexicano" that some find "even better than high-end Mexico City restaurants"; a "quiet" ambiance and staffers who "provide the fascinating history of each dish" make it "enjoyable" despite the slight "dent in your wallet."

Greek Islands Taverna Greek

| 25 | 15 | 21 | $37 |

Ft. Lauderdale | 3300 N. Ocean Blvd. (Oakland Park Blvd.) | 954-565-5505 | www.greekislandstaverna.com

"Opa!" exclaim fans of this "convivial" Ft. Lauderdale Greek offering "authentic" Hellenic fare at "unusually affordable prices"; "decor is not part of the deal" and there's no reserving, but "don't be discouraged" by occasional "lines" because the operation "moves like clockwork" – which also means that service, though "courteous", can feel "rushed."

Grille 66 Seafood/Steak

| 24 | 24 | 24 | $66 |

Ft. Lauderdale | Hyatt Regency Pier 66 | 2301 SE 17th St. (Access Rd.) | 954-728-3500 | www.grille66andbar.com

"Everything is right" at this "quality" surf 'n' turfer in Ft. Lauderdale's Hyatt Pier 66 complex – from the "professional" staffers to the "stylish" space and 1,000-bottle wine list; the "beautiful setting", with views of the Intracoastal and marina, makes the expense "worth it", and harbor rats suggest "wandering among the million-dollar yachts" "before or after dinner" to complete the experience.

Kitchenetta Trattoria Tipica Italiana ⓂItalian

27 | 18 | 22 | $41

Ft. Lauderdale | 2850 N. Federal Hwy. (bet. E. Oakland Park Blvd. & NE 26th St.) | 954-567-3333 | www.kitchenetta.com

"Monster portions" of "delicious" housemade Italian fare – including wood-fired brick-oven flatbreads that are "meals in themselves" – garner "raves" for this reasonably priced Ft. Lauderdale trattoria/enoteca; a "friendly" staff and open kitchen add to its "casual" appeal, but the "concrete" "industrial"-style space can be "deafening" on "busy nights", so conversationalists often "opt for an outdoor table."

La Brochette Bistro Ⓜ Mediterranean

28 | 19 | 26 | $54

Cooper City | Embassy Lakes Plaza | 2635 N. Hiatus Rd. (Sheridan St.) | 954-435-9090 | www.labrochettebistro.com

"Who would expect to find" Broward County's top spot for Food and Service "tucked away" in a Cooper City strip mall "a couple doors down from Winn-Dixie"? ask fans who marvel at the "gastronomical delights" on chef-owner Aboud Kobaitri's moderately expensive, seafood-focused Med menu; the "intimate" "European" environs are conducive to "romantic" meals, and diners are "well cared for" by the "sweet, old-fashioned" staffers.

Market 17 Ⓜ American/Eclectic

26 | 25 | 25 | $58

Ft. Lauderdale | 1850 SE 17th St. (Eisenhower Blvd.) | 954-835-5507 | www.market17.net

"Innovative" American-Eclectic fare made with a "deft" touch and "farm-fresh" ingredients earns kudos for this sophisticated spot in Ft. Lauderdale; "superlative" service, "elegant" environs and a "wonderful wine and cocktail list" also help justify the "expensive" tabs; P.S. a private room hosts "memorable" "dining-in-the-dark" tasting meals.

Sette Bello Italian

26 | 21 | 25 | $52

Ft. Lauderdale | 6241 N. Federal Hwy. (NE 62nd St.) | 954-351-0505 | www.settebellofla.com

At this "authentic" "family-owned" Italian in Ft. Lauderdale, diners feel "welcomed" by a chef-owner who "oversees everything", both in the kitchen (preparing "tasty" pastas and other "reasonably priced" fare) and out ("appearing at tables" to "ask about the food"); the "attention to detail" extends to the "small" room's "pretty" decor and "nice" wine list, with "knowledgeable" staffers ready to "suggest good pairings."

Steak 954 Steak

24 | 26 | 23 | $76

Ft. Lauderdale | W Ft. Lauderdale | 401 N. Ft. Lauderdale Beach Blvd. (bet. Bayshore Dr. & Riomar St.) | 954-414-8333 | www.steak954.com

"A hot spot even for a W Hotel", this "chic" chophouse from Stephen Starr (Buddakan in Philly and NYC, etc.) dazzles the eyes with its "fascinating" 15-ft. jellyfish tank and "gorgeous" beach and ocean views, helping it grab the top Decor rating in Broward; taste buds are also treated to some "inventive twists on traditional steakhouse standards" delivered by an "attentive" crew, making it "worth every [one] of the many dollars."

Thai Spice *Thai*

26 | 22 | 25 | $38

Ft. Lauderdale | 1514 E. Commercial Blvd. (bet. NE 13th Ave. & 15th Terr.) | 954-771-4535 | www.thaispicefla.com

With a "litany" of daily specials recited by a "smiling" staff plus an "extensive" printed menu, there's "way more than pad Thai" at this "excellent" Siamese in a Ft. Lauderdale strip mall, including a recently added bar/lounge space; "fresh orchids" adorning "beautifully presented" plates and an "upscale" setting with "spectacular" "tropical fish tanks" set the scene for "romance", while "fair" prices seal the deal.

3030 Ocean *American/Seafood*

26 | 23 | 24 | $57

Ft. Lauderdale | Harbor Beach Marriott Resort & Spa | 3030 Holiday Dr. (Seabreeze Blvd.) | 954-765-3030 | www.3030ocean.com

"Ultrafresh" fish prepared with "imagination" is the lure at this "upscale" Ft. Lauderdale New American now under the direction of former sous chef Paula DaSilva after the departure of longtime chef Dean Max; it's in the "hectic" lobby of an "oceanfront" Marriott so there could be "noisy conventioneers" or "a family in their bathing suits" nearby, but "get over it" and "ask for a window" with "beautiful" water views or a "quiet table at the rear" away from the "lively" bar.

Valentino's Cucina Italiana 🗷🅜 *Italian*

27 | 16 | 25 | $71

Ft. Lauderdale | 620 S. Federal Hwy. (SE 6th Ct.) | 954-523-5767 | www.valentinoscucinaitaliana.com

The "innovative" fare at this "pricey" Ft. Lauderdale Italian is so "blow-you-away" good that some find themselves "creating excuses to call things 'special occasions'" just to go back again; to cap it all off, service is "excellent" in the spacious setting chicly dressed with wood beams, white linens and cushy seating (a post-Survey move is not reflected in the Decor rating).

Honolulu

TOP FOOD RANKING

Restaurant	Cuisine
29 La Mer	French
Mitch's Sushi Restaurant	Japanese/Seafood
28 Alan Wong's	Hawaii Regional
Sushi Sasabune	Japanese
27 Chef Mavro	French/Hawaii Regional
Michel's	French
Hiroshi Eurasion Tapas	Eurasian
Le Bistro	French
Orchids	Pacific Rim
Hy's Steak House	Steak

OTHER NOTEWORTHY PLACES

Assaggio	Italian
Big City Diner	American
d.k Steak House	Steak
Nobu Waikiki	Japanese/Peruvian
Pineapple Room	Hawaii Regional
Roy's	Hawaii Regional
Sansei	Japanese/Pacific Rim
3660 on the Rise	Pacific Rim
Town	American/Italian
Vino Italian Tapas	Italian

Alan Wong's *Hawaii Reg.* | 28 | 23 | 27 | $79 |

McCully | 1857 S. King St. (McCully St.) | 808-949-2526 | www.alanwongs.com

A "pioneer in Hawaii Regional cuisine", chef Alan Wong "continues to innovate", "plating up the best of local farms and island seas" at this McCully "nirvana", perennially rated a "perfect No. 1" as Oahu's Most Popular Restaurant; the "exceptionally prepared" food boasts "brilliant flavors" and the "wine list is top-notch", and it's all "expertly presented" by a "smart" staff versed in every "culinary nuance"; if a few quibble that it "lacks panache", most agree it's the "dining highlight" of the island.

Assaggio *Italian* | 25 | 23 | 24 | $39 |

Ala Moana | Ala Moana Ctr. | 1450 Ala Moana Blvd. (bet. Atkinson Dr. & Piikoi St.) | 808-942-3446

Hawaii Kai | Koko Marina Ctr. | 7192 Kalanianaole Hwy. (Lunalilo Home Rd.) | 808-396-0756

Kahala | 4346 Waialae Ave. (Kallauea Ave.) | 808-732-1011

Kailua | 354 Uluniu St. (Aarona Pl.) | 808-261-2772

Kapolei | 777 Kamokila Blvd. (Alohike St.) | 808-674-8801

Mililani | Town Center of Mililani | 95-1249 Meheula Pkwy. (Lanikuhana Ave.) | 808-623-5115

www.assaggiohawaii.com

"Never been disappointed" at this Italian chain declare diners who give "kudos" to the "savory, delicious" and "memorable" fare, "pleasant, light" atmosphere and "courteous" service; portions are "plentiful" and "reasonably" priced and the Caesar salad made tableside is "heaven", especially for "garlicphiles" – little wonder this outfit is a "gathering spot for local folk" who live a "hop, skip and a jump" away; P.S. the view of the harbor at the Koko Marina branch is "very relaxing."

Big City Diner *American*   21 | 17 | 22 | $22

Aiea | Pearlridge Shopping Ctr. | 98-211 Pali Momi St. (Moanalua Rd.) | 808-487-8188
Kailua | Kailua Town Ctr. | 108 Hekili St. (Hamakua Dr.) | 808-263-8880
Kaimuki | 3565 Waialae Ave. (11th Ave.) | 808-738-8855
Waipahu | Waipio Shopping Ctr. | 94-800 Ukee St. (Oli Loop) | 808-678-8868
Ward | Ward Entertainment Ctr. | 1060 Auahi St. (Kamakee St.) | 808-591-8891
www.bigcitydinerhawaii.com

"Go with an empty stomach and leave full" urge fans who frequent this "family-friendly" Oahu diner chain with "lively decor", specializing in "ono-licious local grinds" (or "excellent" American "comfort food" with an "authentic" Hawaiian "twist"); the "extensive menu" is packed with "affordable" "simple pleasures", including an "out-of-this-world breakfast", "gigantic burgers" and "insane" kimchi fried rice, all dished out in "customary huge portions" and served "with a smile."

Chef Mavro Ⓜ *French/Hawaii Reg.*   27 | 25 | 28 | $103

Moiliili | 1969 S. King St. (McCully St.) | 808-944-4714 | www.chefmavro.com
"Expert culinarian" George (Mavro) Mavrothalassitis "delivers on all fronts", offering a "spectacular taste of the islands" at his Hawaii Regional–French "true gourmet experience" set in a "nondescript building" in Moiliili where his "wife greets you at the door"; "plan to take your time" – the chef "combines exquisite technique with his passion for local ingredients" ensuring that "every morsel" of the "pricey set menu" (à la carte available upon request) is a "series of unique surprises", while the sommelier does a "fantastic job" with wine pairings, and service is "gracious."

d.k Steak House *Steak*   26 | 23 | 26 | $62

Waikiki | Waikiki Beach Marriott Resort & Spa | 2552 Kalakaua Ave. (bet. Ohua & Paoakalani Aves.) | 808-931-6280 | www.dkrestaurants.com
D.K. Kodama's "clubby" yet "elegant" Waikiki Beach Marriott steakhouse is "one of the best" places on the beach to "savor a real" hunk of dry-aged beef while enjoying the "spectacular sunset"; the meat is "earthy, juicy and well paired" with the "solid" wine selection and a "dizzying array of delicious sides", all toted to table by an "absolutely delightful" staff; if quibblers find the decor a "bit lacking" for that "special night out", for most the "awesome location" more than compensates.

Hiroshi Eurasion Tapas *Eurasian*   27 | 24 | 26 | $56

Restaurant Row | 500 Ala Moana Blvd. (bet. Punchbowl & South Sts.) | 808-533-4476 | www.dkrestaurants.com
"Prepare to be seduced by the flavors" at this "modern" Eurasian tapas "favorite" on Restaurant Row, next to sibling Vino; chef/co-owner Hiroshi Fukui constantly experiments with ingredients from "local farmers", dreaming up "imaginative" combos "to delight the palate" while his business partner (along with restaurateur D.K. Kodama) and "main attraction", master sommelier Chuck Furuya, "happily guides

you"; service is "attentive but not smothering", and happy hour is "amazing", as are the occasional multicourse kaiseki dinners.

Hy's Steak House *Steak*
27 | 25 | 27 | $70

Waikiki | Waikiki Park Heights Hotel | 2440 Kuhio Ave. (bet. Kaiulani Ave. & Kapuni St.) | 808-922-5555 | www.hyshawaii.com

"No postage-stamp portions" here so "bring an appetite" to this "old-school" steakhouse in the Waikiki Park Heights Hotel, an "oasis in the bustle" of the city where you "expect to see the Rat Pack" in the "big leather booths"; the "exceptional" kiawe-grilled beef sets the "gold standard", the wine selection is "terrific", service is "supremely professional" and the live music "fits perfectly" with the "romantic" mood, making for a "memorable experience"; P.S. "save room for the cherries jubilee" prepared tableside.

La Mer *French*
29 | 29 | 29 | $143

Waikiki | Halekulani Hotel | 2199 Kalia Rd. (Lewers St.) | 808-923-2311 | www.halekulani.com

"By far the finest dining experience you will have on Oahu", this "elegant, intimate" French "keeper" in the "stunning" Halekulani Hotel "aspires to Parisian culinary decadence with prices to match", garnering No. 1 ratings among Oahu Restaurants for Food, Decor and Service; the "superbly prepared" prix fixe and tasting menus coupled with a "top-notch wine list", "supreme" setting overlooking Waikiki Beach and "utterly spectacular" sunset views give epicures the "best reasons to open the piggy bank and put on a jacket" or long-sleeve collar shirt (either one required).

Le Bistro *French*
27 | 22 | 25 | $60

Niu Valley | Niu Valley Shopping Ctr. | 5730 Kalanianaole Hwy. (Halemaumau St.) | 808-373-7990

"Leave the strip mall behind" as you enter this "true hidden gem" owned by "talented" Japanese chef Alan Takasaki and his wife, Debbie, serving "fantastic French" fare in an "unlikely" Niu Valley venue; the "service-oriented staff" is "committed" to delivering "beautifully prepared dishes" made with "lots of local ingredients" and an "outstanding" wine list while the "elegant" room retains a "cozy feel", making for a "*magnifique*" and "memorable" experience that's "well worth the price."

Michel's *French*
27 | 27 | 28 | $85

Waikiki | Colony Surf | 2895 Kalakaua Ave. (Poni Moi Rd.) | 808-923-6552 | www.michelshawaii.com

"Romantic, expensive, posh", yes, this "big date" Classic French "throwback" is "worth every penny" sigh sybarites who snag ocean-front seats at this "bastion of fine traditional cooking" in the Colony Surf Hotel at the foot of Diamond Head; "it's the view that captures your heart" – let the "sunset, ships and night lights of Honolulu woo you" as the "music of the surf caresses the shore" and you "feast on the sumptuous" prix fixe menu prepared tableside by "gracious" tuxedo-clad servers; in sum, "simply marvelous."

Mitch's Sushi Restaurant *Japanese/Seafood*
29 | 13 | 24 | $69

Airport | 524 Ohohia St. (Ualena St.) | 808-837-7774 | www.mitchsushi.com

"In-freakin'-incredible!" cheer fin fans who dive into the "outstanding chirashi plates" and "large portions" of the "freshest" fish at this

Japanese seafooder, a reservations-only BYO set in a "nondescript" warehouse near the airport car rentals; it's "not the prettiest" locale, and the "tiny 'dining' area" is reminiscent of "Ralph Kramden's *Honeymooners* apartment", but the master sushi chefs "ensure that every piece is a balanced work of edible art" that's "worth the high price."

Nobu Waikiki *Japanese/Peruvian*

26 | 25 | 24 | $84

Waikiki | Waikiki Parc Hotel | 2233 Helumoa Rd. (Lewers St.) | 808-237-6999 | www.noburestaurants.com

You can always expect an "ethereal meal at one of Nobu Matsuhisa's" namesake restaurants and the Waikiki Parc Hotel branch is "no exception" exult enthusiasts who suggest you "give yourself over" to your "super-attentive" servers who "delight you with a parade" of "original, brilliant" Japanese-Peruvian fusion "taste sensations"; the sushi is like "edible art" while the low-lit atmosphere is "mellow, yet classy", though a few quip that it "takes a sophisticated palate to appreciate the cost."

Orchids ❶ *Pacific Rim*

27 | 28 | 28 | $75

Waikiki | Halekulani Hotel | 2199 Kalia Rd. (Lewers St.) | 808-923-2311 | www.halekulani.com

It's "less formal than La Mer upstairs", but "from the minute" you enter this "spectacular" Pacific Rim seafooder in the "famed" Halekulani Hotel you're "treated like an alii (royalty)" by the "stellar" staff; "with Diamond Head in the background" and a "gorgeous oceanside setting" plus "innovative global-class cuisine" (including the "justifiably famous" Sunday brunch) and the "quiet elegance" of the orchid-filled room, the stage is set for a "wonderful" "open-air experience."

Pineapple Room *Hawaii Reg.*

25 | 20 | 23 | $37

Ala Moana | Macy's, Ala Moana Ctr. | 1450 Ala Moana Blvd. (bet. Atkinson Dr. & Piikoi St.) | 808-945-6573 | www.alanwongs.com

"Affordable Alan Wong! what a concept!" – this is the place to try the famed chef's "scrumptious" Hawaii Regional "creations" "without the super-high price tag" gush fans who make fruitful expeditions to this "surprising find" on Macy's third floor in the Ala Moana Center; a meal is "both a bargain and a treat", the setting is "casual" and service "pragmatic" – it's a "wonderful combination", and while it can get "noisy", the "food makes up for all of it."

Roy's *Hawaii Reg.*

26 | 23 | 25 | $57

Hawaii Kai | 6600 Kalanianaole Hwy. (Keahole St.) | 808-396-7697
Kapolei | Ko Olina Resort & Marina | 92-1220 Aliinui Dr. (Kamoana Pl.) | 808-676-7697
Waikiki | Waikiki Beach Walk | 226 Lewers St. (Kalakaua Ave.) | 808-923-7697
www.royshawaii.com

The "godfather" of Hawaii Regional cuisine "still shines" insist loyalists who patronize Roy Yamaguchi's "epicurean delight" (Honolulu's Most Popular chain), including the "original" Hawaii Kai "mother ship"; "pupu through dessert", "each morsel makes your mouth happy" (try the "terrific" signature blackened ahi and "sublime" chocolate lava cake) and it's all "complemented by a sophisticated wine list", "cordial" service and "cosmopolitan" atmosphere; if wistful sorts say it was "more interesting once upon a time", for most it's "always a treat."

	FOOD	DECOR	SERVICE	COST

Sansei *Japanese/Pacific Rim* | 26 | 20 | 23 | $47 |

Waikiki | Waikiki Beach Marriott Resort & Spa | 2552 Kalakaua Ave. (bet. Ohua & Paoakalani Aves.) | 808-931-6286
Kapalua | Kapalua Resort | 600 Office Rd. (Village Rd.) | 808-669-6286
Kihei | Kihei Town Ctr. | 1881 S. Kihei Rd. (Halelani Pl.) | 808-879-0004
Kohala Coast | Waikoloa Beach Resort | 69-201 Waikoloa Beach Dr. (Queen Kaahumanu Hwy.) | Kamuela | 808-886-6286
www.sanseihawaii.com

The "amazing array of exquisite" sushi coupled with "scrumptious" entrees and cocktails lures loyalists to this "fabulous", "clublike" Japanese–Pacific Rim chainlet; "sit at the sushi bar and leave it to the chefs to prepare fish so fresh, you'd think they just plucked it out of the sea", though get ready to wait "forever if you don't have a reservation"; P.S. "don't forget the early-bird specials" or weekend karaoke.

Sushi Sasabune ⊠ *Japanese* | 28 | 18 | 21 | $106 |

Makiki | 1417 S. King St. (Keeaumoku St.) | 808-947-3800

"OMG . . . omakase!" – for "mindblowingly fresh sushi impeccably prepared", this "spartan" Japanese "favorite" in Makiki is a "must-visit for purists" who follow "perfectionist" Seiji Kumagawa's motto: "trust me"; yes, he can be "bossy" but his "bark may be worse than his bite – and his bites are worth" the steep costs, since "once you put a piece of signature negitoro in your mouth", it's "simply divine."

3660 on the Rise Ⓜ *Pacific Rim* | 26 | 22 | 26 | $57 |

Kaimuki | 3660 Waialae Ave. (Wilhelmina Rise) | 808-737-1177 | www.3660.com

"Away from the hustle and bustle", this Pacific Rim seafooder "surprisingly set in an office building" remains a "Kaimuki treasure" where chef Russell Siu dreams up "amazingly innovative" fare, including his signature "melt-in-your-mouth" ahi katsu, "served with utmost courtesy" by the "welcoming staff"; if a few wonder "what's all the fuss about?", for most it's "well worth leaving the tourist throngs and joining the locals" at this "upscale, modern" place that "will never plateau."

Town ⊠ *American/Italian* | 26 | 19 | 23 | $39 |

Kaimuki | 3435 Waialae Ave. (9th Ave.) | 808-735-5900 | www.townkaimuki.com

Diners leave Ed Kenney's "lively" and "totally non-fancy" New American–Italian "locavore heaven" in Kaimuki with "smiles across their faces", praising the "innovative use of local ingredients" ("not a single cliché could be found on my plate") and the industrial digs' "hip, young yet welcoming vibe"; while it can get "noisy" and "cramped", for most it "never fails to delight" with its "reasonably" priced "taste of urban chic."

Vino Italian Tapas & Wine Bar ⊠Ⓜ *Italian* | 26 | 21 | 24 | $45 |

Restaurant Row | 500 Ala Moana Blvd. (bet. Punchbowl & South Sts.) | 808-524-8466 | www.dkrestaurants.com

"Wine, wine and more wine" lures oenophiles to D.K. Kodama's Italian on Restaurant Row where master sommelier Chuck Furuya's "philosophy" of pairing "food-friendly" pours from Europe and California with chef Keith Endo's "perfectly prepared small plates" hits all of the "high" notes; for a "real adventure", come for an "informal" meal with a "small group of friends" and "sample the extensive variety" of tapas and "little-known varietals" – "what a combination"; P.S. closed Sunday–Tuesday.

Houston

TOP FOOD RANKING

Restaurant	Cuisine
29] Da Marco	Italian
28] Chez Nous	French
Mark's American Cuisine	American
Pappas Bros. Steakhouse	Steak
27] Nino's	Italian
Brasserie Max & Julie	French
Brennan's	Creole
Del Frisco's	Steak
Kiran's	Indian
Brenner's	Steak
Tony Mandola's	Seafood
26] Uptown Sushi	Japanese
Mockingbird Bistro Wine Bar	American
Perry's Steakhouse & Grille	Steak
Vic & Anthony's	Steak
Dolce Vita Pizzeria Enoteca	Italian
Irma's*	Mexican
Morton's	Steak
Backstreet Café	American
Kanomwan	Thai

OTHER NOTEWORTHY PLACES

Américas	S American
Carrabba's	Italian
Etoile	French
Haven	American
Hugo's	Mexican
Indika	Indian
Kata Robata	Japanese
Latin Bites	Peruvian
Le Mistral	French
Oxheart	American
Pass & Provisions	American
Philippe	American/French
RDG + Bar Annie	American/Southwestern
Reef	Seafood
Ristorante Cavour	Italian
Sparrow Bar + Cookshop	American
Tony's	Continental/Italian
Triniti	American
Uchi	Japanese
Underbelly	American

* Indicates a tie with restaurant above

Américas *S American*

24 | 25 | 23 | $47

River Oaks | 2040 W. Gray St. (Shepherd Dr.) | 832-200-1492
The Woodlands | 21 Waterway Ave. (Lake Robbins Dr.) | 281-367-1492
www.cordua.com

"Sample the tastes of South America" at this upscale duo in River Oaks and The Woodlands from the Cordúa family (Amazón Grill, Artista, Churrascos) with "wonderful", "top-notch" cooking and "fanciful" decor; service receives mixed reviews, and beware of acoustics that "can be painful at peak times."

Backstreet Café *American*

26 | 24 | 25 | $39

River Oaks | 1103 S. Shepherd Dr. (bet. Dallas & Gray Sts.) | 713-521-2239 | www.backstreetcafe.net

There's "lots of character" at this "quaint old house" in River Oaks, a perpetual "favorite" for "stellar" midpriced American fare "with something for everyone" backed by "great wines" selected by Sean Beck (also "quite the mixologist"); "the backyard patio is lovely in pleasant weather", and "Sunday brunch is a real treat" too.

Brasserie Max & Julie *French*

27 | 24 | 25 | $44

Montrose | 4315 Montrose Blvd. (Richmond Ave.) | 713-524-0070 | www.maxandjulie.net

The "quintessential" French brasserie, this "lovely" Montrose charmer pairs "fantastic", "authentic" fare with "excellent" Gallic wines; the "atmosphere will make you believe you're in Paris", and it's even more of a kick "when someone else is treating."

Brennan's *Creole*

27 | 28 | 27 | $56

Midtown | 3300 Smith St. (Stuart St.) | 713-522-9711 | www.brennanshouston.com

A "landmark", this Midtown "grande dame" and sib of the famed Commander's Palace in New Orleans is "the place to indulge" in "fabulous" Southwestern-Creole dishes like turtle soup and bananas Foster; it's ranked No. 1 for Service and Decor in Houston thanks to "exceptional hospitality" that "makes you feel like royalty" plus an "absolutely gorgeous" interior cementing its status as a "go-to" for "birthdays and special occasions" or the "amazing" jazz brunch on Sundays; P.S. jackets suggested.

Brenner's Steakhouse *Steak*

27 | 26 | 25 | $59

Memorial | 10911 Katy Frwy. (bet. Brittmoore Rd. & Wycliffe Dr.) | 713-465-2901
River Oaks | 1 Birdsall St. (Memorial Dr.) | 713-868-4444
www.brennerssteakhouse.com

A longtime "tradition" for beef, this steakhouse from the Landry's chain boasts "impressive" cuts and a staff that "waits on you hand and foot"; "you can't beat the" atmosphere either, with both the circa-1936 Memorial branch and its River Oaks offshoot featuring "dark", wood-trimmed quarters deemed "perfect for a special occasion."

Carrabba's Italian Grill *Italian*

23 | 20 | 22 | $29

Briargrove | 1399 S. Voss Rd. (bet. San Felipe St. & Woodway Dr.) | 713-468-0868
Champions | Champions Vill. | 5440 FM 1960 W. (Champion Forest Dr.) | 281-397-8255

(continued)

Carrabba's Italian Grill

Northwest Houston | 7540 Hwy. 6 N. (bet. Longenbaugh & Ridge Park Drs.) | 281-859-9700
Upper Kirby District | 3115 Kirby Dr. (Branard St.) | 713-522-3131
West Houston | 11339 Katy Frwy. (bet. Kirkwood Rd. & Wilcrest Dr.) | 713-464-6595
Webster | 502 W. Bay Area Blvd. (Texas Ave.) | 281-338-0574
Kingwood | 750 Kingwood Dr. (Chestnut Ridge Rd.) | 281-358-5580
Sugar Land | 2335 Hwy. 6 S. (bet. Lexington & Town Center Blvds.) | 281-980-4433
The Woodlands | 25665 I-45 N. Hwy. (bet. Briar Rock Rd. & Valley Wood Dr.) | 281-367-9423
www.carrabbas.com

"Mainstream" Italian cooking comes in "plentiful" portions at this "reasonably priced" franchise ranked a solid bet "for a casual night out" with the family; "long waits" prevail at most locales, although seasoned patrons proclaim "you're best off" with Houston's Briargrove and the Upper Kirby District locations.

Chez Nous ⧄ *French* | 28 | 24 | 27 | $64 |

Humble | 217 S. Ave. G (bet. Granberry & Staitti Sts.) | 281-446-6717 | www.cheznousfrenchrestaurant.com

In the "quiet city of Humble", this "expensive" foodie "mecca" is "worth the drive" thanks to its "outstanding", market-driven French cuisine, "excellent" wines and "superior service"; the setting in an old church is "romantic" enough that you may just see someone "pop the question."

Da Marco ⧄Ⓜ *Italian* | 29 | 24 | 27 | $61 |

Montrose | 1520 Westheimer Rd. (Ridgewood St.) | 713-807-8857 | www.damarcohouston.com

Tuscany comes to Texas via this Montrose Italian – No. 1 for Food and Most Popular in Houston – whipping up "memorable" meals with "sublime", "homemade pastas" and "amazing things with truffles" in an "intimate" setting tended by a "knowledgeable" staff; yes, it's "crowded", and "you'll take a hit in the pocketbook, but you won't mind"; P.S. beer and wine only.

Del Frisco's Double Eagle Steak House *Steak* | 27 | 24 | 26 | $67 |

Galleria | 5061 Westheimer Rd. (bet. McCue Rd. & Post Oak Blvd.) | 713-355-2600 | www.delfriscos.com

You might just "need two stomachs" for the "outrageous", "buttery" steaks "cooked to perfection" at this high-end chophouse chain catering to an "expense-account" clientele with its "extensive wine list", "fine" service and setting akin to a "chic Western saloon"; it's especially "great for a special occasion" "if money is no object."

Dolce Vita Pizzeria Enoteca Ⓜ *Italian* | 26 | 17 | 21 | $32 |

Montrose | 500 Westheimer Rd. (Whitney St.) | 713-520-8222 | www.dolcevitahouston.com

"Fabulous pizzas" with "beautiful blistered crusts" are the main attraction at this Montrose Italian from Marco Wiles (Da Marco), also putting out "innovative" antipasti and well-chosen wines; the room's bustling most nights with a "noisy" crowd, so "go early" or prepare to wait.

Etoile *French*

| | | | E |

Uptown | Uptown Park | 1101 Uptown Park Blvd. (Post Oak Blvd.) | 832-668-5808 | www.etoilecuisine.com

Chef Philippe Verpiand (ex San Diego's Cavaillon) is behind this pricey Uptown Park French restaurant serving updated versions of old-school Gallic favorites exactly composed; the rustic, yet polished, setting is composed of contrasting dark hues and white-washed wood, complemented by lighter touches like plush banquettes and stylish chandeliers.

Haven ⊠ *American*

| 25 | 24 | 24 | $43 |

Upper Kirby District | 2502 Algerian Way (Kirby Dr.) | 713-581-6101 | www.havenhouston.com

Praised as a "pioneer in the eat-local movement", this "cool" Upper Kirby American from Randy Evans features "marvelous", midpriced small and large plates spotlighting artisanal and organic ingredients "in delicious new ways"; service is "attentive", and the setting has a "Texas-gone-green-and-sustainable vibe" with "sleek", "beautiful" decor designed from reclaimed materials.

Hugo's *Mexican*

| 26 | 23 | 23 | $41 |

Montrose | 1600 Westheimer Rd. (Mandell St.) | 713-524-7744 | www.hugosrestaurant.net

This upscale Montrose Mexican is known for its "brilliantly executed", "modern" dishes "with a twist" and "kick-butt" margaritas "shaken at your table"; service is "excellent" and the attractive setting is always "humming with patrons", so "the only drawback is the noise level"; P.S. be sure to reserve ahead for Sunday's "fabulous brunch."

Indika Ⓜ *Indian*

| 26 | 22 | 23 | $42 |

Montrose | 516 Westheimer Rd. (Whitney St.) | 713-524-2170 | www.indikausa.com

"The flavors are fantastic" at this "modern" Montrose Indian attracting "adventurous" eaters with "fabulously inventive" cuisine that's "not your typical tandoori"; an "upscale" contemporary setting, "knowledgeable" service and an "inspired" cocktail list are clues that it's "not cheap", but certainly "worth it" for an "exciting" meal.

Irma's Southwest Grill ⊠ *Mexican*

| 26 | 20 | 23 | $23 |

Downtown | 22 N. Chenevert St. (Ruiz St.) | 713-222-0767 | www.irmashouston.com

"Menus? we don't need no stinkin' menus" is the m.o. at this funky Downtown Mexican where "Irma herself" "tells you what they've got each day" and customers choose from an array of "wonderfully authentic" dishes (don't miss the rightly famous lemonade); it's a "fun" place and a local "institution", though a few find fault with bills that feel a touch "overpriced."

Kanomwan ⊠ *Thai*

| 26 | 6 | 13 | $21 |

Neartown | 736½ Telephone Rd. (Lockwood St.) | 713-923-4230

"Long live Telephone Thai!" as this Neartown BYO Thai is affectionately known by die-hard fans of its "fabulous", "authentic" food at "unbeatable" prices; the service and "humble" setting are strictly no-frills, but it remains an "institution" nonetheless.

Kata Robata *Japanese*　　　　　　　| 25 | 21 | 22 | $41 |

Upper Kirby District | 3600 Kirby Dr. (Richmond Ave.) | 713-526-8858 | www.katarobata.com

"Fantastic sushi" with "modern twists" keeps crowds coming to this Upper Kirby Japanese also sending out "wonderful" small plates from the kitchen (like Kobe beef skewers) "for those who don't like the raw stuff"; though the "beautifully designed" space hosts a "chic" crowd, the bills "leave a surprisingly small dent in the wallet."

Kiran's ⊠ *Indian*　　　　　　　| 27 | 26 | 25 | $51 |

Galleria | 4100 Westheimer Rd. (Mid Ln.) | 713-960-8472 | www.kiranshouston.com

"The kitchen shows a lot of flair" at this Galleria-area venue specializing in "wonderful" Indian fusion cuisine like you might find at "Bombay's top restaurant"; "elegant" surroundings and an "attentive", "well-trained" staff help justify the "expensive" tabs and make it a "lovely place to dine."

Latin Bites Cafe Ⓜ *Peruvian*　　　　　　| – | – | – | E |

Galleria | Woodway Arch Ctr. | 5709 Woodway Dr. (bet. Bering Dr. & Chimney Rock Rd.) | 713-229-8369 | www.latinbitescafe.com

Not your typical strip-mall eatery, this upscale Galleria-area effort serves exacting, artistically composed renditions of Peruvian and other Latin American dishes, many with international influences; the modernist setting is warm and convivial thanks, in part, to a hopping pisco bar.

Le Mistral *French*　　　　　　　| 26 | 24 | 26 | $55 |

West Houston | 1400 Eldridge Pkwy. (bet. Brimhurst & Westerloch Drs.) | 832-379-8322 | www.lemistralhouston.com

"Paris meets Houston" at this "fantastic" upscale French in West Houston where the Denis brothers roll out "exceptional", "traditional" cuisine with especially "beautiful desserts" (the chocolate soufflé is a highlight); "attentive" service and a "warm, cozy" setting evoking "quiet luxury" make it "one of the best" in town.

Mark's American Cuisine *American*　　| 28 | 27 | 27 | $75 |

Montrose | 1658 Westheimer Rd. (Dunlavy St.) | 713-523-3800 | www.marks1658.com

"Magnificent" meals are had at this "delightful", "eccentric" converted church in Montrose where chef Mark Cox crafts "fabulous" New American dishes from "exceptional ingredients"; add in "impeccable" service, and it's "everything you could want in a restaurant", not counting the "expensive" bills.

Mockingbird Bistro Wine Bar *American*　| 26 | 24 | 25 | $50 |

River Oaks | 1985 Welch St. (McDuffie St.) | 713-533-0200 | www.mockingbirdbistro.com

A "gem" "tucked away in a residential neighborhood" near River Oaks, this New American spotlights "wonderful, creative" seasonal cuisine from chef-owner John Sheely plus a wine menu that "shines"; it's a tad "expensive", but a "warm" staff and a "quaint" setting with an "old European feel" create an overall "inviting" mood.

	FOOD	DECOR	SERVICE	COST

Morton's The Steakhouse *Steak*
26 | 24 | 25 | $67

Downtown | 1001 McKinney St. (bet. Fannin & Main Sts.) | 713-659-3700
Galleria | Centre at Post Oak | 5000 Westheimer Rd. (Post Oak Blvd.) |
713-629-1946
www.mortons.com

"Corporate types" clamor for the "massive" steaks and "wonderful" sides and wines at these "manly" outposts of the nationwide chop-house chain; they're "consistent", from the "top-notch" service to the "dark", "noisy" settings and premium prices, and if some find them "nothing special", they're "rarely disappointing" either.

Nino's ⊠ *Italian*
27 | 22 | 25 | $39

Montrose | 2817 W. Dallas St. (La Rue St.) | 713-522-5120 |
www.ninos-vincents.com

Perhaps the menu's "not wildly creative", but this family-owned, mid-priced '70s-era Montrose mainstay is "always a pleasure" thanks to its "dependably *delizioso*" red-sauce dishes; there's a "real Italian feel" to the setting – an old house decorated with plants and pottery – and an ever-present owner who "greets guests warmly" adds to the charm; P.S. it shares a courtyard with sibling Vincent's.

Oxheart *American*
– | – | – | VE

Downtown | 1302 Nance St. (Richey St.) | 832-830-8592 |
www.oxhearthouston.com

In the Warehouse District Downtown, this ambitious, expensive New American – with several veggie-heavy prix fixe and tasting menus (no à la carte) – is the inaugural effort from married young chefs Justin Yu and Karen Man; with an industrial yet comfortable setting that features an open kitchen, it's a cozy place that pairs well with the exacting contemporary fare.

Pappas Bros. Steakhouse ⊠ *Steak*
28 | 25 | 27 | $71

Galleria | 5839 Westheimer Rd. (bet. Augusta & Bering Drs.) |
713-780-7352 | www.pappasbros.com

The "melt-in-your-mouth" steaks "blow the competition away" at this "classy" Galleria chophouse where the "excellent" cuts are matched with an "unbelievable" wine list ("a sommelier's dream"); yes, it's "pricey", but the "impeccable" service and "elegant, masculine" setting make it a "favorite for special occasions."

The Pass & Provisions *American*
– | – | – | E

Montrose | 807 Taft St. (bet. Allen Pkwy. & Dallas St.) | 713-628-9020 |
www.passandprovisions.com

This Montrose New American multitasker offers diners options: a formal, minimalist dining room with a view of an open kitchen plating high-end prix fixe meals (The Pass) and a warmer space decked out with wood reclaimed from a basketball court serving an everyday bistro menu (Provisions); it also has a happening bar area and a good-sized terrace to boot.

Perry's Steakhouse & Grille *Steak*
26 | 26 | 25 | $55

Champions | 9730 Cypresswood Dr. (Cutten Rd.) | 281-970-5999
Memorial | 9827 Katy Frwy. (bet. Bunker Hill & Gessner Rds.) | 832-358-9000
Clear Lake | 487 Bay Area Blvd. (bet. Sea Liner & Seawolf Drs.) |
281-286-8800

(continued)

Perry's Steakhouse & Grille

Katy | LaCenterra at Cinco Ranch | 23501 Cinco Ranch Blvd. (Grand Pkwy.) | 281-347-3600
The Woodlands | 6700 Woodlands Pkwy. (Kuykendahl Rd.) | 281-362-0569
www.perryssteakhouse.com

An "elegant place for business or special occasions", this chophouse chain is the place to "impress" with "wonderful" steaks, "outstanding" wines and a signature pork chop that's "not to be missed"; "top-notch" service, "attractive" settings and live jazz are added perks, but it's pretty "expensive" "unless you're on an expense account."

Philippe Restaurant + Lounge ☒ *American/French*

24 | 26 | 24 | $54

Galleria | 1800 Post Oak Blvd. (Ambassador Way) | 713-439-1000 | www.philippehouston.com

Very "chic", this Galleria-area entry from "tremendously talented" Philippe Schmit spotlights "top-line" French-American cooking with playful "Texas twists" (e.g. duck-confit tamales, burgundy beef cheeks); the "sexy" space features a first-floor zinc bar with its own menu plus a stylish industrial-contemporary upstairs dining room with near-"flawless" service and moderate-to-pricey bills.

RDG + Bar Annie *American/Southwestern*

24 | 25 | 22 | $59

Galleria | 1800 Post Oak Blvd. (Ambassador Way) | 713-840-1111 | www.rdgbarannie.com

"Old-guard Houston meets Robert Del Grande" at this "swanky" three-in-one concept in the Galleria with a cushy lounge, "noisy" bar and "excellent, creative" American-Southwestern menu presented in a "lavish" dining room; it's certainly a "place to be seen", although some are irked by "pricey" tabs and service "with an attitude."

Reef ☒ *Seafood*

25 | 21 | 22 | $47

Midtown | 2600 Travis St. (McGowen St.) | 713-526-8282 | www.reefhouston.com

"Hottie chef" Bryan Caswell "knows his seafood" gush fans of this midpriced Midtown "hot spot" known for its "fantastic", "creative" fare, "fabulous wines" and infamous deep-fried mac 'n' cheese ("don't miss it"); service can be "mixed" and the "modern" setting is plenty "noisy", but the "superb food makes it all bearable."

Ristorante Cavour *Italian*

▽ 24 | 26 | 25 | $62

Uptown | Hotel Granduca | 1080 Uptown Park Blvd. (Post Oak Blvd.) | 713-418-1004 | www.granducahouston.com

Hidden inside the ritzy Hotel Granduca Uptown, this dining room rolls out "excellent" (if "not the most creative") Italian cuisine in a "quiet", "elegant" setting; a few find the prices and the formal service "a bit precious", but it works for a "special occasion."

Sparrow Bar + Cookshop ☒Ⓜ *American*

- | - | - | M

Midtown | 3701 Travis St. (bet. Alabama & Winbern Sts.) | 713-524-6922 | www.sparrowhouston.com

Occupying the space where her restaurant t'afia enjoyed years of success, this Midtown New American from chef Monica Pope is an effort in studied simplicity featuring globe-trotting influences on its daily-changing menu, which sometimes includes encores from the space's previous incarnation; its approachable feel is fed by warm, industrial decor and aided by a creative cocktail program and wallet-friendly wine choices.

Tony Mandola's *Seafood*
27 | 23 | 25 | $39

River Oaks | 1212 Waugh Dr. (Clay St.) | 713-528-3474 | www.tonymandolas.com

A "home run" for the Mandola family, this River Oaks seafooder attracts "everyone in Houston" thanks to its "diverse" array of "fabulous" Gulf Coast–style dishes with Creole touches plus a handful of Italian favorites; it's a "bit fancy" with "professional" service and an attractive if "corporate" setting, though the consensus is it's "worth every dime."

Tony's ⧄ *Continental/Italian*
26 | 26 | 26 | $74

Greenway Plaza Area | 3755 Richmond Ave. (Timmons Ln.) | 713-622-6778 | www.tonyshouston.com

"One of Houston's oldest and most elegant", this Greenway Plaza "legend" from Tony Vallone provides "true white-tablecloth" dining via "top-notch" Italian-Continental cuisine and "refined" service in a "date"-worthy setting adorned with world-class art; on the downside are "astronomical" prices and service that can be "a little stuffy" "unless they know you"; P.S. jackets suggested.

Triniti *American*
- | - | - | E

Lower Shepherd | 2815 S. Shepherd Dr. (Kipling St.) | 713-527-9090 | www.trinitirestaurant.com

Boasting plenty of local experience, chef Ryan Hildebrand and his team are behind this expensive New American in Lower Shepherd, which groups its artistically ambitious offerings into three categories: savory, sweet and spirits; modern chandeliers, artwork and other design touches are softened by warm woods for an ultimately inviting atmosphere, which includes an open kitchen with surrounding seats.

Uchi *Japanese*
- | - | - | E

Montrose | 904 Westheimer Rd. (Montrose St.) | 713-522-4808 | www.uchirestaurants.com

With inspired, exacting riffs on contemporary Japanese cooking and impeccably fresh seafood, this Montrose offshoot of an Austin hot spot is a tough reservation despite its high prices; soft lighting and warm woods, including some pieces stacked Jenga-like, provide an intimate feel to the space, which peers onto the bustling lower Westheimer scene.

Underbelly ⧄ *American*
- | - | - | E

Montrose | 1100 Westheimer Rd. (Waugh Rd.) | 713-528-9800 | www.underbellyhouston.com

This first solo effort from Chris Shepherd, who wowed foodies at the former Catalan, features a pricey New American menu that showcases the area's rich local bounty as well as nods to Houston's diverse cultural tapestry; the Montrose storefront is set in the middle of bustling Restaurant Row and boasts on-site butchering, which is evident on the plate.

Uptown Sushi *Japanese* 26 | 22 | 22 | $45

Uptown | Uptown Park | 1131-14 Uptown Park Blvd. (Post Oak Blvd.) | 713-871-1200 | www.uptown-sushi.com

This "trendy" Uptown Japanese matches "outstanding" fusion rolls and sushi with creative cocktails; the decor could be a little "less *Miami Vice*", and some find prices on the high side, but it's a "hot spot" nonetheless.

Vic & Anthony's *Steak* 26 | 26 | 27 | $64

Downtown | 1510 Texas Ave. (La Branch St.) | 713-228-1111 | www.vicandanthonys.com

This "classy" Downtown steakhouse near Minute Maid Park "gets it right" with "amazing" meats and "winning" wines deemed "damn expensive" but "worth" it; "top-notch" service and a dark, "romantic" setting (with piano every night but Sunday) cement its status as a "special-occasion" standby.

Las Vegas

* Indicates a tie with restaurant above

	FOOD	DECOR	SERVICE	COST

Aureole *American*

25 | 27 | 24 | $95

Strip | Mandalay Bay Resort | 3950 Las Vegas Blvd. S. (Hacienda Ave.) | 702-632-7401 | www.charliepalmer.com

Capped with a "spectacular" tower that slinkily clad "wine angels" scale "like mountain climbers" to obtain your vino, über-chef Charlie Palmer's "stunning" New American at Mandalay Bay (an outpost of the NYC original) has diners gawking at the "sophisticated", "one-of-a-kind" setting; the "stellar" fare's nearly as inspiring, and is bolstered by prix fixe options, a "grand" wine list and "extraordinary" service – just "don't worry about the cost", and you'll enjoy a "memorable evening."

Bouchon *French*

26 | 25 | 25 | $61

Strip | Venetian Hotel | 3355 Las Vegas Blvd. S., 10th fl. (bet. Flamingo Rd. & Sands Ave.) | 702-414-6200 | www.bouchonbistro.com

"Amazing from start to finish", Thomas Keller's "fab" French bistro in the Venetian (a spin-off of his Napa original) again wins the Most Popular title in Vegas with its "exquisitely prepared" dishes matched by "superb" wines in a "radiant", Adam Tihany–designed room; "outstanding" service is like icing on the gâteau, and though some say it's "hard to find" and "a little pricey", it remains a "best-seller."

Broadway Pizzeria *Pizza*

27 | 17 | 23 | $13

West Side | 840 S. Rancho Dr. (Palomino Ln.) | 702-259-9002 | www.broadwaypizzerialv.com

"Delicious" pizza "just like back East" whets patrons' appetites at this "reasonably priced" West Side pie purveyor, where you can get 'za "by the slice" in true NYC fashion; while the digs are nothing special, the staff is up to speed whether you're dining in or taking out.

Cheesecake Factory *American*

25 | 23 | 23 | $30

Henderson | District at Green Valley Ranch | 160 S. Green Valley Pkwy. (Paseo Verde Pkwy.) | 702-207-6372
Strip | Forum Shops at Caesars Palace | 3500 Las Vegas Blvd. S. (Flamingo Rd.) | 702-792-6888 ●
Summerlin | 750 S. Rampart Blvd. (Alta Dr.) | 702-951-3800
www.thecheesecakefactory.com

A famously "diverse" menu that "reads like a novel" is the gateway to "oversized" portions of "consistently good" American eats topped off with "phenomenal" cheesecakes at these "affordable" eateries, which rank as Vegas' Most Popular chain; sure, the "attractive" digs can get "loud" and "waits are looong", but "excellent" service helps compensate.

Feast Buffet *Eclectic*

20 | 20 | 21 | $19

East Side | Boulder Station Hotel | 4111 Boulder Hwy. (Lamb Blvd.) | 702-432-7777
Henderson | Sunset Station Hotel | 1301 W. Sunset Rd. (Stephanie St.) | 702-547-7777
Henderson | Green Valley Ranch | 2300 Paseo Verde Pkwy. (Carnegie Dr.) | 702-617-6831
North Las Vegas | Texas Station Hotel | 2101 Texas Star Ln. (bet. Lake Mead Blvd. & Rancho Dr.) | 702-631-1000
Northwest | Red Rock Casino | 11011 W. Charleston Blvd. (I-215) | 702-797-7777

(continued)

FOOD DECOR SERVICE COST

(continued)

Feast Buffet

Northwest | Santa Fe Station Hotel | 4949 N. Rancho Dr.
(bet. Lone Mountain Rd. & Rainbow Blvd.) | 702-658-4900
West of Strip | Palace Station Hotel | 2411 W. Sahara Ave. (Rancho Dr.) |
702-367-2411
www.stationcasinos.com

Customers dig into "good food and plenty of it" at these Eclectic buffet-o-ramas, known for providing a "vast" selection (extending out to "another zip code") at sites across the valley; a "polite" staff further bolsters the "pleasant" settings, and while you may have to endure "long lines", most say they're worth it for the "bargain."

Fleur *Eclectic*

25 | 23 | 22 | $70

Strip | Mandalay Bay Resort | 3950 Las Vegas Blvd. S. (Hacienda Ave.) |
702-632-9400 | www.mandalaybay.com

A "gastronomic symphony" awaits patrons of super-chef Hubert Keller's "must-try" Eclectic at the Strip's Mandalay Bay, where "whimsical" small plates offer culinary surprises; the "knowledgeable" staff works well in "appealing" (and relatively "casual") surroundings, and though it's not cheap, it remains a "favorite" for many – especially for lunch.

Florida Café *Cuban*

22 | 17 | 18 | $22

North of Strip | Howard Johnson Hotel | 1401 Las Vegas Blvd. S.
(Park Paseo) | 702-385-3013 | www.floridacafecuban.com

For "savory" Cuban food that "sticks to your ribs at a price that doesn't stick it to you", try this "friendly", north-of-the-Strip "oasis" by the Little White Wedding Chapel; the eats come in "excellent portions", so it's easy to go whole hog and ignore the "strange" location in a HoJo.

Guy Savoy Ⓜ *French*

28 | 27 | 28 | $199

Strip | Caesars Palace Hotel | 3570 Las Vegas Blvd. S. (Flamingo Rd.) |
877-346-4642 | www.caesarspalace.com

Deemed "very close to perfection", this "sublime" New French at Caesars Palace – like its Paris sib – gives diners the chance to "luxuri-ate in the best of everything"; here, "food is art", with the canvas pro-vided by the "exquisite" setting and "fantastic individualized" service, and though you may have to "win a jackpot" to afford the bill, it's an "absolute must" that "defines 'you get what you pay for.'"

Hugo's Cellar *Continental*

26 | 23 | 27 | $61

Downtown | Four Queens Hotel | 202 Fremont St. (4th St.) | 702-385-4011 |
www.fourqueens.com

An "Old Vegas standby", this "classic" Downtowner in the Four Queens casino treats its guests "like royalty", with "roses for the ladies" heightening the ultra-"romantic" atmosphere; the "upscale", wine cellar–like space and "outstanding" Continental fare add to the "throwback" feel, and though the "premium prices" are relatively modern, diners are convinced there's "nothing like it."

I Love Sushi *Japanese*

27 | 23 | 25 | $31

Henderson | 11041 S. Eastern Ave. (Sunridge Heights Pkwy.) |
702-990-4055

"Locals" love this "affordable" Henderson Japanese offering "super-fresh" sushi and an "amazing" selection of "inventive" rolls in an "exuberant" atmosphere; add in "skilled" chefs and "waitresses in kimonos" delivering "on-the-ball" service, and no wonder it's "often busy."

Jean Philippe Patisserie *Bakery* | 25 | 22 | 20 | $22 |

Strip | Bellagio Hotel | 3600 Las Vegas Blvd. S. (Flamingo Rd.) | 702-693-8788
Strip | Aria Hotel | 3730 Las Vegas Blvd. S. (Harmon Ave.) | 702-590-8550 ◗
www.jpchocolates.com

"Skip breakfast, lunch and dinner and make a beeline straight for dessert" at this "chic" Strip-side French bakery/cafe pair, where "delicate" pastries and other "unique" treats delight with "incredible colors and flavors" (and the sidekick sandwiches are "tasty" too); the Bellagio location warrants a visit "just to see the chocolate fountain alone" (it also has sculptures made of the stuff, like its sister site in CityCenter's Aria), and though it may be "pricey" for the genre, it's a definite "wow."

Joël Robuchon *French* | 29 | 28 | 28 | $227 |

Strip | MGM Grand Hotel | 3799 Las Vegas Blvd. S. (Tropicana Ave.) |
702-891-7925 | www.mgmgrand.com

"An experience from the moment you sit down", this "one-of-a-kind" dazzler at the MGM Grand – brought to you by chef extraordinaire Joël Robuchon – ranks No. 1 for Food in Vegas, with "stunning" New French cuisine that's "as close to heaven as you can get", plus "wonderful", purple-accented decor and "flawless" service; *bien sûr*, you may "faint when the bill arrives", but as to whether it's worth it – "yes, yes, yes!"

Joe's Stone Crab *Seafood/Steak* | 26 | 23 | 25 | $66 |

Strip | Forum Shops at Caesars Palace | 3500 Las Vegas Blvd. S. (Flamingo Rd.) | 702-792-9222 | www.joes.net

Revelers say this Strip-side version of "Miami's classic" is the "real deal", boasting steaks and seafood (including those "wonderful" stone crabs) that "reign supreme" in a "large" space at the Forum Shops at Caesars; the "terrific" staff delivers "tremendous" (even "over-the-top") service and the atmosphere's "amazing", so while tabs can get "hefty", it offers big-time "value for the money."

Julian Serrano *Spanish* | 26 | 23 | 23 | $61 |

Strip | Aria Hotel | 3730 Las Vegas Blvd. S. (Harmon Ave.) | 702-590-8520 | www.arialasvegas.com

Less expensive than its northerly sib, Picasso, this Spaniard by "master chef" Julian Serrano purveys "tapas as they should be", with a menu of "sublime" small plates (including "fantastic vegetarian" options) plus more substantial offerings like paellas in a "cool", "modern" space off the lobby of CityCenter's Aria; the "refreshing" drinks and "helpful" service also impress, and while it's "a little pricey", fans consider it a "keeper."

Kabuki *Japanese* | 27 | 25 | 25 | $29 |

South of Strip | Town Sq. | 6605 Las Vegas Blvd. S. (Sunset Rd.) |
702-896-7440
Summerlin | Tivoli Vill. | 400 S. Rampart Blvd. (Alta Dr.) |
702-685-7776
www.kabukirestaurants.com

"Wondrous eats from the Land of the Rising Sun" delight diners at this Japanese chainster's south-of-the-Strip and Summerlin outposts, bastions of "very fresh" sushi and other savories – all laid

	FOOD	DECOR	SERVICE	COST

out on a "huge" menu; with "friendly" service, "original" drinks and attractive settings, they recall an "elegant Tokyo meal", though without the high prices.

L'Atelier de Joël Robuchon *French*

| 28 | 26 | 27 | $132 |

Strip | MGM Grand Hotel | 3799 Las Vegas Blvd. S. (Tropicana Ave.) | 702-891-7358 | www.mgmgrand.com

"Although lower-key, it's still Joël Robuchon" say admirers of this New French "studio" in the MGM Grand, the more "affordable" (though still "wildly expensive") of the master's two outposts at the hotel, where you can sit at the counter for a "front-row seat" to the "chefs' show"; indeed, the "outstanding" small plates, accompanied by "finely tuned" service and "sensual" decor, may "redefine" dining for you, creating an "experience you'll recount for a long time."

Le Cirque Ⓜ *French*

| 27 | 27 | 27 | $117 |

Strip | Bellagio Hotel | 3600 Las Vegas Blvd. S. (Flamingo Rd.) | 702-693-7223 | www.bellagio.com

This Bellagio spin-off of the celebrated NYC original is a "first-class" destination in its own right, presenting "superb" New French cuisine and a "tremendous" wine list in a "whimsical", Adam Tihany–designed space that conjures up an "adult trip to the circus"; "attentive but not intrusive" service prevails, and while prices are as "grand" as the setting, it may well be the "dinner of your life."

Lotus of Siam *Thai*

| 28 | 15 | 23 | $33 |

East of Strip | Commercial Ctr. | 953 E. Sahara Ave. (bet. Maryland Pkwy. & State St.) | 702-735-3033 | www.lotusofsiamlv.com

It may be in an "unassuming" strip mall, but "don't let the outside fool you" – this longtime east-of-the-Strip spot filled with "locals and foodies from across the country" is "off the hook" with "unusual, ultratasty" Northern Thai specialties elevated by a "clarity in the bright sauces and fresh ingredients", as well as a wine list that "could challenge the big dogs"; savants just suggest "disregarding the decor", an easy feat given the "gracious" staff ("ask for recommendations") and "embarrassingly modest" prices.

Marché Bacchus *French*

| 24 | 25 | 23 | $44 |

Northwest | 2620 Regatta Dr. (Coral Shores Dr.) | 702-804-8008 | www.marchebacchus.com

"Transporting you out of the desert and onto the shores of a lake", this waterside eatery in the Northwest is the "perfect date spot" – especially with an "excellent" on-site wine shop where "you can pick a bottle" to accompany your meal (with "just a $10 corkage fee"); the "lovely" French bistro fare, "discreet" service and "reasonable" rates more than satisfy, so locals feel "lucky" to have it.

Michael Mina *American*

| 27 | 25 | 26 | $104 |

Strip | Bellagio Hotel | 3600 Las Vegas Blvd. S. (Flamingo Rd.) | 702-693-7223 | www.michaelmina.net

"It's impossible to get a bad meal" at San Francisco chef Michael Mina's "exceptional" New American in the Bellagio, where diners dive into "magical seafood morsels" – including "must-have" lobster pot pie – in a "serene" room offering a "welcome oasis from the cacophony of the Strip"; "polished" service enchants too, and

	FOOD	DECOR	SERVICE	COST

though you may have to "break open your cookie jar" for the privilege, it's a "special-occasion treat."

Michael's *Continental*

29	28	29	$116

South of Strip | South Point Hotel | 9777 Las Vegas Blvd. S. (Silverado Ranch Blvd.) | 702-796-7111 | www.southpointcasino.com

"Old-school elegance" is alive and well at this "absolutely superb", "quite pricey" south-of-the-Strip Continental at the South Point Hotel, where the "outstanding" black-tie service – rated No. 1 in Vegas – "makes you feel like you're a long-lost friend"; the "magnificent" dishes ("many prepared tableside") are matched by "upscale", "Victorian"-style surroundings, and though some say it's a little "hard to find", the "level of perfection is worth the hunt."

Mon Ami Gabi *French*

24	25	23	$46

Strip | Paris Hotel | 3655 Las Vegas Blvd. S. (Flamingo Rd.) | 702-944-4224 | www.monamigabi.com

With a patio providing "incredible" views of the Bellagio fountains – plus "second-to-none" people-watching – this French bistro and steakhouse at the Strip's Paris Las Vegas promises a "lively" time; thankfully, "you don't feel like you have to mortgage the house" to enjoy the scenery, "delicious" food or "pleasant" service, and that suits the frequent "crowds" just fine.

Monta Ramen *Japanese*

25	16	21	$13

West Side | 5030 Spring Mountain Rd. (bet. Decatur Blvd. & Hauck St.) | 702-367-4600

Monta Chaya *Japanese*

Henderson | 9310 S. Eastern Ave. (Serene Ave.) | 702-331-5151 www.montaramen.com

Even if you "swore you'd never eat ramen after college", you may happily do so again at this "shoebox-sized" West Side (and Henderson) Japanese, where diners slurp down "stunningly good" noodles bathed in "savory, slow-simmered broths"; it's "always busy", but a "friendly" staff keeps things humming, and all in all there's "so much bang for your buck, it's ridiculous."

Mundo *Mexican*

23	25	22	$37

Downtown | World Market Ctr. | 495 S. Grand Central Pkwy. (Bonneville Ave.) | 702-270-4400 | www.mundolasvegas.com

A striking space – mixing old-world Mexico and Vegas glam – sets the scene at this "upscale" Downtowner in the Las Vegas Design Center, which melds "traditional flavors" with "top-of-the-line ingredients" for a "different take on south-of-the-border cuisine"; moderate prices, "knowledgeable" service and "wowing" cocktails fit the bill too, plus it has an "awesome" location near the Smith Center.

Nobu *Japanese*

27	23	24	$88

East of Strip | Hard Rock Hotel | 4455 Paradise Rd. (bet. Flamingo Rd. & Harmon Ave.) | 702-693-5090

Strip | Caesars Palace Hotel | 3570 S. Las Vegas Blvd. (Flamingo Rd.) | 702-785-6628
www.noburestaurants.com

Diners "dream" of the dinners at Nobu Matsuhisa's Japanese "hot spot" in the Hard Rock Hotel and Caesars Palace, proffering "melt-

	FOOD	DECOR	SERVICE	COST

in-your-mouth" sushi and "mind-blowing" cooked dishes like the "star"-quality miso black cod, plus omakase options; a "helpful" staff distributes everything in a "cool", "hopping" space ripe for "celeb sightings" – *hai*, it's "ultraexpensive", but "how could you not love it?"

Peppermill ● *Diner*
| 22 | 22 | 22 | $25 |

Strip | 2985 Las Vegas Blvd. S. (Convention Center Dr.) | 702-735-4177 | www.peppermilllasvegas.com

A 24/7 bastion of "Old Vegas kitsch", this mainstay on the Strip rocks "1970s-flashback" decor ("if you have any bell-bottoms or leisure suits, wear them") while slinging "massive" portions of "sturdy" diner victuals at "reasonable" prices; service that's "sassy with a smile" heightens the groovy feel, while "glitz at its zenith" (along with "old-school cocktails") can be found at the adjoining Fireside Lounge – a Sin City "essential."

Picasso *French*
| 28 | 29 | 28 | $137 |

Strip | Bellagio Hotel | 3600 Las Vegas Blvd. S. (Flamingo Rd.) | 702-693-7223 | www.bellagio.com

"Who wouldn't want to eat surrounded by original Picassos?" wonder fans of chef Julian Serrano's "life-changing" New French at the Bellagio, where the "unsurpassed" setting – rated tops for Decor in Vegas – complements its "astonishing" art collection with "spectacular views of the fountains"; meanwhile, a "top-notch" staff serves prix fixe dinners as "opulent and rich" as the locale, and if this "masterpiece" commands a "master price", it's earned for delivering the "meal of your dreams."

Ping Pang Pong ● *Chinese*
| 22 | 16 | 16 | $25 |

West Side | Gold Coast Hotel & Casino | 4000 W. Flamingo Rd. (Wynn Rd.) | 702-247-8136 | www.goldcoastcasino.com

"If this weren't in the Gold Coast, you'd think you were in Hong Kong" – yet this West Side Chinese is Vegas all the way, with a big variety of "delicious" dim sum and other "tasty" bites purveyed in "nicely decorated" Sino digs; prices that harken to the Sin City of yesteryear complete the picture.

Pink's Hot Dogs ● *Hot Dogs*
| 20 | 13 | 17 | $14 |

Strip | Planet Hollywood Resort | 3667 Las Vegas Blvd. S. (Harmon Ave.) | 702-405-4711 | www.planethollywoodresort.com

"In the tradition of Pink's in Los Angeles", this Planet Hollywood outpost of the La Brea "legend" serves "sensational chili dogs" and other "snappy" franks laden with "just about anything"; there's only "outdoor seating on the Strip" ("great for people-watching"), and if some think these wieners are "pricier than they should be", late-night noshers say they're "just the thing after a long evening at the tables."

P.J. Clarke's New York Chophouse ● *American*
| 20 | 21 | 20 | $41 |

Strip | Forum Shops at Caesars Palace | 3500 Las Vegas Blvd. S. (Flamingo Rd.) | 702-434-7900 | www.pjclarkes.com

It's "not the original", but this offshoot of the venerable NYC watering hole – conveniently located in the Forum Shops at Caesars Palace – apes its progenitor's look and feel, with "masculine" decor, capable service and a "can't-go-wrong" American menu (big on burgers, steaks and

| | | FOOD | DECOR | SERVICE | COST |

oysters); it's certainly choice for "casual" drinks, and the sensible prices are the right chaser.

Prime Steakhouse *Steak*

| 27 | 27 | 27 | $103 |

Strip | Bellagio Hotel | 3600 Las Vegas Blvd. S. (Flamingo Rd.) | 702-693-7223 | www.bellagio.com

"What more can you say" about this "absolutely first-rate" steakhouse from Jean-Georges Vongerichten, where the filets are the "finest quality", the wine list "outstanding" and the "courteous" staff makes "everyone feel rich" – regardless of whether they win at the tables; let's not forget the "lovely" "chocolate-and-blue" setting or the views of the Bellagio's "dancing fountains", and though it's all quite "costly", "you're on vacation so enjoy"; P.S. no shorts, and no children under five allowed.

Raku ●⊠ *Japanese*

| 28 | 20 | 23 | $57 |

West Side | Seoul Plaza | 5030 Spring Mountain Rd. (Decatur Blvd.) | 702-367-3511 | www.raku-grill.com

Japanese food "like you've never had before" is the province of this "cozy" West Side robata grill, which instills its "exquisite", "high-end" small plates (no sushi) with "bold, complex flavors" and "elevates them to another level"; solid service and late hours are added benefits, so it's a "destination for foodies" as well as "chefs on their off-hours."

Sage ⊠ *American*

| 28 | 27 | 25 | $82 |

Strip | Aria Hotel | 3730 Las Vegas Blvd. S. (Harmon Ave.) | 877-230-2742 | www.arialasvegas.com

"Intriguing flavor combinations" beguile at this "top-quality" New American in CityCenter's Aria, a showcase for Chicago chef Shawn McClain's "unique" fare and "farm-to-table philosophy"; "fantastic" drinks, "personal" service and "smashing" decor – tricked out with "sexy lighting" – enhance the experience, and with prices that may not reach the stratospheres attained by other upper-tier options, it leads fans to extend some "sage advice": try it.

Sen of Japan ● *Japanese*

| 28 | 19 | 26 | $53 |

West Side | 8480 W. Desert Inn Rd. (Durango Dr.) | 702-871-7781 | www.senofjapan.com

The "holy grail of Vegas sushi places", this West Side Japanese slices up "sensational", "highly nuanced" fin fare "without the Strip's hype or prices"; comfortable digs and "enthusiastic, prompt" service complete the package, and if you follow the experts and "ask for the omakase", you'll be fed "till your heart's content."

Settebello Pizzeria Napoletana *Pizza*

| 26 | 18 | 21 | $22 |

Henderson | District at Green Valley Ranch | 140 S. Green Valley Pkwy. (Paseo Verde Pkwy.) | 702-222-3556 | www.settebello.net

It's "worth the trek to Henderson" for a taste of the "real Neapolitan pizza" baked up by this "authentic" spot, the original location of a small chain (with Italian pizzaiolo certification), where a "wood-burning oven" creates "charred-crust" pies that "burst with fresh flavors"; the "relaxed" atmosphere gets a boost from "friendly" service, and though it may be "a bit pricey" for 'za, remember – this ain't your typical slice.

| | FOOD | DECOR | SERVICE | COST |

Steak House *Steak*
28 | 24 | 27 | $71

Strip | Circus Circus Hotel | 2880 Las Vegas Blvd. S. (bet. Desert Inn Rd. & Sahara Ave.) | 702-794-3767 | www.circuscircus.com

Maintaining a "standard that few have ever reached", this "hidden gem" of a steakhouse – surprisingly located in the "low-roller heaven" of Circus Circus – is a meat eater's mecca, dispensing "fantastically prepared cuts" in a "private-club" setting; with "top-rate" service, it offers "terrific value" for the quality, so "if you can get past the kiddies and the clowns, you're in for a great meal."

StripSteak *Steak*
27 | 24 | 25 | $90

Strip | Mandalay Bay Resort | 3950 Las Vegas Blvd. S. (Hacienda Ave.) | 702-632-7414 | www.michaelmina.net

"Serious meat eaters" have a field day with the buttery, "mouthwatering" steaks proffered by this bastion of beef in the Strip's Mandalay Bay – another feather in the cap of San Fran celeb-chef Michael Mina; "personal" service and a "hip" vibe complement the "bright", modern setting, and despite "very expensive" tabs, it's a "must while you're in Vegas."

SW Steakhouse *Steak*
27 | 26 | 27 | $101

Strip | Wynn Hotel | 3131 Las Vegas Blvd. S. (bet. Desert Inn Rd. & Sands Ave.) | 702-248-3463 | www.wynnlasvegas.com

Aces for "grilled-to-perfection" steaks and a "not-to-be-missed" view of the show on the lake, this "wonderful" meatery at Wynn Las Vegas is "outstanding in every way" – making it a natural for "special celebrations"; overseeing the "elegant" setting is an "exceptional" crew, and though you may need to "bring your black card to support payment", most deem it a "spectacular place to dine."

Texas de Brazil *Brazilian/Steak*
27 | 25 | 25 | $55

South of Strip | Town Sq. | 6533 Las Vegas Blvd. S. (Sunset Rd.) | 702-614-0080 | www.texasdebrazil.com

"Only a T. rex wouldn't get enough meat" at this outpost of the Brazilian churrascaria chain in the Town Square complex, where servers "keep coming to your table" with "fantastic", rodizio-style steaks and other carnivoria; there's also a "luxe" salad bar and "superb" service bolstering the "classy-without-being-pretentious" atmosphere, so even if it's a little "expensive", diners "enjoy it every time."

Todd English P.U.B. ◗ *American*
21 | 21 | 20 | $37

Strip | Crystals at CityCenter | 3720 Las Vegas Blvd. S. (Harmon Ave.) | 702-489-8080 | www.toddenglishpub.com

With its "modern, pub-inspired" looks and "convivial" atmosphere, Todd English's tavern in Crystals at CityCenter is popular for its "honest" American eats and "wicked" beer list; the "noise level" isn't for everyone, but "attentive" service, moderate prices and a patio option appease.

Via Brasil *Brazilian/Steak*
27 | 26 | 26 | $58

Summerlin | 1225 S. Fort Apache Rd. (Charleston Blvd.) | 702-804-1400 | www.viabrasilsteakhouse.com

"Bring your appetite" to this Brazilian steakhouse in Summerlin, where "well-seasoned, delicious" meats are delivered to your table "hot off the skewer"; diners also dig the "awesome" staff and "relaxed" setting (yep, those are waterfalls), with relatively reasonable tabs for the feast – so "wear loose clothes" and come on down.

Long Island

Restaurant	Cuisine
28] North Fork Table & Inn	American
27] Onsen Sushi	Japanese
Stone Creek Inn	French/Mediterranean
Lake House	American
Mosaic	American
Peter Luger	Steak
Franina Ristorante	Italian
Kitchen A Trattoria*	Italian
Kotobuki	Japanese
Chachama Grill	American
26] Orto	Italian
Maroni Cuisine	Eclectic/Italian
Salvatore's	Pizza
Thai Angel	Thai
Vintage Prime*	Steak
Starr Boggs	American/Seafood
Kitchen A Bistro	French/Mediterranean
Jedediah Hawkins Inn	American
La Piccola Liguria	Italian
Mirabelle, Restaurant	French

OTHER NOTEWORTHY PLACES

Arata Sushi	Japanese
Besito	Mexican
Brass Rail	American
Bryant & Cooper	Steak
Dario's	Italian
Dave's Grill	Continental/Seafood
Giulio Cesare Ristorante	Italian
Il Mulino New York	Italian
Jimmy Hays	Steak
J. Michaels Tuscan	Italian/Steak
La Plage	Eclectic
La Volpe Ristorante	Italian
Nick & Toni's	Italian/Mediterranean
1 North Steakhouse	Steak
Rothmann's	Steak
Ruth's Chris Steak House	Steak
1770 House Restaurant & Inn	American
Stresa	Italian
Topping Rose House	American
Vine Street Café	American

---

* Indicates a tie with restaurant above

	FOOD	DECOR	SERVICE	COST

Arata Sushi Ⓜ *Japanese*

| 25 | 18 | 23 | $37 |

Syosset | 18 Cold Spring Rd. (Jackson Ave.) | 516-921-8154
The "unique" sushi rolls are nothing short of "outstanding" and a variety of the hot dishes are "amazing" too at this "pleasant", dimly lit Syosset Japanese, where a chef's-selection omakase menu appeals to adventurous diners; "quick service" keeps things moving, prices are moderate and the fish is sublimely "fresh", prompting fans to enthuse "we're hooked."

Besito *Mexican*

| 23 | 23 | 21 | $45 |

Roslyn | Harborview Shoppes | 1516 Old Northern Blvd. (bet. Northern Blvd. & Remsen Ave.) | 516-484-3001
Huntington | 402 New York Ave. (bet. Carver & Fairview Sts.) | 631-549-0100
www.besitomexican.com
"Holy guacamole!" – the tableside treat is a "must" at this "hip", "happening" "designer Mexican food" eatery in Huntington and Roslyn, where the margaritas could "have you dancing on the tables" (there's also a "major tequila offering"); the "chic" decor strikes a "romantic" chord, even though some will want to "bring a flashlight", and most aren't too troubled by "high prices" while downing "warm, cinnamony" churros at meal's end.

Brass Rail *American*

| 25 | 19 | 22 | $46 |

Locust Valley | 107 Forest Ave. (bet. Birch Hill Rd. & Weirs Ln.) | 516-723-9103 | www.thebrassraillocustvalley.com
The "varied" menu of "inventive" American comforts offers "something for everyone" at chef-owner Kent Monkan's Locust Valley "gem", an "upscale gastropub" where plates range from "small bites" to full entrees for every budget and appetite, and there's a "well-chosen" wine list; an 1880s bar anchors the "cozy, clubby" space, which gets "crowded" on weekends with diners who are "happy to have reservations."

Bryant & Cooper Steakhouse *Steak*

| 26 | 20 | 23 | $69 |

Roslyn | 2 Middle Neck Rd. (Northern Blvd.) | 516-627-7270 | www.bryantandcooper.com
A "carnivore's dream", this Roslyn "classic" steakhouse is "as good as it gets" thanks to "perfectly grilled" "prime" cuts and "excellent" seafood served in an "old-world" setting bustling with "professional" waiters; the "see-and-be-seen" vibe isn't for everyone, nor is the "noise level" – and you might have to "cash in a CD" to foot the bill – but "true connoisseurs" consider it "worth every penny."

Chachama Grill *American*

| 27 | 19 | 25 | $51 |

East Patchogue | Swan Nursery Commons | 655 Montauk Hwy. (Country Rd.) | 631-758-7640 | www.chachamagrill.com
Chef Elmer Rubio "never disappoints", creating "delicious", "inventive" New American fare at this "little bit of heaven" in East Patchogue where the "classy" staff treats everyone "like family"; "don't judge it by the strip-mall locale", because once inside, the peach-hued decor and soft lighting make for a "surprisingly upscale" atmosphere, and though tabs can get "NYC" pricey, the prix fixe deal (Sunday–Thursday) is "the best, hands down."

	FOOD	DECOR	SERVICE	COST

Dario's ⊠ *Italian* | 25 | 17 | 24 | $56 |

Rockville Centre | 13 N. Village Ave. (bet. Merrick Rd. & Sunrise Hwy.) | 516-255-0535

"The regular menu is just a starting point" at this "upscale" Italian in Rockville Centre, where "excellent" specials, including the "outstanding" veal chop, are the main event; if the "dimly lit" decor "could use an up-grade", the "gracious" service from tuxedoed waiters does not, and "high prices" don't deter the faithful who frequent this "longtime treasure."

Dave's Grill ⊠Ⓜ *Continental/Seafood* | 25 | 19 | 22 | $58 |

Montauk | 468 W. Lake Dr. (bet. Flamingo Ave. & Soundview Dr.) | 631-668-9190 | www.davesgrill.com

"Stellar" "homestyle" seafood lures fans to this wharfside Montauk Continental, where you could "make a meal" of "outstanding" appetizers alone while savoring a "great view of the marina"; though it can be "pricey", and even diehards express dismay over the "goofy" same-day reservation policy, there's otherwise "no Hamptons attitude", and the "professional" staff provides a "warm welcome" once you've made it through the door; P.S. open Thursday–Sunday in season.

Franina Ristorante Ⓜ *Italian* | 27 | 23 | 25 | $56 |

Syosset | 58 W. Jericho Tpke. (bet. Gordon & Haskett Drs.) | 516-496-9770 | www.franina.com

The "chef is a magician" agree fans who file into this "sophisticated" Syosset Italian to "*mangia*" "amazing, delicious, creative" dishes ranging from classics to more exotic fish and game, all toted to table by "civilized" staffers; while it may seem "expensive for a strip-center lo-cation", the prix fixe is reasonable and the Tuscan decor is "lovely", ensuring a "pleasant evening" that's well "worth it."

Giulio Cesare Ristorante ⊠ *Italian* | 26 | 17 | 24 | $55 |

Westbury | 18 Ellison Ave. (Lafayette Ave.) | 516-334-2982

As "old-school" as they come, this perennial Westbury "favorite" is still serving up "outstanding" Northern Italian fare and "great cock-tails" to an appreciative crowd of "regulars", "celebrities" and other denizens of the "'in' crowd"; though its "dated" old-world decor might "need sprucing up", and prices trend "high", most are too busy being "treated royally" by "excellent" waiters to notice.

Il Mulino New York *Italian* | 25 | 22 | 24 | $69 |

Roslyn Estates | 1042 Northern Blvd. (bet. Searingtown Rd. & The Locusts) | 516-621-1870 | www.ilmulino.com

"Sophisticated" Italian fare is prepared with "flair" at this Roslyn sib-ling to the Manhattan original, a "romantic" indulgence for those with full "expense accounts" and "empty stomachs"; the "elegant yet ca-sual" setting and "first-class treatment" preps diners for the "orgy of food" to come, and if prices seem "prohibitive", it's "worth it" for a "special treat"; P.S. the prix fixe Sunday supper is a "great deal."

Jedediah Hawkins Inn Restaurant *American* | 26 | 26 | 25 | $66 |

Jamesport | Jedediah Hawkins Inn | 400 S. Jamesport Ave. (bet. Main Rd. & Peconic Bay Blvd.) | 631-722-2900 | www.jedediahhawkinsinn.com

Set in the historic, "beautifully renovated" Jedediah Hawkins Inn, this "welcoming" Jamesport New American helmed by chef Richard Kanowsky (whose post-Survey arrival may outdate the Food rating) is a

| | FOOD | DECOR | SERVICE | COST |

"culinary treat" with an unwavering farm-to-table commitment, hawking "fresh, imaginative meals" made with kitchen garden–grown produce, eggs hatched on the premises and locally raised meat; "warm", "professional" staffers enhance the "charming country interior", and while such loveliness comes at a "steep price", it's still a "local favorite."

Jimmy Hays *Steak* 25 | 21 | 22 | $64

Island Park | 4310 Austin Blvd. (Kingston Blvd.) | 516-432-5155 | www.jimmyhayssteakhouse.com

"Excellent beef" may be the prime draw at this "upscale" Island Park steakhouse, but fans also praise its "fabulous" seafood, while some convene for the "really fun" bar scene; dark paneling and historic photos bedeck the "lovely" space and servers are "willing to please", so although it's "pricey", partisans contend it could "rival" any meat mecca in NYC.

J. Michaels Tuscan Steakhouse *Italian/Steak* 26 | 25 | 26 | $76

Northport | 688 Ft. Salonga Rd. (bet. Alsace & Ray Pls.) | 631-651-9411 | www.jmichaelstuscansteakhouse.com

Offering "an interesting twist on a high-end steakhouse", this Northport "keeper" "goes well beyond the usual", delivering "superb" "juicy" chops and "delicious sides" capped with "top-shelf" Italian specialties, "inventive" seafood (think lobster meatballs) and an "outstanding" Sunday brunch (served fall–spring); add in a "beautiful" Tuscan-style setting in a 19th-century home and "friendly" staffers who greet regulars by name and it's no wonder fans cheer it's "a home run."

Kitchen A Bistro ⊄ *French/Mediterranean* 26 | 20 | 25 | $53

St. James | 404 N. Country Rd. (Edgewood Ave.) | 631-862-0151 | www.kitchenabistro.com

A "farm-to-table winner", this "delightful" French-Med in St. James is "never boring" thanks to chef-owner Eric Lomando's "superb" ever-changing menu of Gallic "comfort" classics with "innovative" twists featuring produce "fresh from the backyard garden"; the "fantastic" T-shirt–clad staff and "understated" decor keep the "focus on the food", while the BYO with no corkage fee option helps temper "pricey" tabs; P.S cash only and weekend reservations "a must."

Kitchen A Trattoria 🅑 Ⓜ ⊄ *Italian* 27 | 17 | 25 | $43

St. James | 532 N. Country Rd. (bet. Clinton & Woodlawn Aves.) | 631-584-3518 | www.kitchenatrattoria.com

"The food is the star" at this "casual" Italian counterpart to Kitchen A Bistro "hidden" in St. James where chef-owner Eric Lomando's "innovative", "rustic" offerings "change with the seasons" and a "friendly" staff "never disappoints"; set in a "humble" storefront, it's "cozy and quaint" and the BYO policy "helps keep prices down" – just remember reservations are a must on weekends ("make them now!") and it's cash only.

Kotobuki Ⓜ *Japanese* 27 | 18 | 20 | $39

Roslyn | Harborview Shoppes | 1530 Old Northern Blvd. (Northern Blvd.) | 516-621-5312
Babylon | 86 Deer Park Ave. (Main St.) | 631-321-8387
Hauppauge | 377 Nesconset Hwy. (Brookside Dr.) | 631-360-3969
www.kotobukinewyork.com

"One taste" from the "tantalizing array" of "innovative", "just-plucked-from-the-sea-fresh" sushi and sashimi, not to mention the "incredible" cooked dishes, and it's apparent why this "heavenly" Japanese mini-chain is considered "second to none"; if a few say service is "hit-or-miss", the decor "needs updating" and "peak times" can mean "long waits", true fans counter that once those "reasonably" priced "creative rolls" arrive it's all "worth it."

Lake House ☒ American
27 | 24 | 26 | $59

Bay Shore | 240 W. Main St. (bet. Garner & Lawrence Lns.) | 631-666-0995 | www.thelakehouserest.com

Proving that "good things come in small packages", Eileen and Matthew Connors' "phenomenal" Bay Shore American reels in admirers with "consistently inventive", "beautifully presented" seasonal fare that's in sync with the "serene", "charming setting overlooking the lake"; completing the "memorable" experience is "crisp, attentive service" and an outdoor fire pit where you can sip that "after-dinner scotch."

La Piccola Liguria ☒ Italian
26 | 19 | 26 | $63

Port Washington | 47 Shore Rd. (bet. Mill Pond & Old Shore Rds.) | 516-767-6490

"Known for its looong list of specials", "each one more tempting" than the last, this "wonderful" Port Washington Italian is a "haven for regulars" who thrill to the "perfectly prepared" dishes turned out by the "superb kitchen"; "warm and experienced" servers add to the "old-world" experience, and though tabs are "pricey" that doesn't deter devotees who confide it can be "difficult" to get a reservation.

La Plage ☒ Eclectic
25 | 20 | 23 | $55

Wading River | 131 Creek Rd. (Sound Rd.) | 631-744-9200 | www.laplagerestaurant.net

It's "well worth the effort" to find chef-owner Wayne Wadington's "hidden" "gem by the beach" in Wading River where "creative" Eclectic fare and "knowledgeable" staffers make every visit "a home run"; the "sweet" "vacation-home setting" lends a "casual atmosphere" while "watching the sunset" on the porch ensures a "romantic night", and if some decry "expensive" tabs, the "amazing" lunch prix fixe is among "the best deals in town."

La Volpe Ristorante ☒ Italian
25 | 24 | 25 | $43

Center Moriches | 611 Montauk Hwy. (Brookfield Ave.) | 631-874-3819 | www.lavolperestaurant.net

The chef "does wonders" with Sicilian specialties at the La Volpe family's "excellent" Italian "hidden" away in Center Moriches, where diners can also dig into "outrageously delicious" wood-fired pizza baked next door at its sister operation, Anton Pizzeria; the "top-notch" staff "treats customers like royalty" in the "cozy Tuscan setting", and "reasonable" prices contribute to its standing as a local "gem."

Maroni Cuisine ☒☒☒ Eclectic/Italian
26 | 17 | 25 | $103

Northport | 18 Woodbine Ave. (bet. Main St. & Scudder Ave.) | 631-757-4500 | www.maronicuisine.com

"Make reservations" then "bring your appetite" to this cash-only Eclectic-Italian in Northport where chef-owner Michael Maroni delivers an "out-of-this-world" tasting menu, "a mouthwatering culinary survival race" featuring a "seemingly endless succession" of "delicious" dishes

	FOOD	DECOR	SERVICE	COST

(like "best-in-show" meatballs) all ferried to table by the "superb" staff; the "novel" outdoor courtyard provides a warm-weather alternative to the "tiny", "cramped quarters" and tabs require a "stuffed wallet", but for a "unique" "foodie experience", it's "worth every penny."

Mirabelle, Restaurant M *French*   26 | 24 | 26 | $62

Stony Brook | Three Village Inn | 150 Main St. (Shore Rd.) | 631-751-0555 | www.lessings.com

"As good as it gets" declare disciples of chef Guy Reuge's "sensational" French "favorite" tucked away in Stony Brook's historic Three Village Inn, where the "comfortable", "old-world" atmosphere sets the stage for "special occasions"; "impeccable service" augments the "first-class" experience, and though tabs are "expensive", Mirabelle Tavern, just through the lobby, serves up more "casual fare" at commensurate prices.

Mosaic ⊠M *American*   27 | 22 | 26 | $83

St. James | 418 N. Country Rd. (bet. Clinton & Woodlawn Aves.) | 631-584-2058 | www.eatmosaic.com

"Talented" chef-owners Jonathan Contes and Tate Morris "surprise and delight" diners at this "consistently exceptional" St. James New American serving an "artistically presented" five-course tasting menu that changes daily (no à la carte), enhanced by "amazing pairings" from a "novel" wine list; "small yet inviting", with an "attentive" staff that's "there to please", it's a "unique" "North Shore jewel" that always "delivers."

Nick & Toni's *Italian/Mediterranean*   23 | 21 | 21 | $66

East Hampton | 136 N. Main St. (bet. Cedar St. & Miller Terr.) | 631-324-3550 | www.nickandtonis.com

Still a "crowd-pleaser" after many years, this "sophisticated" East Hampton Italian-Med "takes its cooking seriously" and offers "dependable, tasty" meals to "boldface" names and the "über-trendy" in an "upscale" "farmhouse" setting; while "it's not cheap by a long shot", the staff is "accommodating", so just make sure to "reserve far in advance."

North Fork Table & Inn *American*   28 | 24 | 27 | $81

Southold | North Fork Table & Inn | 57225 Main Rd. (bet. Boisseau & Laurel Aves.) | 631-765-0177 | www.northforktableandinn.com

Southold's "shining star" is again rated No. 1 for Food and Service on Long Island thanks to chef Gerry Hayden's "wonderfully imaginative" American prix fixe menus featuring locally sourced ingredients and Claudia Fleming's "orgasmic" desserts – all "masterpieces of culinary design, taste and complexity" and presented by a "superb" staff; the "spare" "country setting" makes for an "elegant" yet "understated ambiance", and though you'll need to "save your pennies", the more wallet-friendly Lunch Truck in the parking lot offers "delicious" treats like lobster rolls.

1 North Steakhouse M *Steak*   21 | 19 | 21 | $37

Hampton Bays | 1 North Rd. (bet. Montauk & Sunrise Hwys.) | 631-594-3419 | www.1northsteakhouse.com

"Bring your appetite" because a truly "excellent porterhouse" is the signature cut at this popular "go-to" steakhouse in Hampton Bays; if a few are less impressed, the staff is "friendly" and "courteous" and besides, the prices are "very affordable for the quality", meaning legions of fans "would go again."

Onsen Sushi *Japanese*

| 27 | 16 | 25 | $31 |

Oakdale | 597 Montauk Hwy. (Dale Dr.) | 631-567-1688 | www.onsensushi.com

Fans "can't say enough" about this Japanese "hidden diamond" set in an Oakdale strip mall where the "innovative dining experience" revolves around "beautiful preparations" of "wonderful sashimi and sushi" as well as "inventive" cooked dishes that "invigorate the senses"; the bamboo-walled digs may not be much to look at, but service is "out of this world" and the "friendly" owner "has so much enthusiasm", plus prices are moderate, making it "a must-go."

Orto Ⓜ🍴 *Italian*

| 26 | 23 | 23 | $50 |

Miller Place | 90 N. Country Rd. (bet. Honey Ln. & Sylvan Ave.) | 631-473-0014 | www.restaurantorto.com

"This ain't your grandma's spaghetti and meatballs" say supporters of the "superb", "innovative" cuisine at this "delightful" Miller Place Italian from Eric Lomando (Kitchen A) set in an "upscale" yet "rustic" country cottage – think "creaky" floors, a fireplace and exposed-wood-beamed ceilings; prix fixe options help defray "special-occasion prices", while the "knowledgeable" staff and "warm" ambiance round out the recipe for "quiet, leisurely fine dining"; P.S. cash only.

Peter Luger Steak House 🍴 *Steak*

| 27 | 18 | 22 | $71 |

Great Neck | 255 Northern Blvd. (Tain Dr.) | 516-487-8800 | www.peterluger.com

Long Island's "steakhouse of steakhouses", this Great Neck outpost of the legendary Brooklyn original is an "institution" in its own right renowned for its "perfectly prepared" beef and "wish-you-had-room-for-it desserts", which make it the region's Most Popular restaurant; the "men's club" decor may be in "need of an update", waiters "can be a bit short" and you'll need to "refinance the house" to pay the tabs, but fans insist it's all "part of the charm"; P.S. major credit cards not accepted (only cash, checks, debit cards and their own house credit card).

Rothmann's Steakhouse *Steak*

| 25 | 23 | 22 | $69 |

East Norwich | 6319 Northern Blvd. (Oyster Bay Rd.) | 516-922-2500 | www.chasrothmanns.com

A "Long Island classic", this century-old East Norwich chophouse (once owned by Burt Bacharach) is a "meat lover's" mecca renowned for its "terrific" steaks, "endless" wine list and "excellent" service, all delivered in a "richly decorated, clublike" setting; the "packed" bar scene is also a draw for some, and though you might leave with your "wallet a lot lighter", it's "worth every penny" for a "special night out"; P.S. Sunday brunch is a "tremendous experience."

Ruth's Chris Steak House *Steak*

| 25 | 22 | 24 | $66 |

Garden City | 600 Old Country Rd. (Clinton Rd.) | 516-222-0220 | www.ruthschris.com

"Excellent" steaks on plates "sizzling with butter" are the hallmarks of this Garden City outpost of the über-"reliable" chophouse chain that also dishes out "terrific" sides and selections from a "great wine list"; the "posh, polished" setting and "gracious" service make it a "favorite" spot for a "business meeting" or "to impress a date", though an "expense account" definitely helps with the "pricey" tabs.

Salvatore's Ⓜ☞ *Pizza* | 26 | 12 | 20 | $20 |

Port Washington | 124 Shore Rd. (bet. Manhasset Ave. & Manorhaven Blvd.) | 516-883-8457

The Pie at Salvatore's ☞ *Pizza*

Bay Shore | 120 E. Main St. (2nd Ave.) | 631-206-1060
www.salvatorescoalfiredpizza.com

"Always busy and for good reason", these family-owned pizza parlors in Port Washington and Bay Shore lure loyalists with coal-fired brick-oven pies boasting "amazing thin crusts" and a "limited menu" of calzones, homemade pasta and "nice salads"; sure, the old-fashioned atmosphere is "basic" and it's cash only, but the "pleasant" staff makes it a "friendly neighborhood gathering place."

1770 House Restaurant & Inn *American* | 23 | 24 | 23 | $59 |

East Hampton | The 1770 House | 143 Main St. (Dayton Ln.) | 631-324-1770 | www.1770house.com

There's "charm to spare" at this "civilized" dining room set in an "elegant old" East Hampton "relic" (a 17th-century home converted to an inn circa 1770), which serves "innovative" Americana that "changes with the harvests"; though "it's a splurge", few doubt it's "worth it" for such a "memorable" means to "eat, drink and be merry" – and if money is an object, there's somewhat cheaper fare at the "rustic" tavern downstairs.

Starr Boggs *American/Seafood* | 26 | 23 | 23 | $63 |

Westhampton Beach | 6 Parlato Dr. (Library Ave.) | 631-288-3500 | www.starrboggsrestaurant.com

Chef-owner Starr Boggs' "sceney", always-"packed" Westhampton Beach longtimer boasts "top-notch", "inventive" seafood and other American fare served up by "pleasant" staffers in an "elegant" but "relaxed atmosphere"; the "comfortable" digs sport original Warhols and a "lovely patio", and while it's definitely a "splurge", regulars reveal the "prix fixe is the best deal going"; P.S. open seasonally.

Stone Creek Inn *French/Mediterranean* | 27 | 24 | 25 | $65 |

East Quogue | 405 Montauk Hwy. (Wedgewood Dr.) | 631-653-6770 | www.stonecreekinn.com

"Setting the standard for East End dining" according to fans, this "upscale" East Quogue French-Med housed in a "lovely old Victorian" "never fails to please" with a "sophisticated", "consistently terrific" menu and "top-notch service"; whether for a "special occasion" or just a "nice dinner out" it's deemed an "all-time favorite" that's "worth the trip"; P.S. the three-course prix fixe is a "steal!"

Stresa *Italian* | 25 | 22 | 25 | $56 |

Manhasset | 1524 Northern Blvd. (bet. Deepdale Dr. & Shelter Rock Rd.) | 516-365-6956 | www.stresarestaurant.com

"Consistently excellent" Italian fare draws a "country club set" to this "civilized" Manhasset stalwart, where "professional" servers treat guests "like royalty" and the "beautifully decorated" room affords choice "celeb-watching"; wallet-watchers note that the "great" prix fixe lunch is a "pleasure" and "much less expensive" than the "pricey" dinner options.

	FOOD	DECOR	SERVICE	COST

Thai Angel *Thai*

| 26 | 22 | 21 | $25 |

Islandia | 1812 Veterans Hwy. (bet. Blydenburgh Rd. & Sycamore Ln.) |
631-348-2555 | www.thaiangelli.com

"Once you enter, you are transported to Thailand" at this Islandia strip-
mall spot where rice-paper parasols, rich red walls and Southeast
Asian tchotchkes set the mood for "flawless" fare including "don't-
miss pad Thai" and a "wide variety" of curries; the "super-fast" staff is
"sweet" and "inexpensive" prices are made even better with "awesome" lunch specials – no wonder supporters declare it's "the best."

Topping Rose House Restaurant *American*

| - | - | - | VE |

Bridgehampton | Topping Rose House | 1 Bridgehampton-Sag Harbor Tpke.
(Lumber Ln.) | 631-537-0870 | www.toppingrosehouse.com

Celebrity chef Tom Colicchio (NYC's Craft, Colicchio & Sons) goes
country at this tony Bridgehampton beachhead in a renovated 1842
Greek Revival mansion, with an airy dining room plus outdoor seating
on its wraparound porch; the seasonal New American menu draws
from Long Island farms, fishing operations and vintners, as well as the
restaurant's own on-premise kitchen garden; P.S. an overnight stay at
the on-site inn extends the experience.

Vine Street Café *American*

| 25 | 21 | 23 | $64 |

Shelter Island | 41 S. Ferry Rd. (Cartwright Rd.) | 631-749-3210 |
www.vinestreetcafe.com

A "favorite summertime destination" on Shelter Island, this "class-
act" American set in a "quaint" whitewashed building displays a
"thoughtful dedication" in its "simple", "excellent" fare made with local seafood and produce as well as its "well-chosen" wine list; it's
"pricey" and can be "noisy" at times, but the staff is "friendly" and
insiders suggest reserving in advance for the "quiet" back porch;
P.S. closed Tuesday and Wednesday in the winter.

Vintage Prime Steak House *Steak*

| 26 | 22 | 24 | $63 |

St. James | 433 N. Country Rd. (Clinton Ave.) | 631-862-6440 |
www.vintageprimesteakhouse.com

Vintage Bar & Grill *Steak*

Jericho | 399 Jericho Tpke. (Merry Ln.) | 516-364-4641 |
www.vintagejericho.com

Some of the "best steaks in Suffolk County" can be found at this
"classy", "charming little roadside" chophouse in St. James (there's a
newer Nassau County offshoot in Jericho) where "old-school" means
the prime "quality meats" are dry-aged and cut on-site and there's a
"nice" wine list to match; service is "efficient", the "dark" digs boast a
vintage Western feel and if prices can "break the bank", carnivores
nevertheless call it "a wonderful experience."

Los Angeles

TOP FOOD RANKING

Restaurant	Cuisine
29 Asanebo	Japanese
28 Sushi Zo	Japanese
Hamasaku	Japanese
Mélisse	American/French
Matsuhisa	Japanese
Providence	American/Seafood
Angelini Osteria	Italian
Urasawa	Japanese
27 Gjelina Take Away	American
Michael's on Naples	Italian
Michael's Pizzeria	Pizza
Shiro	French/Japanese
Bazaar by José Andrés	Spanish
Sushi Masu	Japanese
Saam at The Bazaar	Eclectic
M.B. Post	American
Piccolo	Italian
Kiwami	Japanese
Hatfield's	American
Katsu-ya	Japanese

OTHER NOTEWORTHY PLACES

Bäco Mercat	Sandwiches
Bar Amá	Tex-Mex
Bestia	Italian
Bouchon	French
Brent's Deli	Deli
Connie & Ted's	Seafood
Father's Office	American
Gjelina	American
Hinoki & The Bird	Japanese
Lazy Ox	Eclectic
Lukshon	Asian
Mo-Chica	Peruvian
Osteria Mozza	Italian
Pikey	Pub Food
Rivera	Pan-Latin
Spago	Californian
Sugarfish	Japanese
Tar & Roses	American
Trois Mec	Eclectic/French
Waterloo & City	British

Angelini Osteria Ⓜ *Italian*
28 | 19 | 24 | $55

Beverly Boulevard | 7313 Beverly Blvd. (bet. Fuller Ave. & Poinsettia Pl.) | 323-297-0070 | www.angeliniosteria.com

"Rustic perfection" sums up the menu at this "convivial" Beverly Boulevard trattoria, where "king of authentic Italian" Gino Angelini makes "taste buds sing" with his "mouthwatering" meats, pastas and "not-to-be-missed" whole branzino; yes, the "noisy" quarters are so "cramped" you can "vicariously enjoy what your neighbors are eating", but unfazed fans will gladly pay "high prices" for "a foolproof meal."

Asanebo Ⓜ *Japanese*
29 | 18 | 25 | $91

Studio City | 11941 Ventura Blvd. (bet. Carpenter & Radford Aves.) | 818-760-3348 | www.asanebo-restaurant.com

"Amazing", "top-tier omakase" featuring the "freshest fish from around the world" plus other "innovative" dishes make this modest Studio City Japanese from "master" chef Tetsuya Nakao LA's No. 1 for Food; sure, it's in a "dumpy strip mall" and you might have to "take out a mortgage to indulge", but acolytes insist "you won't regret it."

Bäco Mercat Ⓢ *Sandwiches*
25 | 18 | 21 | $36

Downtown | 408 S. Main St. (Winston St.) | 213-687-8808 | www.bacomercat.com

"Addicting" bäco sandwiches ("the love child of a taco and a pita") and other "complex" Spanish-inspired dishes suit a "sophisti-cated" "hipster" following at this "delightfully creative" hit from Downtown "pioneer" Josef Centeno (Bar Amá); "solid" service, "reasonable prices" and an "extensive libations list" distract from the "funky" room's "energized" "din."

Bar Amá *Tex-Mex*
▽ 23 | 17 | 21 | $38

Downtown | 118 W. Fourth St. (bet. Main & Spring Sts.) | 213-687-8002 | www.bar-ama.com

The family recipes of celebrated chef-owner Josef Centeno (Bäco Mercat) yield "delicious takes on Tex-Mex" in a "casual", wood-planked space at this "creative" Downtown newcomer; it's also "ele-vating" the cantina genre with "innovative" tequila-based cocktails, though some find slightly "pricey" tabs less inspiring.

Bazaar by José Andrés *Spanish*
27 | 27 | 25 | $83

Beverly Hills | SLS at Beverly Hills | 465 S. La Cienega Blvd. (Clifton Way) | 310-246-5555 | www.thebazaar.com

"An experience like no other", this "culinary Disneyland" in the SLS Hotel from José Andrés presents "wild", "whimsical" Spanish-inspired small plates and "fantastic" drinks "that look like they were made in chemistry class" in an "extravagant", "noisy" Philippe Starck–designed setting out of *Alice in Wonderland* (complete with a pink patisserie for dessert); "trust the waiters to advise" and then "be prepared to spend hours" and "beaucoup bucks" here.

Bestia Ⓜ *Italian*
25 | 24 | 23 | $59

Downtown | 2121 E. Seventh Pl. (Santa Fe Ave.) | 213-514-5724 | www.bestiala.com

Husband-and-wife team Ori Menashe (ex Angelini Osteria) and Genevieve Gergis "are a force to be reckoned with" at this "new fave" in Downtown's Arts District, a "hot" destination for "on-point" "rustic Italian" fare from an open kitchen; "urban-trendy" digs and "cool" servers are more reasons it's "so crowded" and "deafening" – "not that you need to talk with food like this!"; P.S. "reservations are difficult."

Bouchon *French*
25 | 25 | 24 | $63

Beverly Hills | 235 N. Canon Dr. (bet. Dayton Way & Wilshire Blvd.) | 310-271-9910 | www.bouchonbistro.com

If you can't make it to the Yountville original, Thomas Keller's "civilized" Beverly Hills bistro showcases "terrific" French fare and "kitchen savvy" "worthy of its provenance"; add "professional" service, "magnificent decor" and "a celebrity or two", and it sizes up as "expensive but worth it."

Brent's Deli *Deli*
26 | 15 | 22 | $23

Northridge | 19565 Parthenia St. (bet. Corbin & Shirley Aves.) | 818-886-5679
Westlake Village | 2799 Townsgate Rd. (Westlake Blvd.) | 805-557-1882
www.brentsdeli.com

"Come hungry, leave stuffed" after noshing on "huge sandwiches" and other "fabulous", "real-deal" deli fare that's "worthy of NYC status" at this "bustling" Northridge vet and its "more modern" Westlake Village offshoot; conditions are "often crowded", but given the "efficient" service and "good value", "what's not to love?"

Connie & Ted's *Seafood*
- | - | - | M

West Hollywood | 8171 Santa Monica Blvd. (Havenhurst Dr.) | 323-848-2722 | www.connieandteds.com

Popular from day one, this casual seafooder in West Hollywood from Michael Cimarusti (Providence) features a medium-priced menu served in a room that looks lifted from the Maine shoreline; it sports bright-orange seats, polished wood tables and an open kitchen and raw bar with everything on display.

Father's Office ❶ *American*
23 | 16 | 15 | $25

Culver City | Helms Bldg. | 3229 Helms Ave. (bet. Venice & Washington Blvds.) | 310-736-2224
Santa Monica | 1018 Montana Ave. (bet. 10th & 11th Sts.) | 310-736-2224
www.fathersoffice.com

"It's all about the burger" at this "dark, crowded" American gastropub duo in Santa Monica and Culver City famed for its "decadent" blue-cheese patties and "world-class selection of beers on tap"; no menu substitutions (or ketchup) are allowed, and "you're on your own to find a table" so "get there early" or prepare to wait.

Gjelina ❶ *American*
26 | 21 | 18 | $46

Venice | 1429 Abbot Kinney Blvd. (bet. California & Milwood Aves.) | 310-450-1429 | www.gjelina.com

"A must" on the "hipster" "farm-to-table" circuit, this "fabulous" Abbot Kinney American features "delicious, unique" pizzas and other "shareable" "ultrafresh" plates in a "loud", "sceney" setting; while service can be "spotty" and the "waits" are a "pain", most "can't wait to go back"; P.S. "try to get a seat on the patio."

Gjelina Take Away *American*

27 | 15 | 19 | $25

Venice | 1429 Abbot Kinney Blvd. (bet. California & Milwood Aves.) | 310-450-1429 | www.gjelina.com

"You'll never forget the pork belly sandwich" say those who swear by this all-day Venice take-out spin-off of Gjelina offering the same "tremendous" seasonal American food (including "excellent pizzas") without the need for "month-in-advance" reservations; it's "a little expensive for lunch every day" and service can be "slow", but reviewers recommend it "if you don't mind sitting on milk crates."

Hamasaku Ⓩ *Japanese*

28 | 18 | 25 | $66

West LA | 11043 Santa Monica Blvd. (bet. Bentley & Camden Aves.) | 310-479-7636 | www.hamasakula.com

The "incredible", "innovative" rolls are named for celebs at this "high-class" West LA Japanese from Michael Ovitz also featuring "clever" small plates; an "impeccable" staff treats everyone – from plebs to Hollywood luminaries – "like a VIP" in the serene space, but know "your wallet will take a hit."

Hatfield's *American*

27 | 25 | 26 | $75

Melrose | 6703 Melrose Ave. (Citrus Ave.) | 323-935-2977 | www.hatfieldsrestaurant.com

"Simply sublime", this "elegant", expensive Melrose New American from husband-and-wife team Quinn and Karen Hatfield serves "carefully crafted", "locally sourced" fare (including a "wonderful" tasting menu) and desserts that strike a "high note of creativity"; it's "an oasis of calm" with the staff "moving seamlessly about" an "understated" modern dining room – in sum, "an all-around wonderful experience."

Hinoki & The Bird Ⓩ Ⓜ *Japanese*

23 | 26 | 23 | $78

Century City | The Century | 10 Century Dr. (Ave. of the Stars) | 310-552-1200 | www.hinokiandthebird.com

"Refined, but not precious" sums up the "inventive" Japanese cuisine at this "pricey" Century City entry from David Myers dispensing small and large plates in a "beautiful" rustic room scented with hinoki wood (it "smells like a wonderful sauna"); with interesting seasonal cocktails, the "bar area is a scene" too.

Katsu-ya *Japanese*

27 | 15 | 20 | $44

Encino | 16542 Ventura Blvd. (Hayvenhurst Ave.) | 818-788-2396
Northridge | 9709 Reseda Blvd. (Superior St.) | 818-678-1700
Studio City | 11680 Ventura Blvd. (Colfax Ave.) | 818-985-6976
www.katsu-yagroup.com

A "trailblazer for modern sushi", chef-owner Katsuya Uechi's Studio City "original" and its Encino and Northridge offshoots are famed for "exquisite" "rock-star" sushi and "innovative chalkboard specials"; sure, "you'll have to wait", service can be "rushed" and the settings could "use a face-lift", but even so, most find it's one of the "best for the price" and the food surpasses any "hassle."

Kiwami *Japanese*

27 | 20 | 24 | $53

Studio City | 11920 Ventura Blvd. (Carpenter Ave.) | 818-763-3910 | www.katsu-yagroup.com

An "upscale version" of sibling Katsu-ya, this Studio City "jewel" impresses guests with "sublime" sushi, sashimi and "beautifully prepared" small plates; the vibe is "cool" without being "trendy", and though bills can be "painfully high" – especially for the hard-to-reserve private omakase with Katsuya himself – it's regarded as one of "the best" in town; P.S. check out the "great deals" at happy hour.

Lazy Ox Canteen ● Eclectic
24 | 16 | 20 | $41

Little Tokyo | 241 S. San Pedro St. (bet. 2nd & 3rd Sts.) | 213-626-5299 | www.lazyoxcanteen.com
Dubbed a "foodie paradise", this "exhilarating" little spot in Little Tokyo "wows" with an ever-"evolving" Eclectic menu featuring "amazing" "out-of-the-box" small plates based on "unique" seasonal ingredients and "all things pig", plus a "great burger"; prices are "moderate", servers are "informed" and the vibe is "cool", even if the "ear-splitting" music could "scare off anyone over 28."

Lukshon �Ⓢ Asian
24 | 23 | 22 | $48

Culver City | Helms Bldg. | 3239 Helms Ave. (bet. Venice & Washington Blvds.) | 310-202-6808 | www.lukshon.com
Sang Yoon (Father's Office) does Southeast Asian at his "gem" in Culver City's Helms Building that turns out a "clever menu" of "spicy" small plates in a "sleek" setting of teak and stainless metal; a "pleasant patio", "attentive service" and "unusual" drinks help take the edge off tabs that "can add up quickly."

Matsuhisa Japanese
28 | 18 | 24 | $89

Beverly Hills | 129 N. La Cienega Blvd. (bet. Clifton Way & Wilshire Blvd.) | 310-659-9639 | www.nobumatsuhisa.com
Devotees make the "pilgrimage" to Nobu Matsuhisa's "original temple of seafood", this "still-amazing" 27-year-old Beverly Hills Japanese offering "sushi perfection" and "incredible" Peruvian-influenced fare to a "beautiful" crowd; service earns high marks while the digs are "simple and without pretense", and despite what some describe as "eyeball-popping" prices, most agree it's "worth a visit."

M.B. Post American
27 | 22 | 24 | $47

Manhattan Beach | 1142 Manhattan Ave. (bet. Center Pl. & 12th St.) | 310-545-5405 | www.eatmbpost.com
"Nearly every dish is a hit" at this "not-so-hidden gem" in Manhattan Beach from chef David LeFevre (ex Water Grill) turning out "amazing", "innovative" "farm-to-table" small plates – "the bacon-cheddar biscuits are a must" – and "fun cocktails" in a "cool" setting crafted from reclaimed wood; it's not cheap and many find it "incredibly loud", "but the food makes up for it"; P.S. "brunch is fantastic" too.

Mélisse �SⓂ American/French
28 | 26 | 27 | $121

Santa Monica | 1104 Wilshire Blvd. (11th St.) | 310-395-0881 | www.melisse.com
"Something magical happens" at Josiah Citrin's Santa Monica destination offering "exquisite" tasting menus of "fresh, market-driven" French-American cuisine (plus a "top-notch" vegetarian version) and "heavenly" wine pairings; "everything is totally polished", from the "impeccable" service (ranked No. 1 in Los Angeles) to the "elegant" setting, and while some quip that you'll need to "sell that screenplay to afford it", most agree you'll be "richly rewarded" for the expense.

FOOD | DECOR | SERVICE | COST

Michael's on Naples Ristorante *Italian*   27 | 24 | 26 | $58

Long Beach | 5620 E. Second St. (bet. Ravenna & Tivoli Drs.) |
562-439-7080 | www.michaelsonnaples.com

Helmed by "ever-present" owner Michael Dene, this upscale Long
Beach "gem" "deserves the accolades" for its "excellent", "genuine"
Italian cuisine and "top-notch" wine list, served by a "charming", "professional"
staff; a "sophisticated" setting with "rooftop dining" and
live music also help make it an "amazing destination restaurant";
P.S. the tasting menus are "well worth the price."

Michael's Pizzeria *Pizza*   27 | 21 | 25 | $25

Long Beach | 210 E. Third St. (bet. Long Beach Blvd. & Pine Ave.) |
562-491-2100
Long Beach | 5616 E. Second St. (Ravenna Dr.) | 562-987-4000
www.michaelspizzeria.com

An offshoot of the venerable Michael's on Naples, this "fabulous" Long
Beach pizzeria duo loads up its "heavenly", "authentic" Neapolitan
pies with "fresh", homemade mozz, plus more "creative" items like
clams, egg and baby artichokes; given "excellent service" and "modest
prices", the "simple", "noisy" settings are easily excused.

Mo-Chica ●☒ *Peruvian*   23 | 16 | 18 | $42

Downtown | 514 W. Seventh St. (bet. Grand Ave. & Olive St.) |
213-622-3744 | www.mo-chica.com

Fans want to go "mo-often" to this midpriced Downtowner on Seventh
Street's Restaurant Row, where Ricardo Zarate (Picca, Paiche) creates
his "modern takes on Peruvian food" with "lots of unique small plates
to mix up"; the servers "know the menu inside and out", and "well-
done" cocktails help fuel a "happening" vibe ("noisy" to some).

Osteria Mozza *Italian*   27 | 23 | 23 | $67

Hollywood | 6602 Melrose Ave. (Highland Ave.) | 323-297-0100 |
www.osteriamozza.com

"Melt-in-your-mouth" pastas and a "to-die-for" mozzarella bar "speak
volumes" about the "extraordinary" eating at this "high-end" Hollywood
Italian from powerhouse pair Nancy Silverton and Mario Batali;
"knowledgeable" servers tend to a "celebrity clientele" that packs the
"elegant" space, and one bite of burrata ("wow!") will render the
"deafening" noise and "huge prices" "worth it."

Piccolo *Italian*   27 | 23 | 25 | $71

Venice | 5 Dudley Ave. (Speedway) | 310-314-3222 | www.piccolovenice.com
"Journey to Italy" via this "romantic" "jewel" just off Venice beach,
where "sublime" Venetian cuisine, "amazing" wines and "smart" service
make for a "thoroughly delightful" time; yes, it's "pricey", but admirers
insist it's also "one of LA's best."

The Pikey ● *Pub Food*   ▽ 18 | 22 | 18 | $37

Hollywood | 7617 W. Sunset Blvd. (Stanley Ave.) | 323-850-5400 |
www.thepikeyla.com

Hearty gastropub fare plus inventive cocktails crafted from an extensive
list of spirits (absinthe, anyone?) make this "trendy", well-priced
Hollywood spot a happy-hour crowd-pleaser; tiled floors, dark
wooden booths and "sharp" servers in suspenders add to the
authentic English feel.

	FOOD	DECOR	SERVICE	COST

Providence *American/Seafood* | 28 | 26 | 27 | $124 |

Hollywood | 5955 Melrose Ave. (Cole Ave.) | 323-460-4170 |
www.providencela.com

"Seafood is the star" at this "sophisticated", "upscale" New American in Hollywood helmed by "brilliant" chef Michael Cimarusti who turns out "delectable", "wildly creative" prix fixe feasts in a "minimalist setting" that's an "oasis of tranquility"; add in "warm", "intelligent" service that "treats you like royalty" and "you won't want to leave after your meal"; P.S. "save room for the cheese cart."

Rivera *Pan-Latin* | 26 | 24 | 23 | $62 |

Downtown | Met Lofts | 1050 S. Flower St. (11th St.) | 213-749-1460 |
www.riverarestaurant.com

"A knockout every time", this Downtown Pan-Latin from "genius" chef John Sedlar presents "playful", "high-concept, beautifully executed" dishes that "look like art and taste like heaven" alongside "brilliant" cocktails in a "chic" dining room; service "always pleases" too, and although some complain it "needs to tone down the noise", ultimately it's a "favorite" that's "worth the high prices."

Saam at The Bazaar by José Andrés 🅰🅼 *Eclectic* | 27 | 26 | 26 | $132 |

Beverly Hills | SLS at Beverly Hills | 465 S. La Cienega Blvd. (Clifton Way) | 310-246-5545 | www.thebazaar.com

Chef José Andrés will "delight all your senses" with his "exquisite" Eclectic tasting menu – "22-plus courses of molecular gastronomy at its best" – served in an "oasis of calm" inside the Bazaar in Beverly Hills; while it's "pricey", most agree it's an "incredible experience" "worth every penny"; P.S. for a "once-in-a-lifetime" event, big spenders advise "get the wine pairing and stay the night at the SLS Hotel."

Shiro 🅼 *French/Japanese* | 27 | 20 | 27 | $54 |

South Pasadena | 1505 Mission St. (bet. Fair Oaks & Mound Aves.) | 626-799-4774 | www.restaurantshiro.com

The "catfish is epic" at this "intimate" French-Japanese in South Pasadena where the "expertly prepared" deep-fried whole fish is so "*umami*-yummy" that "it's hard to order anything else"; "amazing" service is another plus, and while the setting strikes some as "stark" and others find the tabs "a bit high", fans insist it's "worth the drive"; P.S. open Wednesdays–Sundays.

Spago *Californian* | 27 | 25 | 26 | $80 |

Beverly Hills | 176 N. Canon Dr. (Wilshire Blvd.) | 310-385-0880 |
www.wolfgangpuck.com

"Beautifully redone", Wolfgang Puck's Beverly Hills "classic" still attracts a "who's who" crowd thanks to its "consistently excellent", "creative" Californian cuisine, "intense wine list", "on-point" service and "wonderful new environs" designed by Barbara Lazaroff; a few grouse about "smaller plates" and "higher prices", but to most it remains the "standard by which all other top-notch restaurants are judged."

Sugarfish by Sushi Nozawa *Japanese* | 26 | 20 | 22 | $42 |

Downtown | 600 W. Seventh St. (Grand Ave.) | 213-627-3000
Beverly Hills | 212 N. Canon Dr. (bet. Clifton & Dayton Ways) | 310-276-6900

(continued)

Sugarfish by Sushi Nozawa

Brentwood | 11640 W. San Vicente Blvd. (bet. Darlington & Mayfield Aves.) | 310-820-4477

Marina del Rey | The Waterside | 4722¼ Admiralty Way (Mindanao Way) | 310-306-6300

Santa Monica | 1345 Second St. (Santa Monica Blvd.) | 310-393-3338

Calabasas | The Commons at Calabasas Shopping Ctr. | 4799 Commons Way (bet. Civic Center Way & Commons Way) | 818-223-9966

Studio City | 11288 Ventura Blvd. (Vineland Ave.) | 818-762-2322
www.sugarfishsushi.com

Ranked as LA's Most Popular restaurant, chef Kazunori Nozawa's "fantastic" Japanese mini-chain pleases "sushi snobs" who "line up" to enjoy its "traditional", "melt-in-your-mouth" fish on "amazing" warm rice, offered à la carte or in set menus ("order one of the 'trust me' options and you can't go wrong"); an "inviting", "modern" ambiance and "fast, efficient" service help offset the "no-reservations" policy, and most find prices "affordable" given the quality.

Sushi Masu Ⓜ *Japanese*

27 | 15 | 25 | $48

West LA | 1911 Westwood Blvd. (bet. La Grange & Missouri Aves.) | 310-446-4368

"Lots of loyal regulars" count on this West LA Japanese, a "quiet, neighborhood" "gem" for "fresh, delish", "expertly prepared" sushi at an "ideal cost/quality ratio"; though the simple space is "not fancy", chef Hiroshi Masuko is an "engaging host" who "makes you feel at home"; P.S. "sit at the bar" if you can.

Sushi Zo Ⓩ *Japanese*

28 | 14 | 20 | $117

West LA | 9824 National Blvd. (Castle Heights Ave.) | 310-842-3977

The "incredible parade" of "exceptional" sushi makes a visit to this omakase-only West LA Japanese feel "like a trip to Tokyo", complete with almost "over-attentive" service; aficionados "who don't care too much about ambiance" are rewarded with "bits of bliss" that "make it hard to know when to stop" – no wonder it's "zo expensive."

Tar & Roses *American*

24 | 19 | 22 | $53

Santa Monica | 602 Santa Monica Blvd. (6th St.) | 310-587-0700 | www.tarandroses.com

"A culinary treat" "from start to finish", this "addictive" Santa Monica "up-and-comer" from chef-owner Andrew Kirschner (Joe's, Wilshire) turns out "memorable" New American plates both small and large via a wood-burning oven; tables can be "hard to come by" since the "elevated gastropub" setting is "always busy" (and "noisy"), so "book well in advance."

Trois Mec Ⓩ *Eclectic/French*

- | - | - | E

Hollywood | 718 N. Highland Ave. (Melrose Ave.) | no phone | www.troismec.com

A trio of celebrity chefs – Ludo Lefebvre, Jon Shook and Vinny Dotolo – oversees this hot ticket in a tiny 26-seat space in a mini-mall behind a gas station at the corner of Melrose and Highland; expect pricey French-Eclectic creations cooked by Lefebvre in the open kitchen – that is, if you can score a much-coveted reservation.

	FOOD	DECOR	SERVICE	COST

Urasawa 🅂🅼 *Japanese*

28 | 24 | 27 | $514

Beverly Hills | 218 N. Rodeo Dr. (Wilshire Blvd.) | 310-247-8939

Truly "memorable", this intimate Beverly Hills Japanese showcases an "amazing" omakase-only parade of small plates and sushi crafted by "perfectionist" chef Hiro Urasawa; "nothing is spared" when it comes to service either, so if you can "afford the luxury", it's "an experience worth having at least once in your lifetime."

Waterloo & City ◐ *British*

23 | 19 | 21 | $43

Culver City | 12517 W. Washington Blvd. (Mildred Ave.) | 310-391-4222 | www.waterlooandcity.com

"LA meets London gastropub" at this "hip" Culver City "favorite" from "innovative chef" Brendan Collins spotlighting a "sophisticated" Modern British menu "heavy on meat" with "lots of surprises", elevated by "awesome" beers and a "nicely curated" cocktail list; prices are "reasonable", the servers are "savvy" and the space has a pleasantly "ramshackle feel", although it's frequently "jam-packed."

Miami

TOP FOOD RANKING

	Restaurant	Cuisine
29	Naoe	Japanese
28	Palme d'Or	French
	Zuma	Japanese
	Palm	Steak
27	Il Gabbiano	Italian
	OLA	Pan-Latin
	Pascal's on Ponce	French
	Michy's	American/French
	Prime One Twelve	Seafood/Steak
	Nobu Miami Beach	Japanese
	Azul	European
	Matsuri	Japanese
	Michael's Genuine	American
	Yakko-San	Japanese
	Joe's Stone Crab	Seafood
	Red	Steak
26	Oishi	Japanese/Thai
	Frankie's	Pizza
	La Dorada*	Seafood/Spanish
	Francesco	Peruvian

OTHER NOTEWORTHY PLACES

AltaMare	Mediterranean/Seafood
Bazaar/José Andrés	Eclectic/Spanish
BLT	Steak
Bourbon	Steak
Bulla	Spanish
DB Bistro Moderne	French
Eating House	American
Escopazzo	Italian
Estiatorio Milos	Greek
1500°	American/Steak
Florida Cookery	American
Forge	American
Hakkasan	Chinese
J&G Grill	American
Katsuya by Starck	Japanese
Makoto	Japanese
Pubbelly	Asian
Scarpetta	Italian
Sugarcane	Eclectic
Yardbird	Southern

* Indicates a tie with restaurant above

AltaMare *Mediterranean/Seafood*   24 | 20 | 23 | $54

South Beach | 1233 Lincoln Rd. (bet. Alton Ct. & Alton Rd.) | Miami Beach | 305-532-3061 | www.altamarerestaurant.com

Claudio the owner is always on hand, "ensuring all are satisfied" with the "beautifully executed" Med-accented seafood, meats and "home-made" pasta emanating from the open kitchen of this SoBe spot; if it's gotten more "pricey", it still pleases "locals" who "love" the "stylish" space on a "mellow stretch" of Lincoln Road that's "convenient for movies", theater and shopping.

Azul 🖾 *European*   27 | 27 | 26 | $76

Brickell Area | Mandarin Oriental Hotel | 500 Brickell Key Dr. (SE 8th St.) | 305-913-8358 | www.mandarinoriental.com

This "perennial favorite" in Brickell Key's Mandarin Oriental pleases its well-heeled clientele with a Modern European menu that incorporates American and Asian accents; cuisine aside, its "attentive but unobtrusive" service, "serious" wine list and "sleek" setting with "spectacular bay views" help make it a "special-occasion" "delight" – "even if prices are close to those for nearby condos."

Bazaar by José Andrés *Eclectic/Spanish*   - | - | - | E

South Beach | SLS Hotel South Beach | 1701 Collins Ave. (17th St.) | Miami Beach | 305-455-2999 | www.thebazaar.com

DC-based culinary magician José Andrés makes his mark in South Beach at the SLS Hotel with this Spanish-Eclectic set in a spacious, sexy deco-esque room dominated by a huge seashell-encrusted chandelier, offering traditional tapas as well as more forward-thinking small plates with Caribbean and Latin twists; either way, prices are high and reservations can be as difficult to obtain as snowshoes on Ocean Drive.

BLT Steak *Steak*   25 | 23 | 23 | $71

South Beach | The Betsy Hotel | 1440 Ocean Dr. (bet. 14th & 15th Sts.) | Miami Beach | 305-673-0044 | www.bltsteak.com

"A bit more hip" than old-school meat palaces, this Betsy Hotel outpost of a "quality-brand" steakhouse chain excels with its "perfectly charred" chops, "inventive" sides and "terrific" wine list – that's icing on the cake for fans who admit "they had me at the popovers"; tabs are "steep" and some "don't love the lobbyish atmosphere", but most deem it a "refined" escape from the SoBe "riffraff."

Bourbon Steak *Steak*   25 | 27 | 25 | $83

Aventura | Turnberry Isle Hotel & Resort | 19999 W. Country Club Dr. (Aventura Blvd.) | 786-279-6600 | www.michaelmina.net

From its "gorgeous" setup designed by Tony Chi to its "decadent" chops, "delish" burgers and "addictive" fries, Michael Mina's steakhouse in Aventura's Turnberry Isle Hotel strikes fans as "ahead of the herd"; a "passionate" staff (a "rare find in Miami") mixes "well-balanced drinks" and helps diners navigate an "extensive" wine list that's loaded with "treasures" – and they'll gladly accept your "gold card" at meal's end.

Bulla *Spanish*   - | - | - | E

Coral Gables | 2500 Ponce de Leon Blvd. (Andalusia Ave.) | 305-441-0107 | www.bullamiami.com

This upscale tapas-y-cerveza hot spot in Coral Gables pairs sophisticated Spanish and Catalan small plates with the casual ambiance of a good-timey watering hole; a large rectangular bar and open kitchen dominate the wood-and-tile-wrapped dining area, plus there's a Moorish-looking terrace lounge.

DB Bistro Moderne *French* | 26 | 25 | 25 | $76 |

Downtown | JW Marriott Marquis Miami | 255 Biscayne Boulevard Way (bet. SE 2nd & 3rd Aves.) | 305-421-8800 | www.danielnyc.com
Proof positive that NYC's Daniel Boulud is a "genuine food god" is the "perfectly prepared" French fare at this "chic" spot in Downtown Miami's JW Marriott Marquis; service is "attentive" and the "airy" Yabu Pushelberg–designed trifecta of dining room, lounge and out-door terrace is "beautiful", so if you "can handle the tab", "what's not to like?"; P.S. "burger fanatics" shouldn't miss the $34 sirloin, foie gras and truffle burger.

Eating House Miami Ⓜ *American* | - | - | - | M |

Coral Gables | 804 Ponce De Leon Blvd. (8th St.) | 305-448-6524 | www.eatinghousemiami.com
Miami-raised chef and rising star Giorgio Rapicavoli dusts his ambi-tious New American creations with flavors from all over the globe at his midpriced Coral Gables gathering spot; the low-key interior fea-tures walls decked with graffiti art, while the chef's own DJ mixes oc-casionally provide the soundtrack.

Escopazzo ◑Ⓜ *Italian* | 25 | 19 | 24 | $62 |

South Beach | 1311 Washington Ave. (bet. 13th & 14th Sts.) | Miami Beach | 305-674-9450 | www.escopazzo.com
SoBe "insiders", "locavores" and "gourmets" know that this "nonde-script storefront" on "busy" Washington Avenue houses a "hidden jewel", where chef-owner Giancarla Bodoni "does wonders" with the "fresh, organic ingredients" that go into "one-of-a-kind" Italian creations; her "love and creativity justify high prices", so consider the "über-friendly" service, "quiet", "low-key" vibe and large wine selection pure gravy.

Estiatorio Milos *Greek* | - | - | - | VE |

South Beach | 730 First St. (Washington Ave.) | Miami Beach | 305-604-6800 | www.milos.ca
Fish flown in almost daily from the Mediterranean and displayed like jewels on a bed of ice compete with spare-no-expense decor featuring white marble floors, raw exposed wood and ancient-looking pot-tery at this über-posh Greek mini-chain outpost in SoBe; the sea-food is as breathtakingly expensive as it is impeccably fresh, with many species starting at $50 a pound and going up, and there's an epic wine list to match.

1500° *American/Steak* | 24 | 22 | 20 | $71 |

Miami Beach | Eden Roc Renaissance | 4525 Collins Ave. (W. 41st St.) | 305-674-5594 | www.1500degreesmiami.com
Set in Miami Beach's storied Eden Roc Hotel, this "classy" venue is named for the temperature at which chef Paula DaSilva (*Hell's Kitchen* finalist and 3030 Ocean alum) cooks "juicy", "melt-in-your-mouth" steaks, a "specialty" on the "creative" New American menu; it's expen-sive and service is "erratic", but diners appreciate being able to "speak without shouting" in the "pretty" dining room or on the "breezy" patio.

	FOOD	DECOR	SERVICE	COST

Florida Cookery *American*
| - | - | - | M |

South Beach | The James Royal Palm | 1545 Collins Ave. (bet. 15th & 16th Sts.) | Miami Beach | 305-604-5700 | www.florida-cookery.com
As the name indicates, Kris Wessel taps into traditional Florida cooking at this airy, streamlined American hidden inside the South Beach James Royal Palm Hotel; just as the midpriced menu puts newfangled spins on old-fashioned regional recipes – think alligator empanadas, seared frogs' legs and grilled wild boar chops – the sleek wood walls and plush linen banquettes are as contemporary as it gets.

Forge Restaurant & Wine Bar *American*
| 24 | 26 | 24 | $78 |

Miami Beach | 432 41st St. (bet. Royal Palm & Sheridan Aves.) | 305-538-8533 | www.theforge.com
This Miami Beach "landmark" was "reinvented" several years ago with an "over-the-top", "*Alice in Wonderland*"-esque "makeover" of its many "special rooms" and an updated New American menu bearing the "magic touch" of chef Dewey LoSasso; yet it has "stayed true to its roots" as a playground for "celebrities" and other "monied" types and still boasts a "museumlike wine cellar", so most find it "better than ever."

Francesco 🗷 *Peruvian*
| 26 | 17 | 23 | $55 |

Coral Gables | 325 Alcazar Ave. (bet. Salzedo St. & SW 42nd Ave.) | 305-446-1600 | www.francescorestaurantmiami.com
According to fans, the "best ceviche in Miami" is to be found at this "first-rate" Peruvian in Coral Gables dishing up "expensive" but "consistently amazing" seafood and other dishes, some "authentic", others with Italian touches; the small space gets "tightly packed" and the "decor could use a refresh", but the "owner is always on-site and it shows" in the overall "welcoming" vibe.

Frankie's Pizza 🗷⇗ *Pizza*
| 26 | 7 | 20 | $14 |

Westchester | 9118 Bird Rd. (92nd Ave.) | 305-221-0221 | www.frankiespizzaonline.com
Since the 1950s, the Pasquarella family has been slinging square (read: "not your standard") pies at this cheap, cash-only pizza joint in Westchester, and folks who've "been going since they were little runts" insist "that should tell you" it's "worth" it; there's a "few picnic tables" in back, but it's "primarily a take-out" spot – indeed, they ship 'half-baked' pies anywhere in the country.

Hakkasan *Chinese*
| 26 | 27 | 24 | $78 |

Miami Beach | Fontainebleau Miami Beach | 4441 Collins Ave. (W. 44th St.) | 786-276-1388 | www.fontainebleau.com
"Wow, so *this* is Chinese food" declare converts whose "eyes are opened" by the "incredible" modern Cantonese fare at the Miami Beach outpost of the London original hidden in the "sprawling" Fontainebleau; assets include "superior" dim sum, "knowledgeable" service and "chic" environs that are surprisingly "intimate" given the "big" space – just expect to pay "crazy money" to enjoy it all.

Il Gabbiano ●🗷 *Italian*
| 27 | 26 | 27 | $81 |

Downtown | One Miami Tower | 335 S. Biscayne Blvd. (SE 3rd St.) | 305-373-0063 | www.ilgabbianomia.com
From the antipasti to the after-dinner limoncello (both gratis), this Downtown destination exhibits "true Italian class"; expect an "in-

spired menu", "extensive" wine list, "stellar" service and "elegant" digs that extend to a "beautiful" outdoor terrace where diners can "gaze at Biscayne Bay or into their companion's eyes" – welcome distractions from tabs that reflect the "top-notch" quality.

J&G Grill *American*   — | — | — | VE

Bal Harbour | St. Regis Bal Harbour Resort | 9703 Collins Ave. (96th St.) | 305-993-3333 | www.jggrillmiami.com

Jean-Georges Vongerichten lends a subtle Asian touch to this über-elegant and über-pricey beachfront New American at the stunning St. Regis Bal Harbour, where well-heeled patrons can choose a protein, pair it with a sauce and have it grilled to order; the glass-enclosed dining room mixes city sophistication (cool gray hanging lanterns and linen-wrapped booths) with tropical beauty (palm trees outside every window), while a fairly deep wine list adds extra appeal.

Joe's Stone Crab *Seafood*   27 | 20 | 23 | $68

South Beach | 11 Washington Ave. (bet. 1st St. & S. Pointe Dr.) | Miami Beach | 305-673-0365 | www.joesstonecrab.com

"Rob a bank, sell the house, [do] whatever it takes" to afford the "succulent" stone crabs that again make this "legendary" SoBe eatery Miami's Most Popular – though "the irony is that everything else on the menu is reasonably priced", and standouts like fried chicken and Key lime pie are equally "to die for"; "looong waits" and "rushed" service from "track-star" waiters racing through the "gigantic" space are the norm, but you can "avoid the madness" by heading to the take-out cafe; P.S. it has limited summer hours, so it's best to call ahead.

Katsuya by Starck ● *Japanese*   — | — | — | E

South Beach | SLS Hotel South Beach | 1701 Collins Ave. (17th St.) | Miami Beach | 305-455-2995 | www.sbe.com

The minimalist, black-and-white Philippe Starck decor at this pricey Japanese venue in the swanky SLS South Beach deftly showcases the uniquely personal fare of master sushi chef Katsuya Uechi, who mixes traditional fresh-fish preparations with more eclectic takes; a larger-than-life pair of geisha's eyes gazes seductively from behind the sushi bar, as at the chain's other locations in LA and Houston, while her lips can be found upstairs at the Dragon Room Lounge.

La Dorada ● *Seafood/Spanish*   26 | 21 | 26 | $77

Coral Gables | 177 Giralda Ave. (Ponce de Leon Blvd.) | 305-446-2002 | www.ladoradamiami.com

This Coral Gables Spaniard offers "elegant, wonderfully simple preparations" of seafood that tastes as fresh as if it were "flown in daily from the Mediterranean" – via "first-class airfare", judging by the cost; however, wallet-watchers say the "awesome" prix fixe lunch is a "great value", while "friendly service", a "good wine selection" and live music on weekends are further pluses.

Makoto *Japanese*   ▽ 25 | 26 | 25 | $60

Bal Harbour | Bal Harbour Shops | 9700 Collins Ave. (96th St.) | 305-864-8600 | www.makoto-restaurant.com

Pennsylvania powerhouse Stephen Starr pleases Miamians with his "top-class" Japanese sushi and robata effort in chichi Bal Harbour, helmed by chef Makoto Okuwa, a Morimoto protégé; its "sleek", "sedate" setting with a sexy outdoor patio is "so cool you'll forget you're in a mall", but be aware: prices are as posh as the eats.

Matsuri ⓜ _Japanese_   27 | 20 | 21 | $36

South Miami | 5759 Bird Rd. (bet. Red Rd. & SW 58th Ave.) | 305-663-1615

"Luscious" fish so "fresh" it "tastes like it swam into the restaurant" is the big lure at this longtime South Miami strip-mall mecca for "true sushi aficionados", but it also dishes up "good cooked items" (brush up on your kanji and "ask for the Japanese-language menu" for more "unique" offerings); the "austere" setting isn't always warmed by service that can swing from "attentive" to "abrupt" – but "who cares with prices like this?"

Michael's Genuine Food & Drink _American_   27 | 20 | 23 | $56

Design District | Atlas Plaza | 130 NE 40th St. (bet. 1st & 2nd Aves.) | 305-573-5550 | www.michaelsgenuine.com

The name of this "trendy" Design District "hot spot" is "a statement of intent that they deliver on" via chef-owner Michael Schwartz's "ambitious" yet "down-to-earth" small, medium and large plates of locally sourced New American "comfort" food, backed by "inspired" treats from "genius" pastry chef Hedy Goldsmith and a "well-considered" wine list; staffers can seem "a touch snooty" at times but their "efficiency" compensates, plus there's a "lovely" outdoor courtyard and "decent" prices.

Michy's ⓜ _American/French_   27 | 19 | 25 | $63

Upper East Side | 6927 Biscayne Blvd. (69th St.) | 305-759-2001 | www.michysmiami.com

Chef Michelle Bernstein is "at the top of her game" at this "pricey" Upper East Side "showcase" for "novel takes" on French–New American comfort food; though opinion diverges on the decor – "funky" vs. "Aunt Mildred's living room" – most applaud the staff's "attention to detail."

Naoe ⓜ _Japanese_   29 | 23 | 28 | VE

Brickell Area | Courvoisier Centre | 661 Brickell Key Dr. (Brickell Ave.) | 305-947-6263 | www.naoemiami.com

"I can't believe this exists in Miami" since it would be "outstanding even in Japan" gush fans of this culinary star in Brickell Key, rated the city's tops for Food and Service; Kevin Cory's "creative" omakase meals include a bento box "revelation" and "impossibly good" sushi, all presented with "warm", "personal" care by "charming" manager Wendy Maharlika and a helper, and though it's not cheap (price varies according to the day's offerings and how many courses you opt for), it's so "worth it" – just book "well in advance"; P.S. two seatings, Tuesday–Sunday.

Nobu Miami Beach _Japanese_   27 | 22 | 22 | $83

South Beach | Shore Club | 1901 Collins Ave. (19th St.) | Miami Beach | 305-695-3232 | www.noburestaurants.com

"Beautiful fish and beautiful people" dazzle at this "über-hip" "pregame warm-up for SoBe's clubs", part of Nobu Matsuhisa's far-flung fusion empire renowned for its "incredible" Japanese-Peruvian cuisine crowned by "sushi to die for" (indeed, the bill alone "may kill you"); the space is "beyond minimalist compared to the rest of the Shore Club's glitz" and critics contend service is "not up to par with the prices", but "have a sake, chill" and "keep your eyes open – you'll be surprised who you might see."

Oishi Thai *Japanese/Thai*
26 | 22 | 24 | $44

North Miami | 14841 Biscayne Blvd. (146th St.) | 305-947-4338 | www.oishithai.com

"Delicious" sushi shares billing with "exotic" Thai creations at this North Miami strip-maller, "admirably run" by a onetime Nobu chef; a "cool" modern Asian look, servers who "do everything they can to make for an enjoyable meal" and an optimal "quality/price ratio" further boost its appeal.

OLA *Pan-Latin*
27 | 22 | 25 | $66

South Beach | Sanctuary Hotel | 1745 James Ave. (bet. 17th & 18th Sts.) | Miami Beach | 305-695-9125 | www.olamiami.com

"Ceviche is king" at this "quiet" Pan-Latin respite from the "craziness of SoBe", offering a "superb" culinary "trip from Mexico to Argentina"; set in the boutique Sanctuary Hotel well "off the main drag", it has a "trendy" yet "comfortable" vibe, a "thoughtful" wine list parsed by a "knowledgeable" crew and a "delightful" terrace.

The Palm *Steak*
28 | 20 | 25 | $73

Bay Harbor Islands | 9650 E. Bay Harbor Dr. (96th St.) | 305-868-7256 | www.thepalm.com

"Top-quality meat cooked right", "great sides" and "strong drinks" are what you can expect "every time" at this Bay Harbor Islands outpost of the "quintessential NY steakhouse" chain; caricatures line the walls and "local bigwigs" fill the seats of the "clubby" environs, which are overseen by "old-school waiters" and host an "amiable bar scene", but it doesn't come cheap: "my credit card won't allow me near the place."

Palme d'Or ⑤Ⓜ *French*
28 | 27 | 27 | $92

Coral Gables | Biltmore Hotel | 1200 Anastasia Ave. (Columbus Blvd.) | 305-913-3201 | www.biltmorehotel.com

"The prize of Coral Gables, if not all of Miami/Dade", is this "superb" New French stunner boasting a "well-considered" wine list and "seamless" service in a "luxurious", "refined" setting, though a recent chef change may outdate the Food rating; "not cheap" understates things, especially if you go all out and "stay the night" at the "beautiful" Biltmore Hotel for the "ultimate romantic evening."

Pascal's on Ponce ⑤ *French*
27 | 20 | 25 | $66

Coral Gables | 2611 Ponce de Leon Blvd. (Valencia Ave.) | 305-444-2024 | www.pascalmiami.com

"Creativity abounds" in the "*magnifique*" New French fare at chef-owner Pascal Oudin's "unassuming" storefront bistro "just off the Mile" in Coral Gables; the space is about as "small" as the bills are "big", but "first-rate" service and "soufflés so light that you won't gain a pound" help explain why most find it "always a treat."

Prime One Twelve ◐ *Seafood/Steak*
27 | 23 | 22 | $87

South Beach | 112 Ocean Dr. (1st St.) | Miami Beach | 305-532-8112 | www.mylesrestaurantgroup.com

"Super sexy" yet "serious", this South Beach surf 'n' turfer dishes up "monstrous" portions of "amazing" food, but it's just as well known for hosting the "scene of scenes", with "Bentleys, Ferraris and Lambos" pulling up out front and "wannabes" "rubbing elbows" ("literally, they pack 'em in") with "movie stars", "sports legends" and "models" inside; downsides include "noise", "long waits", variable service and "black-card" tabs, but hey, "you'll have a story to tell."

Pubbelly ●Ⓜ *Asian* | 24 | 22 | 22 | $38 |

Miami Beach | 1418 20th St. (Bay Rd.) | 305-532-7555 | www.pubbelly.com

"Porktastic!" squeal fans of this pig-centric Miami Beach gastropub that pairs "rich", "creative" Asian fusion fare with a strong selection of craft brews and wine; the "'in' crowd" that throngs the rustic "hole-in-the-wall" digs declares it a "great spot to start, end or make an evening" thanks to its small- and large-plate options, moderate prices and "down-to-earth service."

Red, The Steakhouse *Steak* | 27 | 25 | 24 | $83 |

South Beach | 119 Washington Ave. (1st St.) | Miami Beach | 305-534-3688 | www.redthesteakhouse.com

As the name implies, this "classy" South Beach steakhouse is a true "red meat/red wine lover's paradise" with its "juicy", "velvety" Angus beef and "extensive wine collection" displayed behind a glass wall – though the "extravagant" price tags require a lot of green; an "attentive" staff, a "cool ambiance" and a "stylish" "contemporary" look complete the "first-rate" experience.

Scarpetta *Italian* | 25 | 26 | 23 | $79 |

Miami Beach | Fontainebleau Miami Beach | 4441 Collins Ave. (W. 44th St.) | 305-674-4660 | www.fontainebleau.com

"Spaghetti with oomph", the "best polenta this side of heaven" and other "outstanding" Italian cuisine make diners "happy to have Scott Conant's talents in Miami" at this Fontainebleau Hotel spin-off of the Manhattan original; yes, it's "pricey", but "you get what you pay for", including "thoughtful, efficient" service and a "captivating" setting complete with "fantastic" water views and *Top Model*"-like patrons.

Sugarcane Raw Bar Grill ● *Eclectic* | 25 | 24 | 20 | $50 |

Downtown | 3252 NE First Ave. (32nd St.) | 786-369-0353 | www.sugarcanerawbargrill.com

A "happening scene" unfolds at this Downtowner where the "excellent" Eclectic small plates offer "something for everyone", and the airy "Havana"-esque decor transports the "attractive" crowd to an "island paradise"; just know that bills can climb and the "360-degree" indoor-outdoor bar can be a "real meat market."

Yakko-San ● *Japanese* | 27 | - | 21 | $31 |
(fka Hiro's Yakko-San)

North Miami Beach | Intracoastal Mall | 3881 NE 163rd St. (Sunny Isles Blvd.) | 305-947-0064 | www.yakko-san.com

"Feel like Andrew Zimmern" sampling the "unusual" "izakaya-style" small plates and "inspired" sushi at this "adventurous" Japanese eatery in a North Miami Beach strip center; the modern setting, sporting a large sushi bar, dependable service and "low" prices – especially during happy hour – are further pluses.

Yardbird ● *Southern*

| - | - | - | M |

South Beach | 1600 Lenox Ave. (16th St.) | Miami Beach | 305-538-5220 |
www.runchickenrun.com

Putting the 'South' in South Beach, this newfangled Southern comfort-fooder from exec chef Jeff McInnis (ex Gigi) vends down-home dishes with contemporary twists for not a lot of scratch; the rather large nest is feathered with rustic elements like butcher-block tables and tractor-seat stools and includes a well-stocked bourbon bar.

Zuma ● *Japanese*

| 28 | 27 | 24 | $83 |

Downtown | EPIC Hotel | 270 Biscayne Blvd. Way (Brickell Ave.) |
305-577-0277 | www.zumarestaurant.com

"Book way ahead" to secure a seat at the Epic Hotel's "it" spot Downtown because this overseas import (and "international sensation") draws throngs with its "Zen mastery" of modern izakaya-inspired Japanese fare plus sushi, robata grill items and more; "fabulous views" can be had from the terrace overlooking the Miami River, or you can just watch the "beautiful people" burning many "benjamins" in the "stunning" dining room and "vibrant" sake bar/lounge.

Minneapolis/St. Paul

TOP FOOD RANKING

Restaurant	Cuisine
29 Travail	American
Alma	American
La Belle Vie	French/Mediterranean
28 Lake Elmo Inn	American
Lucia's	American
Capital Grille	Steak
Craftsman	American
Meritage	American/French
Matt's Bar	Burgers
Manny's Steak	Steak

OTHER NOTEWORTHY PLACES

Axel's	Steak
Bachelor Farmer	Scandinavian
Big Bowl	Asian
Borough	American
Doolittle's	American
5-8 Club	Burgers
Heidi's	American
Kincaid's	Seafood/Steak
112 Eatery	Eclectic
Saffron	Mediterranean/Mideastern

Alma *American*   29 | 25 | 28 | $55

Dinkytown | 528 University Ave. SE (6th Ave.) | Minneapolis | 612-379-4909 | www.restaurantalma.com

"Alma does the soul good" rave reviewers of this Dinkytown "gem" where ingredients from "local farmers" inspire "exceptional" New American cooking by chef-owner Alexander Roberts that's "always a pleasure"; "elegant" yet "unpretentious" with a "superb" staff, it's "a bit expensive but worth it" for a "romantic evening", "entertaining business guests" or "just dinner with friends."

Axel's *Steak*   26 | 23 | 25 | $33

Chanhassen | 560 W. 78th St. (Laredo Dr.) | 952-934-9340
Mendota | 1318 Sibley Memorial Hwy. (D St.) | 651-686-4840
www.axelsrestaurants.com

Fans "love the popovers" and "delicious steaks and seafood" at these "reliable old" meateries where the portions are so generous, you can "count on leftovers"; it's "cozy" and kid-friendly with a "helpful" staff, so many dub it a "solid" "favorite" where they're "never disappointed."

Bachelor Farmer *Scandinavian*   25 | 24 | 25 | $48

Warehouse | 50 Second Ave. N. (1st St.) | Minneapolis | 612-206-3920 | www.thebachelorfarmer.com

"Eco-friendly local providers" fuel the "clever" "contemporary" Scandinavian menu at this "hot" Warehouse District pick with "outstanding" service, "cool digs" and a "hipster-meets-foodie" scene; it's "high-priced" and "hard to get a reservation", though the "secret" Marvel "speakeasy downstairs" is a slightly more accessible option; P.S. those bachelor owners are sons of Minnesota's governor.

Big Bowl *Asian* | 25 | 22 | 23 | $21 |

Edina | Galleria | 3669 Galleria (France Ave.) | 952-928-7888
Minnetonka | Ridgedale Ctr. | 12649 Wayzata Blvd. (Plymouth Rd.) | 952-797-9888
Roseville | Rosedale Ctr. | 1705 Hwy. 36 (bet. Fairview & Snelling Aves.) | 651-636-7173
www.bigbowl.com

"Build-your-own stir-fries" packing "loads of fresh veggies" and other "tasty" Chinese and Thai dishes come "as advertised" with "large portions for the right price" at these "contemporary" Asian chain links with "prompt", "efficient" service; offering "unique" cocktails too, they're "pleasing" choices for a "relaxed evening with friends", since "you just can't go wrong" here.

Borough *American* | - | - | - | E |

Warehouse | 730 Washington Ave. N. (7th Ave.) | Minneapolis | 612-354-3135 | www.boroughmpls.com

This Warehouse District foodie magnet (from Travail alums) attracts savvy diners with its American home-cooking-gone-haute menu; the glammed-up industrial dining room features huge street-facing windows, a lower-level lounge serves craft cocktails and bites from an edited bar menu and there's a loading-dock patio for fair-weather dining.

The Capital Grille *Steak* | 28 | 26 | 27 | $50 |

Downtown Mpls | La Salle Plaza | 801 Hennepin Ave. (8th St.) | Minneapolis | 612-692-9000 | www.thecapitalgrille.com

"Exemplary" steak and "all the trimmings" (plus a "great wine list") come with "impeccable" service at this "trusted" Downtown chain link with a "luxurious feel"; sure, you "pay for the quality", but it's "tops" for a "group on business" or a "tête-à-tête with someone special."

The Craftsman *American* | 28 | 24 | 26 | $41 |

South Minneapolis | 4300 E. Lake St. (43rd Ave.) | Minneapolis | 612-722-0175 | www.craftsmanrestaurant.com

Both the "innovative", "locally grown" New American fare and the cocktails "change with the seasons" at this South Minneapolis "neighborhood" "find"; set in an Arts and Crafts–style space with a "well-done" patio and service that "couldn't be better", "it's definitely an experience" that's "worth every dime."

Doolittle's Woodfire Grill *American* | 26 | 24 | 24 | $23 |

Eagan | 2140 Cliff Rd. (Nicols Rd.) | 651-452-6627
Golden Valley | 550 Winnetka Ave. N. (Golden Valley Rd.) | 763-542-1931
www.doolittlesrestaurants.com

Enticing with a "wonderful aroma", the "chicken on the wood-fire grill is outstanding" and the rest of the "diverse menu" also pleases at this "reasonably priced" American, with branches in Eagan and Golden Valley, that's a "frolic" when you want to feel like you're "eating around a campfire"; "friendly" service enhances the "nice ambiance", keeping it a "favorite" for many.

	FOOD	DECOR	SERVICE	COST

5-8 Club *Burgers*

`25` `16` `21` `$15`

Champlin | 6251 Douglas Ct. (bet. 109th & 110th Aves.) | 763-425-5858
Maplewood | 2289 Minnehaha Ave. (McKnight Rd.) | 651-735-5858
South Minneapolis | 5800 Cedar Ave. (58th St.) | Minneapolis |
612-823-5858
www.5-8club.com

"Unbeatable" burgers are the big draw of this "comfortable" (if slightly
"divey") tavern mini-chain, voted Most Popular in Minneapolis, that's
"famous" for its "must-have" Juicy Lucy – a half-pounder stuffed with
cheese; "service can vary" when "busy", but overall it's "easy on the
wallet" with a "neighborly", "working-class atmosphere", and the
"food definitely makes up for the decor."

Heidi's *American*

`26` `24` `23` `$53`

Lyn-Lake | 2903 Lyndale Ave. S. (29th St.) | Minneapolis | 612-354-3512 |
www.heidismpls.com

This "vibrant" New American from Stewart and Heidi Woodman
"rocks" say customers who commend the "inventive" plates with "flavor and depth beyond your imagination" served in a "stunning" environment that's as "hip and urban" as the boho Lyn-Lake neighborhood;
coming through with "exciting" cocktails and "well-informed" service
and delivering "terrific value" for the somewhat "expensive" tabs, it's
an all-around "home run."

Kincaid's *Seafood/Steak*

`26` `26` `26` `$45`

Bloomington | 8400 Normandale Lake Blvd. (84th St.) | 952-921-2255
Downtown SP | 380 St. Peter St. (bet. 5th & 6th Sts.) | St. Paul |
651-602-9000
www.kincaids.com

"Classic" chain links in Downtown St. Paul and Bloomington, these
meateries "still pull in a lot of power players" for "rewarding" steaks
and seafood served in "sharp" surroundings lightened up with large
windows; "terrific" service and "wonderful", "twice-daily happy
hours" are additional assets, so despite murmurs that it's "a little
pricey" and "predictable", its target audience calls it "first-class for
business or pleasure."

La Belle Vie *French/Mediterranean*

`29` `27` `29` `$84`

Loring Park | 510 Groveland Ave. (Hennepin Ave.) | Minneapolis |
612-874-6440 | www.labellevie.us

"Just close your eyes" and pick any of the "modern", "exquisite" Med-
New French dishes (or go for the "brilliant" tasting menu) at this "wonderful little gem" in Loring Park, "top of the heap when it comes to
fine dining", complete with a "formal look" in a "grande dame of an old
apartment building", and earning the Twin Cities' No. 1 rating for
Service ("phenomenal"); sure it's a "splurge", so "bring your best credit
card" and get set for a "memorable" evening; P.S. the "gorgeous" bar
is "less stuffy" with a more affordable menu.

Lake Elmo Inn *American*

`28` `24` `27` `$38`

Lake Elmo | 3442 Lake Elmo Ave. (Upper 33rd St.) | 651-777-8495 |
www.lakeelmoinn.com

The word's out on this "hidden secret" in Lake Elmo (an "agricultural
community" on the east side of St. Paul) providing a "first-class", "traditional" yet creative American menu in a "really quaint" setting; ser-

vice that's "unobtrusive but intuitive" draws returnees for "special occasions", and while it's on the "pricey" side, weekly specials appeal to the "budget-conscious"; P.S. the "fab Sunday brunch with bottomless champagne" is the "best deal."

Lucia's ☑ American
| 28 | 23 | 26 | $31 |

Uptown | 1432 W. 31st St. (Hennepin Ave.) | Minneapolis | 612-825-1572 | www.lucias.com

Praised as a "prairie home-cooking companion", this "pioneering" "Uptown favorite" by chef-owner Lucia Watson follows the "Alice Waters tradition" of "slow food" based on "locally sourced products", with its "marvelous" "weekly changing" American menu that's "short", "well crafted" and an "excellent value"; "relaxing" for an "intimate dinner" (or "lovely" lunch), the "small", "comfortable" room "allows for special attention", leading customers to come back "again and again" (and sample the "well-stocked wine bar" and bakery too).

Manny's Steakhouse Steak
| 28 | 25 | 27 | $68 |

Downtown Mpls | W Minneapolis, The Foshay | 825 Marquette Ave. (9th St.) | Minneapolis | 612-339-9900 | www.mannyssteakhouse.com

"A steak man's steakhouse", this "high-rolling" Downtown locale in the W Hotel "hits the spot when you need a bludgeon of beef", greeting you with a "meat cart" that lets you "pick your favorite cut", "massive" sides and "stiff" drinks in an "old-time dinner-club" atmosphere; rounded out with a "phenomenal" wine list and "service par excellence", it all adds up to an "A+ meal" that's a "fantastic splurge" – "so if you have $$$ or an expense account, go for it!"

Matt's Bar ⌿ Burgers
| 28 | 15 | 21 | $13 |

South Minneapolis | 3500 Cedar Ave. S. (35th St.) | Minneapolis | 612-722-7072 | www.mattsbar.com

"You haven't lived" until you try the Jucy Lucy say fans of the "killer" burger ("cheese on the inside") at this '50s-era South Minneapolis "neighborhood bar" that's "cramped, dark and cheap-looking" (the way "I love it"); though "you'll have a wait during busy times", the servers "know their customers", the "price is right" and everything is "exactly as it should be", "attitude and all."

Meritage ☑ American/French
| 28 | 27 | 27 | $49 |

Downtown SP | Hamm Bldg. | 410 St. Peter St. (6th St.) | St. Paul | 651-222-5670 | www.meritage-stpaul.com

This "little bit of France in the saintly city" of Downtown St. Paul is "tops" for "upscale" brasserie fare with a "delightful", seasonal New American spin, provided with "impeccable" service in a "bistro-style" setting (with "lovely" sidewalk seating) in close proximity to the Ordway Center; the tab is justly "spendy", especially if you opt for an "amazing" tasting menu with wine, though the "outstanding oyster bar" is a more affordable option.

112 Eatery ● Eclectic
| 27 | 23 | 25 | $42 |

Warehouse | 112 N. Third St. (1st Ave.) | Minneapolis | 612-343-7696 | www.112eatery.com

"Eat where the chefs eat" at this "self-assured" Warehouse District Eclectic by Isaac Becker delivering "pitch-perfect flavor combinations" (including "terrific takes on comfort-food favorites") in a "casual",

"convivial" atmosphere with "excellent" service; it's a "tough reservation", but "lucky" diners love that there's a "price point for everyone
with top-notch food at every tier" – plus it's "open late."

Saffron Restaurant & Lounge ⊠ *Mediterranean/Mideastern*

28 | 25 | 26 | $42

Warehouse | 123 N. Third St. (1st Ave.) | Minneapolis | 612-746-5533 |
www.saffronmpls.com

"Meze, meze, meze" shout "lucky" lovers of this "contemporary"
Warehouse District hang serving "brilliant", "fragrant" and sometimes "adventurous" Med–Middle Eastern plates that can "change
your entire outlook on hummus"; "relaxed yet classy", it also boasts
"inventive" cocktails and "cordial" service (including tableside visits
by the "extremely nice" owners) that support the upscale tabs.

Travail Kitchen & Amusements ⊠Ⓜ *American*

29 | 19 | 26 | $41

Robbinsdale | 4154 W. Broadway Ave. (bet. 41st & 42nd Aves.) |
763-535-1131

The "stellar", "must-do" tasting menu takes you on a "fascinating"
"culinary journey" (touching the "outer edge of molecular gastronomy")
at this "unexpected" chef-owned New American in Robbinsdale, voted
No. 1 for Food in the Twin Cities, and dubbed one of the "best values"
too; "efficient, personalized" service and shared tables add to the
"über-cool" vibe, though you need to "line up early" since it "doesn't
take reservations" – the only reservation foodies have about the place.

Nashville

TOP FOOD RANKING

	Restaurant	Cuisine
28	Etch Restaurant	Eclectic
	Mitchell Delicatessen	Sandwiches
	Miel	American/French
	Margot Cafe & Bar	French/Italian
	Silly Goose*	American
	Chef's Market Cafe	Southern
27	Catbird Seat	American
	Morton's	Steak
	Marché Artisan Foods	European
	Kobe Steaks	Japanese/Steak

OTHER NOTEWORTHY PLACES

Restaurant	Cuisine
Amerigo	Italian
Blackstone Restaurant	American/Pub Food
Capitol Grille	American/Southern
City House	Italian
Flyte World Dining & Wine	American
Husk Nashville	Southern
Kayne Prime	Steak
Lockeland Table	American/Southern
Loveless Cafe	Southern
Pancake Pantry	American
Puckett's Grocery	Southern
Rolf & Daughters	American
Sunset Grill	American
Watermark	American

Amerigo *Italian* — 23 | 21 | 22 | $24

Brentwood | 1656 Westgate Circle (Moores Ln.) | 615-377-7070
Midtown | 1920 West End Ave. (20th Ave.) | 615-320-1740
www.amerigo.net

Links in "one of the better Italian chains in the Nashville area", these Brentwood and Midtown ristorantes are "local favorites", with "helpful" staffers serving up "consistently terrific" classics in "large" portions; "fair" prices and a "classy" ambiance help make them just the thing for a "luncheon meeting" or an "enjoyable dinner" with family and friends.

**Blackstone Restaurant &
Brewery** *American/Pub Food* — 19 | 19 | 20 | $20

West End/Vanderbilt | 1918 West End Ave. (bet. 19th & 20th Aves.) | 615-327-9969 | www.blackstonebrewery.com

The "upscale pub food" served at this West End American is certainly "above average", but to suds-lovers the "excellent" micro-

---

* Indicates a tie with restaurant above

brews are the "big draw"; prices are "fair", staffers are "prompt and friendly" and the "relaxed" setting incorporates the on-site brewery's stainless-steel tanks.

Capitol Grille *American/Southern* 26 | 27 | 26 | $47

Downtown | Hermitage Hotel | 231 Sixth Ave. N. (Union St.) | 615-244-3121 | www.capitolgrillenashville.com

Wheeler-dealers celebrating "special occasions" fill this "grand" Downtown "jewel" in the "beautifully restored" Hermitage Hotel, where executive chef Tyler Brown oversees a kitchen turning out "top-notch" Southern classics with "creative" twists made from farm-fresh ingredients; "outstanding" service comes with the "luxurious" setting, along with an "expensive bill", of course; P.S. gents (and ladies), don't miss a peek at its "famous" art deco men's room.

The Catbird Seat Ⓢ Ⓜ *American* 27 | 22 | 27 | $161

Midtown | 1711 Division St. (18th Ave.) | 615-810-8200 | www.thecatbirdseatrestaurant.com

An "adventure for the senses" awaits at this American Midtowner where Erik Anderson creates "innovative" tasting menus, and serves them (along with "thorough explanations") from the "dinner in the round"–style counter; the "culinary experience" spans several hours, the cost can edge toward the "stratosphere" and "getting a reservation is tough", but it's "worth it" for a "special night."

Chef's Market Cafe & Take Away Ⓢ *Southern* 28 | 21 | 24 | $15

Goodlettsville | 900 Conference Dr. (Northgate Circle) | 615-851-2433 | www.chefsmarket.com

About 20 minutes north of Downtown, this Goodlettsville Southerner is a local "favorite" offering an "exciting variety" of "exceptional cafeteria-style food" that includes "addicting" desserts and "plenty of healthy options"; "good prices", an "always-smiling" staff and a "fun" vibe amid "interesting", European-inspired decor are pluses.

City House *Italian* 26 | 25 | 25 | $36

Germantown | 1222 Fourth Ave. N. (bet. Madison & Monroe Sts.) | 615-736-5838 | www.cityhousenashville.com

"A locavore's dream", this "trendy", midpriced Germantown "rustic" Italian uses area ingredients in "house-cured salami", "best-in-town" belly-ham pizza and other "astonishing creations" served alongside "artisanal" cocktails; the "excellent" staffers "steer you in the right direction", and regulars know to sit in front of the open kitchen to watch chef Tandy Wilson's "exquisite technique."

Etch Restaurant Ⓢ *Eclectic* 28 | 27 | 27 | $49

SoBro | 303 Demonbreun St. (bet. Almond St. & 3rd Ave.) | 615-522-0685 | www.etchrestaurant.com

At this "delightful", "cutting-edge" SoBro Eclectic – rated No. 1 for Food in Nashville – chef Deb Paquette (of the late, lamented Zola) presents an "incredible array of flavor, texture and olfactory experiences" via a "creative", "expertly prepared" menu; factor in a "knowledgeable" staff that's "helpful with wine pairings" and a "NY-chic" setting, and the upscale prices are quite "reasonable" for the quality; P.S. insiders suggest seats overlooking the open kitchen for "an entertaining view" of the action.

Flyte World Dining & Wine ⊠Ⓜ *American*   27 | 24 | 26 | $50

Gulch | 718 Division St. (8th Ave.) | 615-255-6200 | www.flytenashville.com

"Farm-to-table" ingredients turn up in "excellent, inventive cuisine" matched with "a wonderful wine list" at this "high-end" Gulch American; "modern but warm" surrounds and "knowledgeable servers" ready with "recommendations for pairings" are part of the top-flyte experience that makes it one of "the most sought-after reservations" in town.

Husk Nashville *Southern*   – | – | – | E

SoBro | 37 Rutledge St. (bet. Lea Ave. & Middleton St.) | 615-256-6565 | www.husknashville.com

Located in a historic brick mansion on Rutledge Hill in SoBro, this upscale Southern eatery – sibling of Charleston's famed Husk – displays a fanatical devotion to regional ingredients, which are cooked on a unique ember-fired grill; the bright and airy minimalist interior combines elements of the past (original hardwood floors, molding) and the present (modern art, bold purple accents), plus there's a happening bar/lounge and patio.

Kayne Prime Steakhouse *Steak*   27 | 26 | 24 | $69

Gulch | 1103 McGavock St. (11th Ave.) | 615-259-0050 | www.mstreetnashville.com

At this "top-of-the-crop" Gulch chophouse, "terrific" steaks headline a "wonderful, creative" menu and "well-made" cocktails are poured from a large bar backed by huge picture windows with city skyline views; an "accommodating" staff patrols the "beautiful", neutral-toned contemporary space, and though it may be "expensive", most deem it "a real treat."

Kobe Steaks *Japanese/Steak*   27 | 24 | 27 | $30

West End/Vanderbilt | Parkview Towers | 210 25th Ave. N. (bet. Brandau & Elliston Pls.) | 615-327-9081 | www.kobesteaks.net

The "entertaining" hibachi chefs cook "juicy" steaks "right in front of you" at this midpriced Vanderbilt Japanese steakhouse; regulars say the "comfortable", modern space lends itself to a "romantic dinner" or "night out with a group", especially since it's "within walking distance" of music venues and more.

Lockeland Table ⊠ *American/Southern*   26 | 27 | 24 | $27

East Nashville | 1520 Woodland St. (16th St.) | 615-228-4864 | www.lockelandtable.com

In "trendy" East Nashville, this moderately priced "gem" serves a seasonal menu of "terrific" Southern-accented American fare and "incredible" pizzas; the pleasant staff ensures that guests "feel at home" in the rustic, renovated storefront space that makes a "nice date spot."

Loveless Cafe *Southern*   24 | 22 | 23 | $16

West Nashville | 8400 Highway 100 (Pasquo Rd.) | 615-646-9700 | www.lovelesscafe.com

This West Nashville roadhouse slinging "quintessential Southern cuisine" ("fried chicken and biscuits to die for", "smoky, tender pulled pork") is a "tradition that everyone must experience"; with "friendly" staffers, "fair" prices and a "country" vibe, it's no wonder it can get "crowded", but the "eclectic" on-site shops hawking everything from antiques to specialty food "keep you entertained while you wait" for a table.

Marché Artisan Foods ⓜ *European* — 27 | 23 | 23 | $22

East Nashville | 1000 Main St. (10th St.) | 615-262-1111 |
www.marcheartisanfoods.com

Inside a "bustling, casual" space that includes a small deli, this affordable East Nashville bistro with European flair starts the day with "divine breakfasts" that segue into light lunches and "seasonal, inspired"
dinners capped with "wonderful housemade" desserts; servers are
"friendly and efficient", but regulars advise to "get there early or late"
or "expect to wait."

Margot Cafe & Bar ⓜ *French/Italian* — 28 | 25 | 26 | $42

East Nashville | 1017 Woodland St. (11th St.) | 615-227-4668 |
www.margotcafe.com

Situated in a converted East Nashville service station, this "homey",
European-inflected cafe whips up a "Tuscan- and Provençal-inspired
menu" that changes daily and includes "standard-setter" Sunday
brunch fare; staffers give "attention when you need it", and though it
can be "pricey", it's "worth a visit."

Miel ⓜ *American/French* — 28 | 24 | 25 | $51

Sylvan Park | 343 53rd Ave. N. (bet. Charlotte & Elkins Aves.) |
615-298-3663 | www.mielrestaurant.com

At this upscale Sylvan Park bistro, a "delicious", frequently changing menu of farm-to-table American and French classics keeps fans
"coming back"; service is "accommodating", but the contemporary,
"renovated-meat-market" space is "fairly small", so reservations
are "a must."

Mitchell Delicatessen *Sandwiches* — 28 | 21 | 25 | $11

East Nashville | 1402 McGavock Pike (bet. Geneiva & Riverside Drs.) |
615-262-9862 | www.mitchelldeli.com

This "fantastic neighborhood" deli in East Nashville stacks "fresh
produce, local meats and cheeses" between "tasty, crusty bread"
to give "loyal customers" exactly "what a sandwich should be",
particularly the much buzzed about Asian flank steak version
(available only as a special on certain days); add in excellent service and bonuses like a salad bar plus regional gourmet items for
sale, and folks "keep coming back"; P.S. a move to larger digs down the
street is in the works.

Morton's The Steakhouse *Steak* — 27 | 25 | 26 | $56

Downtown | 618 Church St. (Capitol Blvd.) | 615-259-4558 |
www.mortons.com

"Melt-in-your-mouth" steaks are accompanied by an "enormous"
wine selection at this "top-notch" Downtown chain link where "attentive" servers "impress" amid "old-world" surroundings; since tabs can
be "pricey", some save it for a "special night out" or when "someone
else is purchasing", but budget-minders "sit in the bar and order" from
the "bang-for-your-buck" happy-hour menu.

Pancake Pantry *American* — 24 | 17 | 22 | $13

Belmont/Hillsboro Village | 1796 21st Ave. S. (Belcourt Ave.) |
615-383-9333 | www.thepancakepantry.com

The line can sometimes "wind down the street" at this Hillsboro
Village flapjackery, but the stacks of "fluffy pancakes" loaded with

"unique options" are "worth the wait"; the decor may be "nothing to write home about", but prices are "cheap", and the "efficient" staff "keeps the tables turning quickly."

Puckett's Grocery & Restaurant *Southern* | 22 | 21 | 21 | $16 |

Downtown | 500 Church St. (5th Ave.) | 615-770-2772
Franklin | 120 Fourth Ave. S. (B'way) | 615-794-5527
www.puckettsgrocery.com

It's "like eating in an old general store" at these Southern siblings with a "hometown feel" in Downtown Franklin and Nashville, where affordable "country cooking" done "the right way" is accompanied by "friendly" service; there's also "fantastic" live music most nights, which means it can be "loud", but all in all, it's a "fun place to take out-of-town guests"; P.S. yes, there's also a small specialty market on-site.

Rolf & Daughters *American* | - | - | - | E |

Germantown | 700 Taylor St. (7th Ave.) | 615-866-9897 |
www.rolfanddaughters.com

Inventive cocktails and plates shared at a convivial bar or at communal tables make this upscale Germantown New American a popular group gathering spot, and it also works for an intimate dinner date, with additional seating at private tables and a warmly lit setting in a renovated old factory; heartier housemade pastas and meaty dishes round out the menu.

Silly Goose 🗗 Ⓜ *American* | 28 | 24 | 25 | $20 |

East Nashville | 1888 Eastland Ave. (Chapel Ave.) | 615-915-0757 |
www.sillygoosenashville.com

"Farm-to-table" fanatics flock to this "funky" East Nashville American "find" offering a "unique" lineup of "amazing" sandwiches, salads, entrees and more that incorporate "local, organic ingredients"; its "tiny" digs, no-rezzies rule and rep as one of the area's "best dining experiences for your money" mean "you might have to wait awhile" for a table.

Sunset Grill *American* | 25 | 22 | 25 | $34 |

Belmont/Hillsboro Village | 2001 Belcourt Ave. (20th Ave.) |
615-386-3663 | www.sunsetgrill.com

"Perfect for both business and fun", this "vibrant but relaxed" "Nashville landmark" is a "go-to" whether dining with "clients, friends, family" or a "date" on account of its "consistently excellent", wide-ranging American menu that aims to cover "everyone's cravings and budget"; a "friendly, efficient" staff offers tips on the "amazing wine list" and there's an abbreviated list of "amazing-value" dishes on a late-night menu, further reasons it's a "mainstay" of the scene.

Watermark Restaurant 🗗 *American* | 26 | 25 | 26 | $62 |

Gulch | 507 12th Ave. S. (11th Ave.) | 615-254-2000 |
www.watermark-restaurant.com

In the "increasingly glamorous" Gulch neighborhood, this "crisp-white-tablecloth" American is a "favorite for business dinners and special events" thanks to a "diverse menu" prepared with "Southern flair" and served by an "impeccable" staff; the "upscale" experience comes with commensurate tabs, but the bar menu is a relative bargain, leading most to judge it "excellent in every way."

New Jersey

TOP FOOD RANKING

	Restaurant	Cuisine
28	Nicholas	American
	Restaurant Lorena's	French
27	CulinAriane	American
	De Lorenzo's Tomato Pies	Pizza
	Shumi	Japanese
	Steve & Cookie's by the Bay	American
	Chef's Table	French
	Scalini Fedeli	Italian
	Drew's Bayshore Bistro	American
26	Le Rendez-Vous	French
	Belford Bistro	American
	Restaurant Serenade	French
	Cafe Panache	Eclectic
	Peter Shields Inn	American
	Saddle River Inn	American/French
	Cafe Matisse	Eclectic
	Blue Bottle Cafe	American
	Chez Catherine	French
	La Riviera Gastronomia	Italian
	Sono Sushi	Japanese
	Washington Inn*	American

OTHER NOTEWORTHY PLACES

Restaurant	Cuisine
Amanda's	American
Andre's	American
Bernards Inn	American
Blue Morel	American
Cheesecake Factory	American
Cucharamama	S American
David Burke Fromagerie	American
Due Mari	Italian
Elements	American
Fascino	Italian
Frog and the Peach	American
Maritime Parc	American/Seafood
Ninety Acres at Natirar	American
Peacock Inn	American
Pluckemin Inn	American
Rat's Restaurant	French
Ryland Inn	American
Stage Left	American
Ursino	American
Varka	Greek/Seafood

* Indicates a tie with restaurant above

	FOOD	DECOR	SERVICE	COST

Amanda's *American* — 25 | 24 | 24 | $48

Hoboken | 908 Washington St. (bet. 9th & 10th Sts.) | 201-798-0101 |
www.amandasrestaurant.com

"Classy is the key word" that captures this "upscale" Hoboken New
American where a "thoughtful" wine list is matched with "creative"
cuisine that "seduces you" amid the "genteel" surrounds of a "lovely"
Victorian brownstone; the "romantic" vibe is a "dater's delight", but
it's "not too stuffy to take your kids" for "special occasions" – either
way, expect a "warm welcome" from the "attentive" staff.

Andre's ⓈⓂ *American* — 25 | 24 | 24 | $54

Newton | 188 Spring St. (bet. Adams & Jefferson Sts.) | 973-300-4192 |
www.andresrestaurant.com

Chef-owner André de Waal "works at the art of food", pairing his "creative", seasonal American menu with "top-notch" wines at this "upscale" Newton "gem"; "folksy but professional" service matches the
"intimate" setting that strikes "the right balance between formal and
casual"; P.S. open Wednesday–Saturday only.

Belford Bistro *American* — 26 | 19 | 24 | $46

Belford | 870 Main St. (Lenison Ave.) | 732-495-8151 |
www.belfordbistro.com

At their "cozy" Belford "gem", chefs Kurt Bomberger and Crista Trovato
have fans swooning over "creative", "excellent" American fare where
the "knowledgeable staff seems to read minds"; "reservations are a
must", for the "small" strip-mall space is usually "crowded", and while
it's "a little pricey", "BYO makes it a relative bargain."

Bernards Inn *American* — 25 | 25 | 25 | $67

Bernardsville | The Bernards Inn | 27 Mine Brook Rd. (Quimby Ln.) |
908-766-0002 | www.bernardsinn.com

Set in a "charming" Bernardsville inn, this "elegant" New American
exudes "old-money" "sophistication" – from the "excellent" seasonal menu to the "extensive" wine list to the "professional" service; for those who find the dining room "stuffy" (or strictly for
"special occasions"), the library bar offers an "informal" alternative, with a lighter menu and prices that will still allow you to "send
your kid to college."

Blue Bottle Cafe ⓈⓂ *American* — 26 | 20 | 23 | $46

Hopewell | 101 E. Broad St. (Elm St.) | 609-333-1710 |
www.thebluebottlecafe.com

A "real gem" in the Princeton area, this Hopewell BYO draws "serious
foodies" with its "excellent" New American fare served with "artistic"
flair – plus "standout" desserts; it's "pricey but worth it", with "polished, unpretentious" service, and if it looks a bit like a "double-wide
trailer" on the outside (and a "country cafe" within), that's hardly an
issue when the food is such a "star"; P.S. reservations are a "must."

Blue Morel *American* — 24 | 22 | 23 | $62
(fka Copeland)

Morristown | The Westin Governor Morris | 2 Whippany Rd. (Lindsley Dr.) |
973-451-2619 | www.bluemorel.com

Set inside Morristown's Westin Governor Morris, this "high-end"
"modern" American might "save you a trip to NYC" with its "per-

fectly prepared" dishes and "impressive" raw seafood choices; there's also a "vibrant bar scene" fueled by "inventive cocktails", and "gracious" service, but "be warned" – the experience "does not come cheap."

Cafe Matisse Ⓜ *Eclectic*

26 | 25 | 26 | $73

Rutherford | 167 Park Ave. (bet. Highland Cross & Park Pl.) | 201-935-2995 | www.cafematisse.com

"Demanding foodies" revel in the "complex flavors" of "beautifully presented" Eclectic tasting menus at this "classy" Rutherford "jewel box", where the "passionate" staff "describes each dish with detail" and makes guests "feel special"; some cringe at the "NY prices", but loyalists declare it a "masterful meal deserving of its namesake"; P.S. the attached wine shop makes BYO a breeze.

Cafe Panache *Eclectic*

26 | 24 | 25 | $59

Ramsey | 130 E. Main St. (bet. Island Ave. & Spruce St.) | 201-934-0030 | www.cafepanachenj.com

A "go-to place for special occasions", this Ramsey Eclectic delivers "artful presentations" of "inventive", "seasonal" fare in an "elegant setting" that's "always packed"; while it's undoubtedly "high-end", BYO "helps keep the price down", and "attentive", "professional" service caps an all-around "delightful evening."

Cheesecake Factory ● *American*

21 | 21 | 20 | $28

Hackensack | Shops at Riverside | 197 Riverside Sq. (Hackensack Ave.) | 201-488-0330

Short Hills | Short Hills Mall | 1200 Morris Tpke. (John F. Kennedy Blvd.) | 973-921-0930

Wayne | Willowbrook Mall | 1700 Willowbrook Blvd. (Rte. 46) | 973-890-1400

Bridgewater | Bridgewater Commons | 400 Commons Way (Rte. 206) | 908-252-0399

Edison | Menlo Park Mall | 455 Menlo Park Dr. (Rte. 1) | 732-494-7000

Freehold | Freehold Raceway Mall | 3710 Rte. 9 (Raceway Mall Dr.) | 732-462-6544

Cherry Hill | Marketplace at Garden State Park | 931 Haddonfield Rd. (bet. Garden Park Blvd. & Marlton Pike) | 856-665-7550 www.thecheesecakefactory.com

There are "no surprises" at this "wildly popular" American chain, just "steady" food "turned up a notch" and served in "button-bursting portions" from a menu the size of "*War and Peace*"; though critics cite "long waits" and find the "decibels as high as the calorie count", many more call it a "fail-safe" choice where "you know what you're getting" and it's "always good."

The Chef's Table ⓈⓂ *French*

27 | 20 | 25 | $57

Franklin Lakes | Franklin Square Shopping Ctr. | 754 Franklin Ave. (Pulis Ave.) | 201-891-6644 | www.tctnj.com

It's "like being in Paris" (by way of a Franklin Lakes strip mall) at this "fabulous" French BYO bistro, a "tour de force" starring "first-rate" chef Claude Baills and his "superb", "hearty" "classics"; Madame Baills guides the "excellent service", and since the "charming" place is "small", "reservations are a must" (and "hard to get") – still, "dedicated regulars" declare it "marvelous for special occasions."

Chez Catherine 🛇Ⓜ *French*

26 | 23 | 25 | $81

Westfield | 431 North Ave. W. (bet. Broad & Prospect Sts.) | 908-654-4011 | www.chezcatherine.com

"Close to perfect" is how aficionados assess this "fantastic" French cafe adjacent to the Best Western Westfield Inn; lunch has à la carte options, but dinner is strictly prix fixe, and while opinions on the "formal" setting range from "elegant" to "tired", most agree the service is "outstanding" and the "food is inspiring" – even if "special-occasion" prices have some wondering, "are they based on the euro?"; P.S. jackets are recommended.

Cucharamama Ⓜ *S American*

25 | 22 | 22 | $46

Hoboken | 233 Clinton St. (3rd St.) | 201-420-1700 | www.cucharamama.com

"Creatively delicious" cuisine, including "great" breads from a wood-burning oven, offers an "education in South American" cooking from chef and food historian Maricel Presilla at this "destination-worthy" Hoboken Pan-Latin, a sibling of nearby Zafra; although some find the digs "tight", "attentive" service, an "eclectic" vibe and "lively" cocktails help make "every meal a good time."

CulinAriane 🛇Ⓜ *American*

27 | 22 | 25 | $59

Montclair | 33 Walnut St. (Pine St.) | 973-744-0533 | www.culinariane.com

"Great things happen" in the kitchen of *Top Chef* contestant Ariane Duarte, whose "lovingly prepared" dishes make this Montclair American BYO a "local gem"; with service that's "beyond gracious", plus an "intimate" space and limited hours (Wednesdays–Saturdays), it's no surprise that reservations are "tough" to get, but even with "NYC prices", converts say this "true standout" "should be on everyone's list."

David Burke Fromagerie Ⓜ *American*

25 | 24 | 24 | $70

Rumson | 26 Ridge Rd. (Ave. of 2 Rivers) | 732-842-8088 | www.fromagerierestaurant.com

It's "art on a plate" rave fans who "keep coming back" for chef David Burke's "well-executed" American "innovations" at this Rumson "fine-dining" destination; with "heads-up" service and a "handsome, roomy" setting, there's "a lot to like here", and though tabs are "pricey", you "can't beat the value" on the "popular" Tuesday burger night; P.S. there's frequent live music too.

De Lorenzo's Tomato Pies Ⓜ *Pizza*

27 | 20 | 22 | $19

Robbinsville | Washington Town Ctr. | 2350 Rte. 33 (Robbinsville Edinburg Rd.) | 609-341-8480 | www.delorenzostomatopies.com

Though now in Robbinsville, this decades-old Trenton-born "classic" (operated by one branch of a famous 'za clan) still attracts legions of fans thanks to its "absolutely delicious" pizza with crust that's "perfectly charred", and salads that are "no slouch either"; you can still "expect long waits" in the new digs, which are a "dressed up" version of the old, and while it's BYO, insiders advise "birch beer goes best with the pie."

Drew's Bayshore Bistro *American*

27 | 18 | 23 | $47

Keyport | 25 Church St. (Front St.) | 732-739-9219 | www.bayshorebistro.com

Chef Andrew Araneo's "truly amazing" Cajun-accented New American cuisine "exceeds expectations" at his BYO "gem" in Keyport, where many of the dishes come with a "kick" and are probably "not for dieters"; "fair" prices and "pleasant" service are more reasons why diners agree it's "well worth the visit"; P.S. a recent move to its current location is not reflected in the Decor score.

Due Mari *Italian*   26 | 24 | 24 | $57

New Brunswick | 78 Albany St. (Neilson St.) | 732-296-1600 | www.duemarinj.com

The vibe is "classy" and "metropolitan" at this "elegant" New Brunswick Italian from consulting chef Michael White and the Altamarea Group, where an "innovative" menu features "beautiful" seafood and "exceptional" pastas, which are "impeccably" served by a "helpful" staff; while it's "certainly not cheap", the overall "outstanding experience" makes it a "good choice" for a "special occasion."

Elements *American*   25 | 24 | 24 | $68

Princeton | 163 Bayard Ln. (bet. Birch & Leigh Aves.) | 609-924-0078 | www.elementsprinceton.com

Fans attest it's a "revelation" to dine on culinary "magician" Scott Anderson's "innovative, unforgettable" New American tasting menu featuring local, sustainable ingredients at this "foodie destination" in Princeton; add "amazing" cocktails, "attentive yet unobtrusive" service and an "elegant", "contemporary" room, and most agree there's "little not to love about this place" – except maybe the "NY prices."

Fascino 🍴 *Italian*   26 | 22 | 24 | $54

Montclair | 331 Bloomfield Ave. (bet. Gates Ave. & Willow St.) | 973-233-0350 | www.fascinorestaurant.com

A "win from start to finish", this "upscale" Montclair Italian from Ryan DePersio is a "consistent" "favorite" for its "elegant", "innovative" interpretations of "traditional" dishes (and his mom's "alluring" desserts); the "comfortable" setting (recently brightened and refreshed, possibly outdating the Decor rating) "permits quiet conversation", while service is "gracious", and though it's "expensive", a BYO policy and an "out-of-this-world" tasting menu can make it seem like "a steal."

The Frog and the Peach *American*   25 | 23 | 24 | $59

New Brunswick | 29 Dennis St. (Richmond St.) | 732-846-3216 | www.frogandpeach.com

A "trendsetter" in New Brunswick for several decades, this "gourmet" American helmed by Bruce Lefebvre offers "creative" seasonal cuisine that fans consider a "real must for the foodie in you", with "wines to match", plus "knowledgeable" service in a "charming", diverse space (the garden room is "jungle dining" at its finest); it's "quite pricey", and some fret that it's grown "pretentious", but many deem it "worth every penny" for a "special night out."

La Riviera Gastronomia Ⓜ🍴 *Italian*   26 | 16 | 22 | $31

Clifton | 429 Piaget Ave. (bet. Delaware & Montgomery Sts.) | 973-772-9099

"Don't let the discreet exterior fool you" say fans of this Clifton storefront BYO, where the Calabretta family serves up "incredible" "homestyle" Italian dishes "cooked with love", including housemade pastas, "appetizers that sparkle" and salad dressing that alone is "worth the trip" for some; sure, there's "no decor", no reservations and no credit cards, but fans aren't complaining, especially when the staff "makes you feel like family" and "the bill won't raid your wallet."

Le Rendez-Vous Ⓜ *French* 26 | 19 | 23 | $56

Kenilworth | 520 Boulevard (21st St.) | 908-931-0888

The French cuisine is "nothing less than superb" at this "quaint" Kenilworth bistro, where chef-owner Philippe Lièvre presents a "constantly changing" seasonal menu, served by an "attentive" staff; *oui*, it can be "as cramped as the Paris Metro at rush hour", and "it's not cheap" either, but the cost is alleviated by BYO – and fans say "bring your best."

Maritime Parc Ⓜ *American/Seafood* 23 | 24 | 21 | $56

Jersey City | Liberty State Park | 84 Audrey Zapp Dr. (Freedom Way) | 201-413-0050 | www.maritimeparc.com

The "stunning views of the adjacent marina" and "magnificent" Manhattan skyline at this "romantic" New American in Jersey City's Liberty State Park "can't be beat" – especially when you can "enjoy the outdoor seating" in summer; it's "expensive", but the seafood-centric offerings are "well prepared and fresh", and served by an "attentive" staff.

Nicholas Ⓞ Ⓜ *American* 28 | 27 | 28 | $103

Red Bank | 160 Rte. 35 S. (bet. Cooper Blvd. & Frost Ave.) | 732-345-9977 | www.restaurantnicholas.com

Nicholas and Melissa Harary's "epitome" of "exquisite" fine New American dining in Red Bank is truly "second to none" – and once again voted the state's Most Popular restaurant and No. 1 for both Food and Service; the prix fixe–only menus of "flawlessly executed" seasonal fare are "presented beautifully" by a "top-notch" staff in a "modern" setting that's "upscale" yet "welcoming", and while the prices make it strictly a "special treat" for most, the "bar menu is a pretty good deal."

Ninety Acres at Natirar Ⓜ *American* 25 | 27 | 24 | $72

Peapack | 2 Main St. (bet. Olde Dutch Rd. & Ramapo Way) | 908-901-9500 | www.ninetyacres.com

Follow the "long and winding road" to this "breathtaking", "palatial" Peapack estate, where the carriage house is now a culinary institute serving chef David C. Felton's "excellent", "inventive" New American cuisine sourced from an on-site farm, alongside an "extensive" wine list; fans tout kitchen-side seating (with a "fun" chef's-choice prix fixe) and a "fantastic" outdoor patio, and while tabs are "extravagant", most agree it's a "special place in every way."

The Peacock Inn Restaurant *American* 26 | 26 | 26 | $72

Princeton | Peacock Inn | 20 Bayard Ln. (bet. Boudinot & Nassau Sts.) | 609-924-1707 | www.thepeacockinn.com

Everything is "top-notch" at this "elegant" Princetonian, from the "excellent" "farm-to-table" American cuisine by Nicholas alum Manuel Perez to the "lovely", "warm" setting in a "luxury" inn near campus; "impeccable" service completes the package, but given the cost, some go only when "someone else is paying."

Peter Shields Inn *American*

26 | 27 | 25 | $60

Cape May | 1301 Beach Ave. (Trenton Ave.) | 609-884-9090 |
www.petershieldsinn.com

Set in a "gorgeous" 1907 beachfront manse, this Cape May American is a "real winner" thanks to the "amazing views", "elegant" digs and "superbly prepared" "classic" fare; "comfortable", "well-spaced seating" and "attentive service" help make for a "quiet retreat", and while tabs are "on the pricey side", a BYO option helps "hold down costs."

Pluckemin Inn ☒ *American*

25 | 24 | 24 | $63

Bedminster | 359 Rte. 206 S. (Pluckemin Way) | 908-658-9292 |
www.pluckemininn.com

"Far from the madding crowd", this "pretty country inn" in Bedminister is "special occasion"–worthy, serving "imaginative", "sophisticated" American fare in a restored farmhouse, where a three-story tower showcases an "astounding" wine list; though "casually elegant" is the presiding vibe, some prefer a "less formal" experience in the tavern or on an outdoor patio.

Rat's Restaurant Ⓜ *French*

25 | 27 | 24 | $61

Hamilton | Grounds for Sculpture | 16 Fairgrounds Rd. (Sculptors Way) |
609-584-7800 | www.ratsrestaurant.org

A "make-believe" "château" nestled in the "gorgeous" gardens of a sculpture park – "what could be more charming?" posit admirers of this "magical" Hamilton French, voted New Jersey's No. 1 for Decor, where "enthusiastic" waiters serve "sublime" cuisine in a "most civilized manner"; an outdoor patio is a good spot to enjoy a "marvelous" Sunday brunch, and while it's "quite expensive", many deem it "worth the price", especially if you "stroll the grounds afterward."

Restaurant Lorena's Ⓜ *French*

28 | 23 | 26 | $61

Maplewood | 168 Maplewood Ave. (bet. Baker St. & Depot Plaza) |
973-763-4460 | www.restaurantlorena.com

Chef-owner Humberto Campos Jr.'s "attention to detail" ensures "artistry in every dish" at this Maplewood "jewel" showcasing his "sublime" French cuisine in a "cozy", "romantic" setting; "exquisite" service adds to a "gourmet experience" that's worthy of a "special occasion", with tabs to match (but a BYO policy helps "keep total costs down"); P.S. jackets are recommended.

Restaurant Serenade *French*

26 | 25 | 25 | $75

Chatham | 6 Roosevelt Ave. (Main St.) | 973-701-0303 |
www.restaurantserenade.com

Offering a "civilized dining experience", this "high-end" Chatham destination "deserves all the accolades" for its "creative presentations" of "phenomenal" French cuisine and "extensive" wine list; though "pants with deep pockets are suggested" given the "expensive" tabs, the "quiet", "romantic" ambiance and "first-class" service make it many diners' "go-to for special occasions."

The Ryland Inn *American*

25 | 24 | 24 | $80

Whitehouse | 115 Old Hwy. 28 (bet. Clark Ln. & Lamington Rd.) |
908-534-4011 | www.rylandinnnj.com

Chef Anthony Bucco (ex New Brunswick's Stage Left) is "breathing new life" into this "venerable" Whitehouse favorite, with "beautiful"

American fare sourced from local farms and prepared "with an emphasis on creativity"; the thoroughly renovated 18th-century building affords "elegance" in a "country setting", while a "superb" tasting menu and "attentive" service help make it seem "worth every crazy penny."

Saddle River Inn 🅼🅼 *American/French* 26 | 25 | 25 | $63

Saddle River | 2 Barnstable Ct. (Allendale Rd.) | 201-825-4016 | www.saddleriverinn.com

"Always top of the class", this "elegant" "gem" in Saddle River is a "longtime favorite" for "superb", "sophisticated" Americana with "French flair"; the "cozy", "beautifully restored" barn makes for a "warm, comfortable atmosphere", and service is "unbelievable", and though all of this "charm" comes with "pricey" tabs, the BYO policy helps keep things a bit more "affordable"; P.S. the ratings may not reflect a recent change in ownership.

Scalini Fedeli 🅼 *Italian* 27 | 24 | 25 | $73

Chatham | 63 Main St. (bet. Parrott Mill Rd. & Tallmadge Ave.) | 973-701-9200 | www.scalinifedeli.com

What "white-linen Italian should be", this Chatham "special-occasion destination" from chef Michael Cetrulo is "excellent from start to finish", with "beautiful presentations" of "creative, delicious" dishes, "top-notch" service and "elegant" Tuscan decor in an 18th-century farmhouse; not surprisingly, all this "refinement" is "expensive", but BYO on weeknights sans corkage "helps to keep the cost down"; P.S. dinner is prix fixe only.

Shumi 🅼 *Japanese* 27 | 16 | 22 | $48

Somerville | 30 S. Doughty Ave. (Veterans Memorial Dr.) | 908-526-8596

"Snag a seat at the convivial bar" and join the "devoted patrons" of this "top-notch" Somerville sushi specialist where the chef is "dedicated to his craft and it shows" in the "quality and freshness" of every morsel; while the no-frills space is in a somewhat "bizarre location" ("one challenge: find it"), and tabs aren't cheap, BYO is a plus and fans say it's "definitely worth the trip."

Sono Sushi *Japanese* 26 | 20 | 23 | $35

Middletown | Village Mall | 1098 Rte. 35 S. (bet. New Monmouth Rd. & Penelope Ln.) | 732-706-3588 | www.sonosushi.net

Fans attest to the "enduring quality" of this Middletown Japanese's "fresh, flavorful" sushi and "authentic" cooked fare, which makes up for "strip-mall surroundings" and digs that some find "dated"; "reasonable" prices, a BYO policy, "charming hospitality" and a "kid-friendly" vibe are further reasons it's been "here for so many years."

Stage Left *American* 25 | 23 | 25 | $69

New Brunswick | 5 Livingston Ave. (George St.) | 732-828-4444 | www.stageleft.com

The "industrious" staff has a "knack" for getting you to performances "on time" at this "sophisticated" New Brunswick "go-to" convenient to the State Theater, where a "wide-ranging yet accessible wine list" accompanies the "delicious" New American fare; while "pricey", fans insist it's "worth every penny" for a "special occasion", and the "mouthwatering burger" makes dining at the bar an appealing "casual option."

	FOOD	DECOR	SERVICE	COST

Steve & Cookie's by the Bay *American*   27 | 24 | 25 | $53

Margate | 9700 Amherst Ave. (Monroe Ave.) | 609-823-1163 |
www.steveandcookies.com

Fans attest "quality is everything" at Cookie Till's "legendary" Margate
New American where "well-trained" servers offer "on-target suggestions" from the menu of "excellent" locally sourced fare and "extensive
wine list"; the mood is "upbeat" in the multiroom space that's usually
packed with an "'in' crowd", which is why regulars recommend "reservations in the summer and on weekends year-round."

Ursino ⌧ *American*   24 | 25 | 22 | $61

Union | Stem Bldg. | 1075 Morris Ave. (bet. Kean Dr. & North Ave.) |
908-249-4099 | www.ursinorestaurant.com

"Attention to detail" is evident in the "innovative", "farm-to-table"
fare at this "special" New American "hidden in a modern building on
campus at Kean University" (it "makes me want to go back to college"
muse fans); the "stylish" setting and "competent" service help justify
"expensive" tabs, and outdoor seating's a "treat" when it's warm.

Varka *Greek/Seafood*   25 | 23 | 23 | $62

Ramsey | 30 N. Spruce St. (Carol St.) | 201-995-9333 |
www.varkarestaurant.com

"Pick your exact piece" from the fresh fish display and the kitchen will
"cook it any way you like" at this "upscale" Greek seafooder in Ramsey
that's known for "top-quality, beautifully prepared" dishes (just prepare for the "sticker shock"); insiders say it generally "gets everything
right, except the noise level" – though summertime patio dining
"eliminates that problem."

Washington Inn *American*   26 | 25 | 25 | $61

Cape May | 801 Washington St. (Jefferson St.) | 609-884-5697 |
www.washingtoninn.com

The "definition of fine dining" for many, this Cape May "classic" "always delivers" with "wonderful" American fare, an "extensive wine
list" and "polished" service; set in a "well-preserved", "romantic"
Victorian plantation house, it boasts several dining rooms, "each with
its own personality", making it "perfect" for a "special dinner", and
while it's "pricey", the "lively bar" has a cheaper menu.

New Orleans

Restaurant	Cuisine
28 Cochon Butcher	Cajun/Sandwiches
Clancy's	Creole
La Provence	Creole/French
Brigtsen's	Contemp. Louisiana
GW Fins	Seafood
Cypress	Creole
Lilette	French
August	French
27 Commander's Palace	Creole
Stella!	American
Bayona	American
Mr. John's	Steak
Boucherie	Southern
Irene's Cuisine	Italian
La Boca	Argentinean/Steak
Sal & Judy's	Creole/Italian
Gautreau's	American/French
Herbsaint	American/French
Château du Lac	French
Nine Roses	Chinese/Vietnamese

OTHER NOTEWORTHY PLACES

Acme Oyster House	Seafood
Atchafalaya	Contemp. Louisiana/Creole
Bistro Daisy	American/Southern
Bon Ton Café	Cajun
Café Du Monde	Coffeehouse/Dessert
Cochon	Cajun
Coquette	American
Dickie Brennan's	Steak
Domenica	Italian
Eleven 79	Creole/Italian
Emeril's	Contemp. Louisiana
Galatoire's	Creole/French
Iris	American
K-Paul's Louisiana Kitchen	Cajun
La Petite Grocery	Contemp. Louisiana/French
Martinique Bistro	French/Seafood
Mr. B's Bistro	Contemp. Louisiana
Patois	American/French
Rue 127	American
Upperline	Contemp. Louisiana

	FOOD	DECOR	SERVICE	COST

Acme Oyster House Seafood

| | 24 | 18 | 22 | $29 |

French Quarter | 724 Iberville St. (bet. Bourbon & Royal Sts.) | 504-522-5973
Metairie | 3000 Veterans Memorial Blvd. (Causeway Blvd.) | 504-309-4056
Covington | 1202 N. Hwy. 190 (bet. Crestwood Blvd. & 17th Ave.) | 985-246-6155
www.acmeoyster.com

It's "a shell of a place" hoot fans of this French Quarter seafood centenarian (with area spin-offs) that "consistently" delivers "fabulous oysters" and other "out-of-this-world", "moderately priced" "Louisiana favorites" with "no pretense" in a "lively", "family-friendly" setting; though it may "seem like a tourist trap" with "lines around the block", "locals love" it too; P.S. "sit at the bar" for the full "shucker experience."

Atchafalaya Contemp. Louisiana/Creole

| | 26 | 23 | 23 | $37 |

Irish Channel | 901 Louisiana Ave. (Laurel St.) | 504-891-9626 | www.atchafalayarestaurant.com

Look for the "giant cast-iron pan" outside this Contemporary Louisianan in the Irish Channel that pleases "adventurous palates" with "divine" "transformations" of Creole staples (though a recent chef change puts the Food rating in question) and a "delectable" Sunday brunch with a "do-it-yourself Bloody Mary bar"; the "high-ceilinged" room adorned with "funky art" exudes a "sultry" "New Orleans vibe", and while the staffers may "get bogged down" by crowds of "locals and a few tourists", they always "thank you on the way out."

August French

| | 28 | 28 | 27 | $73 |

Central Business Dist. | 301 Tchoupitoulas St. (Gravier St.) | 504-299-9777 | www.restaurantaugust.com

John Besh's "unforgettable" CBD flagship "glows with his personality" as the "star" chef's "keen sense of flavors" and devotion to "local ingredients" yield "superb" New French fare "presented like works of art"; a "subtly attentive" staff sees to "well-heeled locals" and "Hollywood celebs" in the "stately but not stuffy" space whose "glittering chandeliers and rich wood accents" "demurely whisper class", and even though dinner prices may require "holding up a bank", Friday lunch is a "steal."

Bayona 🗷 American

| | 27 | 26 | 26 | $59 |

French Quarter | 430 Dauphine St. (bet. Conti & St. Louis Sts.) | 504-525-4455 | www.bayona.com

"New Orleans icon" Susan Spicer "continues to inspire" at this French Quarter New American "slice of heaven" where dishes with "creative" Contemporary Louisiana twists are complemented by a "top-notch wine list" and delivered to the table with "grace"; the mood is "festive" inside the "charming old cottage" or its "Garden of Eden" courtyard, and whether for a "special occasion" or a "surprisingly inexpensive" lunch, it's "not to be missed."

Bistro Daisy 🗷🅼 American/Southern

| | 27 | 23 | 26 | $48 |

Uptown | 5831 Magazine St. (bet. Eleonore St. & Nashville Ave.) | 504-899-6987 | www.bistrodaisy.com

At this "quaint" Uptown "locals' secret" by chef Anton and Diane Schulte, "seasonal ingredients" go into "sophisticated yet unpretentious" takes on New American–Southern fare best enjoyed in tandem with a "wine list that begs you to buy by the bottle"; the "gracious" ser-

	FOOD	DECOR	SERVICE	COST

vice ensures guests "never feel crowded or hurried", keeping the "beautiful little cottage" filled with "smiling people."

Bon Ton Café ☒ Cajun   25 | 22 | 25 | $37

Central Business Dist. | 401 Magazine St. (bet. Natchez & Poydras Sts.) | 504-524-3386 | www.thebontoncafe.com

"Classic", "well-prepared" Cajun (crabmeat au gratin, crawfish étouf-fée) awaits at this CBD "stalwart" that "fills with lawyers and bankers" who still practice the "three-martini power lunch" in "seersucker suits and skirts"; the "chatty" staff can be "opinionated" but "treats you like family" in a "time capsule" of "exposed-brick walls and beamed ceilings", where "nothing changes except the prices"; P.S. closed weekends.

Boucherie ☒ M Southern   27 | 22 | 25 | $34

Carrollton | 8115 Jeannette St. (Carrollton Ave.) | 504-862-5514 | www.boucherie-nola.com

At this "quirky" Carrollton cottage, unstoppable chef/co-owner Nathanial Zimet fashions "innovative but never self-indulgent" up-dates on Southern classics with "unexpected finesse" and offers them at "outrageously reasonable prices"; the "charmingly small" (ok, "cramped") space is "always packed" with "young up-and-comers" ("reservations are a must"), but an "efficient, courteous" staff is quick with "inventive cocktails" and beers from a "thoughtfully curated" list.

Brigtsen's ☒ M Contemp. Louisiana   28 | 23 | 27 | $54

Riverbend | 723 Dante St. (Maple St.) | 504-861-7610 | www.brigtsens.com

"Feel New Orleans in every bite" of "acclaimed chef" Frank Brigtsen's "rich, upscale" Contemporary Louisiana fare at this "hard-to-find" Riverbend cottage "near the levee"; even if the setting's "not for the claustrophobic", most consider it as "cozy" as a "family dining room", overseen by "warm", "wonderful" servers who are "devoid of attitude even though they could get away with it."

Café Du Monde Coffeehouse/Dessert   26 | 20 | 20 | $11

Central Business Dist. | Riverwalk Mktpl. | 500 Port of New Orleans (Poydras St.) | 504-587-0841
French Quarter | French Mkt. | 800 Decatur St. (St. Ann St.) | 504-525-4544 ●⇱
Gretna | Oakwood Mall | 197 Westbank Expwy. (bet. Terry Pkwy. & Whitney Ave.) | 504-365-8600
Kenner | Esplanade Mall | 1401 W. Esplanade Ave. (Delaware Ave.) | 504-468-3588
Kenner | 3245 Williams Blvd. (bet. 32nd & 33rd Sts.) | 504-469-7699
Metairie | 1814 N. Causeway Blvd. (Melrah Dr.) | 985-951-7474
Metairie | Lakeside Shopping Ctr. | 3301 Veterans Memorial Blvd. (bet. Causeway Blvd. & Severn Ave.) | 504-834-8694
Metairie | 4700 Veterans Memorial Blvd. (Lime St.) | 504-888-9770
Covington | 70437 S. Tyler St. (Hyacinth Dr.) | 985-893-0453
www.cafedumonde.com

Tourists "from across the world" join locals winding down "a night on the town" at this 24-hour French Quarter "landmark" whose "light-textured" beignets "heaped with powdered sugar" and "smooth" chic-ory coffee satisfy "sweet cravings" in an "open-air" setting; the service can be "uneven" and every surface "sticky", but focus on the "parade of daily life" for an experience that's as New Orleans "as Mardi Gras and humidity"; P.S. suburban branches minimize "the hassle" but lack the "same atmosphere."

Château du Lac ☒ *French*

27 | 23 | 23 | $46

Old Metairie | 2037 Metairie Rd. (Atherton Dr.) | Metairie | 504-831-3773 | www.chateaudulacbistro.com

"Under the radar" in Old Metairie, this "excellent" bistro from chef Jacques Saleun provides a roster of "classic" "French country fare" and "creative" specials matched by a "knowledgeably selected" wine list; with the help of a "welcoming" staff, it's a "lively" "neighborhood gem" that lets you "escape to France" even when "surrounded by locals."

Clancy's ☒ *Creole*

28 | 24 | 26 | $54

Uptown | 6100 Annunciation St. (Webster St.) | 504-895-1111 | www.clancysneworleans.com

"Old-style New Orleans charm" is alive and well at this Uptown "lo-cals' favorite" serving up "mouthwatering" "haute Creole" fare (like smoked soft-shell crab) and "top-notch martinis" at "somewhat steep" prices; "pitch-perfect" servers "make it their career to know and please" in the "intoxicatingly loud" downstairs dining room that can feel like a "country club without golf", but still "makes you want to be a regular."

Cochon ☒ *Cajun*

27 | 23 | 24 | $43

Warehouse District | 930 Tchoupitoulas St. (Andrew Higgins Dr.) | 504-588-2123 | www.cochonrestaurant.com

The "pig never saw it coming" at this "trendy" Warehouse District Cajun where chefs-owners Donald Link (Cochon Butcher) and Stephen Stryjewski fulfill "porky fantasies" – and "tempt a vegetarian" or two – with "sophisticated home cooking like you can't believe", served amid "boisterous", "industrial yet rustic" surroundings; despite seeming "slightly pricey" to some, it's a kick to "get a ringside seat by the kitchen" and chow down among the faithful on a porcine "pilgrimage."

Cochon Butcher *Cajun/Sandwiches*

28 | 21 | 22 | $20

Warehouse District | 930 Tchoupitoulas St. (Andrew Higgins Dr.) | 504-588-7675 | www.cochonbutcher.com

"A must if you dig the pig", Donald Link's "phenomenal" Warehouse District Cajun earns a resounding "oink" of approval and New Orleans' No. 1 Food rating for its "daring", "decadent" sandwiches, "atypical" daily sides and "well-curated" wine list; the "small", "laid-back" space (right next to Cochon) has "squashed-together" seating and a "constant crowd", so "plan your time of attack carefully" or let the "ultrafriendly" staff send you home with "superb" charcuterie from the "hard-to-resist" deli case.

Commander's Palace *Creole*

27 | 28 | 28 | $65

Garden District | 1403 Washington Ave. (Coliseum St.) | 504-899-8221 | www.commanderspalace.com

"Step into a grand movie" at this "better-than-ever", unapologetically "over-the-top" Garden District Creole and revel in a "shocking, playful and sinful" "gastronomic experience" worthy of "an Oscar" (or at least New Orleans' Most Popular and No. 1 Decor and Service ratings); with a "wine list worth the trip itself" and "impeccable" servers who "actu-ally appear to want to serve", it's no wonder that "locals and tourists

alike" happily invest in a spendy dinner or "delightful" jazz brunch –
after all, this is the "place to bring grandma to assure you're in the
will"; P.S. no shorts or T-shirts; jackets suggested for dinner.

Coquette *American*　　　27 | 26 | 25 | $48

Garden District | 2800 Magazine St. (Washington Ave.) | 504-265-0421 |
www.coquette-nola.com

"Farm-to-table without being ostentatious about it", this "chic" Garden
District bistro by chef/co-owner Michael Stoltzfus impresses a
"young, trendy" clientele with its "ever-changing" New American
menu of "ambrosial", "thought-provoking" dishes backed by "sublime" cocktails; an "enthusiastic" staff ensures that whether soaking
up the "lively" downstairs ambiance or enjoying the "quieter intimacy"
upstairs, fans find it "heavenly on every note"; P.S. the prix fixe lunch
is a "great deal."

Cypress ⊠ Ⓜ *Creole*　　　28 | 22 | 24 | $40

Metairie | 4426 Transcontinental Dr. (bet. Esplanade Ave. & Murphy Dr.) |
504-885-6885 | www.restaurantcypress.com

Smitten surveyors say this "suburban masterpiece" in Metairie "easily
competes" with "New Orleans' finest" thanks to Creole dishes "flavored with a delicate hand" and "specials that never fail to please";
while the "tiny" space "can get noisy", most enjoy the "neighborhood
atmosphere" and suggest that ever-"present" owners, chef Stephen
and manager Katherine Huth, "don't charge enough for the fabulous
food" – no wonder "locals want to keep it their little secret."

Dickie Brennan's Steakhouse *Steak*　　27 | 25 | 26 | $63

French Quarter | 716 Iberville St. (bet. Bourbon & Royal Sts.) |
504-522-2467 | www.dickiebrennanssteakhouse.com

"A traditional steakhouse with a New Orleans flair", this Brennan-
family beef bastion in the French Quarter "does not disappoint" with
its "tender", "immaculate" meat, "perfect sides" and "terrific" drinks
served in a "clubby downstairs cavern" (and at the "fun bar"); the
"young, attentive" staff "exudes Southern hospitality", rounding out
an "extravagant night" that's "worth every dollar."

Domenica *Italian*　　　27 | 25 | 24 | $39

Central Business Dist. | Roosevelt Hotel | 123 Baronne St. (Canal St.) |
504-648-6020 | www.domenicarestaurant.com

At "John Besh's bow to Italy" in the CBD's Roosevelt Hotel, "up-
and-coming" chef Alon Shaya "mans the stoves" to create "imaginative" "culinary adventures" starring "exceptional" pizza, "perfect"
pasta and "house-cured meats"; the "glam", "glossy" and "high-
energy" room is staffed by a "well-trained" team that makes a trip
here "worth every penny" – and a "steal" during the "half-price-
pie" happy hour.

Eleven 79 ⊠ *Creole/Italian*　　　25 | 23 | 23 | $52

Lower Garden Dist. | 1179 Annunciation St. (bet. Calliope & Erato Sts.) |
504-299-1179 | www.eleven79.com

"Politicians and local celebs" indulge in "rich, garlicky" "upscale" Italian
with "Creole touches" at this Lower Garden District "hideaway" by
"New Orleans legend" Joseph Segreto, who "knows his customers"
and watches over the "entertaining" staff; devotees of the "hard-to-

find" "throwback" suggest you "bring someone you're not supposed to be with", ignore the "elevated" prices and be "enveloped" by "old-world charm" worthy of "Mr. Sinatra."

Emeril's Contemp. Louisiana

26 | 25 | 25 | $66

Warehouse District | 800 Tchoupitoulas St. (Julia St.) | 504-528-9393 | www.emerils.com

"Grand master" Emeril Lagasse "puts on a show" at this "up-to-the-hype" Warehouse District "standard-bearer" specializing in "huge portions" of "delectable" Contemporary Louisiana favorites and personal signatures (barbecue shrimp, "sublime" banana cream pie) that will "floor" you with "unexpected flavor"; "gorgeously modern", "jumping with energy" and staffed by "prompt", "intelligent foodies", it's a "high-roller heaven" where "sitting at the chef's bar" is "unforgettable."

Galatoire's M Creole/French

26 | 26 | 27 | $64

French Quarter | 209 Bourbon St. (Iberville St.) | 504-525-2021 | www.galatoires.com

"New Orleans wouldn't be New Orleans without" this century-old French Quarter "institution" where "Southern hospitality" reigns supreme as tux-wearing servers "guide you" to "stellar" seafood and other "pricey" French-Creole "warhorses done with aplomb"; fueled by "copious" drinks, "locals and dignitaries" in "seersucker suits" gather in the "elegantly tiled" main dining room for lunch that's "always a party" – arguably "the most fun you can have over a white tablecloth"; P.S. jackets required after 5 PM and all day Sunday; reservations only accepted upstairs.

Gautreau's ⊠ American/French

27 | 25 | 27 | $58

Uptown | 1728 Soniat St. (Danneel St.) | 504-899-7397 | www.gautreausrestaurant.com

The "elite meet" at this "secluded" Uptown bistro for chef Sue Zemanick's "elegant", "inspired" New American–New French cooking backed by an "outstanding little wine list"; "wonderful host" Patrick Singley oversees a "cordial" staff in the "jewel box" of a converted pharmacy where the "lighting makes everybody look good" and the "dreamy" dinners are "worth the cost" (and the "search").

GW Fins Seafood

28 | 26 | 27 | $53

French Quarter | 808 Bienville St. (bet. Bourbon & Dauphine Sts.) | 504-581-3467 | www.gwfins.com

"Simple" yet "beautifully done", "lighter" preparations of fish "flown in from all areas of the oceans" are "accompanied by an extensive wine list" at this "pricey" French Quarter "seafood mecca" set in a "swanky" "open warehouse space"; the "docentlike" staff "bends over backwards" to keep customers happy, so many wonder why it's relatively "under the radar" when it's such "a catch"; P.S. no T-shirts or flip-flops.

Herbsaint ⊠ American/French

27 | 23 | 25 | $48

Warehouse District | 701 St. Charles Ave. (Girod St.) | 504-524-4114 | www.herbsaint.com

Chef/co-owner Donald Link (Cochon) "makes you swoon" with his "refined yet joyous" New American–New French cooking at this Warehouse District "delight" that "locals swear by" for a "hopping" "business lunch" or "hip", "casually elegant" dinner; there's "gracious service without formality", keeping guests "all smiles" as they share "wonderful small plates", sip "exciting" drinks and watch "passing streetcars on St. Charles Avenue" from the "huge windows."

Irene's Cuisine ☒ Italian   27 | 23 | 25 | $45

French Quarter | 539 St. Philip St. (bet. Chartres & Decatur Sts.) | 504-529-8811

A "glorious" garlic scent wafts from this French Quarter haunt "beloved by locals" for its "fantastic" Italian plates "with a Nola twist"; expect the "personable" staff to "usher you to a romantic sitting room" (with a "rockin' piano bar") when you enter, because "even with a reservation", "you will wait" for a table in the "charming" "speakeasy" space.

Iris ☒ American   25 | 22 | 22 | $50

French Quarter | Bienville House Hotel | 321 N. Peters St. (bet. Bienville & Conti Sts.) | 504-299-3944 | www.irisneworleans.com

With a "gentle touch" that lets "each ingredient shine", chef/co-owner Ian Schnoebelen produces "elevated but not stuffy" New American fare at this "chic" "sleeper" in the French Quarter's Bienville House; Laurie Casebonne welcomes the "young, hip clientele" with an "attentive" team and an "infectious laugh" as "amazing" cocktails fuel an experience that "gets better with each visit."

K-Paul's Louisiana Kitchen ☒ Cajun   26 | 22 | 24 | $53

French Quarter | 416 Chartres St. (bet. Conti & St. Louis Sts.) | 877-553-3401 | www.kpauls.com

"The man who brought Cajun into the mainstream", Paul Prudhomme, and his "one-of-a-kind" French Quarter kitchen are "still going strong" as exec chef Paul Miller delivers "upscale" eats with "in-your-face flavors" along with a "bargain" "order-at-the-counter" lunch Thursday–Saturday; the "professional" servers are "excellent educators" for "tourists" and "foodies" who make their "pilgrimage" to the "down-home", "comfortable" locale, which "deserves repeat visits, even on the same trip."

La Boca ☒ Argentinean/Steak   27 | 22 | 24 | $55

Warehouse District | 857 Fulton St. (St. Joseph St.) | 504-525-8205 | www.labocasteaks.com

"You are *loca* if you don't try La Boca" say carnivores crazy for this Argentine steakhouse in the Warehouse District specializing in "beautifully executed", "less typical cuts" paired with "full-bodied wines" by a "knowledgeable" team; the "bohemian" look evokes "Buenos Aires", and it's "priced reasonably for the caliber", suiting the crowd of "service-industry folks, young foodies" and others who urge "go for a pisco sour", "go in a group of four and do the tasting menu" or just "go and indulge."

La Petite Grocery Ⓜ Contemp. Louisiana/French   26 | 24 | 25 | $47

Uptown | 4238 Magazine St. (General Pershing St.) | 504-891-3377 | www.lapetitegrocery.com

At this "quaint"-looking Uptown bistro, "rock-star" chef/co-owner Justin Devillier combines "clean flavors" into "gustatory pleasures" that "lean to French" with a Contemporary Louisiana bent; "congenial" staffers help make it a "serene" "respite from the busy Magazine

Street scene", so even if tabs get "slightly steep" for some, most simply revel in this little "sliver of utopia."

La Provence ⓜ Creole/French
28 | 28 | 28 | $56

Lacombe | 25020 Hwy. 190 (bet. Bremermann & Raymond Rds.) | 985-626-7662 | www.laprovencerestaurant.com

"When you can't fly to Provence, cross the lake" to Lacombe for John Besh's "rustic" yet "upscale" French-Creole made with "fresh, flavorful ingredients" (many of which are "raised on the property") and served in "charming" "country-manor" surroundings; "sublime" service ensures that an "intimate" evening or even just Sunday brunch is "memorable for all the right reasons" – and the "must-try" prix fixe is an "excellent value" to boot.

Lilette ⓈⓂ French
28 | 25 | 26 | $50

Uptown | 3637 Magazine St. (Antonine St.) | 504-895-1636 | www.liletterestaurant.com

"Beautiful people", "young professionals" and "movie stars" flock to this "expensive but divine" Uptown "corner bistro" to dine on "artistic", "delicious" French fare "carefully crafted" by chef-owner John Harris and presented with "sexy" drinks by "spot-on" servers; an "understated" "blend of old and modern", the "converted storefront" dining room can "get a little loud", so some raters recommend the patio for a "Parisian" experience.

Martinique Bistro ⓜ French/Seafood
26 | 24 | 23 | $47

Uptown | 5908 Magazine St. (bet. Nashville & State Sts.) | 504-891-8495 | www.martiniquebistro.com

"Savvy locals" love chef Eric LaBouchere's "modern", "high-end" versions of French bistro "classics" (particularly seafood) at this Uptown "gem" showcasing "tantalizing local ingredients" on a "frequently changing" menu; while the "well-trained" staff and "warm" atmosphere transport you to a "small French village", "romantics" say "nothing is better" than the "exquisite" "secret garden" on a "sultry" New Orleans night.

Mr. B's Bistro Contemp. Louisiana
26 | 25 | 25 | $48

French Quarter | 201 Royal St. (Iberville St.) | 504-523-2078 | www.mrbsbistro.com

Locals "celebrate birthdays" and "impress out-of-towners" at this "lively" French Quarter "staple" from the Brennan family whose "can't-go-wrong" Contemporary Louisiana repertoire includes a "bucket-list-worthy" brunch, an "affordable" lunch and classics like gumbo ya-ya and the "wonderful" if "messy" BBQ shrimp ("wear your bib or you'll be sorry"); with its "accommodating" service and "clubby", "dark-wood" backdrop, it takes you back to a time "when proper manners were still observed" and a restaurant meal was a "rare treat."

Mr. John's Steakhouse ⓈⓂ Steak
27 | 24 | 26 | $57

Lower Garden Dist. | 2111 St. Charles Ave. (bet. Jackson Ave. & Josephine St.) | 504-679-7697 | www.mrjohnssteakhouse.com

"Satisfy your steak cravings" at this "pricey but well worth it" Lower Garden District "sleeper" delivering both "superb" Italian specialties and "melt-in-your-mouth" meats that arrive "sizzling"; "professional and precise", the staff tends to a "combination of locals and tourists" in an "old New Orleans" setting that exudes "comfortable elegance" and offers "views of St. Charles Avenue."

Nine Roses *Chinese/Vietnamese*   27 | 19 | 22 | $23
(aka Hoa Hong 9)

Gretna | 1100 Stephens St. (O'Connor St.) | 504-366-7665

"Worth the drive across the bridge", this Gretna "favorite" is prized for "delicious", "authentic" Vietnamese dishes on an "endless" menu that "resembles a novel" (although some suggest you "avoid the Chinese" chapters); service is "friendly", and while the "large venue" lacks luster, the "inexpensive", "generous" portions "never disappoint."

Patois Ⓜ *American/French*   26 | 23 | 24 | $48

Uptown | 6078 Laurel St. (Webster St.) | 504-895-9441 | www.patoisnola.com

There's a "buzz" in a "quiet pocket of Uptown" thanks to this "so-cool" French–New American where "talented" chef/co-owner Aaron Burgau crafts a "confident" "farm-to-table" menu bolstered by "eclectic" cocktails, a "standout" Sunday brunch and "good value"; generally strong service "makes you want to tip" the "hipsters" overseeing the "adorable" digs, but "boy is it busy" – and "noisy" – with throngs of "in-the-know tourists" and "discerning locals" who declare it New Orleans' "new breed."

Rue 127 Ⓢ *American*   27 | 23 | 25 | $46

Mid-City | 127 N. Carrollton Ave. (Iberville St.) | 504-483-1571 | www.rue127.com

A "loyal following" has discovered this "hidden" Mid-City shotgun house where "greatness" "comes out of the kitchen" in the form of "simply prepared" but "flawlessly executed" New American from chef-owner Ray Gruezke; "well staffed", the "intimate" (and "tiny") quarters foster a "relaxed fine-dining atmosphere" "perfect for a date" or any time you seek an "exquisite experience" that's somewhat "pricey, but money well spent."

Sal & Judy's Ⓜ *Creole/Italian*   27 | 21 | 25 | $40

Lacombe | 27491 Hwy. 190 (14th St.) | 985-882-9443 | www.salandjudysrestaurant.com

"Be prepared to step back in time" at this "bargain" Creole–Southern Italian in Lacombe where chef-owner Sal Impastato brings "his Italian flair" to "fresh Louisiana produce" in "delicious" dishes that require an "extra car for leftovers"; the "small" setting evokes a "family home" and the staff is "attentive" – though a few feel it caters more to "regulars" who snap up the "hard-to-get reservations."

Stella! *American*   27 | 26 | 27 | $111

French Quarter | Hotel Provincial | 1032 Chartres St. (bet. St. Philip St. & Ursulines Ave.) | 504-587-0091 | www.restaurantstella.com

At this "romantic" "jewel" from chef-owner Scott Boswell "tucked away in the Quarter", the "uncompromising" New American cuisine employs "exotic ingredients" and "seemingly kooky combinations" that become "works of art" "begging to be photographed"; each night the staff performs a "dance" that's "a sight to behold", and even if you "gulp twice when you get the check", acolytes insist the experience warrants the "exclamation point" in the name; P.S. four- and seven-course prix fixe menus only.

Upperline ⓜ *Contemp. Louisiana*   27 | 25 | 26 | $51

Uptown | 1413 Upperline St. (bet. Pitt & Prytania Sts.) | 504-891-9822 |
www.upperline.com

"Original renditions of traditional favorites" impress at this Uptown "hideaway for locals" that "still hits the mark" with an "unusual" Contemporary Louisiana menu and "unmatched hospitality" via "pure New Orleans" "host with the most" JoAnn Clevenger; set in an 1877 townhouse covered with "art ranging from the beautiful to the bizarre", it's a "treasure of the Big Easy" where a meal feels "like visiting a dear old friend."

New York City

TOP FOOD RANKING

	Restaurant	Cuisine
29	Le Bernardin	French/Seafood
	Bouley	French
28	Per Se	American/French
	Daniel	French
	Eleven Madison	French
	Jean Georges	French
	Sasabune	Japanese
	Sushi Yasuda	Japanese
	La Grenouille	French
	Gramercy Tavern	American
	Sushi Seki	Japanese
	Marea	Italian/Seafood
	Degustation	French/Spanish
27	Gotham B&G	American
	Mas (Farmhouse)	American
	Peter Luger	Steak
	Chef's Table/Brooklyn Fare	French
	Soto	Japanese
	Annisa	American
	Picholine	French/Mediterranean
	Kyo Ya	Japanese
	Lucali	Pizza
	Torrisi	Italian
	L'Artusi	Italian
	Scalini Fedeli	Italian

OTHER NOTEWORTHY PLACES

ABC Kitchen	American
Aureole	American
Babbo	Italian
Balthazar	French
Betony	American
Blue Hill	American
Carbone	Italian
Del Posto	Italian
Eataly	Italian
Four Seasons	American
Grocery	American
Katz's Deli	Deli
Keens	Steak
Lafayette	French
Milos	Greek/Seafood
Minetta Tavern	French
Modern	American/French
Momofuku Ssäm	American
Nobu	Japanese

NoMad	American/European				
Red Rooster	American				
River Café	American				
Telepan	American				
21 Club	American				
Union Square Cafe	American				

ABC Kitchen *American*

26 | 24 | 23 | $59

Flatiron | ABC Carpet & Home | 35 E. 18th St. (bet. B'way & Park Ave. S.) | 212-475-5829 | www.abckitchennyc.com

An "eco-friendly delight" from Jean-Georges Vongerichten, this "refreshingly" "whimsical" American in the Flatiron's ABC Carpet & Home "continues to amaze" as chef Dan Kluger's "organic sourcing" and "farm-to-table approach" yield an "exquisite", "seasonal menu" presented by a "knowledgeable" staff; access to the "energized space" remains a "challenge", but "keep on trying" for a rez – it's "worth it."

Annisa *American*

27 | 24 | 26 | $87

W Village | 13 Barrow St. (bet. 7th Ave. S. & W. 4th St.) | 212-741-6699 | www.annisarestaurant.com

"Anita Lo's care and craft" continue to "pay off" at this "high-end" West Village "gem", a "civilized respite" renowned for its "brilliant, Asian-inspired" New American fare, "superb service" and "understated elegance"; a "smart", "soothing" space where you "can actually have a conversation" rounds out this "rare treat."

Aureole *American*

26 | 24 | 25 | $88

W 40s | Bank of America Tower | 135 W. 42nd St. (bet. B'way & 6th Ave.) | 212-319-1660 | www.charliepalmer.com

A rare "civilized" "oasis" near Times Square, Charlie Palmer's "first-class" New American "does not disappoint" those anticipating "inspired" cuisine, a "fabulous wine list", "pampering" service and an overall "polished" milieu; the "formal" main dining room's prix fixe-only pricing is an "indulgence" for "expense-accounters", but going à la carte in the "vibrant" front bar is "lighter on the wallet."

Babbo ● *Italian*

27 | 23 | 24 | $82

G Village | 110 Waverly Pl. (bet. MacDougal St. & 6th Ave.) | 212-777-0303 | www.babbonyc.com

"Year after year", the Batali-Bastianich team's Village "standard-bearer" for "elevated Italian" cooking "lives up to its rep" with a "daring and fulfilling" menu that highlights "unrivaled pasta" in "warm" carriage-house surrounds filled with "energized" "music and hubbub"; it's still "worth the Byzantine reservations policy" and "big bucks" for a "dynamic" outing that's "not to be missed."

Balthazar ● *French*

24 | 23 | 21 | $57

SoHo | 80 Spring St. (Crosby St.) | 212-965-1414 | www.balthazarny.com

There's "never a dull moment" at Keith McNally's "high-profile" SoHo brasserie, where the "belle epoque" decor, "heady Parisian atmosphere" and "memorable" French fare ("can't-be-beat" breakfasts included) are a "magnet" for a "SoHo microcosm" of "locals", "moneyed tourists" and stray "celebrities"; the "controlled chaos" comes with "rushed" service and "daunting" decibels, but it's a certified "classique."

Betony ⎇ *American* — | — | — | E

W 50s | 41 W. 57th St. (bet. 5th & 6th Aves.) | 212-465-2400 | www.betony-nyc.com

Helmed by Eleven Madison Park alums, this upscale arrival in Midtown's former Brasserie Pushkin space puts forth playful, artfully plated New American dishes matched with a creative cocktail list; the quiet upstairs dining room is suited to intimate dinners, while a bar area with vaulted ceilings is prime for a pre-curtain tipple before heading to nearby Carnegie Hall.

Blue Hill *American* 27 | 23 | 26 | $89

G Village | 75 Washington Pl. (bet. MacDougal St. & 6th Ave.) | 212-539-1776 | www.bluehillfarm.com

Dan Barber's "farm-to-table" "temple", this "top-tier" Village American "consistently wows" with "heavenly" "locavore" cuisine that "brings together the best ingredients and makes them shine"; a "serene", "sophisticated" venue where the staff "couldn't be more engaged", it's "well worth" the rez drama and "high-end" cost ("what's good enough for Mr. President . . .").

Bouley ⎇ *French* 29 | 27 | 28 | $116

TriBeCa | 163 Duane St. (bet. Hudson St. & W. B'way) | 212-964-2525 | www.davidbouley.com

"Engaging all the senses", David Bouley's TriBeCa "masterpiece" presents "superb", "French-decadence-at-its-best" cuisine, "consistently superior" service and a "beautiful", "formal" (jackets required) setting that add up to a "wonderful overall experience"; it's "among NYC's true elite", with prices to match, but when you seek an "unforgettable" repast, it's "hard to beat"; P.S. the $55 lunch prix fixe is a "bargain."

Carbone ◉ *Italian* ▽ 21 | 21 | 21 | $93

G Village | 181 Thompson St. (bet. Bleecker & Houston Sts.) | 212-254-3000 | www.carbonenewyork.com

Among NYC's "hottest" tickets, the Torrisi boys' "upscale" ode to Italo-American nostalgia in the Village's erstwhile Rocco's space delivers "fine" red-sauce classics theatrically presented by "jovial" tuxedoed waiters; it's an "upbeat", "celeb"-sprinkled "scene" with a '60s soundtrack, and while some find its "stagey" touches a bit much – ditto the "lotta moolah" prices – "when you see Jake Gyllenhaal and Jerry Seinfeld, you know the place has got to be good."

Chef's Table at Brooklyn Fare ⎇ *French* 27 | 20 | 25 | $332

Downtown Bklyn | 200 Schermerhorn St. (bet. Bond & Hoyt Sts.) | Brooklyn | 718-243-0050 | www.brooklynfare.com

Affirming "Brooklyn's continued place" on the "NYC cuisine scene", this 18-seat prep kitchen in a Schermerhorn Street grocery presents Japanese-influenced French cooking from "extraordinary chef" Cesar Ramirez, favoring the "privileged" few who score "elusive" reservations with 20-plus "magical" small plates and "close-to-flawless" service; it may "take a second mortgage" to settle the $255 prix fixe–only tab, but "save up the dough" and "keep redialing" – "you won't regret it."

	FOOD	DECOR	SERVICE	COST

Daniel ⛌ *French*   28 | 28 | 28 | $146

E 60s | 60 E. 65th St. (bet. Madison & Park Aves.) | 212-288-0033 |
www.danielnyc.com

Still the "hautest of haute" after two decades, Daniel Boulud's "magnificent" Eastsider offers a "religious experience" via "otherworldly"
prix fixe–only New French cuisine, an "exquisite", jackets-required
setting and near-"flawless" service; sure, you'll need a "Brinks truck"
to settle the bill, but "it's worth the gold" to "dine in heaven"; P.S. the
comparatively casual lounge offers à la carte dining.

Degustation ● *French/Spanish*   28 | 20 | 24 | $84

E Village | 239 E. Fifth St. (bet. 2nd & 3rd Aves.) | 212-979-1012 |
www.degustation-nyc.com

"Intimate" and "extraordinary" in equal measure, Grace and Jack
Lamb's "tiny" Franco-Spanish East Villager serves up "exquisite",
"smack-in-the-taste-buds" small plates via "friendly" chefs who work
their "magic" in an open, behind-the-bar kitchen; be warned though,
the "dollar-to-calorie ratio" isn't always favorable.

Del Posto *Italian*   26 | 27 | 26 | $111

Chelsea | 85 10th Ave. (bet. 15th & 16th Sts.) | 212-497-8090 |
www.delposto.com

Another "incredible dining experience" delivered by Mario, Joe and
Lidia, this Chelsea "stunner" serves up "masterful" "upscale Italian"
cuisine and "unrivaled" wines in "opulent" balconied environs overseen by a "first-class" crew; yes, the prices can seem "punitive" –
"have a grappa ready when the check arrives" – but hey, it's "cheaper
than flying to Italy."

Eataly *Italian*   23 | 19 | 17 | $41

Flatiron | 200 Fifth Ave. (bet. 23rd & 24th Sts.) | 212-229-2560 |
www.eataly.com

A "sprawling" "cornucopia of Italian delights", this "three-ring-circus"
Flatiron food hall from the Batali-Bastianich team doles out "heavenly"
pastas, pizzas, veggies, fish, cheese, coffee and gelato from stations
set within a gourmet "mercato"; "victims of their own success", it's
also a "daunting" "madhouse" with limited seating, but most agree
"the B and B team did it right."

Eleven Madison Park *French*   28 | 28 | 28 | $254

Flatiron | 11 Madison Ave. (24th St.) | 212-889-0905 |
www.elevenmadisonpark.com

"Magical" is how admirers describe Daniel Humm's French "knockout" next to Madison Square Park, where "well-choreographed",
"theatrical" tasting menus (think "card tricks") feature "exquisite"
dishes and "memorable" wine pairings, served with "perfect precision" by an "amazing" pro staff in "spectacular" "landmark" digs;
you may need to "take out a mortgage" first, but it "doesn't get much
better" than this.

Four Seasons ⛌ *American*   27 | 28 | 27 | $103

E 50s | 99 E. 52nd St. (bet. Lexington & Park Aves.) | 212-754-9494 |
www.fourseasonsrestaurant.com

Midtown's "gold standard" of "classic luxury" draws "elite" folks
with "delectable" New American cuisine, a "timeless" midcentury

modern setting and "flawless service" under the aegis of owners Alex von Bidder and Julian Niccolini; the Grill Room is a magnet for lunchtime "movers and shakers" while the Pool Room is best for "romance", but either way the tabs are "extravagant" and jackets are de rigueur for gents.

Gotham Bar & Grill *American* | 27 | 25 | 26 | $84 |

G Village | 12 E. 12th St. (bet. 5th Ave. & University Pl.) | 212-620-4020 | www.gothambarandgrill.com

"Still going strong" after 30 years, "cooking genius" Alfred Portale's "delightful" Village "destination" scores "high marks" all around, from the "towering", "wickedly delicious" New American cuisine and "professional" service to the "classy, airy" room; it's "a splurge sort of place" for sure, but the $25 prix fixe lunch is a "bargain."

Gramercy Tavern *American* | 28 | 26 | 27 | $120 |

Flatiron | 42 E. 20th St. (bet. B'way & Park Ave. S.) | 212-477-0777 | www.gramercytavern.com

"A classic that seems to maintain its standing effortlessly", Danny Meyer's Flatiron "favorite" promises a "wow experience" featuring chef Michael Anthony's "top-of-the-line" New American cuisine, "superlative" pro service and a "beautiful", "flower-filled" atmosphere; while you'll spend a "handsome sum" to dine in the prix fixe–only main room, the "fabulous à la carte offerings" in the front tavern are a somewhat "more affordable" option.

The Grocery 🖾 Ⓜ *American* | 27 | 18 | 25 | $64 |

Carroll Gardens | 288 Smith St. (bet. Sackett & Union Sts.) | Brooklyn | 718-596-3335 | www.thegroceryrestaurant.com

"Carefully sourced", "superbly executed" New American food served with a "warm, personal touch" makes this enduring Smith Street "jewel" one of "Brooklyn's finest culinary experiences"; given the "no-frills", "closetlike" dining room, insiders say it's "best when you can sit in the back garden."

Jean Georges *French* | 28 | 27 | 28 | $153 |

W 60s | Trump Int'l Hotel | 1 Central Park W. (61st St.) | 212-299-3900 | www.jean-georgesrestaurant.com

"Every bit deserving of its praise", Jean-Georges Vongerichten's CPW culinary "cathedral" persists as a "paragon" of "sophisticated" service and "marvelously inventive" New French cuisine, with "superb wines to match"; the "serene, civilized" (jackets required) setting rounds out the "top-notch dining experience" that's "priced accordingly" – though the $38 prix fixe lunch promises the same "high quality" without "breaking the bank."

Katz's Delicatessen 🍴 *Deli* | 24 | 11 | 14 | $25 |

LES | 205 E. Houston St. (Ludlow St.) | 212-254-2246 | www.katzsdelicatessen.com

Slinging "piled-high" pastrami sandwiches and other "old-time Jewish deli" staples since 1888, this cash-only LES "legend" is generally "packed" with "tourists and locals alike"; the "cafeteria-style" digs evoke a "bygone period" while the "surly-but-lovable" staff is a slice of "real NY", but "for the ultimate" experience, movie buffs suggest "sit at the *When Harry Met Sally* table."

	FOOD	DECOR	SERVICE	COST

Keens Steakhouse *Steak*
26 | 24 | 24 | $76

Garment District | 72 W. 36th St. (bet. 5th & 6th Aves.) | 212-947-3636 | www.keens.com

You don't have to be a carnivore to appreciate the "rich history" of this circa-1885 Garment District "meat house", though "outstanding" steaks and "glorious" mutton chops ("yeah, you read that right") are key to its "charm"; with "seamless" service, a "superb" scotch selection and thousands of antique clay pipes "adorning the ceiling", it "doesn't get more old NY."

Kyo Ya ● *Japanese*
27 | 24 | 25 | $99

E Village | 94 E. Seventh St., downstairs (1st Ave.) | 212-982-4140

With "stunningly good" Kyoto-style dishes "meticulously arranged" on an "array of pottery", the "presentation alone is worth the trip" to this East Village "temple to kaiseki"; "attentive" service helps justify "expensive" tabs, but reservations are a must, given the "intimate" setting.

Lafayette *French*
∇ 19 | 22 | 17 | $72

NoHo | 380 Lafayette St. (Great Jones St.) | 212-533-3000 | www.lafayetteny.com

This much anticipated newcomer from chef Andrew Carmellini (The Dutch, Locanda Verde) offers "classic" French country cooking in the NoHo space that was formerly Chinatown Brasserie (the sprawling setting done up in "pseudo belle epoque style" also includes an on-site bakery and several private rooms); all-day hours make access a bit easier, but brace yourself for crowds and waits at prime times.

La Grenouille ⊠Ⓜ *French*
28 | 28 | 28 | $113

E 50s | 3 E. 52nd St. (bet. 5th & Madison Aves.) | 212-752-1495 | www.la-grenouille.com

With "lavish flower displays" amid "magnificent", "artfully decorated" environs ("where Truman Capote entertained his swans"), the "visual feast is beyond compare" at Charles Masson's "transporting" East Side "NYC classic", which is equally beloved for its "exquisite" haute French cuisine and "seamless" service; the "first-class" experience is "worth your last dollar" – though the $38 upstairs lunch deal is a "bargain."

L'Artusi *Italian*
27 | 23 | 24 | $61

W Village | 228 W. 10th St. (bet. Bleecker & Hudson Sts.) | 212-255-5757 | www.lartusi.com

"Something special" from the Dell'anima team, this West Village Italian "justifiably lures throngs" with "top-notch" cooking matched with an "impressive" wine list (the "hip vibe", "pretty" decor and "snap-to-it" service don't hurt, either); sure, it's pricey and sometimes "overcrowded", but the payoff is "stylish" dining.

Le Bernardin ⊠ *French/Seafood*
29 | 28 | 28 | $169

W 50s | 155 W. 51st St. (bet. 6th & 7th Aves.) | 212-554-1515 | www.le-bernardin.com

Dining doesn't get much more "blissful" than at this "sublime" Midtown French seafooder via Maguy Le Coze and chef Eric Ripert, a near "religious experience" where "exquisite" meals, "meticulous" service and an "impressive", revamped room have again earned it Top Food and Most Popular honors in NYC; granted, the tabs are equally "extraordinary" –

the prix fixe–only dinners start at $130 – but then again, it's "fabulous in every way"; P.S. a no-reserving lounge offers small plates, while a neighboring wine bar and private dining room in the former Palio/Piano Due spaces are in the works.

Lucali ⊉ *Pizza* | 27 | 19 | 19 | $27 |

Carroll Gardens | 575 Henry St. (bet. Carroll St. & 1st Pl.) | Brooklyn | 718-858-4086

"If you can get in", the pies and calzones are mighty darn "awesome" at this Carroll Gardens, Brooklyn, "neighborhood" pizzeria, again voted No. 1 in NYC; it takes neither credit cards nor reservations, and "long waits" are the norm, but the BYO policy is "pretty cool."

Marea *Italian/Seafood* | 28 | 26 | 26 | $105 |

W 50s | 240 Central Park S. (bet. B'way & 7th Ave.) | 212-582-5100 | www.marea-nyc.com

"Memorable" is putting it mildly at chef Michael White's Columbus Circle "stunner", again voted NYC's No. 1 Italian thanks to "exquisite" seafood and pasta dispatched in a "quiet", "contemporary" setting by a "skilled, unobtrusive" team; it draws a "dressed-up" crowd of "celebs" and "one-percenters" who bring an "extra credit card" to settle the "astronomical" checks – though lunch is a "more affordable" option.

Mas (Farmhouse) ◑ *American* | 27 | 25 | 26 | $96 |

W Village | 39 Downing St. (bet. Bedford & Varick Sts.) | 212-255-1790 | www.masfarmhouse.com

"Everything you could ask for in a dining experience", this "cozy" West Village American is a "foodie must", showcasing the "amazing", "farm-to-table" skills of chef Galen Zamarra; "polished" service and an "intimate" ambiance set the stage for "romantic" dalliances, and although decidedly pricey, it's "worth every penny."

Milos ◑ *Greek/Seafood* | 27 | 24 | 24 | $87 |

W 50s | 125 W. 55th St. (bet. 6th & 7th Aves.) | 212-245-7400 | www.milos.ca

"Absolutely delectable" seafood arrives in a "sleek", "airy" room at this "gold-standard" Midtown Hellenic, where the "just-caught" catch is as "impeccable" as the "brisk" service; "by-the-pound pricing" adds up to "sky-high" tabs, but the lunch and pre-theater prix fixes are "experiments in Greek austerity."

Minetta Tavern ◑ *French* | 24 | 21 | 21 | $67 |

G Village | 113 MacDougal St. (Minetta Ln.) | 212-475-3850 | www.minettatavernny.com

Channeling "long-gone better times", Keith McNally's "retro" remodel of a classic 1937 Village tavern is still "sceney" thanks to French cooking that's as "delicious" as the "Madonna-Gwyneth-Sting" celeb-sightings; the "back room" is the place to sit and the "epic" Black Label burger the thing to order, provided you can snag a "difficult reservation."

The Modern *American/French* | 26 | 26 | 25 | $127 |

W 50s | Museum of Modern Art | 9 W. 53rd St. (bet. 5th & 6th Aves.) | 212-333-1220 | www.themodernnyc.com

"Pure class all the way", this Danny Meyer "triumph" is a "truly special" MoMA showcase for "inspired" French–New American cooking served by a "choreographed" team; the "exquisite" view of the sculpture garden helps justify the "steep" prix fixe–only tabs, though "more affordable" small plates are available à la carte in the "busy" front bar.

Momofuku Ssäm Bar ● *American* 25 | 17 | 20 | $50

E Village | 207 Second Ave. (13th St.) | 212-254-3500 | www.momofuku.com

"Truly creative", David Chang's "cool" East Villager rolls out a "mad-value", Asian-accented American menu that's highlighted by a "to-die-for" bo ssäm pork shoulder feast; "stark" looks and "loud" decibels come with the territory, as do "long lines."

Nobu *Japanese* 27 | 23 | 24 | $84

TriBeCa | 105 Hudson St. (Franklin St.) | 212-219-0500

Nobu 57 *Japanese*

W 50s | 40 W. 57th St. (bet. 5th & 6th Aves.) | 212-757-3000

Nobu, Next Door *Japanese*

TriBeCa | 105 Hudson St. (Franklin St.) | 212-334-4445 www.noburestaurants.com

Nobu Matsuhisa's 20-year-old TriBeCa flagship "has lost none of its luster", still offering "exceptional" Japanese-Peruvian fare to an "attractive" crowd in a "theatrical", David Rockwell–designed space; its "more casual" next-door offshoot and more "touristy" Midtown outlet are "just as delicious" – and just as "expensive."

NoMad *American/European* 27 | 26 | 24 | $89

Chelsea | NoMad Hotel | 1170 Broadway (28th St.) | 347-472-5660 | www.thenomadhotel.com

"All the hype is justified" at Daniel Humm and Will Guidara's NoMad Hotel "stunner", offering a "first-rate" American-European menu led by what may be the "best chicken dish on the planet"; the multiroom setting is "stylish", the service "suave" and the bar scene "sexy", so even though it's "definitely not cheap", it's still virtually "impossible to get a table" here.

Per Se *American/French* 28 | 28 | 29 | $325

W 60s | Time Warner Ctr. | 10 Columbus Circle (60th St. at B'way) | 212-823-9335 | www.perseny.com

"Unpretentious perfection" starts with the "superb" nine-course tasting menu at chef Thomas Keller's "flawless" French–New American in the Time Warner Center and continues with "inspiring" Central Park views and "approachable", "amazingly well-orchestrated" service (again voted No. 1 in NYC); granted, the $295 set price may be "astronomical", but overall this jackets-required destination is "hard to top" for a "bucket-list" indulgence.

Peter Luger Steak House ✐ *Steak* 27 | 16 | 21 | $83

Williamsburg | 178 Broadway (Driggs Ave.) | Brooklyn | 718-387-7400 | www.peterluger.com

Voted NYC's No. 1 steakhouse for the 30th year in a row, this circa-1887 Williamsburg, Brooklyn, "landmark" offers a "classic, straightforward" menu (highlighted by a "terrific" aged porterhouse) that "hasn't changed" in eons but still draws big "crowds"; "gruff" service and a "no-frills, boys'-club" ambiance are "part of the experience", and don't forget to bring "plenty of cash" – it doesn't accept credit cards.

	FOOD	DECOR	SERVICE	COST

Picholine *French/Mediterranean* | 27 | 25 | 26 | $103

W 60s | 35 W. 64th St. (bet. B'way & CPW) | 212-724-8585 | www.picholinenyc.com

Thanks to "sophisticated" French-Med fare dispatched in a "classy" setting by an "impeccable" team, Terry Brennan's "oasis of calm" near Lincoln Center continues to draw a "loyal clientele", especially among "cheese lovers" who save room for the "unusual" selections; granted, the tabs will cost you "big bucks", but the payoff is a "thoroughly elegant dining experience."

Red Rooster *American* | 22 | 22 | 22 | $52

Harlem | 310 Lenox Ave. (bet. 125th & 126th Sts.) | 212-792-9001 | www.redroosterharlem.com

"Cock of the walk" Marcus Samuelsson rolls out an "outstanding", Southern-accented American menu at this "jumping Harlem joint" where the scene's "lively" and the people-watching "superb"; "efficient" service and frequent live music in Ginny's Supper Club downstairs are other reasons why it's perpetually "crowded."

River Café *American* | 26 | 27 | 26 | $130

Dumbo | 1 Water St. (bet. Furman & Old Fulton Sts.) | Brooklyn | 718-522-5200 | www.rivercafe.com

The "million-dollar views" of Lower Manhattan are "indispensable" at Buzzy O'Keeffe's "true NY classic" on the Dumbo, Brooklyn, waterfront, refurbished following Hurricane Sandy and still maintaining the "highest standards" via "glorious" New American cuisine from a "professional staff" in a "romantic" setting; granted, the prix fixe–only dinners are a "splurge", but then again, the dining here is truly "memorable."

Sasabune 🗷Ⓜ *Japanese* | 28 | 11 | 21 | $115

E 70s | 401 E. 73rd St. (bet. 1st & York Aves.) | 212-249-8583

"Trust the chefs" at Kenji Takahashi's "outstanding" UES Japanese offering "unforgettable", omakase-only meals featuring "delicate", "skillfully prepared" sushi; even though the digs are "cramped" and the service "rushed", devotees happily shell out "bank loan"–worthy sums for such a "high-quality" experience.

Scalini Fedeli 🗷 *Italian* | 27 | 25 | 26 | $93

TriBeCa | 165 Duane St. (bet. Greenwich & Hudson Sts.) | 212-528-0400 | www.scalinifedeli.com

"Abundant with marvelous choices", the prix fixe–only menus at Michael Cetrulo's TriBeCa Italian feature "outstanding" dishes bolstered by an "equally lavish" wine cellar; "dedicated" staffers, "old-world" decor and "very expensive" tabs are all part of the "la dolce vita" package.

Soto ●🗷 *Japanese* | 27 | 19 | 21 | $104

W Village | 357 Sixth Ave. (bet. Washington Pl. & W. 4th St.) | 212-414-3088

It's "uni heaven" at this West Village Japanese, where chef Sotohiro Kosugi turns out "wonderfully creative" urchin dishes plus "beyond-all-expectations" sushi and "amazing" omakase; "efficient" service and a "tranquil", "minimalist" setting help calm nerves jangled by the "splurge" pricing.

	FOOD	DECOR	SERVICE	COST

Sushi Seki ●🖾 *Japanese*

28 | 14 | 22 | $80

E 60s | 1143 First Ave. (bet. 62nd & 63rd Sts.) | 212-371-0238

Transforming "pristine fish" into "phenomenal sushi", "master-of-his-art" chef Seki "never disappoints" at this "something-special" East Side Japanese; "late-night" hours draw night owls who don't mind the "costly" tabs and "needs-a-face-lift" decor.

Sushi Yasuda 🖾 *Japanese*

28 | 22 | 24 | $88

E 40s | 204 E. 43rd St. (bet. 2nd & 3rd Aves.) | 212-972-1001 | www.sushiyasuda.com

Even though "chef Yasuda is gone", the "raw talent" in the kitchen perseveres at this "top-of-the-line" Japanese near Grand Central known for its "succulent" sushi; don't be misled by the "austere decor", it's "not inexpensive" – though the $28 prix fixe is a big-time bargain and there's now a no-tipping policy.

Telepan *American*

26 | 22 | 25 | $73

W 60s | 72 W. 69th St. (bet. Columbus Ave. & CPW) | 212-580-4300 | www.telepan-ny.com

Greenmarket cuisine "wizard" Bill Telepan oversees this "high-level" UWS New American, where "perfectionist" plates are served in a "soothing" townhouse setting by "first-rate" staffers; granted, it's "costly" (the $28 prix fixe lunch aside), but the "serious foodies" and "Lincoln Centric" types who love it "don't mind paying the price."

Torrisi Italian Specialties *Italian*

27 | 19 | 24 | $80

NoLita | 250 Mulberry St. (bet. Prince & Spring Sts.) | 212-965-0955 | www.torrisinyc.com

"Exceptional dining" awaits at this "real-deal" NoLita nook, where "original" takes on Italian-American eats are "done to perfection" and presented by an "attentive" staff at a $60 prix fixe–only price; the "cozy" setting may verge on "cramped", but it's "worth the work to get a reservation" – the overall experience is "amazing."

21 Club 🖾 *American*

23 | 25 | 25 | $75

W 50s | 21 W. 52nd St. (bet. 5th & 6th Aves.) | 212-582-7200 | www.21club.com

"Dine surrounded by history" at this circa-1929 Midtown former speakeasy, a "NY icon" where tuxedoed "career waiters" make you "feel like one of the *Mad Men*" within "delightful" "throwback" digs including a "legendary" barroom hung with "model planes and miscellaneous knickknacks" and private rooms upstairs that are "outstanding" for parties; just "dress up" (jackets required) and expect a "hefty bill" for American "country club cuisine (but better)" – though there's always the "best-in-town" deal of a $42 pre-theater prix fixe.

Union Square Cafe *American*

27 | 23 | 26 | $72

Union Sq | 21 E. 16th St. (bet. 5th Ave. & Union Sq. W.) | 212-243-4020 | www.unionsquarecafe.com

"Still going strong", this Union Square "tent pole in Danny Meyer's restaurant empire" bases its "well-earned reputation" on "stellar", Greenmarket-fresh New American food served by "engaging" staffers in a "refined" setting made for "intimate conversation"; it's a "special-occasion" place with appropriately "costly" tabs, and though scoring a reservation can be tough, insiders advise "dining at the bar."

Orange County, CA

TOP FOOD RANKING

	Restaurant	Cuisine
29	Bluefin	Japanese
	Marché Moderne	French
28	Basilic	French/Swiss
	Blake's Place	BBQ
	Gabbi's Mexican	Mexican
	Park Ave	American
27	Il Barone	Italian
	La Sirena*	Mexican
	Napa Rose	Californian
	Ramos House	American

OTHER NOTEWORTHY PLACES

Anaheim White House	Italian
Broadway by Amar Santana	American/Eclectic
Brunos Trattoria	Italian
Charlie Palmer	American
Mastro's Ocean Ranch	Seafood/Steak American
South of Nick's	Mexican
3-Thirty-3 Waterfront	American
21 Oceanfront	Seafood
230 Forest Avenue	Californian

Anaheim White House *Italian*

25	24	25	$57

Anaheim | 887 S. Anaheim Blvd. (Vermont Ave.) | 714-772-1381 | www.anaheimwhitehouse.com

"The staff treats you like royalty" at this "regal" Anaheim landmark "just down the road from the land of Mickey and Donald", where chef-owner Bruno Serato is lauded for both his "beautifully pre-pared" Italian steakhouse fare and community work with needy kids; critics may find the decor "dated" and "stuffy", but an "older clientele" appreciates the "formal" yet "festive" ambiance that makes it "great for celebrations."

Basilic ⊠ Ⓜ *French/Swiss*

28	22	27	$53

Newport Beach | 217 Marine Ave. (Park Ave.) | 949-673-0570 | www.basilicrestaurant.com

Intrepid eaters say "you'll never forget" the "superb", "pricey" French-Swiss fare that "deserves its reputation" at this "hard-to-find" Balboa Island "jewel box" by chef-owner Bernard Althaus; a "thoughtful" wine list, "wonderful" service and "quaint, romantic" ambiance are further assets, though since it only seats 24, "definitely make reservations"; P.S. "Raclette Night is a must-do."

---

* Indicates a tie with restaurant above

	FOOD	DECOR	SERVICE	COST

Blake's Place *BBQ*
28 | 19 | 25 | $15

Anaheim | 2905 E. Miraloma Ave. (Red Gum St.) | 714-630-8574 | www.blakesplacebbq.com

This "bustling local favorite" in Anaheim has an "IQ for BBQ" say carnivores who "crave" its "tender" brisket and ribs with "real wood-smoke pit flavor", slathered in "incredible" sauce and conveyed by an "on-the-ball" crew; those indulging off-site say it's "even better as takeout" and the catering's "well worth it."

Bluefin *Japanese*
29 | 23 | 26 | $53

Newport Coast | Crystal Cove Promenade | 7952 E. PCH (Reef Point Dr.) | 949-715-7373 | www.bluefinbyabe.com

"Way beyond a sushi bar", this "busy" Newport Coast Japanese – voted OC's No. 1 for Food – showcases chef-owner Takashi Abe's "phenomenal" fish and other "yummy" creations for a mostly local clientele; the "fast" service and "fabulous", waterfall-enhanced modern decor make the most of the Crystal Cove Promenade space, and though some think it's "pricey", the omakase lunch is still a "deal."

Broadway by
26 | 27 | 29 | $57

Amar Santana ❶ *American/Eclectic*

Laguna Beach | 328 Glenneyre St. (Forest Ave.) | 949-715-8234 | www.broadwaybyamarsantana.com

Amar Santana's "swanky", NYC-themed New American–Eclectic "oasis" in Laguna Beach is rated tops for Service in OC thanks to an "impeccable" staff that ferries tasting-menu items and small plates (plus "unique" cocktails and a Cal-heavy wine list) while navigating a "lively" space featuring chef's-table seats overlooking the kitchen; costs are proportionate, and some cite a "noisy" scene, but to most, it's "raised the bar."

Brunos Trattoria *Italian*
- | - | - | M

Brea | Birch St. Promenade | 6001 Washington Blvd. (Hargis St.) | 310- 280-3856 | www.brunosbrea.com

Chef-partner Peter Serantoni pays homage to his childhood in Venice, Italy, with thoughtful Northern Italian fare in a chic Brea setting with brick walls and leather banquettes; highlights include handmade pastas, artisanal salumi and signature cocktails made with Med spirits.

Charlie Palmer at Bloomingdale's
24 | 25 | 23 | $56

South Coast Plaza *American*

Costa Mesa | South Coast Plaza | 3333 Bristol St. (Anton Blvd.) | 714-352-2525 | www.charliepalmer.com

When the "beautiful" people crave a "classy respite" from South Coast Plaza, Charlie Palmer's "elegant" New American comes through with an "inventive and delicious" menu served amid "soothing", "modern decor"; "top-notch" service adds to the "highly civilized" air that suits "expense accounts", while shallow pockets adore the "bargain"-priced three-course lunch; P.S. oenophiles can take home bottles from the "incredible" selection at the on-site Next Vintage shop.

Gabbi's Mexican Kitchen *Mexican*
28 | 24 | 23 | $33

Orange | 141 S. Glassell St. (bet. Almond & Chapman Aves.) | 714-633-3038 | www.gabbipatrick.com

Those "in the know" head to this upmarket, "rustic"-looking storefront (with "no sign outside") for the "haute" side of Mexican cuisine in Old

FOOD DECOR SERVICE COST

Towne Orange, where the "next-level" plates by chef/co-owner Gabbi Patrick are not only "delightful" but "works of art", and the desserts are "delicious" too; long waits are "accurate indicators" of its popularity, and while it's slightly "pricey" for the genre, guests assure "you'll go away loving every bit."

Il Barone Ristorante 🗷 *Italian*

27 | 22 | 24 | $41

Newport Beach | 4251 Martingale Way (Corinthian Way) | 949-955-2755 | www.ilbaroneristorante.com

The "chef's specials" alone are "worth the drive" to this Newport Beach Italian out by the airport where presiding couple chef Franco Barone and manager Donatella Barone treat guests to "superb", slightly "pricey" fare in a "lovely" ambiance; given the "warm, gracious hospitality" and "over-the-top" service, fans say it's "spot-on" when you're "celebrating."

La Sirena Grill *Mexican*

27 | 17 | 22 | $18

Irvine | 3931 Portola Pkwy. (Culver Dr.) | 714-508-8226
Laguna Beach | 347 Mermaid St. (Park Ave.) | 949-497-8226 🗷

"Eat without the guilt" at this casual "fresh-Mex" chainlet offering "bold takes" on the classics crafted from local, organic and sustainable ingredients like a "not-to-be-missed" blackened-salmon burrito; though the tabs are higher than the competition, allies appreciate the "quality" eats as well as the "friendly" crew that dishes it out; P.S. Downtown Laguna Beach has outdoor seating only.

Marché Moderne *French*

29 | 25 | 27 | $61

Costa Mesa | South Coast Plaza | 3333 Bristol St. (Anton Blvd.) | 714-434-7900 | www.marchemoderne.net

"*C'est magnifique!*" trumpet fans of this "expensive" "gem" in South Coast Plaza (OC's Most Popular restaurant) featuring such "exquisite" French fare – from "decadent" classics to "inventive" small plates – that "you almost want a reverse gastric banding so you can eat the entire menu"; add in a "charming" staff and "gorgeous" setting with a patio and "a view of the Christian Louboutin store across the way", and "what more could you ask for?"; P.S. the three-course prix fixe lunch is a "flat-out steal."

Mastro's Ocean Club *Seafood/Steak*

26 | 26 | 23 | $78

Newport Coast | Crystal Cove Promenade | 8112 E. PCH (Reef Point Dr.) | 949-376-6990 | www.mastrosrestaurants.com

"If you're going to 'do it up', do it here" at this "flashy" "high-end" Crystal Cove chophouse where "excellent" steaks and seafood are paired with "appropriately old-school service and strong martinis" in luxe digs packed with "beautiful people"; it's a tad "superficial" to some, and "unless your bank account is in the six figures" it can be way "too expensive" to boot; P.S. don't miss the serious "pickup action" at the bar.

Napa Rose *Californian*

27 | 26 | 28 | $68

Anaheim | Disney's Grand Californian Hotel & Spa | 1600 S. Disneyland Dr. (bet. Ball Rd. & Katella Ave.) | 714-300-7170 | www.disneyland.com

An "elegant escape" within the Disneyland theme park, this "special-occasion" dining room spotlights Andrew Sutton's "breathtaking" seasonal Californian cuisine and "amazing" wines from "the best list within a walk of the Matterhorn"; the Craftsman-style setting boasts

	FOOD	DECOR	SERVICE	COST

"exceptional" service and a surprisingly "kid-friendly" vibe – just "bring two checkbooks" to foot the bill.

Park Ave Ⓜ American | 28 | 24 | 27 | $41 |

Stanton | 11200 Beach Blvd. (bet. Katella & Orangewood Aves.) | 714-901-4400 | www.parkavedining.com

A "gem" in Stanton, this "sophisticated" American from David Slay supplies "simple comfort food done perfectly", crafted from "fresh" ingredients from the "lovely" garden out back and matched with "phenomenal" cocktails; adding to the charm is the "swank" "midcentury Googie setting", "superb" hospitality and "reasonable" pricing.

Ramos House Café Ⓜ American | 27 | 24 | 25 | $38 |

San Juan Capistrano | 31752 Los Rios St. (Ramos St.) | 949-443-1342 | www.ramoshouse.com

Set in a "beautiful" old cottage on the train tracks in Old San Juan Capistrano, this New American is a "treasure" serving "elaborate", "incredible" Southern-style lunches and brunches from chef John Q. Humphreys, along with massive Bloody Marys, on the tree-shaded patio; "knowledgeable" service cements the "pleasurable", albeit "pricey", experience; P.S. the buttermilk biscuits alone are "worth the drive."

The Ranch American | ▽ 28 | 29 | 28 | $45 |

Anaheim | 1025 E. Ball Rd. (Lewis St.) | 714-687-6336 | www.theranch.com

Fine dining meets "country-western" at this "upscale ranch" in Anaheim serving "incredibly creative" rustic American cuisine and "impressive" wines in an abode of dark woods, leather and upscale cattle-country touches; "yes, it's in an industrial area", but the ambiance and service are "excellent", and it's especially "fun" for a date; P.S. an attached saloon features live and DJ'd country music and dancing Wednesday–Sunday.

South of Nick's Mexican | ▽ 24 | 24 | 24 | $32 |

San Clemente | 110 N. El Camino Real (Ave. Del Mar) | 949-481-4545 | www.thenicko.com

"Creative, modern" spins on Mexican classics and a "kicking" bar with an elite list of sipping tequilas are the draw at this sibling of Nick's in a historic Spanish Colonial Revival building that was once the office of San Clemente's founder, Ole Hanson; additionally, the staff is "friendly" and weekend breakfasts are a welcome hangover cure.

3-Thirty-3 Waterfront ● American | 23 | 23 | 21 | $38 |

Newport Beach | 333 Bayside Dr. (PCH) | 949-673-8464 | www.3thirty3nb.com

This "trendy" Newport Beacher is where "cougars", "sugar daddies" and young ones collide for "tasty" New American small plates and cocktails served against a backdrop of "knock-your-socks-off" waterfront vistas; some quibble about "slow" service and "loud" acoustics, but most don't mind since prices are moderate and it's mostly "about the scene."

21 Oceanfront Seafood | 25 | 23 | 23 | $54 |

Newport Beach | 2100 W. Oceanfront (21st Pl.) | 949-673-2100 | www.21oceanfront.com

"Gorgeous views" of the ocean set the scene at this lavish, long-established Newport Beach seafooder where "superb" servers ferry "fabulous" fish and steaks to a deep-pocketed crowd; although a few find fault with the "old-school" looks and "no-surprises" menu, on the whole most deem it "worth a try" for a "special occasion."

230 Forest Avenue *Californian*   25 20 22 $42

Laguna Beach | 230 Forest Ave. (PCH) | 949-494-2545 | www.230forestavenue.com

Chef-owner Marc Cohen's "lively" Californian in the heart of Laguna Beach is "frequented by locals" and tourists who come for the "unique", "delicious" menu abetted by "top-notch" service and "great people-watching" in "trendy" surroundings; despite the "cramped quarters" ("be prepared to sit in the laps of the couple next to you"), "fair prices" make it a "winner."

Orlando

TOP FOOD RANKING

Restaurant	Cuisine
29 Cress	Eclectic
Victoria & Albert's	American
28 Nagoya Sushi	Japanese
Chatham's Place	Continental
Norman's*	New World
Christner's	Steak
Viet Garden	Thai/Vietnamese
Jiko – The Cooking Place	African
Texas de Brazil	Brazilian
Lee & Rick's Oyster Bar	Seafood
27 Ruth's Chris	Steak
Seito Sushi	Japanese
Pho 88	Vietnamese
4 Rivers Smokehouse	BBQ
Prato	Italian
Palm	Steak
Black Bean Deli	Cuban
Fleming's Prime	Steak
Ming Bistro	Chinese
Capital Grille	Steak

OTHER NOTEWORTHY PLACES

Bahama Breeze	Caribbean
Bosphorous	Turkish
Cask & Larder	Southern
Charley's	Steak
Cheesecake Factory	American
Chef's Table at Edgewater	American
Dragonfly	Japanese
Enzo's Restaurant	Italian
Flying Fish Café	Seafood
K Restaurant	American
Luma on Park	American
Primo	Italian/Mediterranean
Ravenous Pig	American
Roy's	Hawaiian
Rusty Spoon	American
Sanaa	African/Indian
Seasons 52	American
Table Orlando	American
Todd English's Bluezoo	Seafood
Vines Grille & Wine Bar	Steak

---

* Indicates a tie with restaurant above

Bahama Breeze ● *Caribbean*   24 | 25 | 24 | $29

International Drive | 8849 International Dr. (Austrian Row) | 407-248-2499
Lake Buena Vista | 8735 Vineland Ave. (Apopka Vineland Rd.) |
407-938-9010
East Orlando | 1200 N. Alafaya Trail (Ashton Manor Way) | 407-658-6770
Altamonte Springs | 499 E. Altamonte Dr. (Palm Springs Dr.) | 407-831-2929
Kissimmee | Orange Lake Shopping Ctr. | 8160 W. Irlo Bronson Memorial Hwy.
(Orange Lake Blvd.) | 407-390-0353
www.bahamabreeze.com

"Step away from the everyday" at this "top-quality" chain – Orlando's
Most Popular restaurant – where the "music will whisk you to the islands" and the "fruity" tropical drinks, "delicious" Caribbean cooking
and "beautiful" "resort"-like surroundings will keep you there; "prices
are reasonable" and "service is usually attentive", making the fittingly
"breezy vibe" that much more "enjoyable."

Black Bean Deli 🗷 *Cuban*   27 | 13 | 23 | $11

Winter Park | 325 S. Orlando Ave. (Fairview Ave.) | 407-628-0294 |
www.blackbeandeli.com

For "Cuban done right", diners point to this Winter Park "hole-in-the-
wall" where the "kitchen creates miracles", sending out "outstanding"
fare, including some of the "best black beans" (of course); it's an "excellent value for the dollar", and since the "tiny" digs have limited
seating, most suggest you "get it to go", adding "timely" service makes it
"delicious for a quickie"; P.S. a much larger Colonial Drive outpost is
imminent at press time.

Bosphorous Turkish Cuisine *Turkish*   25 | 23 | 21 | $30

Bay Hill/Dr. Phillips | The Marketplace | 7600 Dr. Phillips Blvd.
(Sand Lake Rd.) | 407-352-6766
Winter Park | 108 S. Park Ave. (Morse Blvd.) | 407-644-8609
www.bosphorousrestaurant.com

"Save the airfare to Istanbul" and head instead to this moderate Winter
Park Turkish (with a Dr. Phillips sequel), where the "delicious", "well-
prepared" fare, like "incredible", "puffy" lavosh bread and "orgasmi-
cally good" hummus, is "perfect for sharing"; the casual dining room
is pleasant, and sidewalk seating is "nice too", so though "friendly"
service can be "somewhat slow", fans suggest you simply appreciate
that there's "no rush."

The Capital Grille *Steak*   27 | 25 | 26 | $70

International Drive | Pointe Orlando | 9101 International Dr.
(Pointe Plaza Ave.) | 407-370-4392 | www.thecapitalgrille.com
Millenia | The Mall at Millenia | 4200 Conroy Rd. (Millenia Blvd.) |
407-351-2210 | www.capitalgrille.com

"Done-to-perfection" steaks and "well-prepared sides" result in "delicious" meals at this "special-occasion" chophouse chain's Orlando outposts; "professional" service and "classy surroundings" further make it
"upscale in every regard", so "expense-account" tabs are to be expected.

Cask & Larder 🅼 *Southern*   - | - | - | M

Winter Park | 565 W. Fairbanks Ave. (Orange Ave.) | 321-280-4200 |
www.caskandlarder.com

Seasonal ingredients and housemade beers are the focus of this midpriced Winter Park spot, where chef-owners James and Julie Petrakis

(Ravenous Pig) put their innovative spin on Southern favorites; brick walls and wood floors lend a casual, homey vibe, and whole-animal feasts (reserve 72 hours in advance) add group-dining appeal.

Charley's Steak House Steak   26 | 23 | 25 | $59

International Drive | 8255 International Dr. (Sand Lake Rd.) | 407-363-0228
Kissimmee | 2901 Parkway Blvd. (Irlo Bronson Memorial Hwy.) |
407-239-1270
www.charleyssteakhouse.com

"Come hungry" to this Kissimmee and International Drive chophouse duo where "cooked-to-perfection" cuts are "as tender as butter" and served in portions so "huge" you'll leave "feeling stuffed"; "the staff delivers even when stretched thin", and "classy", white-tablecloth surrounds boost the "special-occasion" appeal, all of which makes "expensive" tabs easier to digest.

Chatham's Place ☒ Continental   28 | 24 | 27 | $61

Bay Hill/Dr. Phillips | 7575 Dr. Phillips Blvd. (Sand Lake Rd.) | 407-345-2992 |
www.chathamsplace.com

A "charming little hideaway", this spendy Dr. Phillips Continental is "well attended by locals" who savor "carefully prepared", "top-notch" dishes featuring produce from the chef's own garden and enjoy wine from an "excellent selection"; "impeccable" service and a "classy", "romantic" space further justify its status as an "all-time favorite."

Cheesecake Factory American   25 | 24 | 24 | $30

Millenia | Mall at Millenia | 4200 Conroy Rd. (Millenia Blvd.) | 407-226-0333
Winter Park | Winter Park Vill. | 520 N. Orlando Ave. (Gay Rd.) |
407-644-4220
www.thecheesecakefactory.com

"Bring your appetite and your sweet tooth" to these "moderately priced" chain links in Millenia and Winter Park best known for "enormous portions (think tomorrow's lunch)" of "delicious" American fare off a "huge, book-size menu"; "dependable" service and an "upbeat", "inviting" scene – plus "out-of-this-world" cheesecake, of course – help most overlook "noisy" conditions and "huge waits to get in."

Chef's Table at the Edgewater Hotel &   28 | 23 | 28 | $84
Tasting Room ☒Ⓜ American

Winter Garden | Edgewater Hotel | 99 W. Plant St. (bet. Boyd & Main Sts.) |
407-230-4837 | www.chefstableattheedgewater.com

A "true dining experience" awaits at this "quaint" Winter Garden New American where chef Kevin Tarter "describes all menu items tableside" and "puts his heart" into the "outstanding" seasonal prix fixes (no à la carte); his sommelier wife, Laurie, adds even more "personal touches" and service is "astonishingly good" overall, so fans suggest you "settle in" and "plan to spend several hours" enjoying an "intimate" meal; P.S. the adjoining Tasting Room is a less costly alternative with small plates and a "great bar."

Christner's Prime Steak & Lobster ☒ Steak   28 | 23 | 26 | $65

Winter Park | 729 Lee Rd. (Alloway St.) | 407-645-4443 |
www.christnersprimesteakandlobster.com

"Top-of-the-line" say fans bedazzled by the "high-quality", "mouthwatering" cuts "served on a sizzling plate" at this "popular" Winter

Park chophouse also known for its "prime" lobster, "expansive" wine list and "old-fashioned", "supper club"-like surrounds; with "first-class" service, "expense-account" tabs are a given, so many suggest saving it for "when you want to impress someone."

Cress ☒Ⓜ Eclectic
29 | 26 | 28 | $41

DeLand | 103 W. Indiana Ave. (bet. Florida Ave. & Woodland Blvd.) | 386-734-3740 | www.cressrestaurant.com

"Incredible talent" Hari Pulapaka ("geeky math professor" by day, chef-owner by night) "never fails to delight" at this "rare jewel in DeLand", wowing with "innovative", "globally inspired" Eclectic cooking that highlights "crazy refined flavors" and earns No. 1 Food honors in the Orlando area; servers who "know their menu" work the "intimate", "romantic" space, and while it's not cheap, it's labeled "one of the best" around.

Dragonfly Robata Grill & Sushi Japanese
27 | 26 | 24 | $38

Bay Hill/Dr. Phillips | Dellagio Plaza | 7972 Via Dellagio Way (bet. Della Dr. & Sand Lake Rd.) | 407-370-3359 | www.dragonflysushi.com

"Mingle with the hip crowd" at this Japanese izakaya on Dr. Phillips' Restaurant Row that "hits the spot" with a "variety" of "interesting" "tapas-style" dishes, including "excellent sushi rolls" and "flavorful" specialties from the robata grill; "modern" environs with cork floors and dark-wood tables appeal, as does generally "attentive" service, and though what's "reasonable" to some is "expensive" to others, all appreciate the "great happy hour."

Enzo's Restaurant on the Lake ☒Ⓜ Italian
27 | 24 | 26 | $49

Longwood | 1130 S. Hwy. 17-92 (bet. Laura St. & Wildmere Ave.) | 407-834-9872 | www.enzos.com

"Upscale dining with down-home flavors" sums up this "romantic" Longwood "fixture", a "wonderful celebration place" that "captures the essence of Italian cuisine" in "excellent" cooking from a "kitchen that doesn't seem capable of sending out a bad meal"; "friendly yet professional servers" further sweeten the "scenic" lakeside setting, making "pricey" tabs less than surprising.

Fleming's Prime Steakhouse & Wine Bar Steak
27 | 25 | 27 | $63

Bay Hill/Dr. Phillips | Dellagio Plaza | 8030 Via Dellagio Way (bet. Della Dr. & Sand Lake Rd.) | 407-352-5706
Winter Park | 933 N. Orlando Ave. (Lee Rd.) | 407-699-9463
www.flemingssteakhouse.com

Diners "indulge" in "top-notch" steaks and one of the "best burgers in town" at this "reliable" chophouse chain with branches in Dr. Phillips and Winter Park, where a "modern" and "less stodgy" vibe makes it a "far hipper destination" than some of its kin; "professional, friendly" service adds to the "high-end" experience, and if tabs seem too "expensive", try the "lower-priced" bar menu.

Flying Fish Café Seafood
26 | 24 | 26 | $57

Epcot Area | Disney's BoardWalk Inn | 2101 Epcot Resorts Blvd. (Buena Vista Dr.) | Lake Buena Vista | 407-939-3463 | www.disneyworld.com

An "oasis in the middle of chaos", this spendy Disney BoardWalk seafooder has diners "flying high" with "innovative", "well-prepared" plates, including the "memorable" potato-wrapped snapper, plus "selections for landlubbers" too; also winning praise are "experienced", "accommodating" staffers who "add to the evening" and a "welcoming (if sometimes noisy) atmosphere."

4 Rivers Smokehouse 🗷 *BBQ*   27 | 20 | 24 | $19

Longwood | Longwood Village Shopping Ctr. | 1869 W. State Rd. 434 (bet. Raymond Ave. & Springwood Circle) | 407-474-8377
Winter Garden | Tri-City Shopping Ctr. | 1047 S. Dillard St. (Colonial Dr.) | 407-474-8377
Winter Park | 1600 W. Fairbanks Ave. (bet. Harold & Jackson Aves.) | 407-474-8377
www.4rsmokehouse.com

'Cue fans "go ga-ga" over the "heavenly" Texas-style BBQ at this counter-serve chainlet, a local "sensation" thanks to "humongous" portions of "smoked-to-perfection brisket", "simply divine" pulled pork and a "variety of delicious sides" all washed down with "retro sodas" ("no booze"); yes, "lines can be long" and it's often "crowded", but "reasonable" tabs and "gracious" service help, so most still give it a "definite thumbs-up."

Jiko – The Cooking Place *African*   28 | 28 | 28 | $59

Animal Kingdom Area | Disney's Animal Kingdom Lodge | 2901 Osceola Pkwy. (Sherberth Rd.) | Lake Buena Vista | 407-938-4733 | www.disneyworld.com

The "diverse", "African-inspired specialties" are "crazy good" say fans of this "must-visit" in Disney's Animal Kingdom Lodge, where the offerings are "exotic enough to be original" but still "accessible" enough for "picky eaters" and are augmented by a "fantastic" South African-focused wine list; a wall that "changes colors like a sunset" makes the "beatifully designed", "transportive setting" "even more magical", and service is "terrific" too, so it comes "highly recommended" – "if you have the money", of course.

K Restaurant 🗷 *American*   26 | 21 | 24 | $49

College Park | 1710 Edgewater Dr. (bet. New Hampshire & Yates Sts.) | 407-872-2332 | www.kwinebar.com

"Creative", "cleanly crafted" plates prepared with "locally sourced ingredients" (including some from the backyard garden) result in a "joy-of-eating experience" at this College Park New American from "experimental" chef-owner Kevin Fonzo; the "remodeled house" setting is "inviting", and service is "attentive", so "high" prices don't deter devotees who vow they'll "definitely be back."

Lee & Rick's Oyster Bar *Seafood*   28 | 12 | 24 | $26

Kirkman Road | 5621 Old Winter Garden Rd. (Kirkman Rd.) | 407-293-3587 | www.leeandricksoysterbar.com

"Food of the gods" comes in the form of "awesome" "shucked-to-order" oysters swear acolytes of this Kirkman Road seafood eatery, where diners who "sit at the concrete bar" are rewarded by "buckets (that's right, buckets)" of the bivalves (served by the dozen at tables) and the opportunity to "b.s." with the "friendly" staffers; "don't get dressed up" because the "dive" digs have "all the charm of a men's washroom", but hey, "that's how they keep the numbers manageable."

Luma on Park *American*   26 | 27 | 25 | $45

Winter Park | 290 S. Park Ave. (bet. Lyman & New England Aves.) |
407-599-4111 | www.lumaonpark.com

A "chic", "ultramodern" dining room with a "buzzy atmosphere" provides the backdrop for "innovative", "beautifully crafted" New American
plates at this "high-end" Winter Park "hot spot", where the "always-
changing" seasonal menu gets a boost from "delicious" cocktails and
an "extensive wine list"; add in "knowledgeable" staffers who make
you their "number-one priority" and it's no surprise many make it a
"special-occasion" destination.

Ming Bistro *Chinese*   27 | 14 | 21 | $19

Mills 50 | 1212 Woodward St. (Colonial Dr.) | 407-898-9672

"Hungry locals" hit up this Mills 50 Chinese for "incredible" "authentic" fare, including some of "the best dim sum in town"; the "minimal"
decor verges on "shabby", but "service is pleasant", and with "easy-
on-the-wallet" tabs, most leave "with smiles on their faces."

Nagoya Sushi *Japanese*   28 | 22 | 26 | $35

Bay Hill/Dr. Phillips | The Marketplace | 7600 Dr. Phillips Blvd.
(Sand Lake Rd.) | 407-248-8558
Winter Springs | Willa Springs Shopping Ctr. | 5661 Red Bug Lake Rd.
(Tuskawilla Rd.) | 407-478-3388
www.nagoyasushi.com

"Don't give up" trying to locate this "hard-to-find" Dr. Phillips Japanese
(with a Winter Springs sibling) advise admirers who say the reward is
"fresh", "outstanding sushi and bento" "well served" by "friendly" staffers; moderate tabs are a further plus, so the only complaint is that the
"hole-in-the-wall" digs seem a bit "too small" given its "popularity."

Norman's *New World*   28 | 27 | 28 | $94

South Orlando | Ritz-Carlton Grande Lakes | 4012 Central Florida Pkwy.
(John Young Pkwy.) | 407-393-4333 | www.normans.com

"Impeccable" service will make you "feel like a queen" at this high-end
dining room in South Orlando's "impressive" Ritz-Carlton Grande
Lakes where chef Norman Van Aken sends out "exquisite" New World
cuisine; elegant, marble-walled surroundings further contribute to the
"world-class" experience, making it easy to "forget Mickey, Donald
and a million screaming kids are just a few blocks away."

The Palm *Steak*   27 | 24 | 26 | $71

Universal Orlando | Hard Rock Hotel | 5800 Universal Blvd. (Major Blvd.) |
407-503-7256 | www.thepalm.com

"Tender" "perfectly cooked" chops, "juicy" lobsters and some of the
"best cocktails in town" bring an "upper-crust" crowd to this "high-
end" NY-based steakhouse set in Universal's Hard Rock Hotel; the
caricature-enhanced space has a "pleasant atmosphere" and the "attentive" staff is there when "you want to be pampered", so it fits the
bill on "splurge nights."

Pho 88 *Vietnamese*   27 | 16 | 21 | $16

Mills 50 | 730 N. Mills Ave. (Park Lake St.) | 407-897-3488 |
www.pho88orlando.com

"Authentic" offerings mean there's "no faux pho" at this Mills 50
Vietnamese say fans cheering the "kick-butt" eats; the casual space

may not inspire the same praise, but service rates well, and with "wallet-friendly" prices, it's considered an overall "find."

Prato *Italian*
27 | 28 | 26 | $37

Winter Park | 124 N. Park Ave. (Morse Blvd.) | 407-262-0050 | www.prato-wp.com

The "meatballs deserve a standing ovation" rave fans of this "beautifully decorated" Winter Park Italian turning out "hearty, rustic" "foodie cuisine"; the "cool, hip atmosphere" makes it feel like a "real Manhattan-style joint", while service gets high marks too, and with approachable prices, it's quickly becoming a "favorite."

Primo *Italian/Mediterranean*
28 | 24 | 26 | $63

South Orlando | JW Marriott Grande Lakes | 4040 Central Florida Pkwy. (John Young Pkwy.) | 407-393-4444 | www.grandelakes.com

"Not a typical hotel restaurant" attest admirers of Melissa Kelly's "upscale" Italian-Mediterranean inside South Orlando's JW Marriott Grande Lakes, where the "excellent", "inventively prepared" cuisine highlights local ingredients; further incentives include a "warm, knowledgeable" staff and "beautiful" Tuscan-style dining room, leaving some wondering why "no one seems to know about it."

Ravenous Pig ⊠ *American*
26 | 25 | 25 | $40

Winter Park | 1234 N. Orange Ave. (Minnesota Ave.) | 407-628-2333 | www.theravenouspig.com

Live "a foodie's dream" at this "simply marvelous" Winter Park gastropub, where chefs-owners James and Julie Petrakis offer a "constantly evolving" but "consistently fabulous" menu of "innovative" American cuisine, "from pub food to complex main dishes", all served alongside "creative" "Prohibition era–inspired cocktails", "awesome microbrews" and a "thoughtful wine list"; they "pay close attention to every detail of service", and the "charming" wood-enhanced space has a "true big-city feel", so most fully "embrace the pig."

Roy's *Hawaiian*
27 | 26 | 27 | $54

Bay Hill/Dr. Phillips | Plaza Venezia | 7760 W. Sand Lake Rd. (Dr. Phillips Blvd.) | 407-352-4844 | www.roysrestaurant.com

"Aloha at its finest" can be found at this Restaurant Row link in Roy Yamaguchi's upscale Hawaiian chain, a "special-event favorite" that "never disappoints", from the "flavorful" and "innovative" fusion fare to the "gracious", "accommodating" staffers; true, it's "on the pricey side", but the "festive", "friendly atmosphere" helps ease the pain.

Rusty Spoon *American*
25 | 22 | 25 | $36

Downtown Orlando | 55 W. Church St. (Orange Ave.) | 407-401-8811 | www.therustyspoon.com

"Fine dining without the stuffiness or price" brings chowhounds to this Downtown Orlando gastropub where the "rustic, inspired" New American offerings are made with local ingredients; further pluses include "personable" staffers and a "cozy" earth-toned setting.

Ruth's Chris Steak House *Steak*
27 | 25 | 26 | $72

Bay Hill/Dr. Phillips | Fountains Plaza | 7501 W. Sand Lake Rd. (bet. Dr. Phillips Blvd. & Turkey Lake Rd.) | 407-226-3900
Lake Mary | 80 Colonial Center Pkwy. (County Rd. 46A) | 407-804-8220

	FOOD	DECOR	SERVICE	COST

(continued)

Ruth's Chris Steak House

Winter Park | Winter Park Vill. | 610 N. Orlando Ave. (Webster Ave.) |
407-622-2444
www.ruthschris.com

"*Magnifique*" proclaim fans of this "special-occasion" chophouse chain
known for "melt-in-your-mouth delicious" steaks and a "classy", "clubby
atmosphere"; "pampering" service is another part of the package – as
are prices considered "reflective" of the "high-class" experience.

Sanaa *African/Indian* | 25 | 26 | 27 | $36 |

Animal Kingdom Area | Disney's Animal Kingdom Villas | 2901
Osceola Pkwy. (Epcot Center Dr.) | Lake Buena Vista | 407-939-3463 |
www.disneyworld.com

"Get a seat by the window" for "fantastic views" of the "exotic ani-
mals" roaming right outside at this midpriced eatery in Disney's
Animal Kingdom Lodge, where the "exciting ambiance" is matched by
"well-prepared" African-Indian fare that offers an "adventure in flavors"; "impeccable" service "adds to the experience", further ensuring
a "wonderful meal all around."

Seasons 52 *American* | 27 | 26 | 26 | $40 |

Bay Hill/Dr. Phillips | Plaza Venezia | 7700 W. Sand Lake Rd.
(bet. Della Dr. & Dr. Phillips Blvd.) | 407-354-5212
Altamonte Springs | 463 E. Altamonte Dr. (Palm Springs Dr.) | 407-767-1252
www.seasons52.com

"Even the most season-ed diners" "rave" about these Dr. Phillips and
Altamonte chain links, where the "well-presented" New American
dishes are all 475 calories or fewer (including the "perfectly sized"
shot-glass sweets) so you can "enjoy a delicious dinner and dessert"
"without breaking the nutrition bank"; the "inviting" dining rooms
have a "very Frank Lloyd Wright feel" and service is "professional", so
even if a few heartier eaters may "want to stop by Burger King on the
way home", most deem it a "winner."

Seito Sushi *Japanese* | 27 | 23 | 24 | $33 |

Baldwin Park | 4898 New Broad St. (Jake St.) | 407-898-8801
Bay Hill/Dr. Phillips | Phillips Crossing | 8031 Turkey Lake Rd.
(Sand Lake Rd.) | 407-248-8888
www.seitosushi.com

Some of the "freshest sushi and sashimi" is offered alongside "excellent hot dishes" at this "happening" Dr. Phillips Japanese (with a Baldwin
Park twin); "knowledgeable" staffers tend the "trendy", "modern"
digs, and while it's not cheap, it's "not crazy expensive" either, all of
which makes it pretty "hard to beat."

The Table Orlando 🗲Ⓜ *American* | - | - | - | VE |

Bay Hill/Dr. Phillips | Rialto | 8060 Via Dellagio Way (Sand Lake Rd.) |
407-900-3463 | www.thetableorlando.com

Determined diners vie for pricey berths at this intimate Dr. Phillips
New American, where guests gather around a lone communal table to
partake of a five-course prix fixe meal with wine pairings (no à la
carte); there is only one seating, at 7 PM on Friday and Saturday, and
each evening kicks off with vino and nibbles at the bar before getting
down to business at the eponymous table.

	FOOD	DECOR	SERVICE	COST

Texas de Brazil *Brazilian*

28 | 25 | 27 | $63

International Drive | 5259 International Dr. (Touchstone Dr.) |
407-355-0355 | www.texasdebrazil.com

Expect to be "rolled out" of this I-Drive link of the Brazilian churrascaria chain, a "high-end" "meat lover's paradise" where "strolling gauchos" deliver a "never-ending selection" of "deliciously prepared", "mouthwatering" meat "until you scream '*no mas*'"; the "huge", "heavenly" salad bar completes the "pig-out" experience, and while it doesn't come cheap, most are satisfied since you get "lots of food for lots of bucks."

Todd English's Bluezoo *Seafood*

25 | 25 | 24 | $59

Epcot Area | Walt Disney World Swan and Dolphin |
1500 Epcot Resorts Blvd. (Buena Vista Dr.) | Lake Buena Vista |
407-934-1111 | www.thebluezoo.com

A "stunning restaurant with food to match", this "hip" seafooder in Disney World's Dolphin resort wins kudos for its "elegant but not stuffy" setting and "creative", "delicious" offerings from celeb chef Todd English; other pros include "attentive" staffers, an "extensive wine list" and "top-shelf ambiance", all of which help make "expensive" tabs easier to swallow.

Victoria & Albert's *American*

29 | 28 | 29 | $136

Magic Kingdom Area | Disney's Grand Floridian Resort & Spa |
4401 Floridian Way (bet. Maple Rd. & Seven Seas Dr.) |
Lake Buena Vista | 407-939-3862 | www.victoria-alberts.com

A "once-in-a-lifetime experience", this Grand Floridian "celebration destination" earns "superlatives all around", from chef Scott Hunnel's "exquisite", "beautifully presented" New American prix fixes to the "impeccable" staff – it's voted No. 1 in Orlando for Service – and an "über-romantic, high-end" setting where "elegance rules" (jackets are required for men); you may "need to hock one of your kids" to pay, but those "trying to impress" say there's "no finer place."

Viet Garden *Thai/Vietnamese*

28 | 16 | 23 | $17

Mills 50 | 1237 E. Colonial Dr. (Shine Ave.) | 407-896-4154 |
www.vietgardenorlando.com

Take an "enjoyable adventure" abroad courtesy of "excellent" "traditional" dishes at this Mills 50 Vietnamese-Thai, where highlights include "the best peanut sauce" and "crave"-worthy garden rolls; "plain surroundings" are boosted by "attentive" servers and it's "well priced", both of which help it "stand out from the competition."

Vines Grille & Wine Bar *Steak*

25 | 24 | 22 | $54

Bay Hill/Dr. Phillips | Fountains Plaza | 7533 W. Sand Lake Rd.
(bet. Dr. Phillips Blvd. & Turkey Lake Rd.) | 407-351-1227 |
www.vinesgrille.com

"Delicious" steaks and "can't-beat" live music (nightly) make this Dr. Phillips chophouse a "first-rate" choice say regulars also singling out the "great wine selections"; LED fireplaces and dark-wood walls enhance the upscale-casual space, and though it's on the "expensive" side, fans still make it a "standard dining-out place."

Palm Beach

TOP FOOD RANKING

	Restaurant	Cuisine
28	Marcello's La Sirena	Italian
	Chez Jean-Pierre	French
27	11 Maple Street	American
	Captain Charlie's	Seafood
	Café L'Europe	Continental
	Casa D'Angelo	Italian
26	Abe & Louie's	Steak
	Trattoria Romana	Italian
	Café Boulud	French
	Chops Lobster Bar	Seafood/Steak

OTHER NOTEWORTHY PLACES

Bonefish Grill	Seafood
Buccan	Eclectic
Café Chardonnay	American
Coolinary Café	American
Kee Grill	Seafood/Steak
Little Moir's	Seafood
Malcolm's: The Art of Food	Eclectic/Seafood
Max's Harvest	American
Seasons 52	American
32 East	American

Abe & Louie's *Steak*   26 | 24 | 25 | $66

Boca Raton | 2200 W. Glades Rd. (NW Sheraton Way) | 561-447-0024 |
www.abeandlouies.com

The bone-in filet is "as good as it gets" ("you could cut it with a fork"),
the "sides are a great match" and the wine list is "impressive" at this
Boston-bred beef palace in Boca favored for "power lunches" and
"special occasions"; the "clubby" environs are "comfy" and "well-man-
aged" by "experienced" pros – "when you have a reservation for 8 PM,
you sit down at 8 PM" – so while it costs "big bucks", most feel it
delivers big-time.

Bonefish Grill *Seafood*   22 | 19 | 21 | $36

Lake Worth | 9897 Lake Worth Rd. (Rte. 441) | 561-965-2663
Stuart | Stuart Ctr. | 2283 SE Federal Hwy. (Monterey Rd.) |
772-288-4388
Palm Beach Gardens | 11658 U.S. 1 (Donald Ross Rd.) |
561-799-2965
Boca Raton | Boca Grove | 21065 Powerline Rd. (Sunstream Blvd.) |
561-483-4949
Boynton Beach | Renaissance Commons Shopping Ctr. |
1880 N. Congress Ave. (Gateway Blvd.) | 561-732-1310
www.bonefishgrill.com

"Just-out-of-the-water fish in many forms" "draws droves" to these
"delightful", "easygoing" seafooders ("hard to believe it's a chain");

"longish waits, even with a reservation" and "noise" are balanced by "prompt and courteous" service and "competitive prices"; P.S. the "Bang Bang shrimp is bang-on."

Buccan *Eclectic*
25 | 23 | 21 | $52

Palm Beach | 350 S. County Rd. (Australian Ave.) | 561-833-3450 | www.buccanpalmbeach.com

"An instant hit", this "utterly hip" Eclectic helmed by Clay Conley (ex Miami's Azul) is "exactly what Palm Beach needs", drawing a "beautiful" "young crowd" that makes it a "zoo on weekend nights"; the mix of "imaginative" small bites (think hot dog panini, bacon-wrapped Florida peaches), wood-fired pizzas and entrees can add up, but that doesn't faze many since it's "not easy to snag a prime-time table" or happy-hour berth at the bar.

Café Boulud *French*
26 | 26 | 26 | $75

Palm Beach | Brazilian Court Hotel | 301 Australian Ave. (Hibiscus Ave.) | 561-655-6060 | www.danielnyc.com

"Beautiful people" "break out their diamonds and gold" at this "un-Florida" "class act" in the Brazilian Court Hotel that ranks as Palm Beach's Most Popular spot thanks to "sophisticated" French fare that "does Daniel [Boulud] proud", backed by "excellent" wines and a staff operating at "the peak of hospitality" in the "casually elegant" interior or on the "lush" terrace; sure, it's "pricey", but the prix fixe lunch and weekend brunch are "bargains."

Café Chardonnay *American*
25 | 22 | 23 | $59

Palm Beach Gardens | Garden Square Shoppes | 4533 PGA Blvd. (Military Trail) | 561-627-2662 | www.cafechardonnay.com

This "classy" American in a "nondescript" Palm Beach Gardens strip mall "must be doing something right" because after more than 25 years it's still many folks' "first choice" for a "night on the town"; the "innovative" food is served by "skilled" staffers, the "charming" space is conducive to "conversations" and there's a "wonderful wine list" to boot, key ingredients for those celebrating "special occasions."

Café L'Europe *Continental*
27 | 27 | 27 | $78

Palm Beach | 331 S. County Rd. (Brazilian Ave.) | 561-655-4020 | www.cafeleurope.com

"Bump elbows with the country's wealthiest people" at this "fine-dining icon" that's "still hitting all the right notes" after three decades with its "scrumptious" Continental cuisine, huge wine list and "superb" staff – rated tops in Palm Beach – that treats diners "like royalty"; add in an "old-world" setting filled with fresh flowers and "lovely" music via a "magical pianist", and it's "worth" the "astronomical" tabs.

Captain Charlie's Reef Grill *Seafood*
27 | 14 | 23 | $36

Juno Beach | Beach Plaza | 12846 U.S. 1 (bet. Juno Isles Blvd. & Olympus Dr.) | 561-624-9924

"Don't be put off by the dumpy strip-mall exterior" or no-reservations policy – this "wildly popular" Juno Beach seafooder is a "classic not to be missed" on account of its "strikingly fresh fish" in "creative" preparations; "professional" service and a "large" list of wines "at ridiculously low prices" offset the "spartan surroundings and noise."

	FOOD	DECOR	SERVICE	COST

Casa D'Angelo *Italian*

27 | 22 | 24 | $61

Boca Raton | 171 E. Palmetto Park Rd. (bet. Mizner Blvd. & N. Federal Hwy.) | 561-996-1234 | www.casa-d-angelo.com

Chef-owner Angelo Elia's "outstanding" Northern Italian fare, including a "wide variety of homemade pasta", takes diners on a "delightful" "journey to Italy" without leaving Boca; it's "expensive" (i.e. an excuse to "wear your Valentino") but the chef accommodates requests, and the romantic setting, along with "warm" service and a buzzing bar scene help explain why it's "beloved" by many – reservations are highly recommended.

Chez Jean-Pierre Bistro 🗗 *French*

28 | 22 | 26 | $74

Palm Beach | 132 N. County Rd. (bet. Sunrise & Sunset Aves.) | 561-833-1171 | www.chezjean-pierre.com

"*Mais oui*" exclaims the "very Palm Beach" crowd that flocks to this "family-run" "country kitchen" for chef Jean-Pierre Leverrier's "consistently awesome" French fare including "outstanding Dover sole" and profiteroles with "chocolate sauce worth drowning in"; the "elegant" space is lined with "unique" modern art and warmed by "attentive" service, and while it helps to have "money to burn", most say it "always delivers"; P.S. closed July through mid-August.

Chops Lobster Bar *Seafood/Steak*

26 | 25 | 26 | $71

Boca Raton | Royal Palm Pl. | 101 Plaza Real S. (1st St.) | 561-395-2675 | www.chopslobsterbar.com

From "excellent steaks" and "fabulous" "flash-fried lobster" to "top-notch" service, this "happening" Boca branch of an Atlanta-based surf 'n' turfer "rarely misses"; the full menu is offered in both the "clubby" steakhouse side and in the replica of NYC's famed Oyster Bar complete with vaulted, tiled ceiling, and there's a lively "bar scene" with live music most nights; of course, some balk at "billfold-fracturing" tabs, but most feel it's "worth it."

Coolinary Café 🗗 *American*

- | - | - | M

Palm Beach Gardens | Donald Ross Vill. | 4650 Donald Ross Rd. (bet. Central Blvd. & Military Trail) | 561-249-6760 | www.coolinarycafe.com

There's often a wait to get in for a taste of chef-owner Tim Lipman's creative, farm-to-fork plates served alongside unique wines and craft beers at his moderately priced New American in Palm Beach Gardens; it's a tiny sliver of a space with an open kitchen behind a small counter where banter with the cooks and servers is par for the course.

11 Maple Street Ⓜ *American*

27 | 22 | 25 | $66

Jensen Beach | 3224 NE Maple Ave. (Jensen Beach Blvd.) | 772-334-7714 | www.11maplestreet.net

This "out-of-the-way" New American in "funky" Jensen Beach is a place to "escape the hustle" while enjoying chef-owner Mike Perrin's "inventive" seafood-strong menu, featuring mostly small plates presented like "works of art" and "costing about the same"; set in a "quaint" "Old Florida house", it has a "lovely" vibe and "friendly" staffers who are "knowledgeable" about the food and substantial wine list.

Kee Grill *Seafood/Steak*

| 24 | 21 | 22 | $47 |

Juno Beach | 14020 U.S. 1 (Donald Ross Rd.) | 561-776-1167 |
www.keegrilljunobeach.com
Boca Raton | 17940 N. Military Trail (Maxwell Dr.) | 561-995-5044 |
www.keegrillbocaraton.com

"Consistent quality and value" are the hallmarks of this Boca–Juno
Beach eatery offering "finely prepared fish dishes" along with land-
based options and "wonderful sides" like spinach soufflé ("heaven in
a ramekin"); the "tropical island" digs get "jammed" by an "older
crowd" during the "terrific" early-bird special so "don't linger" because the staff, though "friendly", will "take the water glass out of your
hand" (it's more relaxed later on in the evening).

Little Moir's Food Shack ☒ *Seafood*

| 26 | 15 | 21 | $36 |

Jupiter | Jupiter Sq. | 103 U.S. 1 (E. Indiantown Rd.) |
561-741-3626

Little Moir's Leftovers Café ☒ *Seafood*

Jupiter | Abacoa Bermudiana | 451 University Blvd. (Military Trail) |
561-627-6030
www.littlemoirsfoodshack.com

Fish fanciers "queue up" at this "funky", "colorful" seafood "shack",
with two outlets in different Jupiter malls, for "a wide array" of "killer"
Florida catch at "reasonable" prices; "friendly" service and an "eclectic collection of craft beer" enhance its "laid-back" charm.

Malcolm's: The Art of Food *Eclectic/Seafood*

| - | - | - | E |

Palm Beach | The Omphoy Ocean Resort & Spa | 2842 S. Ocean Blvd.
(Lake Ave.) | 561-540-6444 | www.malcolmsrestaurant.com

This elegant venue in Palm Beach's Omphoy Resort builds its upscale seafood-centric dishes on an Eclectic range of influences
(e.g. Mediterranean, Latin, European); providing deft accompaniment
to the food is the extensive selection of international wines as well as
the sweeping sea views from the earth-toned dining room's huge bank
of floor-to-ceiling windows.

Marcello's La Sirena ☒ *Italian*

| 28 | 19 | 26 | $66 |

West Palm Beach | 6316 S. Dixie Hwy. (bet. Franklin & Nathan Hale Rds.) |
561-585-3128 | www.lasirenaonline.com

There are "no surprises" at this venerable West Palm Beach "icon",
just "unforgettable" Italian "soul food" – which rates as the No. 1
meal in the county – accompanied by a wine list full of "character"
and "professional" service, making it perfect for "special occasions"; its "old-style, white-tablecloth" setting can get "crowded",
but tables are in better supply if you "eat later than the senior set";
P.S. closed in summer.

Max's Harvest *American*

| - | - | - | M |

Delray Beach | Pineapple Grove | 169 NE Second Ave. (bet. 1st & 2nd Sts.) |
561-381-9970 | www.maxsharvest.com

Restaurateur Dennis Max brings a modern American menu tuned to
local and heritage foods with a smart wine selection to Delray's
Pineapple Grove; reservations are prudent in season, regardless of
where you want to sit in the four-part space: lush back patio and
bar, front sidewalk tables or a pair of inner rooms, one with views of
an open kitchen.

Seasons 52 *American*

23 | 24 | 23 | $42

Palm Beach Gardens | 11611 Ellison Wilson Rd. (PGA Blvd.) | 561-625-5852
Boca Raton | 2300 NW Executive Center Dr. (Glades Rd.) | 561-998-9952
www.seasons52.com

"Guilt-free" food (all items are under 475 calories) that "actually tastes exciting" – like "out-of-this-world" flatbreads and "cute" desserts in shot glasses – is the "unique concept" behind this "health-oriented but not health-nutty" chain featuring seasonal New American fare; "warm decor", "well-trained service", "interesting" wines and "active" bars with nightly entertainment further explain why they're "very popular."

32 East *American*

25 | 21 | 23 | $55

Delray Beach | 32 E. Atlantic Ave. (bet. 1st & Swinton Aves.) |
561-276-7868 | www.32east.com

Chef Nick Morfogen "continues to surprise and impress" with his "nightly changing" dinner menu featuring seasonal, local ingredients at this New American "favorite" in Delray Beach; service is "above par", and though tabs are "on the pricey side", it draws a "young, energetic" crowd that turns the inside into a "festive" "zoo" – those who prefer not to "scream" can sit outside and watch "*tout* Delray" stroll by on "fashionable" Atlantic Avenue.

Trattoria Romana *Italian*

26 | 21 | 22 | $63

Boca Raton | 499 E. Palmetto Park Rd. (NE 5th Ave.) | 561-393-6715 |
www.trattoriaromanabocaraton.com

A real "class act", this Boca Italian puts out "terrific" "old-fashioned" fare (with a "don't-miss" antipasto bar) that keeps it perpetually "crowded"; there's a hopping bar pouring cocktails and wine that "makes waits a lot more enjoyable", although some take issue with "expensive" prices and service that seems to "favor regulars."

Philadelphia

TOP FOOD RANKING

	Restaurant	Cuisine
29	Fountain	Continental/French
	Vetri	Italian
	Birchrunville Store	French/Italian
	Bibou	French
28	Sycamore	American
	Fond	American
	Paloma	French/Mexican
	Bluefin	Japanese
	Vedge	Vegan
	Sketch	Burgers
	Talula's Table	European
	Morimoto	Japanese
	Amada	Spanish
	Sovana Bistro	French/Mediterranean
	Little Fish	Seafood
	Domani Star	Italian
	Ela	American
	Capogiro	American/Dessert
	Majolica*	American
27	Zahav	Israeli

OTHER NOTEWORTHY PLACES

Restaurant	Cuisine
Alma de Cuba	Nuevo Latino
Barbuzzo	Mediterranean
Barclay Prime	Steak
Buddakan	Asian
Capital Grille	Steak
Chickie's & Pete's	Pub Food
Dmitri's	Greek
Han Dynasty	Chinese
Il Pittore	Italian
Iron Hill Brewery	American
Le Virtù	Italian
Modo Mio	Italian
Noord	Scandinavian
Osteria	Italian
Sbraga	American
Serpico	American
Talula's Garden	American
Tashan	Indian
Tinto	Spanish
Vernick Food & Drink	American

* Indicates a tie with restaurant above

	FOOD	DECOR	SERVICE	COST

Alma de Cuba *Nuevo Latino*
| 25 | 26 | 24 | $50 |

Rittenhouse | 1623 Walnut St. (bet. 16th & 17th Sts.) | 215-988-1799 |
www.almadecubarestaurant.com

You almost "expect Papa Hemingway" to appear at Stephen Starr and
Douglas Rodriguez's "upscale", "special-occasion" Nuevo Latino, still
"trendy" after a decade-plus in Rittenhouse; brace yourself for "inva-
sive noise levels" generated by "high rollers" who "come for the moji-
tos" in the "dim" lounge but stay for the "bold flavors" "from land and
sea" (e.g. "amazing" ceviche) and "world-class" desserts, all served
by a "prompt, attentive" staff in the sleek, contemporary space.

Amada *Spanish*
| 28 | 25 | 25 | $53 |

Old City | 217-219 Chestnut St. (bet. 2nd & 3rd Sts.) | 215-625-2450 |
www.amadarestaurant.com

Iron Chef Jose Garces' "rustic yet swanky" Spanish "crown jewel" in
Old City "still gets a big *olé*" for its "fabulous" tapas, "perfectly
crafted" sangria and "attentive" service, though it also gets a few jeers
for "noise levels" approaching a "soccer match"; fans recommend
"bringing a group to justify over-ordering", and since "noshing" makes
you "run up a bill", consider the "pig roast" (which must be ordered 72
hours in advance) or "tasting menus."

Barbuzzo ● *Mediterranean*
| 27 | 21 | 24 | $43 |

Washington Square West | 110 S. 13th St. (Sansom St.) | 215-546-9300 |
www.barbuzzo.com

You'd get "fresher" produce only "in the middle of a farmer's field"
gush fans of Marcie Turney and Valerie Safran's Med "gem" in
Washington Square West, offering "beautiful" fare featuring "locally cultivated ingredients" and "knowledgeable" service; the rustic, narrow space feels a bit "cramped" to some, but most find it
"well worth it", especially the budino dessert, which is "so good it
should be illegal."

Barclay Prime *Steak*
| 26 | 25 | 26 | $76 |

Rittenhouse | The Barclay | 237 S. 18th St. (Locust St.) | 215-732-7560 |
www.barclayprime.com

"Big-business types on expense accounts" and other high rollers head
to Stephen Starr's "meat mecca" on Rittenhouse Square, where
"mouthwatering steaks" are ferried by "professional" servers in a "hip
library" setting, and bartenders pour "terrific drinks" at the "chic
bar"; while some decry "overpriced" wines and the "gimmicky $100
cheesesteak", really, "any place where you can pick out your own knife
is automatically awesome."

Bibou ⓂⱫ *French*
| 29 | 21 | 27 | $55 |

Bella Vista | 1009 S. Eighth St. (Kimball St.) | 215-965-8290 |
www.biboubyob.com

Go ahead and "bring your best bottle" to this "intimate" BYO bistro
housed in a former row house in Bella Vista, where Pierre Calmels
creates "soulfully designed" French fare boasting flavors both
"subtle and bold", while his wife, Charlotte, will "treat you like
mom" did; it's almost "impossible to get a reservation", especially
on Sundays, when it offers an "amazing" $45 prix fixe, and remember
it's cash only.

Birchrunville Store Cafe 🅂 Ⓜ⇗ *French/Italian*   29 | 25 | 28 | $57

Birchrunville | 1403 Hollow Rd. (Flowing Springs Rd.) | 610-827-9002 |
www.birchrunvillestorecafe.com

"Take a GPS" and head into the "rolling hills of Chester County's horse country", home to Francis Trzeciak's French-Italian "gem" that's "hard to find and harder to forget", thanks to his "inspired" cuisine that was "farm-to-fork before it was cool", served by an "excellent" staff in an "intimate", high-ceilinged setting that lets you "pretend you are in Provence"; BYO makes the "steep" tabs "more palatable" (just don't forget to bring cash).

Bluefin 🅂 *Japanese*   28 | 19 | 23 | $43

East Norriton | 2820 Dekalb Pike (Germantown Pike) | 610-277-3917 |
www.restaurantbluefin.com

It can be "hard to get a reservation" at Yong Kim's Japanese BYO housed in an East Norriton strip mall, thanks to what many say is the "freshest, most creative sushi in the 'burbs", including "insanely delicious" rolls that "melt like butter"; spacious, contemporary digs and "smiling", "friendly" service are other pluses, and given the "awesome" fare and "reasonable" prices, many "can't help but over-order."

Buddakan ● *Asian*   27 | 27 | 25 | $57

Old City | 325 Chestnut St. (4th St.) | 215-574-9440 | www.buddakan.com

Still "buzzing" after many years, Stephen Starr's "sexy", "swanky" Old City Asian earns Philadelphia's Most Popular title thanks to "creative", "exceptionally flavorful" food (oh those "amazing" edamame ravioli) served by a "professional" staff in a "beautiful", "Buddhist-chic" setting; sure, the "lively crowd" and "thumping" "techno-beats" prompt some to "pray to Buddha for peace" and your wallet will end up "significantly lighter", but most agree the experience is "well worth it."

The Capital Grille *Steak*   26 | 25 | 26 | $65

Avenue of the Arts | 1338 Chestnut St. (Broad St.) | 215-545-9588
King of Prussia | 236 Mall Blvd. (Goddard Blvd.) | 610-265-1415
www.thecapitalgrille.com

An "upscale crowd" indulges its "carnivorous cravings" at this "clubby" national steakhouse chain, a "slice of red meat heaven" where the "awesome" steaks are "expertly prepared", "superb" bartenders pour "terrific" drinks and the "service is always stellar"; most agree it's "worth the splurge", so "bring lotsa money" for a "night to remember."

Capogiro Gelato Artisans *American/Dessert*   28 | 16 | 21 | $9

East Passyunk | 1625 E. Passyunk Ave. (Morris St.) | 215-462-3790
Rittenhouse | 117 S. 20th St. (Sansom St.) | 215-636-9250 ●
University City | Radian | 3925 Walnut St. (40th St.) | 215-222-0252 ●
Washington Square West | 119 S. 13th St. (Sansom St.) | 215-351-0900 ●
www.capogirogelato.com

Sweet tooths swoon over this dessert chain's "decadent", "silky rich" gelato made with seasonal, local ingredients, served by a "congenial" staff "generous with samples" of the "myriad flavors"; many tout it as a post-dinner stop to "really impress a date" (though it also serves a limited menu of New American fare), and while a few carp about "pricey", "small portions", for most it's a "treat" well worth the "extra time on the treadmill."

Chickie's & Pete's ❶ *Pub Food* | 23 | 22 | 22 | $26 |

Eastwick | 8500 Essington Ave. (Bartram Ave.) | 215-492-0569
Northeast Philly | 4010 Robbins Ave. (Mulberry St.) | 215-338-3060
South Philly | 1526 Packer Ave. (15th St.) | 215-218-0500
Bensalem | Parx Casino | 2999 Street Rd. (Tillman Dr.) | 267-525-7333
Warrington | 500 Easton Rd. (bet. Garden & Maple Aves.) | 215-343-5206

Chickie's & Pete's Cafe ❶ *Pub Food*

Northeast Philly | Boulevard Plaza | 11000 Roosevelt Blvd. (Plaza Dr.) |
215-856-9890
www.chickiesandpetes.com

"Crab fries rule" at this "high-decibel", Philadelphia-centric sports bar (ranked the city's Most Popular chain), which is "loaded with TVs" to "yell at" and "decent" fried food to douse with "beer, beer, beer"; though critics dismiss it as a "Chuck E. Cheese's for adults", with takes on the service ranging from "friendly" to "subpar", most consider it a "great place to get together with friends" – as long as they're "Philly fans."

Dmitri's *Greek* | 25 | 16 | 21 | $33 |

Northern Liberties | 944 N. Second St. (Laurel St.) | 215-592-4550
Queen Village | 795 S. Third St. (Catharine St.) | 215-625-0556 ⏁
Rittenhouse | 2227 Pine St. (23rd St.) | 215-985-3680
www.dmitrisrestaurant.com

Afishionados gladly sit "elbow-to-elbow" to savor "awesome seafood" "prepared as simply as possible" at this "informal" Greek taverna chainlet, whose prices are "friendly to the wallet" and help most overlook what some describe as "consistently inconsistent" service from a "hipster" staff; the Queen Village original is BYO and cash-only, while Northern Liberties is also BYO but accepts credit cards and Fitler Square takes plastic and has a liquor license (got that?).

Domani Star *Italian* | 28 | 19 | 25 | $35 |

Doylestown | 57 W. State St. (bet. Hamilton & Main Sts.) | 215-230-9100 |
www.domanistar.com

While the meatballs may be "to die for", "every dish on the menu is a hit" at this "convivial" Italian BYO in Downtown Doylestown, where the "fresh", "tasty" fare is "served with a smile" and "lives up to the prices" (especially the Sunday–Thursday dinner prix fixe, a "steal" of a deal); some report "cramped", "noisy" environs, but most declare it a "winner."

Ela ❶Ⓜ *American* | 28 | 24 | 25 | $50 |

Queen Village | 627 S. Third St. (Bainbridge St.) | 267-687-8512 |
www.elaphilly.com

Jason Cichonski is "wowing everyone" at his upscale-casual Queen Village New American with "inventive", "molecular cuisine" featuring "interesting pairings of textures and flavors" (the "liquid cookie dough dessert is to die for"); while some caution that "small plates lead to expensive dinners", it's nonetheless a "great neighborhood spot" that impresses "without trying to be too cool for school."

Fond ⊠Ⓜ *American* | 28 | 20 | 27 | $49 |

East Passyunk | 1537 S. 11th St. (Tasker St.) | 215-551-5000 |
www.fondphilly.com

"Over-the-top terrific" sums up surveyors' sentiments about this intimate East Passyunk corner bistro (in new digs, which may outdate its

FOOD DECOR SERVICE COST

Decor rating), where "every bite" of Lee Styer's New American cooking and Jessie Prawlucki's "heavenly desserts" "takes your breath away"; although it's not cheap, "special occasions" are well supported by Tory Keomanivong's "enthusiastic", "genuinely caring" servers, leading to an overall "memorable" experience.

Fountain Restaurant *Continental/French* `29` `28` `28` `$82`

Logan Square | Four Seasons Hotel | 1 Logan Sq. (Benjamin Franklin Pkwy.) | 215-963-1500 | www.fourseasons.com
Philadelphia's No. 1 for Food, Decor and Service, the Four Seasons' "formal but comfortable" French-Continental standout makes you "feel like royalty" with "fabulous" "feasts" of "succulent, creative" fare and "impeccable" service in a "beautiful" setting; "you feel rich just being there", though maybe less so after you leave – but "go ahead and splurge" since most agree it's the "standard by which all other restaurants should be judged."

Han Dynasty *Chinese* `25` `15` `19` `$26`

Manayunk | 4356 Main St. (bet. Grape & Levering Sts.) | 215-508-2066
Old City | 108 Chestnut St. (Front St.) | 215-922-1888
University City | 3711 Market St. (38th St.) | 215-222-3711
Exton | 260 N. Pottstown Pike (Waterloo Blvd.) | 610-524-4002
Royersford | Limerick Square Shopping Ctr. | 70 Buckwalter Rd. (Rte. 422) | 610-792-9600
www.handynasty.net
Aficionados advise be sure to "grab your water" and "take extra tissues" to cope with the "tongue-numbing", dial-by-number "heat" at Han Chiang's "affordable" Sichuan chainlet, where some fans would "probably trade" their "first-born child" for the "ecstasy-inducing" dan dan noodles; while the contemporary surroundings leave little impression, opinions of the owner range from "amusing to annoying."

Il Pittore *Italian* `26` `24` `25` `$63`

Rittenhouse | 2025 Sansom St. (bet. 20th & 21st Sts.) | 215-391-4900 | www.ilpittore.com
"Bring your bonus check" to experience chef Chris Painter's "inventive" takes on modern Italian cuisine at his and Stephen Starr's "intimate" storefront "splurge" in Rittenhouse; the "portions are small to allow for several courses" (you may find yourself "ordering more than you should"), and meals are enhanced by "smooth wine pairings" provided by a "lovely" staff that keeps an eye on you "without going overboard."

Iron Hill Brewery & Restaurant *American* `22` `21` `22` `$28`

Chestnut Hill | 8400 Germantown Ave. (bet. Gravers Ln. & Highland Ave.) | 215-948-5600 ☣
Phoenixville | 130 Bridge St. (Starr St.) | 610-983-9333
West Chester | 3 W. Gay St. (High St.) | 610-738-9600
Media | 30 E. State St. (Church St.) | 610-627-9000
North Wales | Shoppes at English Vill. | 1460 Bethlehem Pike (bet. Enclave Blvd. & Welsh Rd.) | 267-708-2000
Lancaster | Franklin & Marshall College | 781 Harrisburg Ave. (bet. Dillerville Rd. & Prince St.) | 717-291-9800
www.ironhillbrewery.com
"There's no better place to be Friday at 5" than these "always-busy" local brewpubs whose "bright, open" (maybe a little "corporate") settings permit prime viewing of the brewing process while amping the

"noise"; surveyors tout the "inventive" "comfort food" "for the masses" and "down-to-earth" service but add "the beer alone is worth the trip" – so "make sure to get the sampler and a designated driver."

Le Virtù *Italian*   27 | 22 | 23 | $49

East Passyunk | 1927 E. Passyunk Ave. (bet. McKean & Mifflin Sts.) | 215-271-5626 | www.levirtu.com

"Craveable fresh pasta", "housemade salumi" – "you cannot wrong with anything" on the "rustic" menu at this "casual" yet "elegant" Abruzzese "destination" in East Passyunk where "the pig head sits in the kitchen in full view" (on weekends) to remind that this is "not your standard red-sauce Italian"; while some think the "servers need more personality", others "feel well cared for", and the "lovely" outdoor garden is an added bonus.

Little Fish BYOB *Seafood*   28 | 16 | 23 | $44

Bella Vista | 746 S. Sixth St. (Fitzwater St.) | 267-455-0172 | www.littlefishbyob.com

Making a big "splash" despite its "tiny" dimensions, Chadd Jenkins' "solid" BYO Bella Vista seafooder hooks fish lovers with its "creative" chalkboard menu and a "superior" Sunday tasting menu full of "fabulous surprises"; fans describe it as a "perfect little hole-in-the-wall" with a "quaint" "Village feel" and "helpful" staff, suggesting "make reservations early" – "you won't be sorry, if you can get in."

Majolica ⓜ *American*   28 | 21 | 25 | $49

Phoenixville | 258 Bridge St. (bet. Gay & Main Sts.) | 610-917-0962 | www.majolicarestaurant.com

Cognoscenti urge you to "let your bouche be amused" by chef Andrew Deery's "artistic" treatment of New American cuisine – "amazing flavors not usually found in the suburbs" – at the pricey, "trendsetting" Phoenixville BYO he runs with his wife, Sarah Johnson; between the "lovely, intimate" dining room and "warm" service with "no rush", most say it's an "unpretentious indulgence" that's "worth the trip" for a "special night out."

Modo Mio ⓜ✏ *Italian*   27 | 17 | 24 | $40

Northern Liberties | 161 W. Girard Ave. (Hancock St.) | 215-203-8707 | www.modomiorestaurant.com

"Every dish pops with flavor" on the moderately priced four-course Italian 'turista' menus at Peter McAndrews' "modest" BYO trattoria near Northern Liberties, which many deem one of the "best deals in the city"; the service is "knowledgeable", although a few find it "quirky", while others complain that the space's "horrific acoustics" make "lip-reading" necessary; P.S. don't forget cash, and "reservations are a must."

Morimoto *Japanese*   28 | 27 | 26 | $74

Washington Square West | 723 Chestnut St. (bet. 7th & 8th Sts.) | 215-413-9070 | www.morimotorestaurant.com

"Omakase: just do it" urge boosters of this "one-of-a-kind" Japanese from Stephen Starr and Iron Chef Masaharu Morimoto in Washington Square West, where legions are tempted to "close their eyes in rapturous delight" over the "heavenly" fare – but if they did, they'd miss the "color-changing", "postmodern" setting; "knowledgeable" service is another plus, and despite "splurge" pricing, many leave "screaming 'I want Mor-imoto!'"

Noord ☒ *Scandinavian*

| - | - | - | E |

East Passyunk | 1046 Tasker St. (11th St.) | 267-909-9704 | www.noordphilly.com

Garrulous, globe-trotting chef Joncarl Lachman (ex Chicago's Home Bistro) helms this spare, white-tablecloth BYO in burgeoning East Passyunk whose menu plunders the bounty of the North Sea; the somewhat upscale offerings include nods to the chef's Dutch heritage, like Amsterdam-style mussels, augmented by refined takes on home-spun Nordic favorites, such as smørrebrød (house-smoked fish on dark rye) and lohikeitto (salmon chowder).

Osteria *Italian*

| 27 | 25 | 26 | $55 |

North Philly | 640 N. Broad St. (Wallace St.) | 215-763-0920 | www.osteriaphilly.com

"Tuscany" is just a "cab ride" away courtesy of this "pricey" North Philly "treasure" where the "bustle and warmth" is "conducive to conversation" and chef Jeff Michaud's "robust", "inventive" Italian cooking makes "every mouthful a delight", from "savory, crispy" pizzas and "house-cured" salumi to "creative" handmade pastas matched with a "mouthwatering wine list"; "knowledgeable" service orchestrates a "*fantastico*" experience in which the Vetri Family's "golden touch is apparent."

Paloma Mexican Haute Cuisine ☒☒ *French/Mexican*

| 28 | 21 | 25 | $54 |

Bella Vista | 763 S. Eighth St. (Catharine St.) | 215-928-9500 | www.palomafinedining.com

Fans predict "you'll keep coming back" to this "cozy", white-tablecloth Bella Vista BYO for chef-owner Adán Saavedra's "inventive" "haute" French fare "laced" with the "flavors and spices of Mexico" and topped off with his wife Barbara's "homemade desserts" (the "spicy sorbets alone are worth the visit" to some); "charming" service, "reasonable" prices and a "quiet" setting with "ample room" "between tables" seal the deal.

Sbraga *American*

| 27 | 24 | 24 | $64 |

Avenue of the Arts | 440 S. Broad St. (Pine St.) | 215-735-1913 | www.sbraga.com

A "*Top Chef* creates a top restaurant" is the story line of Kevin Sbraga's New American located "steps from the Kimmel Center", where the TV "winner" provides "affordable fine dining" with a "bargain" prix fixe of "mind-bending" small plates; an open kitchen anchors the "trendy" rustic space (which can get "noisy"), while the "friendly", "knowl-edgeable" staff works hard to ensure a "memorable evening."

Serpico *American*

| - | - | - | E |

South St. | 604 South St. (6th St.) | 215-925-3001 | www.serpicoonsouth.com

Peter Serpico, the former lieutenant of David Chang's Momofuku empire, partners with Stephen Starr at this sophisticated, upscale Asian-inspired New American on South Street; the sexily low-lit, white-brick space, anchored by a bustling open kitchen, includes ringside seating at an expansive chef's counter.

Sketch *Burgers*
28 | 20 | 24 | $15

Fishtown | 413 E. Girard Ave. (Columbia Ave.) | 215-634-3466 |
www.sketch-burger.com

"Super-messy burgers" and other "comfort-food" classics are "worth the hike" to this Fishtown "joint" where diners doodle while they wait and seating options include "vintage church pews"; Kobe beef and even vegan patties plus sauces that add "the right amount of sloppy, fatty goodness" are a testament to the kitchen's "creativity", and while it all "might cost a few bucks more", "passionate" service seals the deal.

Sovana Bistro Ⓜ *French/Mediterranean*
28 | 23 | 26 | $53

Kennett Square | 696 Unionville Rd. (Rte. 926) | 610-444-5600 |
www.sovanabistro.com

Enthusiasts encourage city folk to "get in your Zipcars" because this "contemporary" Kennett Square destination is "worth the ride" for "surprising, original" French-Med fare that reflects "great use of locally grown or raised" ingredients – predictably, the "tiny tables" are "packed at all hours"; accounting for the "quality" eats, "first-class" service and optional BYO, "prices are not bad", but "bring extra cash" anyway.

Sycamore Ⓜ *American*
28 | 22 | 25 | $45

Lansdowne | 14 S. Lansdowne Ave. (Baltimore Ave.) | 484-461-2867 |
www.sycamorebyo.com

Local ingredients shine on the "wonderfully inventive" New American tasting and prix fixe menus at this BYO "gem" in a "low-key" Lansdowne storefront where the "owner's belief in service is inspiring"; a "first-class" cheese course, "wonderful" toffee pudding dessert and "incredible" "cocktail mixers" are pluses, leaving "high prices" as the only complaint.

Talula's Garden *American*
27 | 27 | 25 | $63

Washington Square West | 210 W. Washington Sq. (Walnut St.) |
215-592-7787 | www.talulasgarden.com

"Oohs and ahs" fill the "farmhouse-chic" confines of this "spectacular" collaboration between Aimee Olexy (Talula's Table) and Stephen Starr in Washington Square West, where the "wonderfully inventive" American cuisine showcases the "best ingredients the season has to offer", including a "can't-miss cheese plate"; "impeccable" servers "lead you to exactly what you want", and in summer the "gorgeous garden" is "perfect" for a "magical meal" that's "well worth" the "high price."

Talula's Table *European*
28 | 24 | 28 | $140

Kennett Square | 102 W. State St. (Union St.) | 610-444-8255 |
www.talulastable.com

"The tough part is getting in" to Aimee Olexy's "outstanding" European BYO in a Kennett Square market, where groups of ten to 12 sit at the titular table for the "superb" eight-course prix fixe (no à la carte) that delivers an "educating experience for the taste buds"; you'll need "deep pockets" and reservations "a year in advance", but the "staff couldn't be friendlier" and most agree it "deserves all the accolades it receives."

Tashan *Indian*
25 | 25 | 23 | $51

Avenue of the Arts | 777 S. Broad St. (Catharine St.) | 267-687-2170 |
www.mytashan.com

"Bollywood buzz with upscale Indian" fare sums up this eatery on Avenue of the Arts that "could make an Indian foodie out of anyone"

FOOD | DECOR | SERVICE | COST

with its "creative spin" and nontraditional approach; far from "lamb vindaloo territory", this is fusion gone "to nirvana" in a "snazzy" setting where servers who are "excited to share their knowledge" help make the "pricey" experience "worth every penny."

Tinto *Spanish*

27 | 24 | 24 | $56

Rittenhouse | 114 S. 20th St. (Sansom St.) | 215-665-9150 | www.tintorestaurant.com

This "impeccable" Rittenhouse Basque is Iron Chef "Jose Garces at his best", showcasing "innovative" pintxos (small plates) that are "huge in flavor" and "remain true to Spanish spirit", enhanced by selections from an "amazing wine list" and served in an "intimate", "comfortable" bi-level space; "informed" staffers help create a "convivial", "more personal" vibe than at some of his other operations, and though it's "not cheap", most consider it a "winner."

Vedge 🅼 *Vegan*

28 | 28 | 28 | $47

Washington Square West | 1221 Locust St. (Camac St.) | 215-320-7500 | www.vedgerestaurant.com

Rich Landau and Kate Jacoby make you "forget images of hippies and heavy-handed meat substitutes" with "inventive, delectable" vegan small plates featuring "astoundingly fresh" veggies at their "elegant" successor to Horizons, set in a "charming old mansion" in Washington Square West; "gorgeous" decor and "excellent" service add to its allure, and while a few gripe about "pricey" "small portions", the "extraordinary" fare makes even "hard-core carnivores" "consider giving up meat."

Vernick Food & Drink 🅼 *American*

- | - | - | E

Rittenhouse | 2031 Walnut St. (21st St.) | 267-639-6644 | www.vernickphilly.com

Chef Gregory Vernick (who spent years working with Jean-Georges Vongerichten) is behind this bi-level American in a Rittenhouse brownstone, serving a pricey menu of simple, polished classics; the chic, Euro-inspired setting includes a small counter at the open kitchen and sunny window seating on the second floor.

Vetri 🅼 *Italian*

29 | 25 | 28 | $202

Washington Square West | 1312 Spruce St. (bet. Broad & 13th Sts.) | 215-732-3478 | www.vetriristorante.com

Acolytes attest "heaven on earth" can be found in an "unassuming" townhouse in Washington Square West, home of Marc Vetri's flagship Italian, a "gastronomic tour de force" that's "high-end" "without being ostentatious", offering "sublime" cuisine and "professional" service; while you may have to "raid your 401(k)" given the figures listed on the prix fixe–only menu, it's on just about "everyone's bucket list."

Zahav *Israeli*

27 | 24 | 26 | $51

Society Hill | 237 St. James Pl. (2nd St.) | 215-625-8800 | www.zahavrestaurant.com

A "breath of fresh international air", Michael Solomonov's "one-of-a-kind" Society Hill Israeli "blends traditional food" (think "heavenly hummus") with "modern techniques" for "delectable combinations" to "keep your tongue guessing"; a "responsive" staff elevates the "casual" setting and guides diners through the journey – a "splurge", but an "adventure" that acolytes assert "everyone must try."

Phoenix/Scottsdale

TOP FOOD RANKING

Restaurant	Cuisine
29 Binkley's	American
Kai	Eclectic
28 Pane Bianco	Sandwiches
Mastro's City Hall	Steak
Dick's Hideaway	Southwestern
Nobuo at Teeter House	Japanese
Vincent Market Bistro	French
27 Romeo's Euro Cafe	Mediterranean
Mastro's Steakhouse	Steak
Rokerij	Southwestern/Steak

OTHER NOTEWORTHY PLACES

Capital Grille	Steak
Chompie's	Deli
Fleming's Prime	Steak
FnB Restaurant	American
Grimaldi's Pizzeria	Pizza
P.F. Chang's	Chinese
Pizzeria Bianco	Pizza
Rancho Pinot	American
ShinBay	Japanese
Vincent's on Camelback	French/Southwestern

Binkley's Restaurant ⊠Ⓜ *American*   29 | 22 | 28 | $82

Cave Creek | 6920 E. Cave Creek Rd. (Vermeersch Rd.) | 480-437-1072 | www.binkleysrestaurant.com

"Fasten your seat belts" at this "expensive" Cave Creek New American – voted the Phoenix/Scottsdale area's No. 1 for Food – because chef-owner Kevin Binkley conducts a "culinary magical mystery tour" focusing on customized tasting menus with "surprising combinations" and "beautifully prepared small plates" inspired by molecular gastronomy; the "romantic", "out-of-the-way" setting, "flawless" service and "expert wine pairings" also help make it the "best excuse for a splurge."

The Capital Grille *Steak*   27 | 26 | 26 | $51

Camelback Corridor | Biltmore Fashion Park | 2502 E. Camelback Rd. (bet. Orange Dr. & 24th St.) | Phoenix | 602-952-8900

North Scottsdale | Promenade Shopping Ctr. | 16489 N. Scottsdale Rd. (Frank Lloyd Wright Blvd.) | Scottsdale | 480-348-1700
www.thecapitalgrille.com

"Classic" and "classy", these steakhouse chain branches exude an "old-school feel" with "dark wood", "crisp linens" and an "upscale" clientele; "fabulous steaks", "to-die-for sides" and "top-notch wines" match the "fantastic" service, so it's a good fit when "you want to impress others" – and you have the cash to burn.

	FOOD	DECOR	SERVICE	COST

Chompie's *Deli*

23 | 18 | 20 | $15

North Scottsdale | Mercado Del Rancho | 9301 E. Shea Blvd. (92nd St.) | 480-860-0475
Chandler | Chandler Village Ctr. | 3481 W. Frye Rd. (Chandler Village Dr.) | 480-398-3008
North Phoenix | Paradise Valley Mall | 4550 E. Cactus Rd. (Tatum Blvd.) | Phoenix | 602-710-2910
www.chompies.com

This "kosher-style" mini-chain is the "closest thing to a New York deli" in Arizona say fans who inhale "delicious", "piled-high" corned beef and pastrami sandwiches, along with bagels, matzo ball soup and other Jewish "comfort foods"; "friendly", "fun" service and "reasonable prices" are also part of the ritual.

Dick's Hideaway *Southwestern*

28 | 23 | 24 | $21

North Phoenix | Sunprite Ctr. | 6008 N. 16th St. (Bethany Home Rd.) | Phoenix | 602-241-1881 | www.richardsonsnm.com

"Watch the cooks working behind the bar" as they prepare "incredible" New Mexico–style Southwestern grub at this "small", "busy" North Phoenix spot, an offshoot of Richardson's; moderate prices and "fast" service add extra luster to a "precious gem."

Fleming's Prime Steakhouse & Wine Bar *Steak*

27 | 25 | 26 | $52

Chandler | 905 N. 54th St. (bet. Harrison St. & Ray Rd.) | 480-940-1900
North Scottsdale | Market St. at DC Ranch | 20753 N. Pima Rd. (Market St.) | Scottsdale | 480-538-8000
Scottsdale | 6333 N. Scottsdale Rd. (Lincoln Dr.) | 480-596-8265
www.flemingssteakhouse.com

"Consistency is the name of the game" at these "lively" links of the national chophouse chain, where the "scrumptious steaks" are "cooked to perfection", the cocktails are "potent" and the wines by the glass are "excellent"; "top-level" service and "beautiful surroundings" help justify the "hefty" price points.

FnB Restaurant Ⓜ *American*

26 | 20 | 26 | $43

Scottsdale | 7125 E. Fifth Ave. (Craftsman Ct.) | 480-284-4777 | www.fnbrestaurant.com

Chef-owner Charleen Badman "does magic with vegetables and a mesquite grill" at this upscale New American, conjuring up an "ever-changing menu" of "unexpected" entrees, buttressed by an "extensive", Arizona-centric wine list; after a post-Survey move within Old Town, it's more spacious, which may outdate the Decor rating.

Grimaldi's Pizzeria *Pizza*

23 | 21 | 22 | $17

Chandler | The Falls at Ocotillo | 1035 W. Queen Creek Rd. (Alma School Rd.) | 480-812-2100
Chandler | Casa Paloma Shopping Ctr. | 7131 W. Ray Rd. (56th St.) | 480-785-1600
Gilbert | SanTan Vill. | 2168 E. Williams Field Rd. (Santana Frwy.) | 480-814-7722
North Scottsdale | Scottsdale Quarter | 15147 N. Scottsdale Rd. (bet. Butherus Dr. & Greenway Hayden Loop) | Scottsdale | 480-596-4070
North Scottsdale | Market St. at DC Ranch | 20715 N. Pima Rd. (Market St.) | Scottsdale | 480-515-5588

(continued)

Grimaldi's Pizzeria

Old Town | 4000 N. Scottsdale Rd. (Indian School Rd.) | Scottsdale | 480-994-1100

Peoria | Park West | 9788 W. Northern Ave. (Agua Fria Frwy.) | 623-486-4455

www.grimaldispizzeria.com

Get a "taste of NY" at these straight-outta-Brooklyn pizzerias, where the coal-fired pies are topped with "flavorful sauce" and "high-quality ingredients"; "delightful" old-school decor and "courteous service" help justify tabs "on the high side" for pizza.

Kai ⓈⓂ *Eclectic* | 29 | 29 | 29 | $83 |

Chandler | Sheraton Wild Horse Pass Resort & Spa | 5594 W. Wild Horse Pass Blvd. (Maricopa Frwy.) | 602-225-0100 | www.wildhorsepassresort.com

There's "nothing like" this "upscale" Chandler beacon in the Sheraton Wild Horse Pass Resort, where the "imaginative" Native American-influenced Eclectic fare (e.g. "fantastic" buffalo filet mignon) is "fabulous in every way"; diners can bask in the "beautiful" traditional decor, mountain views and "flawless", "phenomenal" service", and if the cost makes it a "once-in-a-lifetime" experience for some, fans say it's "well worth it."

Mastro's City Hall Steakhouse *Steak* | 28 | 26 | 26 | $62 |

Fashion Square | 6991 E. Camelback Rd. (Goldwater Blvd.) | Scottsdale | 480-941-4700 | www.mastrosrestaurants.com

A "shrine to great steaks", this Fashion Square destination offers its "melt-in-your-mouth" meat alongside "shrimp cocktail like no other", lobster mac 'n' cheese that's "pure gluttony" and "never a bad wine"; if settling the bill "requires a small fortune", the payback is "superb service" and dining among the city's "who's who."

Mastro's Steakhouse *Steak* | 27 | 26 | 26 | $66 |

North Scottsdale | La Mirada Shopping Ctr. | 8852 E. Pinnacle Peak Rd. (Pima Rd.) | Scottsdale | 480-585-9500 | www.mastrosrestaurants.com

Some carnivores "find it difficult to eat steak anywhere but here" at this North Scottsdale chophouse thanks to "buttery" cuts like "unbelievable filet mignon and porterhouse" as well as "dependable" seafood alternatives, "sides large enough to share" and "well-made" cocktails; "consistent" service, "upscale" decor and a "terrific bar scene" add to an "above-and-beyond" experience that commands "premium prices."

Nobuo at Teeter House Ⓜ *Japanese* | 28 | 25 | 25 | $54 |

Downtown Phoenix | Heritage Sq. | 622 E. Adams St. (bet. 6th & 7th Sts.) | Phoenix | 602-254-0600 | www.nobuofukuda.com

Fans say "you can't get better" Japanese cuisine than at this "remarkable" (and expensive) Downtown izakaya, where chef Nobuo Fukuda is the "master" of "surprising combinations and wonderful presentations", including "magical" creations like edible fish bones and (literally) smoking small plates; the "lovely decor" and "historic setting" contribute to the overall "understated elegance"; P.S. it's a teahouse at lunchtime.

	FOOD	DECOR	SERVICE	COST

Pane Bianco *Sandwiches*   28 | 17 | 22 | $17

Central Phoenix | 4404 N. Central Ave. (bet. Cambell & Turney Aves.) |
Phoenix | 602-234-2100 | www.pizzeriabianco.com

This "special" Central Phoenix sandwich shop from Chris Bianco
(Pizzeria Bianco) uses "high-quality" local ingredients and "crusty"
homemade bread for lunch indulgences like a caprese (tomato, mozzarella and basil), while "amazing pizzas" emerge at dinner; modest
prices and "picnic-style seating" keep it "casual."

P.F. Chang's China Bistro *Chinese*   23 | 24 | 23 | $22

Chandler | Chandler Fashion Ctr. | 3255 W. Chandler Blvd.
(bet. Chandler Village Dr. & Price Rd.) | 480-899-0472
Fashion Square | The Waterfront | 7135 E. Camelback Rd. (Scottsdale Rd.) |
Scottsdale | 480-949-2610
Mesa | 6610 E. Superstition Springs Blvd. (Power Rd.) | 480-218-4900
North Scottsdale | Kierland Commons | 7132 E. Greenway Pkwy.
(Scottsdale Rd.) | Scottsdale | 480-367-2999
Peoria | Arrowhead Fountain Ctr. | 16170 N. 83rd Ave. (Paradise Ln.) |
623-412-3335
Tempe | 740 S. Mill Ave. (bet. 7th St. & University Dr.) | 480-731-4600
www.pfchangs.com

This "constantly busy" chain offers "reliable, tasty" fare that's "not real
Chinese but real-good Americanized Chinese" (the "wonderful chicken-
lettuce wraps" are a "must"), along with an "extensive cocktail list", all at
"not-so-outrageous" prices, which makes it the Phoenix/Scottsdale
area's Most Popular dining option; "solid service" and "delightful" "contemporary" decor are additional cogs in a "well-run machine."

Pizzeria Bianco Ⓢ *Pizza*   26 | 20 | 21 | $24

Downtown Phoenix | Heritage Sq. | 623 E. Adams St. (7th St.) |
Phoenix | 602-258-8300
Phoenix | Town & Country Mall | 4743 N. 20th St. (Camelback Rd.) |
602-368-3273
www.pizzeriabianco.com

"Huge crowds" congregate at chef-owner Chris Bianco's "legendary"
Downtown pizzeria (with a newer outlet at Town & Country Mall) for
"unforgettable" pies that are full of "smoky flavor" and crafted with
"attention to detail"; "attentive" servers navigate the "rustic", "elbow-
to-elbow" dining room, and there's a wine bar next door where you can
"sip while you wait."

Rancho Pinot ⓈⓂ *American*   27 | 19 | 25 | $52

Scottsdale | Lincoln Village Shopping Ctr. | 6208 N. Scottsdale Rd.
(bet. Lincoln & McDonald Drs.) | 480-367-8030 | www.ranchopinot.com

Even though the "delicious seasonal menu" changes at this Scottsdale
New American, the "fish, meat and poultry are all done well" year-round
by chef-owner Chrysa Robertson, and "spectacular" wines are another
constant; while some say the "cowboy-inspired decor" is "so-so", most
find the "high" prices "in line with the quality" and "elegant" service.

Rokerij *Southwestern/Steak*   27 | 25 | 25 | $31

North Phoenix | 6335 N. 16th St. (bet. Bethany Home Rd. & Maryland Ave.) |
Phoenix | 602-287-8900 | www.richardsonsnm.com

Spicy Hatch green chiles take "center stage" in the "amazing New
Mexican" dishes at this midpriced North Phoenix "neighborhood

	FOOD	DECOR	SERVICE	COST

gem" where the "delicious" Southwestern menu includes a "great piece of prime rib"; it's "small" and can be "cramped" during peak times, but "happy hour in the basement can't be beat."

Romeo's Euro Cafe *Mediterranean*
27 | 21 | 23 | $23

Gilbert | 207 N. Gilbert Rd. (Cullumber Ave.) | 480-962-4224 | www.eurocafe.com

"Order anything, but plan on sharing" at this modestly priced Gilbert taverna where chef-owner Romeo Taus creates "masterpieces" on a "huge menu" of "exquisite" Mediterranean fare; "friendly", "attentive" servers brighten the "bustling" atmosphere; P.S. save room for the "excellent" desserts from the "fabulous" in-house bakery.

ShinBay Ⓜ *Japanese*
▽ 27 | 27 | 28 | $70

Scottsdale | Scottsdale Seville | 7001 N. Scottsdale Rd. (Indian Bend Rd.) | 480-664-0180 | www.shinbay.com

Though "expensive", the prix fixe omakase dinners are "worth it" at this "fantastic" Scottsdale Japanese from "genius" chef Shinji Kurita; "excellent" sake, "amazing service" and a serene setting add to the experience; P.S. reservations must be made at least 24 hours in advance.

Vincent Market Bistro *French*
28 | 23 | 25 | $26

Camelback Corridor | 3930 E. Camelback Rd. (bet. 38th Pl. & 40th St.) | Phoenix | 602-224-0225 | www.vincentsoncamelback.com

One of the "best bangs for your buck" in town, this "friendly" French "oasis", a sibling and neighbor to Vincent's on Camelback, delivers a "marvelous" and "reasonably priced" bistro menu for breakfast, lunch and dinner; "cute", transporting decor transforms it into an "outpost of Paris."

Vincent's on Camelback Ⓩ *French/Southwestern*
24 | 21 | 24 | $55

Camelback Corridor | 3930 E. Camelback Rd. (40th St.) | Phoenix | 602-224-0225 | www.vincentsoncamelback.com

It's "always a treat to wine and dine" at Vincent Guerithault's "classic" (and spendy) Camelback Corridor bistro, where "wonderful" Southwestern-French fusion (think duck tamales) pairs with "a nice selection of wine"; a "charming" ambiance and "old-style" country decor combine with "warm", "attentive" service for a "special night out."

Portland, OR

TOP FOOD RANKING

Restaurant	Cuisine
29 Painted Lady	Pacific NW
28 Le Pigeon	French
Genoa	Italian
Evoe	European/Sandwiches
Cabezon	Seafood
Lardo	Sandwiches
Andina	Peruvian
Noho's	Hawaiian
Lovely's Fifty Fifty	Pizza
Nostrana	Italian

OTHER NOTEWORTHY PLACES

Flying Pie	Pizza
Gustav's	German
Heathman	French/Pacific NW
Higgins	Pacific NW
Jake's Famous Crawfish	Seafood
McMenamins	Pub Food
Ox	Argentinean
Paley's Place	Pacific NW
Pok Pok	Thai
Woodsman Tavern	American

Andina *Peruvian* **28 | 26 | 26 | $40**

Pearl District | Pennington Bldg. | 1314 NW Glisan St. (bet. 13th & 14th Aves.) | Portland | 503-228-9535 | www.andinarestaurant.com
An array of "lovely flavors" "tickle your taste buds" at this Pearl District "destination", where "adventurous" eaters tuck into "delicious, modern" Peruvian fare – plus a "huge selection" of "inventive, colorful" tapas – and wash it down with "amazing" "regional cocktails"; "warm" service matches the "boisterous", "gorgeous" environs, and though "pricey", there's no denying it's the "real deal."

Cabezon *Seafood* **28 | 25 | 27 | $36**

Hollywood | 5200 NE Sacramento St. (52nd Ave.) | Portland | 503-284-6617 | www.cabezonrestaurant.com
This "family-run" Hollywood "neighborhood gem" offers a "wonderful", daily changing menu of "creative" fin fare, as well as a number of "options for those who don't want seafood"; a "friendly" staff makes you "feel welcome" in the wooden-raftered interior (and at the sidewalk tables), and if some find the bill a tad "spendy", most agree it's "worth it."

Evoe Ⓜ *European/Sandwiches* **28 | 21 | 25 | $21**

Hawthorne | Pastaworks | 3731 SE Hawthorne Blvd. (bet. 37th & 38th Aves.) | Portland | 503-232-1010 | www.pastaworks.com
"Every bite" of chef Kevin Gibson's "unusual, creative" sandwiches and small plates is a "burst of flavor" insist insiders who "sit at the

counter" of this Hawthorne "gem" and watch as the European-inspired dishes "come together"; it's set in a "simple, small" space in an "odd location" (inside the gourmet grocery Pastaworks), but a "large collection" of wines by the glass, modest prices and that "exquisite" chow overcome all; P.S. closes at 7 PM; closed Monday–Tuesday.

Flying Pie Pizzeria *Pizza*

27 | 21 | 24 | $21

Montavilla | 7804 SE Stark St. (78th Ave.) | Portland | 503-254-2016
Gresham | 1600 NW Fairview Dr. (Burnside Rd.) | 503-328-0018
Lake Oswego | 3 Monroe Pkwy. (Boones Ferry Rd.) | 503-675-7377
Milwaukie | 16691 SE McLoughlin Blvd. (Naef Rd.) | 503-496-3170
www.flying-pie.com

"You'll never leave hungry" from this "quality" pizza chainlet, where the "out-of-this-world" pies "heaped high" with "fresh" meat and veggies are "not a solo" venture ("bring friends") – and come at tabs that lead frequent fliers to advise "you get way more than you pay for"; they skew "noisy", but the "smiling service is always a plus", as are the "laid-back", "family-oriented" vibe and "offbeat" video games.

Genoa ⓜ *Italian*

28 | 26 | 28 | $85

Belmont | 2832 SE Belmont St. (bet. 28th & 29th Aves.) | Portland | 503-238-1464 | www.genoarestaurant.com

A "beloved" Belmont "institution" for "romantic", "unhurried" evenings full of "food artistry", this "formal" Italian "wows" with an "exquisite" five-course prix fixe menu of "imaginatively prepared", "consistently superb" plates (no à la carte); the "impeccable service" includes a sommelier at the "top of his game", and while it's "expensive", it's "well worth it."

Gustav's *German*

25 | 24 | 24 | $25

Hollywood | 5035 NE Sandy Blvd. (50th Ave.) | Portland | 503-288-5503
Clackamas | 12605 SE 97th Ave. (Sunnyside Rd.) | 503-653-1391
Tigard | 10350 SW Greenburg Rd. (Oak St.) | 503-639-4544
www.gustavs.net

"*Wunderbar!*" declare devotees of this "busy" local chainlet revered for its "gut-busting" platters of "hearty", "full-flavored" German fare, "awesome deals" ("happy hour? yes, please") and "super-friendly" service; the "festive" atmosphere, fueled by "some of the best imported beers" on tap, may just "make you want to wear lederhosen" – no wonder it's ranked the Most Popular restaurant in Portland.

Heathman Restaurant & Bar *French/Pacific NW*

26 | 25 | 26 | $47

Downtown | Heathman Hotel | 1001 SW Broadway (Salmon St.) | Portland | 503-790-7752 | www.heathmanrestaurantandbar.com

"Elegance without pretense" takes center stage at this "romantic" venue in Downtown's Heathman Hotel, where "inventive" "French-inflected" Pacific NW fare is served – and whose "terrific" breakfasts, high teas and "cool happy hours" also have a fanbase; "impeccable" service and a seemingly "bottomless" wine cellar add to the "high-end enjoyment."

Higgins Restaurant & Bar ● *Pacific NW*

27 | 24 | 27 | $46

Downtown | 1239 SW Broadway (Jefferson St.) | Portland | 503-222-9070 | www.higginsportland.com

"Uniformly superb" NW dishes comprising the "freshest local ingredients" have kept "godfather of sustainability" Greg Higgins and his

Downtown bistro near the "top of the Portland food chain" for years; "outstanding" Oregon wines "add another dimension to meals", while the "classy" yet "relaxed" vibe in the "always-busy" dining room ("make reservations!") is echoed by a staff of "total pros"; P.S. the "lively" bar boasts an "astonishing beer list" – and "less-expensive" tabs.

Jake's Famous Crawfish *Seafood* 27 | 24 | 26 | $38

West End | 401 SW 12th Ave. (Stark St.) | Portland | 503-226-1419 | www.jakesfamouscrawfish.com

This "legendary Portland seafood palace" is "still delivering the goods" after 100-plus years in its "clubby" West End digs, where "fresh, delicious" fish comes accompanied by "professional" service; it gets a "little pricey", which explains why the "bargain" lunch specials and "amazing" happy hours are especially "popular" – and that's when you'll see a "healthy amount of locals" among a "lot of tourists" in the eatery that spawned the McCormick & Schmick's chain.

Lardo *Sandwiches* 28 | 21 | 27 | $17

Hawthorne | 1212 SE Hawthorne Blvd. (12th Ave.) | Portland | 503-234-7786
West End | 1205 SW Washington St. (12th Ave.) | Portland
www.lardopdx.com

Having originally peddled his "melt-in-your-mouth" pork products and "delicious" fries from one of the "cutest" food trucks around, "talented" chef Rick Gencarelli is now firmly rooted at this brick-and-mortar sandwich shop in Hawthorne and the West End (not reflected in the Decor score); expect "awesome" pig-centric sammies, plus plenty of indoor/outdoor seating and plenty of beer on tap.

Le Pigeon *French* 28 | 22 | 25 | $46

Lower Burnside | 738 E. Burnside St. (8th Ave.) | Portland | 503-546-8796 | www.lepigeon.com

"Impeccable" French cuisine that blends "whimsy, precision and inventiveness" attracts an "eclectic crowd" to this "snug joint" in Lower Burnside, where "loyal minions" snag seats at communal tables or at the counter to watch "highly skilled" (and "tattooed") chef Gabriel Rucker turn out "genius dishes" from an "ever-changing menu"; while some find it "pricey" for the tight fit, most are "drooling to go back."

Lovely's Fifty Fifty Ⓜ *Pizza* 28 | 22 | 26 | $25

Mississippi | 4039 N. Mississippi Ave. (bet. Mason & Shaver Sts.) | Portland | 503-281-4060 | www.lovelysfiftyfifty.com

At this "cute, kitschy" Mississippi joint, "gorgeous" wood-fired pizzas with "unconventional", locally sourced toppings share space on a gently priced menu with "delicious" salads and "killer" housemade ice cream (including salted caramel – "OMG!") made all the better by "great service"; naturally, it's almost "always jammed" with a "lively" crowd, but no matter: loyalists just "love this place."

McMenamins Bagdad *Pub Food* 24 | 23 | 22 | $22

Hawthorne | 3702 SE Hawthorne Blvd. (37th Ave.) | Portland | 503-236-9234

McMenamins Barley Mill Pub *Pub Food*

Hawthorne | 1629 SE Hawthorne Blvd. (17th Ave.) | Portland | 503-231-1492

McMenamins Black Rabbit Restaurant *Pub Food*

Troutdale | Edgefield | 2126 SW Halsey St. (244th Ave.) | 503-669-8610

(continued)

McMenamins Blue Moon ◐ *Pub Food*
Northwest Portland | 432 NW 21st Ave. (Glisan St.) | Portland | 503-223-3184

McMenamins Chapel Pub *Pub Food*
Humboldt | 430 N. Killingsworth St. (Commercial Ave.) | Portland | 503-286-0372

McMenamins Kennedy School Courtyard Restaurant ◐ *Pub Food*
Concordia | McMenamins Kennedy School | 5736 NE 33rd Ave. (bet. Jessup & Simpson Sts.) | Portland | 503-288-2192

McMenamins Ringlers Annex ◐ *Pub Food*
West End | 1223 SW Stark St. (Burnside St.) | Portland | 503-384-2700

McMenamins Ringlers Pub ◐ *Pub Food*
West End | 1332 W. Burnside St. (bet. 13th & 14th Aves.) | Portland | 503-225-0627

McMenamins St. Johns *Pub Food*
St. Johns | 8203 N. Ivanhoe St. (Richmond Ave.) | Portland | 503-283-8520

McMenamins Zeus Café *Pub Food*
West End | McMenamins Crystal Hotel | 303 SW 12th Ave. (bet. Burnside & Stark Sts.) | Portland | 503-384-2500
www.mcmenamins.com
Additional locations throughout the Portland area

The "solid" if "basic" pub fare "goes down easy" with the "hearty", housemade craft beer at this "reliable" tavern family ranked Most Popular chain in Portland and owned by the McMenamin brothers, who specialize in restoring notable buildings and decking them out with "eclectic" furnishings and colorful murals; opinions on service run the gamut ("swell" to "slow"), but many agree that the environs are "mellow" and the inexpensive menu offers "something for everyone."

Noho's Hawaiian Cafe *Hawaiian* 28 | 22 | 25 | $18
Beaumont | 4627 NE Fremont St. (47th Ave.) | Portland | 503-445-6646
Clinton | 2525 SE Clinton St. (26th Ave.) | Portland | 503-233-5301
www.nohos.com

It's "like a mini-vacation to the islands" at this "authentic" Hawaiian eatery, where the "brilliant" barbecue "always hits the spot" ("Kalua pig makes for a mighty fine Friday night"), as do the "not-too-expensive" prices; while "helpful" servers and surfer-abilia can be expected at both locations, Beaumont features a "great patio", while alcohol-free Clinton can feel a bit "crowded" – though "the food really makes up for it."

Nostrana *Italian* 28 | 24 | 23 | $37
Buckman | 1401 SE Morrison St. (14th Ave.) | Portland | 503-234-2427 | www.nostrana.com

"Wonderful" thin-crust pizza "baked to blistered perfection" in a wood-fired oven attracts acolytes to Cathy Whims' "unpretentious" (some say "pricey") Buckman Italian that also wins converts for "authentic" dishes constructed from "high-quality ingredients handled simply"; though the oft-"crowded" digs can get "noisy at times", the "welcoming, knowledgeable" staff lends the "soaring", "lodge"-like space a "convivial" vibe.

Ox ☒ *Argentinean* | - | - | - | E |

Boise-Eliot | 2225 NE Martin Luther King Jr. Blvd. (bet. Sacramento & Thompson Sts.) | Portland | 503-284-3366 | www.oxpdx.com

The custom-made, wood-fired grill stars at this pricey Boise-Eliot Argentinean that pulls in crowds for its sizzling mash-up of South American and Pacific NW cuisines; like its namesake, the interior is sturdy and serviceable with an exposed-brick wall and simple tables that lend an everyday vibe; P.S. check out the adjacent bar if there's a wait.

The Painted Lady ☒ *Pacific NW* | 29 | 28 | 29 | $85 |

Newberg | 201 S. College St. (2nd St.) | 503-538-3850 | www.thepaintedladyrestaurant.com

"You're in for a remarkable" evening (and the Portland area's top-rated Food, Decor and Service) the "minute you step inside the picket fence" surrounding this wine-country "jewel" set in a "romantic" Newberg Victorian, where the "world-class" Pacific NW tasting menus are "fascinating in their variety, seasonality and freshness"; "well-orchestrated" service and "fabulous" local vinos add to the "stellar" experience; P.S. rezzies required; closed Monday and Tuesday.

Paley's Place Bistro & Bar *Pacific NW* | 27 | 24 | 26 | $58 |

Northwest Portland | 1204 NW 21st Ave. (Northrup St.) | Portland | 503-243-2403 | www.paleysplace.net

Within the "intimate" confines of a "charming" Victorian dwelling, "master chef" Vitaly Paley prepares "sophisticated", "always-surprising" Pacific NW fare replete with European flourishes and made from what fans call the "freshest" local ingredients in NW Portland; happily, he's backed by a "professional" staff and a "consummate hostess" "running the front of the house with ease" – his wife, Kimberly; P.S. reservations are "essential", especially for seats on the "gracious veranda."

Pok Pok *Thai* | 27 | 20 | 23 | $24 |

Division | 3226 SE Division St. (32nd Ave.) | Portland | 503-232-1387 | www.pokpokpdx.com

Pok Pok Noi *Thai*

Sabin | 1469 NE Prescott St. (bet. 14th Pl. & 15th Ave.) | Portland | 503-287-4149 | www.pokpoknoi.com

A "culinary mecca" say fans of this "gutsy" Division Thai and its "more casual, less crowded" Sabin offshoot where chef-owner Andy Ricker turns out "lip-smacking", "mind-blowing street food", like "unbelievably good chicken wings", plus "creative beverages" featuring "brilliant" drinking vinegars; sure, they're a "little pricey" for the genre, and the "cramped" Division digs are "mad busy", but the "hipster staff" is "prompt" and many agree they're area "musts"; P.S. sib Whiskey Soda Lounge (across the street from Pok Pok) offers drinks and nibbles.

The Woodsman Tavern *American* | 24 | 23 | 24 | $36 |

Division | 4537 SE Division St. (46th Ave.) | Portland | 971-373-8264 | www.woodsmantavern.com

Stumptown Coffee founder Duane Sorenson is the brains behind this Division "source of hyper-buzz", where a "professional" staff of "hairy guys and pretty gals" proffers "delicious" New American plates and inventive cocktails at modest tabs; the "cavernous" space features dark woods and vintage mountain landscapes that feed the rustic vibe.

San Antonio

TOP FOOD RANKING

Restaurant	Cuisine
28 Bistro Vatel	French
27 Sorrento	Italian
Bohanan's	Steak
Dough	Pizza
Silo	American
Il Sogno	Italian
Sandbar	Seafood
Grey Moss Inn	American
26 Biga on the Banks	American
Perry's Steakhouse & Grille	Steak

OTHER NOTEWORTHY PLACES

Arcade Midtown Kitchen	American
Bliss	American
Boudro's	Seafood/Steak
Citrus	American/Eclectic
Feast	American
Granary 'Cue & Brew	BBQ/Eclectic
La Gloria	Mexican
Monterey	American
Nao	Latin American
Rudy's	BBQ

Arcade Midtown Kitchen Ⓜ *American*   - | - | - | M

Near North | Pearl | 303 Pearl Pkwy. (Ave. A) | 210-233-1212 |
www.arcadesatx.com

This Near North American inside the Pearl complex offers up a seasonally changing menu of plates from its open kitchen, with influences taken from Southwestern, Southern, Italian and Mediterranean cuisines; the airy interior reuses former brewery goods, turning beer cases into lighting fixtures, and a garage door opens the bar onto an arched patio.

Biga on the Banks   *American*   26 | 26 | 25 | $50

River Walk | 203 S. St. Mary's St. (Market St.) | 210-225-0722 |
www.biga.com

"First-rate all the way" – and San Antonio's Most Popular restaurant – this "sophisticated" River Walk respite puts out an "excellent", "innovative" mix of New American and Southwest fare from chef-owner Bruce Auden in "industrial-chic" surroundings; add an "accommodating" staff and it's worth the "splurge"; P.S. look for pre- and post-theater prix fixe dinners as well as half-price options on entrees on weekends.

Bistro Vatel Ⓜ *French*   28 | 20 | 25 | $46

Olmos Park | 218 E. Olmos Dr. (bet. Judson & McCullough Aves.) |
210-828-3141 | www.bistrovatel.com

It may be a "low-key" bistro in an Olmos Park strip mall, but "lovely" fish, steaks and other "super", "high-quality" French fare from Damien

Watel earn it San Antonio's No. 1 Food rating; a "cozy atmosphere" and "good-value" pricing inspire repeat visits; P.S. the prix fixe menu is "a deal."

Bliss ⊠ Ⓜ *American*   − | − | − | E

Southtown | 926 S. Presa St. (bet. Devine & Sadie Sts.) | 210-225-2547 | www.foodisbliss.com

The first solo venture of well-respected chef Mark Bliss (Silo), this stylishly updated filling station in Southtown fuels appetites with high-octane, high-end New American dishes like chicken-fried oysters and seared scallops on cheesy grits, as well as daily creative extras; the space is enhanced with modern art and natural light, and the stove-side chef's table offers a glimpse of the calm control a well-run kitchen can be.

Bohanan's Prime Steaks & Seafood *Steak*   27 | 23 | 26 | $72

Downtown | 219 E. Houston St., 2nd fl. (bet. Navarro & St. Mary's Sts.) | 210-472-2600 | www.bohanans.com

A "classic steakhouse done right", this "much-loved" Downtown entry "exceeds expectations" with "outstanding" beef, a "stellar bar with well-made cocktails" and an "old-school" vibe; "expensive" tabs hardly faze the "expense-account" clientele; P.S. the bar is on the ground floor and stays open later with a light menu.

Boudro's on the Riverwalk *Seafood/Steak*   24 | 22 | 22 | $40

River Walk | 421 E. Commerce St. (bet. Losoya & Presa Sts.) | 210-224-8484 | www.boudros.com

It's always a "party" at this River Walk spot where "tourists and locals" angle for an outside seat for "mouthwatering" seafood and steaks with Texas touches, "famous" tableside guac and "strong drinks" that "will have you down for the count"; "exceptional people-watching" and "attentive service" seal the deal; P.S. "make reservations."

Citrus *American/Eclectic*   ∇ 26 | 24 | 24 | $45

Downtown | Hotel Valencia | 150 E. Houston St. (St. Mary's St.) | 210-230-8412 | www.hotelvalencia.com

"More than a hotel restaurant", this "chic" entry in Downtown's Valencia proves a "wonderful choice" for business or a date thanks to its "excellent" Eclectic–New American menu; the "upscale" setting also boasts River Walk views from the upper deck.

Dough *Pizza*   27 | 21 | 24 | $26

North Central | Blanco Junction Shopping Ctr. | 6989 Blanco Rd. (Loop 410) | 210-979-6565 | www.doughpizzeria.com

"Mamma mia!", there are "lines out the door every night" at this otherwise unassuming North Central pizzeria plying "superlative", "thin-crust" Neapolitan pies and other "fab" Italian items "with panache", including a "not-to-be-missed" housemade burrata; a "knowledgeable" staff rewards patient diners with "terrific" service, "generous wine pours" and modest bills, making it a "definite must-go."

Feast Ⓜ *American*   − | − | − | M

Southtown | 1024 S. Alamo St. (bet. Cedar & Mission Sts.) | 210-354-1024 | www.feastsa.com

Tongues are wagging about this Southtown small-plates purveyor and its hip New American fare paired with both classic and creative cocktails;

it has a cool, ethereal look with crystal chandeliers and acrylic furniture set against white walls, but pricing is decidedly down-to-earth.

The Granary 'Cue & Brew 🅂🅼 *BBQ/Eclectic*   – | – | – | M

Near North | Pearl | 602 Ave. A (Newell Ave.) | 210-228-0124 |
www.thegranarysa.com

In a renovated house adjacent to the Pearl complex, this Near North hot spot does double duty as a straightforward Texas-style barbecue joint serving meat by the pound or platter at lunchtime, while at dinner it morphs into a more upscale affair, offering an Eclectic assortment of creatively composed plates, some with flavor nods to other countries' barbecue traditions; picnic-style bench seating and house-crafted beer keep things cozy and convivial.

Grey Moss Inn *American*   27 | 26 | 26 | $45

Helotes | 19010 Scenic Loop Rd. (Blue Hill Dr.) | 210-695-8301 |
www.grey-moss-inn.com

With "all the charm of a country inn a short distance from San Antonio", this "delightful hideaway" in Helotes hosts "romantic dinners" galore in its "rustic" interior or its "beautiful" courtyard; the "unique" Texas-accented American menu features "delicious" steaks cooked on an outdoor grill, although some find the bills a touch costly.

Il Sogno 🅼 *Italian*   27 | 23 | 25 | $48

Near North | Pearl | 200 E. Grayson St. (Karnes St.) | 210-223-3900 |
www.pearlbrewery.com

A "don't-miss" antipasti table "tempts" on arrival and leads to "expertly prepared", "innovative" Italian plates from chef Andrew Weissman (Sandbar) at this Near Northerner in the Pearl complex; it's "pricey", but service is "impeccable", making entree into the "always" a-"buzz" industrial dining room "worth waiting" for.

La Gloria *Mexican*   23 | 21 | 16 | $20

Near North | Pearl | 100 E. Grayson St. (Elmira St.) | 210-267-9040 |
www.lagloriaicehouse.com

"Funky" and "informal", this Near North cantina in the Pearl complex from Johnny Hernandez specializes in "wonderful", "fantastically spiced" Mexican street food in small plates that are "fun to share"; admirers overlook uneven service and "not cheap" à la carte pricing, focusing instead on the "picturesque" views from the quieter end of the River Walk.

The Monterey 🅼 *American*   – | – | – | I

Southtown | 1127 S. St. Mary's St. (bet. Pereida & Stieren Sts.) |
210-745-2581 | www.themontereysa.com

"Incredibly inventive" American snacks grab the spotlight at this Southtown spot, a renovated gas station with "limited inside seating" and three times the space on the "great" patio; like the food menu, the considerable wine and beer selection is "affordably priced", just as you would expect from such an "eclectic, casual" environment.

Nao 🅂 *Latin American*   – | – | – | M

Near North | Culinary Institute of America | 312 Pearl Pkwy. (Karnee St.) |
210-554-6484 | www.naorestaurant.com

Ancient foodways and modern gastronomic techniques are woven into artfully composed Latin American dishes by students of the Culinary

	FOOD	DECOR	SERVICE	COST

Institute of America at this moderately priced Near Northerner; creative cocktails and light bites are dispensed from the bar in the warm, contemporary space, though limited seating demands advance reservations.

Perry's Steakhouse & Grille *Steak*

| | 26 | 26 | 25 | $55 |

La Cantera | The Shops at La Cantera | 15900 La Cantera Pkwy. (Loop 1604) | 210-558-6161 | www.perryssteakhouse.com

An "elegant place for business or special occasions", this chophouse chain is the place to "impress" with "wonderful" steaks, "outstanding" wines and a signature pork chop that's "not to be missed"; "top-notch" service, "attractive" settings and live jazz are added perks, but it's pretty "expensive" "unless you're on an expense account."

Rudy's *BBQ*

| | 25 | 16 | 20 | $16 |

Selma | 15560 I-35 N. (Pasatiempo) | 210-653-7839
Leon Springs | 24152 I-10 W. (Boerne Stage Rd.) | 210-698-2141
Westside | 10623 Westover Hills Blvd. (Hwy. 151) | 210-520-5552
www.rudysbbq.com

You can smell the smoke from "a mile away" at these "solid-as-a-rock" chain pit stops doling out "tender" BBQ brisket ("go for the extra moist") and "mouthwatering ribs" sided with "amazing" "signature creamed corn"; most are set in refurbished gas stations, so you can line up "cafeteria-style", "order by the pound" and fill up your tank on the way out – talk about "true fast food."

Sandbar Fish House & Market ⓈⓂ *Seafood*

| | 27 | 23 | 23 | $41 |

Near North | Pearl | 200 E. Grayson St. (Karnes St.) | 210-212-2221 | www.sandbarsa.com

"Every single dish is crafted with total precision" and tastes "superb" at this Near North seafooder overseen by Andrew Weissman (Il Sogno); its steel-and-white-tile locale in the Pearl complex is "a little stark" and the tabs are a bit "pricey", but don't let that deter you – it's unquestionably "worth it."

Silo Elevated Cuisine *American*

| | 27 | 25 | 26 | $41 |

Alamo Heights | 1133 Austin Hwy. (Exeter Rd.) | 210-824-8686
Loop 1604 | Ventura Plaza | 434 N. Loop 1604 NW (off Access Rd. 1604) | 210-483-8989
www.siloelevatedcuisine.com

Admirers attest it's "impossible to go wrong" at this Alamo Heights bistro or its Loop 1604 spin-off serving up a "surprising" roster of New American dishes in "chic" surroundings blessed with "cool" bar scenes; tabs are "pricey, but not outrageous" – no wonder both are so "popular."

Sorrento ⓈＺ *Italian*

| | 27 | 17 | 23 | $29 |

Alamo Heights | 5146 Broadway St. (Grove Pl.) | 210-824-0055 | www.sorrentopizzeria.com

"Great" pizza is the highlight of this Alamo Heights Italian with a ristorante component preparing antipasti, pastas and entrees; walletfriendly prices match the "homey, comfortable" environment, with red-checkered tablecloths and "families" galore.

San Diego

TOP FOOD RANKING

	Restaurant	Cuisine
29	Sushi Ota	Japanese
28	Tao	Asian/Vegetarian
	Market Restaurant	Californian
	Tapenade	French
27	Pamplemousse	American/French
	Ruth's Chris	Steak
	Donovan's	Steak
	West Steak	Steak/Seafood
	Blue Water	Seafood
	Mille Fleurs	French

OTHER NOTEWORTHY PLACES

Restaurant	Cuisine
Addison	French
Anthony's Fish	Seafood
A.R. Valentien	Californian
Brigantine Seafood	Seafood
George's Cal. Modern/Ocean	Californian
In-N-Out	Burgers
Island Prime/C-Level Lounge	Seafood/Steak
94th Aero Squadron	American/Steak
Phil's BBQ	BBQ
Wine Vault	Eclectic

Addison ⊠Ⓜ *French*   27 | 27 | 27 | $130

Carmel Valley | Grand Del Mar | 5200 Grand Del Mar Way (Del Mar Way) | 858-314-1900 | www.addisondelmar.com

"First class in every respect", this "extravagant" contemporary French venue draws seekers of "ethereal flavors" to Carmel Valley's "ultra-posh" Grand Del Mar resort, where chef William Bradley's "superior" prix fixe dinners (with "astounding" wine pairings) are considered by many to be among "SoCal's best"; the food is matched by "opulent villa" surroundings where you're "treated like royalty" by a "formal but warm" staff that earns the No. 1 rating for Service in San Diego – though you may have to "pawn the family jewels to afford it."

Anthony's Fish Grotto *Seafood*   24 | 20 | 22 | $31

Downtown | 1360 N. Harbor Dr. (Ash St.) | 619-232-5103
La Mesa | 9530 Murray Dr. (Water St.) | 619-463-0368

Anthony's Fishette *Seafood*

Downtown | 1360 N. Harbor Dr. (Ash St.) | 619-232-5103
www.gofishanthonys.com

"Around for decades", these "classic" midpriced seafooders, voted Most Popular in San Diego, still turn out "famous" chowder and other "delicious" daily catches for "tourists and locals" alike; service is "family-friendly", and though critics call these La Mesa and Downtown spots fairly "dated", they're won over by the "completely unpretentious" feel and "fresh ocean breezes" at the latter locale's more "casual" Fishette adjunct.

A.R. Valentien *Californian*

26 | 26 | 26 | $67

La Jolla | Lodge at Torrey Pines | 11480 N. Torrey Pines Rd. (Callan Rd.) | 858-777-6635 | www.arvalentien.com

Chef Jeff Jackson "works wonders" with the "freshest" of "farm-to-table" ingredients to create a "constantly changing" menu of "incomparable" Cal cuisine at this "unique destination" in La Jolla's Lodge at Torrey Pines; "impeccable" service that's "gracious yet unobtrusive" and a "beautiful, Craftsman-style" setting with "majestic" golf-course views make it a "gift to San Diego" – albeit a "pricey" one.

Blue Water Seafood *Seafood*

27 | 15 | 20 | $21

India Street | 3667 India St. (bet. Chalmers & Washington Sts.) | 619-497-0914 | www.bluewaterseafoodsandiego.com

Fish doesn't get any "fresher" "unless you catch it yourself" say fans of this "bang-for-the-buck" India Street restaurant/market's "delicious, customizable seafood"; there's "no pretension – or ambiance" – so patrons can wait in the "long lines" "wearing drenched wet suits" and dine on "paper plates with plastic utensils."

Brigantine Seafood *Seafood*

24 | 22 | 23 | $35

Del Mar | 3263 Camino Del Mar (Via De La Valle) | 858-481-1166
Coronado | 1333 Orange Ave. (Adella Ave.) | 619-435-4166
La Mesa | 9350 Fuerte Dr. (bet. Grossmont Blvd. & Severin Dr.) | 619-465-1935
Escondido | 421 W. Felicita Ave. (Centre City Pkwy.) | 760-743-4718
Point Loma | 2725 Shelter Island Dr. (Shafter St.) | 619-224-2871
Poway | 13445 Poway Rd. (Community Rd.) | 858-486-3066
www.brigantine.com

For "flavorful, simple" fare that "satisfies your seafood cravings" – think "favorite" fish tacos and "perfectly cooked" fillets – this "upscale chain" meets "high expectations", especially during the "vibrant", "affordable" happy hour; though the "dust needs to be blown off" some locations, the "polite" staff is "speedy" even when there's a "huge crush" of customers.

Donovan's La Jolla ⌧ *Steak*

27 | 25 | 26 | $68

Golden Triangle | 4340 La Jolla Village Dr. (Genesee Ave.) | 858-450-6666
Donovan's San Diego Gaslamp *Steak*
Gaslamp Quarter | 570 K St. (6th Ave.) | 619-237-9700
www.donovanssteakhouse.com

Beef eaters boast "you'll never have a better steak" than at these Golden Triangle and Gaslamp "temples of red meat" where a "superb" team proffers "generous" plates of "tender", "top-quality" cuts "with all the fixin's" and "smooth" martinis at "through-the-roof" prices; the "dark, clubby" decor pleases, though "noisy, upscale crowds" make an "intimate dinner" unlikely.

George's California Modern *Californian*

27 | 27 | 26 | $51

La Jolla | 1250 Prospect St. (bet. Cave St. & Ivanhoe Ave.) | 858-454-4244
George's Ocean Terrace *Californian*
La Jolla | 1250 Prospect St. (bet. Cave St. & Ivanhoe Ave.) | 858-454-4244
www.georgesatthecove.com

With "fantastic" Californian fare from chef Trey Foshee, an "eclectic, extensive" wine list and a "one-of-a-kind" setting boasting "unsurpassed" ocean views, it's no wonder proprietor George Hauer's "tried-and-true performer" in La Jolla "endures with consistency"; the "accommodating" staff "operates like a well-oiled machine", plus the "relaxed" rooftop terrace offers a less "pricey" option for equally "enjoyable" meals.

In-N-Out Burger ● *Burgers* 26 | 18 | 24 | $10

El Cajon | 1541 N. Magnolia Ave. (Bradley Ave.)
Kearny Mesa | 4375 Kearny Mesa Rd. (Armour St.)
Mira Mesa | 9410 Mira Mesa Blvd. (Westview Pkwy.)
Mission Valley | 2005 Camino Del Este (Camino Del Rio)
Carlsbad | 5950 Avenida Encinas (Palomar Airport Rd.)
Rancho Bernardo | 11880 Carmel Mountain Rd. (Rancho Carmel Dr.)
Pacific Beach | 2910 Damon Ave. (Mission Bay Dr.)
Poway | 12890 Gregg Ct. (Community Rd.)
Chula Vista | 1725 Eastlake Pkwy. (Dawn Crest Ln.)
Sports Arena | 3102 Sports Arena Blvd. (Rosecrans St.)
800-786-1000 | www.in-n-out.com
Additional locations throughout the San Diego area

Ranked the Most Popular chain and top Bang for the Buck in San Diego, this "classic-Cal" burger specialist is "beloved" for "fresh-cut fries, fresh-cut produce and fresh beef" that all add up to "heaven on a bun" and can be complemented with grilled cheese, Neapolitan milkshakes and saucy "animal-style" patties from the "secret menu"; a "chipper" counter crew and "extra-clean" locations help offset "long waits" and a sometimes "slow drive-thru."

Island Prime/C-Level Lounge *Seafood/Steak* 26 | 27 | 25 | $46

Harbor Island | 880 Harbor Island Dr. (Harbor Dr.) | 619-298-6802 | www.cohnrestaurants.com

Locals can "show off their hometown" at this Harbor Island waterfronter from Cohn Restaurant Group, with "spectacular" skyline views ("what more decor do you need?") and "flavorful" steak and seafood dishes from chef Deborah Scott; whether in the "upscale" Island Prime or "more casual, less costly" C-Level Lounge, the staff lends a "pleasant" touch.

Market Restaurant & Bar *Californian* 28 | 23 | 26 | $69

Del Mar | 3702 Via de la Valle (El Camino Real) | 858-523-0007 | www.marketdelmar.com

"Everything is spectacular" on "genius" chef-owner Carl Schroeder's "irresistible" menu at this "expensive-but-worth-it" Del Mar "must", where "inventive" Californian dishes (plus sushi in the bar/lounge) drawing on "many cultures" pair with "unknown gems" from a "thoughtful" wine list; you may need to "borrow a Ferrari" to fit in, but most say the "super-relaxed" surrounds and "pro" servers who are "anxious to please" complete the "flawless" night.

Mille Fleurs *French* 27 | 26 | 27 | $76

Rancho Santa Fe | Country Squire Courtyard | 6009 Paseo Delicias (La Granada) | 858-756-3085 | www.millefleurs.com

"*Mon dieu!*" exclaim "stylish" fans of chef Martin Woesle's "delightful" New French creations at this "epitome of culinary indulgence" in Rancho Santa Fe, where "extraordinary" service bolsters the "first-class" (a few say "stuffy") atmosphere in a Provençal "country-home" setting; there's also a "special" patio and "welcoming" piano bar, where those not up for "investment dining" can enjoy a more "accessible" menu.

	FOOD	DECOR	SERVICE	COST

94th Aero Squadron Restaurant *American/Steak*

22 | 22 | 22 | $32

Kearny Mesa | 8885 Balboa Ave. (Ponderossa Ave.) | 858-560-6771 | www.94thaerosquadron.signonsandiego.com

Offering "predictable but always tasty" surf 'n' turf, a "great" Sunday brunch and solid service, this Kearny Mesa "standby" near Montgomery Field invites high-flying fans to dine then "walk to their private plane and take off"; those who find the antiques-packed interior "faded" can enjoy a "lovely landscaped outdoor area", where they can watch jets disembark "with the wind in their hair."

Pamplemousse Grille *American/French*

27 | 22 | 26 | $71

Solana Beach | 514 Via de la Valle (I-5) | 858-792-9090 | www.pgrille.com

Even those "not easily impressed" will be "blown away" by the French–New American "masterpieces", "magisterial" wine list and "sticker-shock prices" at this "class act" in a Solana Beach office complex; "bigger-than-life" chef-owner Jeffrey Strauss is a "great host", guiding "warm yet not intrusive" service in an "elegant, comfortable" space (decorated with "farm paintings") that attracts a "winning" crowd from the nearby racetrack.

Phil's BBQ Ⓜ *BBQ*

26 | 20 | 22 | $22

San Marcos | 579 Grand Ave. (San Marcos Blvd.) | 760-759-1400
Santee | 9816 Mission Gorge Rd. (Cuyamaca St.) | 619-449-7700
Sports Arena | 3750 Sports Arena Blvd. (Hancock St.) | 619-226-6333
www.philsbbq.net

"Wonderful aromas" of "scrumptious", "exceedingly tender" ribs and pulled pork draw lines "longer than Disneyland" to this "affordable" "benchmark BBQ" chainlet where an "eager-to-please" counter staff makes sure queues "move fast"; diners dig in at basic tables equipped with "plenty of paper towels" to mop up the "finger-lickin'" feast.

Ruth's Chris Steak House *Steak*

27 | 24 | 26 | $71

Del Mar | 11582 El Camino Real (Carmel Valley Rd.) | 858-755-1454
Downtown | 1355 N. Harbor Dr. (Ash St.) | 619-233-1422
www.ruthschris.com

Release your inner "caveman" on the "buttery" steaks "cooked to perfection" and paired with "gargantuan" sides, "sinful" desserts and "potent" drinks at these Downtown and Del Mar links in the "high-end" national chain; "superior" service and "fantastic" views from the "contemporary" dining room further support the "splurge" prices.

Sushi Ota *Japanese*

29 | 16 | 21 | $49

Pacific Beach | 4529 Mission Bay Dr. (Bunker Hill St.) | 858-270-5670 | www.sushiota.com

"Sushi purists" will "cry" tears of "pleasure" when "lucky enough" to snag a seat at this "incomparable" Pacific Beach Japanese, where "gracious" chef-owner Yukito Ota and his talented "army" earn the No. 1 Food rating in San Diego with "simply magnificent" seafood "delicacies" and an "innovative" omakase tasting; frequently "hurried" service, a "random" strip-mall location and "shabby" interior certainly don't match the "phenomenal" fare and "pricey" tabs, but guests still need to make a reservation "well in advance."

	FOOD	DECOR	SERVICE	COST

Tao ☒ *Asian/Vegetarian* | 28 | 21 | 24 | $19 |

Normal Heights | 3332 Adams Ave. (Felton St.) | 619-281-6888
Even though you're allowed to "write on the walls" with markers, don't be deceived by the "quirky" atmosphere at this Normal Heights Asian eatery – an affordable "favorite" for its "generous", "spicy" dishes that appeal to carnivores and vegetarians alike; what's more, the staff "always greets you warmly" and is "very willing to accommodate" any special requests.

Tapenade *French* | 28 | 21 | 26 | $61 |

La Jolla | 7612 Fay Ave. (bet. Kline & Pearl Sts.) | 858-551-7500 | www.tapenaderestaurant.com
Francophiles say *"merci"* to this "pricey" La Jolla French destination's "brilliant" chef Jean-Michel Diot, whose "creative" dishes feature "fantastically layered" flavors and "delightful presentations" and are complemented by a "well-balanced" wine list; the atmosphere is "bright" and "serene", and though a few detect a "mildly pretentious" air, most report "first-rate" service attuned to the "classy" clientele.

West Steak & Seafood *Seafood/Steak* | 27 | 25 | 26 | $64 |

Carlsbad | 4980 Avenida Encinas (Cannon Rd.) | 760-930-9100 | www.weststeakandseafood.com
"Terrific fine dining" thrives at this Carlsbad surf 'n' turfer, where "perfectly prepared" steaks and "outstanding" seafood – sided with seasonal produce from the restaurant's private farm – earn raves; upscale decor and "attentive" servers reinforce its "special-occasion" status, though the happy-hour bar menu is an "excellent" deal.

Wine Vault & Bistro ☒☒ *Eclectic* | 27 | 22 | 25 | $45 |

Mission Hills | 3731 India St. (Washington St.) | 619-295-3939 | www.winevaultbistro.com
With "scrumptious, thoughtfully prepared" Eclectic fare, "well-chosen" wine pairings and "bargain" prix fixe meals (no à la carte), "you can't go wrong" at this "hidden treasure" in Mission Hills; diners feel "great camaraderie" with fellow oenophiles in the "simple" setting lined with wine bottles, which is overseen by "dedicated" owners who "truly care about their patrons"; P.S. open Thursday–Saturday only (with winemaker dinners on other nights).

San Francisco Bay Area

Acquerello 🖼Ⓜ *Italian*

28 | 26 | 28 | $107

Polk Gulch | 1722 Sacramento St. (bet. Polk St. & Van Ness Ave.) | San Francisco | 415-567-5432 | www.acquerello.com

For "sumptuous dining" "with all the perks", this "romantic", "extraordinarily refined" Polk Gulch classic is in "a league of its own", proffering "superb", "imaginative" Italian tasting menus complemented by an "amazing" 100-page wine list and "impeccable" "formal service" that leaves the "moneyed crowd" feeling "pampered"; an "elegantly peaceful" former chapel setting and touches such as "footstools for purses" further make it "worth every penny" when "you really want to impress someone."

Ame *American*

26 | 24 | 25 | $77

SoMa | St. Regis | 689 Mission St. (3rd St.) | San Francisco | 415-284-4040 | www.amerestaurant.com

"Culinary enthusiasts" contend it's "worth dressing up" for a "special-occasion" meal at this "high-end" SoMa "destination" in the St. Regis where Terra owners Hiro Sone and Lissa Doumani proffer "gorgeously styled", "seriously delicious" (and "very expensive") New American cuisine infused with "Asian flavors" that's "graciously" served with an "over-the-top sake menu" and "exemplary wine list"; a "quiet", "minimalist" "Zen" setting that "feels like stepping into a meditation room" adds to the appeal of a "memorable evening."

AQ Restaurant & Bar Ⓜ *Californian*

24 | 26 | 22 | $58

SoMa | 1085 Mission St. (7th St.) | San Francisco | 415-341-9000 | www.aq-sf.com

"Creative to the max" is how fans describe this "stylish", upscale SoMa Californian "place of the moment" with both a "seasonal menu and seasonal decor", where chef-owner Mark Liberman is "like a bio-chemist at work" crafting "precisely prepared", "cutting-edge" dishes (think "deconstructed clam chowder"); "superb wine pairings" and a setting with "beautiful high ceilings" and "original brick walls" complete the "lively" scene.

Atelier Crenn 🖼Ⓜ *French*

27 | 24 | 26 | $143

Marina | 3127 Fillmore St. (bet. Greenwich & Moulton Sts.) | San Francisco | 415-440-0460 | www.ateliercrenn.com

"The prettiest food" you may ever eat also "tastes amazing" say those "blown away" by this Marina culinary atelier, where "works of art" blending French cuisine and "molecular gastronomy" are "elegantly presented" on "unusual plates"; "personalized" service in the upscale-minimalist space can include a tableside visit from chef Dominique Crenn herself, and despite "expensive" tabs for "spartan" tasting menu portions, it's deemed a "brilliant dining experience."

Aziza *Moroccan*

26 | 22 | 24 | $59

Outer Richmond | 5800 Geary Blvd. (22nd Ave.) | San Francisco | 415-752-2222 | www.aziza-sf.com

Chef Mourad Lahlou offers a fresh Californian "spin" on Morrocan cuisine at this upscale Outer Richmonder where "inventive", "well-spiced" entrees are "a party for the palate", and even a "simple lentil soup soars" into "gourmet" territory; fans say "don't be fooled" by its "sleepy" location and point to "lovingly crafted" cocktails, "inviting" service and an "intimate" space, adding they'd "go back at the drop of a hat" – or for a "date"; P.S. closed Tuesday.

Benu ⑤Ⓜ *American*   27 | 24 | 28 | $168

SoMa | 22 Hawthorne St. (bet. Folsom & Howard Sts.) | San Francisco | 415-685-4860 | www.benusf.com

"Fine dining at its edgy finest" is how devotees describe this "knock-your-socks-off" SoMa New American, where Corey Lee blends "French technique and Asian flavors" into "rock-star dishes" (stuffed Hokkaido sea cucumber, anyone?); though you may need an "expense account" to pay, "amazing" service ("the wine tasting alone is incredible") in a "Zen-like" space makes for an "outstanding culinary experience"; P.S. "go all the way" with the prix fixe menu, the only option Friday–Saturday, though à la carte is also available Tuesday–Thursday.

Boulevard *American*   27 | 26 | 26 | $71

Embarcadero | Audiffred Bldg. | 1 Mission St. (Steuart St.) | San Francisco | 415-543-6084 | www.boulevardrestaurant.com

"Year after year", chef-owner Nancy Oakes' "spectacular" "San Francisco mainstay" on the Embarcadero "never fails to impress" with its "bridge views" and belle epoque decor as backdrops for "superlative" "big, bold" American fare, "decadent desserts" and a "fantastic" selection of wines, all delivered by a "welcoming", "first-class" staff; there's a "lively" bar scene too, and though it's "noisy" and "costs an arm and two legs", it's still the "gold standard" for "business" and "special occasions" and is itself "reason to have a special occasion."

Cafe Gibraltar Ⓜ *Mediterranean*   28 | 24 | 26 | $45

El Granada | 425 Ave. Alhambra (Palma St.) | 650-560-9039 | www.cafegibraltar.com

The drive to El Granada is "more than justified" by "talented" chef and co-owner Jose Luis Ugalde's "simply spectacular", "one-of-a-kind" fusion menus say fans of this Mediterranean where "seasonal", "organic" dishes are creatively presented with "exotic tableware" and coupled with "terrific", "well-priced" wines; factor in "friendly and professional" service and "amazing" Moorish decor (including "low tables" with "pillows" in back and distant ocean views up front) and there's little wonder why this "gem" is deemed by some "the best (somewhat kept) secret on the coast."

Chez Panisse ⑤ *Californian/Mediterranean*   27 | 25 | 27 | $85

Berkeley | 1517 Shattuck Ave. (bet. Cedar & Vine Sts.) | 510-548-5525 | www.chezpanisse.com

Following a fire, Alice Waters' "inspired" "gastronomic shrine" in Berkeley is again welcoming acolytes who come for "simple" yet "exquisite" "seasonal" Cal-Med prix fixes that "let the ingredients shine" ("even their green garden salad is amazing"), delivered with "exemplary service"; there are "no new surprises" on the menu and the "unique Craftsman-style setting" remains largely the same, so while "the lack of choice" might still miff a few, most locavores insist the place "where it all started" remains "the gold standard"; P.S. scores do not reflect changes after reopening.

	FOOD	DECOR	SERVICE	COST

Chez Panisse Café Ⓢ *Californian/Mediterranean* | 27 | 24 | 26 | $54 |

Berkeley | 1517 Shattuck Ave. (bet. Cedar & Vine Sts.) | 510-548-5049 |
www.chezpanisse.com

Alice Waters' "unpretentious" upstairs "little sister still performs" as
well as its lauded "farm-to-table" sibling downstairs, offering an "unbelievably good" "seasonal" Cal-Med à la carte menu (including
"great" wood-fired pizza), "excellent" wines and "attentive but not intrusive" service at "more affordable" prices; the "homey" setting gets
"crowded", but remains on the "bucket list" of everyone from casual
lunch-goers to gastro-"tourists" looking to "get their food passports
stamped"; P.S. scores don't reflect changes after a devastating fire.

Coi ⓈⓂ *Californian/French* | 27 | 26 | 27 | $228 |

North Beach | 373 Broadway (Montgomery St.) | San Francisco |
415-393-9000 | www.coirestaurant.com

Daniel Patterson's "adventurous", "exquisitely prepared" tasting
menus are a "journey worth taking" assert fans of this North Beach
Californian-French, where "seasonal" ingredients stand out in a "magical" "mélange of flavors and techniques"; service is "impeccable"
while the "minimal" space is an "oasis of calm", and though it may be
"outrageously expensive", many recommend it for a "special occasion" or just to "have your food mind blown."

Commis Ⓜ *American* | 27 | 21 | 26 | $111 |

Oakland | 3859 Piedmont Ave. (Rio Vista Ave.) | 510-653-3902 |
www.commisrestaurant.com

Oakland native James Syhabout's "incredible precision" results in
"stunning", "deliciously inventive" New American prix fixes imbued
with molecular gastronomy at his Lilliputian, high-end Piedmont
Avenue flagship; despite "tiny portions" and "quiet", "spartan" digs
("the servers should be wearing robes"), acolytes insist all "pleasure
points" get "hit", particularly if you opt for the "excellent" wine pairings and dine at the "chef's counter" overlooking the "talented kitchen
staff" in action; P.S. Syhabout's Box and Bells, for casual eating and
drinking, is in the works at 5912 College Avenue.

Coqueta *Spanish* | - | - | - | E |

Embarcadero | Pier 5 (Washington St.) | San Francisco | 415-704-8866 |
www.coquetasf.com

Perched on the edge of Pier 5 with the San Francisco waterfront at its
feet, this convivial eatery from celebrity chef Michael Chiarello
(Bottega) showcases contemporary regional Spanish tapas and *racio-
nes* (family-style large plates); the marble-topped bar focuses on artisanal Spanish and Californian wines, loads of sherry and molecular
cocktails such as frozen sangria, plus a variety of housemade gin and
tonics, all of which can also be enjoyed in the glass-enclosed terrace
or alfresco on the patio along the Embarcadero.

Cucina Paradiso Ⓢ *Italian* | 27 | 23 | 26 | $37 |

Petaluma | 114 Petaluma Blvd. N. (bet. Washington St. & Western Ave.) |
707-782-1130 | www.cucinaparadisopetaluma.com

"Be ready for an old-school Italian welcome" to go along with the "terrific pastas", "homemade baked bread", "locally grown vegetables"
and "affordable" wines being served at this "excellent" Petaluma trat-

toria dubbed "authentic in the best sense of the word"; "lunch or dinner, this place rocks" insist fans, even more so since settling into its "larger", more "sophisticated" Downtown digs.

Delfina Italian — 26 | 20 | 23 | $48

Mission | 3621 18th St. (bet. Dolores & Guerrero Sts.) | San Francisco | 415-552-4055 | www.delfinasf.com

"After all these years" (since 1998), Craig and Anne Stoll's "sterling" Northern Italian in the Mission is "still the standard" for "simple and perfectly cooked" pastas and other "unfussy" but "divine" mains, matched by an "interesting wine list" and "polite", "real" service; there's a "hip crowd", but "waits" for the "too-close" tables "can be a drag", which is why those without a reservation often end up "seated at the bar" – or at their "amazing" pizzeria next door.

Erna's Elderberry House Californian/French — 28 | 28 | 29 | $101

Oakhurst | Château du Sureau | 48688 Victoria Ln. (Hwy. 41) | 559-683-6800 | www.elderberryhouse.com

Delivering a "superlative" dining experience as "inspired and commanding as Yosemite's Half Dome" itself, this culinary "Brigadoon" just outside the park in Oakhurst "delights and surprises" travelers with "exquisite", locally sourced New French–Californian prix fixe dinners proffered in a "magical", "elegant setting" by a "prescient" staff that "makes you feel as if they've personalized the evening just for you"; PS. there's a "wonderful Sunday brunch" for guests who "stay at the château" next door.

Evvia Greek — 28 | 26 | 26 | $56

Palo Alto | 420 Emerson St. (bet. Lytton & University Aves.) | 650-326-0983 | www.evvia.net

It's "as good as any taverna in Greece" attest fans of Palo Alto's "darling little sister" to SF's Kokkari, which might please "Demeter" (goddess of the harvest) herself along with the power-lunching "tech crowd" and special-occasion celebrants digging into the "fantastic", "inspired" "high-end" Mediterranean cuisine (with requisite "high prices"); a "convivial" (if "noisy") "rustic" setting and "doting" service that's like a "hug" from a "Greek mama" complete the picture.

Fleur de Lys 🖂 Ⓜ Californian/French — 27 | 26 | 27 | $101

Downtown | 777 Sutter St. (bet. Jones & Taylor Sts.) | San Francisco | 415-673-7779 | www.hubertkeller.com

Hubert Keller remains "at the top of the game" at his Downtown "flagship" presenting "outstanding" "three-hour"–long French-Californian prix fixes with "perfectly" paired wines in meals that display the "hands of a master"; patrons say "there's no more romantic" setting than the tented room where guests are "treated like kings and queens" "from reception to departure", and while you'll "pay for every bit of it", it remains a "dream night out for any major celebration."

Flour + Water Italian — 26 | 20 | 22 | $49

Mission | 2401 Harrison St. (20th St.) | San Francisco | 415-826-7000 | www.flourandwater.com

"Careful preparation" goes into the "amazing" wood-fired pies and "incredible", high-end pastas by chef Thomas McNaughton at this "lively", "industrial-chic" Italian standout in the Mission; quarters are "tight", the

FOOD DECOR SERVICE COST

music's "loud" and the "difficult" rezzies and waits discourage some, but others say "go early on a slow night" and you might have a shot.

French Laundry *American/French* 28 | 27 | 28 | $297

Yountville | 6640 Washington St. (Creek St.) | 707-944-2380 | www.frenchlaundry.com

"The best French restaurant isn't in Paris, it's in Yountville" declare fans of Thomas Keller and his "iconic" stone farmhouse surrounded by organic gardens, "where no urge or whim goes unattended" by an "impeccable staff" delivering "astounding" French-American tasting menus that merge "art and science" and are matched with "superb" wine pairings; it's also "over the top in formality" and price, and "almost impossible" to get a reservation, but those who do insist "every foodie must try it once" (and "ask for a tour of the kitchen").

Gary Danko *American* 29 | 27 | 29 | $111

Fisherman's Wharf | 800 N. Point St. (Hyde St.) | San Francisco | 415-749-2060 | www.garydanko.com

"In a city of great restaurants", Gary Danko's Wharf-area "classic" is the "all-time favorite" – and once again voted No. 1 in the Bay Area for Food, Service and Popularity thanks to its "sensational", "personalized" New American prix fixe menus and "perfect wine pairings" (plus "the most impressive cheese cart"), all delivered "without a speck of pretentiousness" by a "smart, warm" staff that treats everyone "like royalty"; true, it "isn't cheap" and "reservations are difficult to get" in the "understated, tasteful" room, but for those with the bucks and the necessary "hours" to indulge, devotees urge "just put yourself in their hands, and you won't go wrong."

Hakkasan ● *Chinese* 24 | 26 | 24 | $74

Downtown | 1 Kearny St. (Geary St.) | San Francisco | 415-829-8148 | www.hakkasan.com

"Artful" Chinese food (including "unusual but "tasty" dim sum) that's "almost as seductive as the decor" goes with "amazing" cocktails and strong service at this Downtown "power" place – part of a high-end international chain; while it strikes some as "excessively priced" and "pretentious" ("trying to be LA in SF"), others are smitten by the "clubby", "happening" scene.

Keiko à Nob Hill Ⓜ *French/Japanese* 27 | 24 | 25 | $129

Nob Hill | 1250 Jones St. (Clay St.) | San Francisco | 415-829-7141 | www.keikoanobhill.com

For "sublime food" in an "elegant", "old-world setting", well-heeled diners trek to this "absolutely amazing" Nob Hill sleeper where chef Keiko Takahashi turns out Japanese-influenced French tasting menus showcasing "some of the most delicious, innovative and beautifully prepared dishes" around; the "excellent" staff offers "spot"-on wine pairings from the "impressive" list, and while it's all "worth the price", there's also a "less-formal bar area" offering izakaya à la carte options.

Kiss Seafood Ⓢ Ⓜ *Japanese* 28 | 17 | 25 | $81

Japantown | 1700 Laguna St. (Sutter St.) | San Francisco | 415-474-2866

The "easy-to-miss entrance" is like a "special portal to Japan" gush groupies of this "very traditional" and "very expensive" Japantown "find" where an "adorable" "husband-and-wife" team "work in harmony" proffering "extremely fresh" sushi along with "divine", elegantly presented omakase dinners; "don't come if you're in a rush" or sans reservations, as there are "only 12 seats", and expect to see the chef doing "all the sashimi and cooking right in front of you."

Kokkari Estiatorio *Greek*
28 | 27 | 27 | $59

Downtown | 200 Jackson St. (bet. Battery & Front Sts.) | San Francisco | 415-981-0983 | www.kokkari.com

"*Opa!*" cheer fans of this "still-hot" Downtown taverna that remains the place to "get your Greek on" amid the "power" lunch and dinner crowd feasting on "the best lamb this side of Mount Olympus" and other "spit-roasted marvels" served in a "stylish", "energetic" setting; whether you "sit at the bar" or "by the fireplace", there's "warm", "expert" service, all adding up to a "magnificent experience" that requires you "open your wallet" wide, but leaves diners with "big smiles."

La Ciccia ⓜ *Italian*
27 | 17 | 25 | $50

Noe Valley | 291 30th St. (Church St.) | San Francisco | 415-550-8114 | www.laciccia.com

"If you can score a reservation, take it" urge devotees of this "out-of-the-way" Noe Valley "gem" proffering "incredibly flavorful", "delightfully unique" Sardinian cuisine (including "killer pastas" and seafood); the married owners' "passion" comes across in the food as a "welcoming" staff helps navigate the "brilliant", "reasonably priced" all-Italian wine list and "makes you feel at home" in the "tiny", "crowded" digs; P.S. an enoteca spin-off, La Nebbia, is slated to open at 1781 Church Street.

La Folie Ⓢ *French*
27 | 25 | 27 | $110

Russian Hill | 2316 Polk St. (bet. Green & Union Sts.) | San Francisco | 415-776-5577 | www.lafolie.com

Roland Passot's "shrine" to French "gastronomy" is "anything but folie" declare diners "blown away" at his "chic" Russian Hill "special-occasion" "haven" proffering an "exquisitely prepared" "parade of plates" as "tasty" as they are "beautiful"; it's a "fabulous" "fine-dining" experience "from start to finish", enhanced by brother George's "compact wine list" and service that's "beyond compare", all making it worth the "beaucoup bucks"; P.S. the adjacent lounge serves a late-night bar menu.

La Forêt ⓜ *Continental/French*
27 | 26 | 27 | $65

San Jose | 21747 Bertram Rd. (Almaden Rd.) | 408-997-3458 | www.laforetrestaurant.com

Located only 20 minutes from Downtown San Jose, this historic "special-occasion" restaurant "surrounded by nature" and a meandering creek nonetheless "feels so far away" to the Silicon Valley set that finds the "romantic" "country setting" an "excellent choice" for "dinner anytime" (or a lavish Sunday brunch); the "superb" Continental-French tasting menus and à la carte offerings are capped off by "amazing" soufflés and impressive wines, with "very formal" service to match.

Madrona Manor
Restaurant ⓜ *American/French*
27 | 26 | 27 | $105

Healdsburg | Madrona Manor | 1001 Westside Rd. (Dry Creek Rd.) | 707-433-4231 | www.madronamanor.com

Count on a "memorable dining experience" – with "professional" service and a "massive price tag" to match – at this "charming" Healdsburg restaurant and country inn set in a "beautiful old mansion" surrounded by "estate gardens" where antique furnishings are the backdrop for "fantastic" "modern", candlelit New American–French prix fixes highlighting "local wines" and produce ("the gardener's name is even on the menu"); a few find it a "touch too formal", but concede "if you want "froufrou" in Sonoma, "they do it right"; P.S. closed Monday and Tuesday.

Manresa ☒ *American* — 27 | 26 | 27 | $169

Los Gatos | 320 Village Ln. (bet. Santa Cruz & University Aves.) | 408-354-4330 | www.manresarestaurant.com

"Exciting, unexpected and flawless" is how devotees describe the "special experience" at chef-owner David Kinch's Los Gatos New American, where "sublime", "inventive" tasting menus are inspired and sourced from its own biodynamic gardens; the "hours"-long meals served in the "sophisticated" dining room are elevated by "wonderful" wines and service that's like "precision choreography", and though it's all "horribly expensive", there's a lounge menu too; P.S. closed Monday and Tuesday.

Meadowood, The Restaurant ☒ *Californian* — 27 | 27 | 27 | $293
(aka The Restaurant at Meadowood)

St. Helena | Meadowood Napa Valley | 900 Meadowood Ln. (Silverado Trail) | 707-967-1205 | www.therestaurantatmeadowood.com

"Unforgettable" is how fans describe the "singular experience" of dining at this special-occasion standout in St. Helena's Meadowood resort, where Christopher Kostow's "innovative", bespoke Californian tasting menus are paired with native wines and enhanced by "amazing presentations" and service to match, plus "serene" views overlooking croquet fields and fairways; the initiated swear it's worth the "stratospheric prices" to "experience at least once"; P.S. the bar lounge serves a more affordable three-course menu.

Michael Mina *American* — 27 | 25 | 26 | $104

Downtown | 252 California St. (Battery St.) | San Francisco | 415-397-9222 | www.michaelmina.net

"Artful" New American menus ensure "an adventure each time" for fans of Michael Mina's Downtown destination, which also earns high marks for its "stylish" decor (in the former Aqua digs), "stupendous wine list" and "lovely" service; it's "definitely expensive" and often "noisy", but some can't get enough of the "buzzing" scene.

Quince ☒ *French/Italian* — 26 | 26 | 26 | $101

Downtown | 470 Pacific Ave. (bet. Montgomery St. & Pacific Ave.) | San Francisco | 415-775-8500 | www.quincerestaurant.com

Guests embark on a "gastronomic adventure" at this "outstanding" Downtown Italian-French by chef Michael and Lindsay Tusk, proffering "exquisite" food and service with a focus on "inspired" tasting menus featuring Northern Californian ingredients; "intimate", "elegant" and "very expensive but worth it", it's "at the top of the local game", providing "a total experience."

Saison ☒☒ *American* — 27 | 22 | 26 | $322

SoMa | 178 Townsend St. (bet. 2nd & 3rd Sts.) | San Francisco | 415-828-7990 | www.saisonsf.com

"A unique approach to dining" comes via Joshua Skenes' "fantastic" tasting-menu-only New American eatery – now settled into its tiny, new

SoMa digs with an open kitchen – and "hard-core" foodies insist "you can bet the house that it'll be mind-blowingly good", all delivered with "incredible service"; it's also "stratospheric" in price, though diners can indulge for less on an à la carte salon menu in the cocktail lounge.

Sierra Mar   *Californian/Eclectic*   28 | 29 | 27 | $95

Big Sur | Post Ranch Inn | Hwy. 1 (30 mi. south of Carmel) | 831-667-2200 | www.postranchinn.com

A "bucket-list experience" from start to finish entrances diners "who don't want it to end" when seated in this glassed-in, cliffside aerie "overlooking the Pacific" at Big Sur's Post Ranch Inn, where the "extraordinary architecture" and some of the "best views in California" capture the Bay Area's No. 1 rating for Decor; the setting is a fitting backdrop for "exquisite" (and expensive) Cal-Eclectic cuisine, "world-class wines" and "impeccable" service, and some suggest it's perhaps best appreciated "before sunset" for a "spectacular lunch" or pre-dinner fireside cocktail "on the deck."

Slanted Door   *Vietnamese*   26 | 23 | 22 | $53

Embarcadero | Ferry Building Mktpl. | 1 Ferry Bldg. (The Embarcadero) | San Francisco | 415-861-8032 | www.slanteddoor.com

"Tourists and regulars just keep coming and rightfully so", as Charles Phan's "longtime favorite" provides "extraordinary" "contemporary" Vietnamese cuisine in a "terrific" Embarcadero waterfront location; opinions vary on whether the "modern", "airy" space is "inviting" or too "noisy", and some feel the service can be "rushed", but most affirm the "pricey" tabs are worth it for such a "sensational" meal – "and the views of the bay aren't too bad either."

State Bird Provisions ⬚ *American*   26 | 18 | 23 | $59

Western Addition | 1529 Fillmore St. (bet. Geary Blvd. & O'Farrell St.) | San Francisco | 415-795-1272 | www.statebirdsf.com

The "fabulous concept of dim sum–style service" for "super-creative", "delightful" American dishes is "completely realized" at this "absolute winner" by chef-owners Stuart Brioza and Nicole Krasinski in a "bare-bones" Western Addition storefront; "it's a challenge" to get a reservation (or a seat at the bar), and "can get really expensive if you have no self-control", but given the "refreshing" service, "electric" atmosphere and "unbelievable" food, first-timers "want to come back for more"; P.S. undergoing an expansion at press time.

Sushi Zone ⬚⊄ *Japanese*   27 | 14 | 19 | $34

Castro | 1815 Market St. (Pearl St.) | San Francisco | 415-621-1114 | www.sushizonesf.com

There's a "cult following" for this "extremely small" Castro Japanese where the "mustachioed genius behind the bar" turns out "very fresh" sushi and fusion-y rolls in "good-sized" portions at prices that are "very reasonable"; a "ridiculously long sake list" adds to the appeal, but prepare for a "long wait" on the sidewalk or at the "neighboring bar."

Terra   *American*   27 | 25 | 27 | $91

St. Helena | 1345 Railroad Ave. (bet. Adams St. & Hunt Ave.) | 707-963-8931 | www.terrarestaurant.com

Since 1988, Hiro Sone and Lissa Doumani (also of Ame) have made this "original" St. Helena "treasure" "one of the best places to eat in the wine country", thanks to "complex", "distinctive" and downright "amazing" New American tasting menus (his), "to-die-for" pastries (hers) and an "excellent wine list"; all's presided over by an "impeccable" staff in an "elegant and comfortable" stone farmhouse, while diners desiring à la carte options can find them at the restaurant's Bar Terra next door.

Zuni Café Ⓜ _Mediterranean_

26 | 21 | 23 | $53

Hayes Valley | 1658 Market St. (bet. Franklin & Gough Sts.) | San Francisco | 415-552-2522 | www.zunicafe.com

"Judy Rodgers' menus continue to delight" at this "eclectic" Med "legend" in Hayes Valley, where the brick-oven chicken (for two) with bread salad is the "stuff of dreams" and oysters at the zinc bar are "terrific"; while it can get "a bit frenetic" in the "quirky", "upscalish" two-story space, the staff keeps it "rolling" and the "atmosphere around dinnertime is always good."

Seattle

TOP FOOD RANKING

Restaurant	Cuisine
29 Nishino	Japanese
Staple & Fancy Mercantile*	Italian
Il Terrazzo Carmine	Italian
28 Herbfarm	Pacific NW
Paseo	Cuban/Sandwiches
Tat's Deli	American/Deli
Shiro's Sushi	Japanese
La Medusa	Italian
Le Rêve Bakery*	Bakery/French
Canlis	Pacific NW
Nell's	American
Spinasse	Italian
Buffalo Deli	Deli
Facing East	Taiwanese
Corson Building	Eclectic
Salumi*	Italian/Sandwiches
27 Metropolitan Grill	Steak
Lark	American
Daniel's Broiler	Steak
Kisaku	Japanese

OTHER NOTEWORTHY PLACES

Anthony's HomePort	Pacific NW/Seafood
Aqua by El Gaucho	Seafood
Blue C Sushi	Japanese
Book Bindery	American
Cafe Juanita	Italian
Dahlia Lounge	Pacific NW
Dick's Drive-In	Burgers
Georgian	French/Pacific NW
Harvest Vine	Spanish
La Carta/Mezcaleria Oaxaca	Mexican
Matt's in the Market	Pacific NW/Seafood
Radiator Whiskey	American
Ray's Boathouse	Pacific NW/Seafood
Revel	American/Korean
Seastar	Seafood
Serious Pie	Pizza
Sitka & Spruce	Eclectic
13 Coins	American/Italian
Whale Wins	Euro./Pacific NW
Wild Ginger	Pacific Rim

---

* Indicates a tie with restaurant above

	FOOD	DECOR	SERVICE	COST

Anthony's HomePort *Pacific NW/Seafood* | 25 | 24 | 24 | $37 |

Shilshole | 6135 Seaview Ave. NW (61st St.) | 206-783-0780
Kirkland | 135 Lake St. S. (bet. Kirkland & 2nd Aves.) | 425-822-0225
Des Moines | Des Moines Marina | 421 S. 227th St. (Dock St.) |
206-824-1947
Edmonds | Edmonds Marina | 456 Admiral Way (Dayton St.) | 425-771-4400
Everett | Everett Marina Vill. | 1726 W. Marine View Dr. (18th St.) |
425-252-3333
Tacoma | 5910 N. Waterfront Dr. (Trolley Ln.) | 253-752-9700
Gig Harbor | 8827 N. Harborview Dr. (bet. Burnham Dr. & Peacock Hill Ave.) |
253-853-6353
Bellingham | 25 Bellwether Way (Roeder Ave.) | 360-647-5588
Olympia | 704 Columbia St. NW (Corky Ave.) | 360-357-9700
www.anthonys.com

A "wonderful representation of Washington", this "dependable" fleet
of seafooders (Seattle's Most Popular chain) reels 'em in with "fresh,
local" fin fare and shellfish along with "waterfront settings" that provide "unbeatable" views; though a few carp about "tired" decor need-
ing a "revamp" at some locations, a "congenial", "well-informed" staff
keeps things swimming smoothly, and budget-watchers praise the
"affordable prices" and "sunset dinners" ("a heck of a deal").

Aqua by El Gaucho ❶ *Seafood* | 27 | 26 | 25 | $55 |

Seattle Waterfront | Pier 70 | 2801 Alaskan Way (Broad St.) |
206-956-9171 | www.elgaucho.com

"Succulent seafood" takes center stage at this upscale waterfront spot
and is supported by servers who "know their stuff", a wine list with
bottles at "all price levels" and "spectacular" floor-to-ceiling views of
Elliott Bay; though bargain-hunters say you won't find any here ("it's
pretty spendy"), the "bright, airy" modern room is a "great place" for
"business dinners" or "special occasions."

Blue C Sushi *Japanese* | 21 | 21 | 20 | $21 |

Downtown | Grand Hyatt Hotel | 1510 Seventh Ave. (bet. Pike & Pine Sts.) |
206-467-4022
Fremont | 3411 Fremont Ave. N. (34th St.) | 206-633-3411
University Village | University Vill. | 4601 26th Ave. NE (University Village St.) |
206-525-4601
Bellevue | Bellevue Sq. | 503 Bellevue Sq. (bet. 4th & 8th Sts.) | 425-454-8288
Lynnwood | Alderwood Mall | 3000 184th St. SW
(bet. Alderwood Mall Pkwy. & 33rd Ave.) | 425-329-3596
Tukwila | Westfield Southcenter | 468 Southcenter Mall (bet. Strander Blvd. &
Tukwila Pkwy.) | 206-277-8744
www.bluecsushi.com

Fans of "decent, tasty sushi" and "convenience" like to sit down in
front of the "entertaining" "conveyor belt", grab what looks good and
"immediately start eating" at these "busy" Japanese joints; "modern"
decor featuring "huge screens" playing "anime" and other clips makes
it a "hit with the family", but the budget-minded "pay attention to the
plate colors" that determine prices to "avoid a giant bill."

Book Bindery *American* | 27 | 27 | 25 | $61 |

Queen Anne | 198 Nickerson St. (Etruria St.) | 206-283-2665 |
www.bookbinderyrestaurant.com

Virtuoso chef Shaun McCrain (ex Per Se) shapes a "stunning" contemporary American menu with "subtle" and "intriguing combinations" at

this Queen Anne spot, where a "knowledgeable" staff works "beauti-ful" modern spaces that reveal views of the Lake Washington Ship Canal and the aging barrels of the adjacent Almquist Family Vintners winery; sure, it's a "bit pricey", but insiders insist a "special evening" here that "helps you forget your cares" is worth it.

Buffalo Deli ⓈDeli

28 | 21 | 22 | $21

Belltown | 2123 First Ave. (bet. Blanchard & Lenora Sts.) | 206-728-8759 | www.thebuffalodeli.com

"It's like being in Buffalo" swear supporters of this "super-friendly" Belltown deli, where "high-quality" lunches include "incredible matzo ball" soup and "great, creative" sandwiches (e.g. the famed "beef on weck"), all at a "reasonable price"; since the no-frills place "can get busy", those in the know "call their orders in."

Cafe Juanita Ⓜ Italian

27 | 24 | 26 | $64

Kirkland | 9702 NE 120th Pl. (97th Ave.) | 425-823-1505 | www.cafejuanita.com

"Inventive", "delectable" Northern Italian cuisine that makes the most of "whatever is local and fresh" lures loyalists to chef-owner Holly Smith's Kirkland "gem", where an "impeccable" staff expertly guides diners through the "small" but "surprise"-filled menu and "excellent" wine list (so "listen to your server"); the "intimate", "minimalist" dining room is "nestled" in an "unassuming" building that "sits among trees", a "low-key" setting for an "expensive" but altogether "unforgettable" meal.

Canlis Ⓢ Pacific NW

28 | 28 | 28 | $84

Lake Union | 2576 Aurora Ave. N. (Raye St.) | 206-283-3313 | www.canlis.com

The "next generation of Canlis sons" makes sure that "everything's perfect" at this circa-1950 "Seattle institution", where chef Jason Franey (ex NYC's Eleven Madison Park) reinterprets Pacific NW clas-sics and turns out "perfectly executed" meals that are "outstanding from beginning to end"; in the midcentury modern room framing a "gorgeous Lake Union view", service that's "like choreography" antic-ipates your every need, and while it's all "brutally pricey", you "defi-nitely get what you pay for."

Corson Building Ⓜ Eclectic

28 | 22 | 26 | $66

Georgetown | 5609 Corson Ave. S. (Airport Way) | 206-762-3330 | www.thecorsonbuilding.com

Chef-owner Matthew Dillon (Sitka & Spruce) "showcases the freshest ingredients" in "magnificent", "family-style" dinners served at com-munal tables at this "swoon"-worthy Georgetown Eclectic, which is set in a "funky" 1910 Spanish-style building reminiscent of a European country house; though the "romantic" room can get "noisy" and "it's definitely pricey", the staff's "genuine hospitality" helps make it "worth the splurge"; P.S. hours and menus vary.

Dahlia Lounge Pacific NW

27 | 24 | 25 | $47

Downtown | 2001 Fourth Ave. (Virginia St.) | 206-682-4142 | www.tomdouglas.com

"After all these years", Tom Douglas' first venture is still an "absolute favorite" among fans of this Downtowner's "outstanding", "Asian-infused" Pacific NW cuisine that includes a "rock-your-world" coconut cream pie (get one to go at the bakery next door); the contemporary room's "happy" vibe and "dependable, pleasant" staff are part of the "iconic", if "a tad pricey" experience.

Daniel's Broiler *Steak*

27 | 26 | 26 | $58

Leschi | Leschi Marina | 200 Lake Washington Blvd. (Alder St.) | 206-329-4191
South Lake Union | 809 Fairview Pl. N. (Valley St.) | 206-621-8262
Bellevue | Bank of America Bldg., Bellevue Pl. | 10500 NE Eighth St., 21st fl. (bet. Bellevue Way & 106th Ave.) | 425-462-4662
www.schwartzbros.com

"Perfectly cooked" prime cuts of meat come with sides of "unbeatable views" and "VIP"-worthy service at this "class-act" Seattle-area steakhouse mini-chain; the bill results in some "sticker shock", so the "busy" room is the spot for a "business dinner" or "special occasion", while the budget-minded put away "delicious, filling" appetizers at the "amazing" happy hour.

Dick's Drive-In ●🖨 *Burgers*

24 | 15 | 22 | $9

Capitol Hill | 115 Broadway E. (bet. Denny & Olive Ways) | 206-323-1300
Crown Hill | 9208 Holman Rd. NW (bet. 12th & 13th Aves.) | 206-783-5233
Wallingford | 111 NE 45th St. (bet. 1st & 2nd Aves.) | 206-632-5125
Lake City | 12325 30th Ave. NE (bet. Lake City Way & 125th St.) | 206-363-7777
Queen Anne | 500 Queen Anne Ave. N. (Republican St.) | 206-285-5155
Edmonds | 21910 Hwy. 99 (bet. 216th & 220th Sts.) | 425-775-4243
www.ddir.com

"Unchanged" since the '50s, this "legendary" Seattle chain of "fast-food joints" earns its "cult following" with "always-fresh burgers", "homemade french fries" and "hand-dipped shakes", made with "lightning-fast" speed and for prices that "don't break the bank"; since "everyone goes here", lines can be "long", even up to the 2 AM closing time; P.S. cash only.

Facing East *Taiwanese*

28 | 21 | 22 | $19

Bellevue | Belgate Plaza | 1075 Bellevue Way NE (bet. 10th & 12th Sts.) | 425-688-2986 | www.facingeastrestaurant.com

"Don't worry about the long lines" at this Bellevue strip-mall "favorite": expats and locals alike say it's just part of the "pre-dinner ritual" for those who want to indulge in "interesting", "authentic" Taiwanese fare "not found anywhere" else in town; "reasonable" prices and "fast", "super-friendly" servers help keep the "unpretentious", modern room "packed."

The Georgian *French/Pacific NW*

27 | 29 | 28 | $53

Downtown | Fairmont Olympic Hotel | 411 University St. (bet. 4th & 5th Aves.) | 206-621-7889 | www.fairmont.com

The "old-world surroundings" in this 1924 Italianate dining room in Downtown's Fairmont Olympic Hotel make it a "special place for a special night", with "crystal chandeliers", "high, high ceilings", 11 tints of buttercream paint on the walls and the No. 1 ranking for Decor in Seattle; the "elegant", "outstanding" Pacific Northwest-French fare is delivered by "gracious, welcoming" servers, and while "you pay for the spectacular" experience, fans say it's "worth the splurge"; P.S. the prix fixe lunch is an "unbelievable deal."

Harvest Vine *Spanish*
27 | 23 | 24 | $45

Madison Valley | 2701 E. Madison St. (27th Ave.) | 206-320-9771 | www.harvestvine.com

At this "quaint" Madison Valley *cocina*, fans feel as if they're "being entertained at a great dinner party" when they "sit at the bar" and watch the chefs "work their magic" whipping up "unusual, authentic" (and "expensive") Basque tapas; "unobtrusive" servers patrol an "intimate" space that gets "crowded" and "noisy", though the "romantic" wine cellar filled with "carefully chosen" Spanish bottles provides a "quieter" dining experience.

The Herbfarm Ⓜ *Pacific NW*
28 | 26 | 28 | $215

Woodinville | 14590 NE 145th St. (Woodinville-Redmond Rd.) | 425-485-5300 | www.theherbfarm.com

The "world-class" tasting menu at this Woodinville "culinary retreat" highlights "subtle herbs" and other esoteric Pacific NW ingredients, along with "free-flowing" wine pairings (no à la carte); starting with a "garden tour", an "enchanted evening" here includes a "story" about the night's offerings, "impeccable" service and an "astronomically expensive" bill to match the "unforgettable" experience; P.S. since the "adventure" can last more than four hours, some "stay the night" in the onsite suites.

Il Terrazzo Carmine Ⓢ *Italian*
29 | 27 | 28 | $56

Pioneer Square | 411 First Ave. S. (bet. Jackson & King Sts.) | 206-467-7797 | www.ilterrazzocarmine.com

This "legendary" Pioneer Square Italian is "a must" among "movers and shakers" who dig into "solid, traditional" entrees and sip "grand martinis" or pours from the "extensive" wine list; "hidden" in an office building, the "charming dining room" has a "warm, inviting atmosphere" and features "top-notch" service that's "reminiscent of New York" (as are the "expensive" prices).

Kisaku *Japanese*
27 | 20 | 24 | $35

Wallingford | 2101 N. 55th St. (Meridian Ave.) | 206-545-9050 | www.kisaku.com

The "secret" is out about this Wallingford Japanese "neighborhood treasure", where "master" chef Ryuichi Nakano sates locals with "melt-in-your-mouth" sushi and "superb" contemporary cooked dishes; while families appreciate the "kid-friendly" service and "reasonable prices", the cognoscenti ask for the "off-menu" special rolls or sit at the bar and order the "impeccable" omakase; P.S. closed Tuesdays.

La Carta de Oaxaca Ⓢ *Mexican*
26 | 21 | 21 | $23

Ballard | 5431 Ballard Ave. NW (22nd Ave.) | 206-782-8722

Mezcaleria Oaxaca Ⓢ *Mexican*

Queen Anne | 2123 Queen Anne Ave. N. (bet. Boston & Crockett Sts.) | 206-216-4446
www.lacartadeoaxaca.com

So "authentic" there's an *abuela* "in the kitchen making the tortillas", these "friendly" Ballard and Queen Anne eateries turn out "killer mole" and other Oaxacan specialties; arty "black-and-white images of Mexico" make the "hopping" spots feel a cut above "typical" taquerias, while "reasonable prices" and "must-try" margaritas explain the "long waits" for a table; P.S. the Queen Anne Avenue location specializes in cocktails made from its mescal namesake.

La Medusa ⊠ Ⓜ Italian | 28 | 21 | 25 | $37 |
Columbia City | 4857 Rainier Ave. S. (Edmunds St.) | 206-723-2192 | www.lamedusarestaurant.com

At this "casual" Italian in Columbia City, "creative globe-trotters" in an "open kitchen" concoct some of the "best Sicilian soul food this side of Palermo"; "friendly" servers contribute to the "warm, welcoming" ambiance in the "vibrant" (and "often-crowded") storefront space, where the "reasonably priced" menu on a "large chalkboard" gets updated regularly; P.S. Wednesdays May–October, a moderately priced set menu highlights farmer's market finds.

Lark Ⓜ American | 27 | 22 | 25 | $51 |
Capitol Hill | 926 12th Ave. (bet. Marion & Spring Sts.) | 206-323-5275 | www.larkseattle.com

In the heart of Capitol Hill, John Sundstrom's American "standout" enchants with "inventive", "locally sourced" small plates that are "fun to share"; "professional" yet "personal" service and a "relaxing" vibe make the "tasteful", "rustic" room "feel like it's full of friends", and while all those "incredibly tasty dishes" can make the bill "pricier than expected", most agree the "serious culinary experience" is "worth every penny."

Le Rêve Bakery Bakery/French | 28 | 22 | 24 | $11 |
Queen Anne | 1805 Queen Anne Ave. N. (Blaine St.) | 206-623-7383 | www.lerevebakery.com

"*Incroyable!*" say *amis* who "love" this "amazing bakery" quartered in a "quaint", "little old house" in Queen Anne where "great pastries", "to-die-for" cakes and other reasonably priced goodies are "not only pretty to look at" but "melt-in-your-mouth good"; though service isn't "super-fast", it's "cozy" inside, and the patio is the place to sip a "yummy coffee" and watch locals "stroll by on a sunny day."

Matt's in the Market ⊠ Pacific NW/Seafood | 26 | 21 | 24 | $37 |
Pike Place Market | 94 Pike St., Ste. 32 (1st Ave.) | 206-467-7909 | www.mattsinthemarket.com

"Busy but wonderful", this midrange Pacific NW stalwart on the third floor of Pike Place Market wins fans with its "excellent" seafood and meat offerings (including a "not-to-be-missed" catfish sandwich), as well as "seasonal specials", all made with "inventive flair"; views of Elliott Bay, "cool waiters" and a "deep and wide wine list" help make this the perfect "grand finale" after a "day of sightseeing."

Metropolitan Grill Steak | 27 | 25 | 27 | $69 |
Downtown | 820 Second Ave. (bet. Columbia & Marion Sts.) | 206-624-3287 | www.themetropolitangrill.com

This "old-school" Downtown meatery is a "staple" with the "power lunch" crowd for its "amazing cuts" of dry-aged beef ("don't tell your cardiologist") and "classic sides" such as "to-die-for" mashed potatoes; the "retro steakhouse atmosphere" extends to "comfy booths", "wood and brass" furnishings and "insightful" staffers – just expect a "big bill to go with it" all.

Nell's *American*   28 | 20 | 27 | $44

Green Lake | 6804 E. Green Lake Way N. (2nd Ave.) | 206-524-4044 | www.nellsrestaurant.com

In a "hidden storefront" across from Green Lake, chef Philip Mihalski's "oasis of serenity" wins accolades for "imaginative" American creations made from the "best local, seasonal ingredients" and paired with a "killer wine list"; the basic room looks a tad "tired" to some, but to those who appreciate "relaxed" yet "food-savvy" servers and a "quiet atmosphere", it's a "happy place."

Nishino *Japanese*   29 | 23 | 27 | $54

Madison Park | 3130 E. Madison St. (Lake Washington Blvd.) | 206-322-5800 | www.nishinorestaurant.com

Kyoto-born Nobu alum Tatsu Nishino conceives "delicate, inventive" and altogether "amazing" sushi for deep-pocketed fin fans at his "low-key" Madison Park Japanese; "expert" service and "masterpieces on the walls" by local artist Fay Jones put diners "in a Zen state", but those who want a truly transporting experience know "it's all about" the "straight-from-heaven" omakase menu (just be sure to "order a few days ahead").

Paseo 🗷Ⓜ⇆ *Cuban/Sandwiches*   28 | 12 | 20 | $13

Shilshole | 6226 Seaview Ave. NW (62nd St.) | 206-789-3100
Fremont | 4225 Fremont Ave. N. (bet. 42nd & 43rd Sts.) | 206-545-7440
www.paseoseattle.com

"Man, oh man" moan Cuban cuisine enthusiasts enamored of the signature "chin-dripping-delicious" Caribbean Roast sandwich "bursting with tender, slow-cooked pork" at these "tiny", "tumbledown" shacks in Fremont and Shilshole; there's "limited seating" and they often "run out of the most popular items", but that doesn't stop lines that "go out the door"; P.S. it's cash only, though you won't need much.

Radiator Whiskey *American*   - | - | - | M

Pike Place Market | 94 Pike St. (1st Ave.) | 206-467-4268 | www.radiatorwhiskey.com

Downright cheeky New American eats (think smoked pig head) join over a hundred whiskeys at this gastropub sibling of Matt's, which is also in Pike Place Market; the room itself resembles the inside of a whiskey barrel, what with all the reclaimed wood cladding, and it's often packed with after-work cubicle dwellers and stylish young couples, which makes reservations a dram good idea.

Ray's Boathouse *Pacific NW/Seafood*   25 | 25 | 24 | $45

Shilshole | 6049 Seaview Ave. NW (61st St.) | 206-789-3770 | www.rays.com

"It doesn't get any better" than tucking into "simply outstanding" Pacific NW wild seafood as you "watch the sun set" at this perennial fave boasting "spectacular views" of Shilshole Bay; with service that's "first-class all the way", it's "well worth the money" for a "romantic evening" or impressing "visiting friends"; P.S. "go for Copper River salmon that melts in your blissful mouth" during its limited springtime run.

Revel *American/Korean*

26 | 22 | 22 | $33

Fremont | 403 N. 36th St. (Phinney Ave.) | 206-547-2040 |
www.revelseattle.com

Iron Chef team Rachel Yang and Seif Chirchi's "fusion of French" technique, American flavors and "Korean street food" yields revel-atory
results in the form of "spicy", full-flavored and "reasonably priced"
small plates at this "urban party experience" in Fremont; the industrial-
chic interior can get "noisy" when full, while "custom" drinks at Quoin,
the adjacent 21-and-over lounge, help ease "long waits" for a table.

Salumi 🅂 Ⓜ *Italian/Sandwiches*

28 | 14 | 20 | $17

Pioneer Square | 309 Third Ave. S. (bet. Jackson & Main Sts.) |
206-621-8772 | www.salumicuredmeats.com

Gina Batali (yep, "Mario's sister") "knows what she's doing" at her
Pioneer Square "Italian paradise", where fans wait in "long lines" for
"massive sandwiches" of "insanely good" house-cured salami in addition to other "delicious" deli specialties; just know there's "limited"
communal seating, making takeout a popular option; P.S. open Tuesday-
Friday until mid-afternoon, but "get there early" since popular items
can "run out."

Seastar Restaurant & Raw Bar *Seafood*

27 | 25 | 25 | $52

South Lake Union | 2121 Terry Ave. (bet. Denny Way & Lenora St.) |
206-462-4364

Bellevue | Civica Office Commons | 205 108th Ave. NE (2nd St.) |
425-456-0010

www.seastarrestaurant.com

John Howie's "outstanding", "upscale" seafooders are "definitely
keepers" to admirers of his "stellar" takes on the "freshest" fin fare;
though prices are "expensive", the oyster shucking and sushi making
at the raw bars is a "show in itself", while "high-end service" and
"airy", modern spaces filled with "swells" complete the package;
P.S. Bellevue gets props for "power dinners", while the South Lake
Union outpost is in an up-and-coming area.

Serious Pie *Pizza*

26 | 19 | 21 | $26

Downtown | 316 Virginia St. (bet. 3rd & 4th Aves.) | 206-838-7388 |
www.tomdouglas.com

South Lake Union | 401 Westlake Ave. N. (Harrison St.) | 206-436-0050 |
www.seriouspiewestlake.com

"The name says it all" at this "transformational" pizzeria, where
"wood-fired" "cracker-thin" crusts sport "seriously inventive" toppings of "fresh artisanal ingredients"; servers are "attentive", and
though there are "long waits" and some find the tabs a tad "pricey",
it's all "worth it" to savor "what pizza is supposed to be"; P.S. the "tiny"
Downtown original's "communal tables" mean "you'll get cozy with
your neighbors", while South Lake Union is larger.

Shiro's Sushi *Japanese*

28 | 20 | 25 | $53

Belltown | 2401 Second Ave. (Battery St.) | 206-443-9844 |
www.shiros.com

Shiro Kashiba is semiretired now, but the "true master" still pops in at
his Belltown stalwart, where "purists" say his omakase is one of the
"best sushi experiences" and the "lavish" à la carte menu is "as good
as it gets"; sure, it can be "a little spendy", but the "professional" staff

is "attentive", and the "spartan" room full of Japanese "expats" attracts celebs too, helping make dinner here a "night of entertainment."

Sitka & Spruce *Eclectic*   26 | 23 | 23 | $47

Capitol Hill | Melrose Mkt. | 1531 Melrose Ave. (bet. Pike & Pine Sts.) | 206-324-0662 | www.sitkaandspruce.com

Even simple "seasonal" ingredients become "cutting-edge" at chef-owner Matthew Dillon's "airy, modern" Eclectic set in Capitol Hill's Melrose Market; though it can be "tough to get a last-minute table" and you should "be prepared to spend some money to get full" on the "small plates", the staff is "knowledgeable" and Monday's taco night is a "must-try."

Spinasse *Italian*   28 | 21 | 25 | $54

Capitol Hill | 1531 14th Ave. (bet. Pike & Pine Sts.) | 206-251-7673 | www.spinasse.com

Chef Jason Stratton turns to the Piedmont region for inspiration at his "must-try" Capitol Hill trattoria, where "attentive" servers deliver "delicate, sublime" (and "pricey") pastas paired with "light" sauces and "rustic", meaty ragus; savvy regulars who say the "small" space can get "noisy and crowded" opt for seats at the "kitchen-view" bar so they can "feel like they're cooking with the chef"; P.S. hit the adjacent bar, Artusi, for a "drink while you wait."

Staple & Fancy Mercantile *Italian*   29 | 25 | 26 | $48

Ballard | Kolstrand Bldg. | 4739 Ballard Ave. NW (bet. Dock Pl. & 17th Ave.) | 206-789-1200 | www.ethanstowellrestaurants.com

Ethan Stowell's "spectacular" Italian elicits "OMG"s for the "smashingly good" four-course tasting menu, as well as the "constantly changing dishes" among the "incredible" à la carte options, all at relatively "low" prices; the "great location" on "gentrifying" Ballard Avenue adds to the "adventure", and though the namesake former grocer's space has brick walls, the room is quiet enough to "carry on a conversation."

Tat's Deli ⧆ *American/Deli*   28 | 15 | 22 | $12

Pioneer Square | 159 Yesler Way (2nd Ave.) | 206-264-8287 | www.tatsdeli.com

"Eat these with your sleeves rolled up" warn advocates of the "huge", "sloppy", "yummy" sandwiches at this "piece of the East Coast" in Pioneer Square; there can be "long lines at lunch" (a webcam helps gauge wait times), but the price is right for "satisfying" fare that fans say is "so much better than chains."

13 Coins ❶ *American/Italian*   24 | 21 | 23 | $34

South Lake Union | 125 Boren Ave. N. (bet. Denny Way & John St.) | 206-682-2513
SeaTac | 18000 International Blvd. (bet. 180th & 182nd Sts.) | 206-243-9500
www.13coins.com

Enter a "time warp" at these "funky" SeaTac and South Lake Union 24/7 "landmarks" – which qualify as Seattle's Most Popular – featuring an "extensive menu" of "yummy" Italian classics, standard American lunch fare and "hangover-cure" breakfasts, in addition to "no-fuss service" and "great people-watching" ("especially in the wee hours"); while the "high-backed booths" provide "privacy", regulars often prefer the "swivel seating" at the bar, where they can banter with "witty" chefs who fire up "off-the-menu" requests.

The Whale Wins European/Pacific NW

| - | - | - | M |

Fremont | Fremont Collective | 3506 Stone Way N. (bet. 35th & 36th Sts.) | 206-632-9425 | www.thewhalewins.com

Inside the Fremont Collective retail-and-restaurant space, this mid-range European/Pacific NW venue from Renee Erickson (Boat Street Cafe, The Walrus & the Carpenter) turns out roasted local specialties such as clams and seasonal veggies from a wood-fired oven; the white-and-blue cottagelike room couldn't be more welcoming, what with an art installation suspended from the ceiling that spells out 'hello'; P.S. it shares an entrance with another restaurant, Joule.

Wild Ginger Pacific Rim

| 25 | 24 | 23 | $38 |

Downtown | Mann Bldg. | 1401 Third Ave. (Union St.) | 206-623-4450
Bellevue | The Bravern | 11020 NE Sixth St. (110th Ave.) | 425-495-8889
www.wildginger.net

"Exceptional" Pacific Rim fare - think rave-worthy "duck buns" and other "creative", "rather expensive" dishes with housemade sauces - makes this Downtown and Bellevue duo a "must-go"; the "attentive" staff ably handles the "business lunches" and "pre-symphony crowds" in the "sleek", "sexy" Downtown branch, while the Bellevue location features "happy-hour bargains" and weekend dim sum brunches.

Tampa/Sarasota

TOP FOOD RANKING

	Restaurant	Cuisine
29	Beach Bistro	Floridian
28	Restaurant BT	French/Vietnamese
27	Cafe Ponte	American
	Maison Blanche	French
	SideBern's	Mediterranean
26	Mise en Place	American
	Bern's Steak House	Steak
	Morel	American/Continental
	Mozaic	Mediterranean
	Refinery*	American
	Selva	Peruvian

OTHER NOTEWORTHY PLACES

Bonefish Grill	Seafood
Columbia	Cuban/Spanish
CopperFish	Seafood
Datz	Eclectic
Edison	American
Euphemia Haye	American/European
Indigenous	American
Michael's On East	American
Pané Rustica	Italian
Z Grille	American

Beach Bistro *Floridian*   29 | 26 | 28 | $77

Holmes Beach | Resort Sixty-Six | 6600 Gulf Dr. (66th St.) | 941-778-6444 | www.beachbistro.com

"Always on top of its game", Sean Murphy's Anna Maria Island "jewel" is "one of the best restaurants" around – indeed, it's rated Tampa/Sarasota's No. 1 for Food and Service thanks to its "perfectly pre-pared" Floridian fare complemented by "refined yet warm" service from waiters who show "an obvious desire to please"; some may find tables "too close" in the "cozy" space, but it's nothing a few "fantastic" drinks can't cure – or reserve a spot outside on the beach and "watch the spectacular sunset"; P.S. if "high prices" are a barrier, sit at the "fun" bar, which has more affordable offerings.

Bern's Steak House *Steak*   26 | 22 | 27 | $75

Tampa | 1208 S. Howard Ave. (bet. Marjory & Watrous Aves.) | 813-251-2421 | www.bernssteakhouse.com

"If it's not broken, why fix it?" ask devotees of this circa-1956 "Tampa landmark", ranked the area's Most Popular restaurant and acclaimed for its "incredible, mouthwatering steaks" and "impeccable" service (it's also "a must for any wine lover" thanks to its "biblical" list); the

---

* Indicates a tie with restaurant above

"old-world" "bordello" look may feel "a bit dated" to some, and tabs aren't cheap, but fans say it's "absolutely worth the treat", especially if you finish with a tour of its "famous" wine cellar and a trip to the "intimate upstairs dessert room."

Bonefish Grill *Seafood*

21 | 19 | 21 | $36

Bradenton | 7456 W. Cortez Rd. (75th St.) | 941-795-8020
Sarasota | 3971 S. Tamiami Trail (Liberty Way) | 941-924-9090
Sarasota | Shoppes at University Ctr. | 8101 Cooper Creek Blvd. (University Pkwy.) | 941-360-3171
Bellaire Bluffs | 2939 W. Bay Dr. (Sunset Blvd.) | 727-518-1230
Clearwater | 2519 McMullen Booth Rd. (Enterprise Rd.) | 727-726-1315
St. Petersburg | 5062 Fourth St. N. (51st. Ave.) | 727-521-3434
Brandon | 1015 Providence Rd. (Lumsden Rd.) | 813-571-5553
Tampa | 3665 Henderson Blvd. (Sterling Ave.) | 813-876-3535
Trinity | 10750 State Rd. 54 (Duck Slough Blvd.) | 727-372-7540
Wesley Chapel | The Shoppes at New Tampa | 1640 Bruce B. Downs Rd. (Williamsburg Dr.) | 813-907-8202
www.bonefishgrill.com
Additional locations throughout the Tampa/Sarasota area

This "chain that acts like a local" restaurant "hits all the right notes", with its "consistently good", "well-prepared" seafood in ample quantities (the "Bang Bang Shrimp is a must") served by "professional, friendly" folks in "comfortable" environs that toe the line between "sports bar" and "steakhouse"; while "noisy", it has a "fun bar scene", and though not exactly cheap, it offers "value"-priced specials.

Cafe Ponte *American*

27 | 23 | 26 | $64

Clearwater | Icot Ctr. | 13505 Icot Blvd. (Ulmerton Rd.) | 727-538-5768 | www.cafeponte.com

"Phenomenal", "beautifully plated" New American food is the draw at chef-owner Chris Ponte's Clearwater "treasure" that delivers a "superb" dining experience "in every respect"; servers are "attentive but out of the way" in the "elegant" setting with occasional live piano, and though it's "pricey" overall, regulars say the early-bird prix fixe "represents excellent value."

Columbia Restaurant *Cuban/Spanish*

21 | 21 | 20 | $38

Sarasota | 411 St. Armands Circle (John Ringling Blvd.) | 941-388-3987
Clearwater | 1241 Gulf Blvd. (Gulfview Blvd.) | 727-596-8400
Ybor City | 2117 E. Seventh Ave. (bet. 21st & 22nd Sts.) | 813-248-4961
Tampa International | Tampa International Airport – Concourse E | 4100 George J. Bean Pkwy. (Memorial Hwy.) | Tampa | 813-870-8700

Columbia Café *Cuban/Spanish*

Tampa | 801 Old Water St. (Channelside Dr.) | 813-229-5511
www.columbiarestaurant.com

The "historic" Ybor City original that launched this midpriced Cuban-Spanish mini-chain is "Tampa's Taj Mahal" – you should go at least "once in a lifetime" and bask in its "beautiful", airy "garden"-like setting; otherwise, all locations are marked by generally "courteous" service and "well-prepared" food, with notable standouts being the "impressive" black bean soup and "out-of-this-world" 1905 salad.

CopperFish *Seafood*

| - | - | - | E |

Tampa | 1502 S. Howard Ave. (W. Hills Ave.) | 813-251-6789 | www.copperfishtampa.com

Longtime Tampa restaurateur Gordon Davis' upscale New American seafooder stars super-fresh fish (much of it locally caught) grilled over hardwood and complemented by a range of raw-bar items, local veggies and savvy craft cocktails and wine; conversation buzzes in the warmly decorated, smoke-perfumed dining room and out on the patio – and since it's popular, book ahead.

Datz *Eclectic*

| 24 | 21 | 22 | $26 |

Tampa | 2616 S. MacDill Ave. (bet. Barcelona St. & Palmira Ave.) | 813-831-7000 | www.datztampa.com

A "lengthy and unique" menu (bacon tasting flights, curried vegan stew, fish tacos) is anchored by "original spins on classic deli" sandwiches at this "hip", "casual" Eclectic Tampa "foodie" experience that also appeals to "beer connoisseurs" with its "impressive" brew list; the "hard-working" staff is always "on point" in the "energetic" bi-level space that doubles as a gourmet market – and the next-door bakery is "just as yummy."

Edison 🗷 *American*

| 24 | 19 | 22 | $48 |

Tampa | 912 W. Kennedy Blvd. (bet. Edison Ave. & North Blvd.) | 813-254-7111 | www.edison-tampa.com

"Inventive" is the word that best captures the "always interesting", "delicious" American fare dreamed up at this Tampa food laboratory overseen by "amazing" chef-owner Jeannie Pierola; her entire team is equally as "passionate", so if a few deem it "a bit pricey" and note that the industrial digs are "noisy" and seating "should be more comfortable", most call it an "excellent" dining choice.

Euphemia Haye *American/European*

| 26 | 23 | 24 | $62 |

Longboat Key | 5540 Gulf of Mexico Dr. (Gulf Bay Rd.) | 941-383-3633 | www.euphemiahaye.com

Diehards who "have never been disappointed" by this "long-standing" Longboat Key spot say it's "pricey but perfect for a special occasion" on the strength of its "classic" American and European fare ("amazing" Caesar salad, peppercorn steak that's "pure perfection") served in an "intimate" former home; service is "attentive", but those who call it "stuffy" declare the "fun" upstairs "loft is the place to go" for a "lighter meal", "splendid desserts" or a drink at the bar while listening to live jazz nightly.

Indigenous 🗷Ⓜ *American*

| 23 | 20 | 23 | $53 |

Sarasota | 239 S. Links Ave. (Adams Ln.) | 941-706-4740 | www.indigenoussarasota.com

Sarasotans are flocking to Steve Phelps' "casually classy" "farm-to-market" concept, which displays real "integrity in sourcing ingredients" for its "always-innovative" American creations, making it "worth every penny – maybe more"; service is "terrific", but insiders advise "seating is key", and since it can be "noisy" inside the "Old Florida" bungalow, it's best to "sit outside" for a truly "delightful" experience.

	FOOD	DECOR	SERVICE	COST

Maison Blanche ☑ French
27 | 25 | 26 | $86

Longboat Key | 2605 Gulf of Mexico Dr. (Islands Ct.) | 941-383-8088 | www.maisonblancherestaurants.com

"For a very special evening", Francophiles rely on Jose Martinez's "exemplary" Longboat Key "gem" that's "superior is all respects", from its "sophisticated", "exquisite" Gallic cuisine and "extensive" wine list to the "gracious" staff; the "lovely" all-white setting is très "romantic", and though it's "quite costly", remember: "you get what you pay for"; P.S. closes seasonally during summer.

Michael's On East ☒ American
26 | 25 | 25 | $60

Sarasota | Midtown Plaza | 1212 East Ave. S. (Bahia Vista St.) | 941-366-0007 | www.michaelsoneast.com

"Predictably excellent" describes this "high-class" Sarasota "institution", "known for its great steaks" and other "outstanding" New American cuisine bolstered by a "well-chosen" wine list; an "astute" staff patrols the "over-the-top elegant" premises, which include a "fun" piano bar, and though it's "not for diners on a budget", the monthly changing "cutting-edge" global prix fixe menus are a comparative "deal."

Mise en Place ☒☑ American
26 | 24 | 25 | $61

Tampa | 442 W. Kennedy Blvd. (Grand Central Ave.) | 813-254-5373 | www.miseonline.com

Marty Blitz's "gastronomic tour de force" remains a "long-standing favorite" of fans who say his University of Tampa-area New American is still "hitting on all cylinders" with its "innovative", "carefully designed" menu and "superb" wine pairings that "add to every bite"; an "upscale" yet "welcoming" setting supported by "friendly, professional" service makes it "perfect for a romantic evening or a special occasion", especially given the "reasonable" (for the quality) tabs.

Morel ☑ American/Continental
26 | 18 | 25 | $51

Sarasota | 3809 S. Tuttle Ave. (bet. Bee Ridge & Homasassa Rds.) | 941-927-8716 | www.morelrestaurant.com

"Don't be put off by first sight" of this Sarasota strip-mall bistro because "every patron is individually attended to" by the "old-world" staffers who deliver the "excellent" American-Continental fare (the signature mushroom soup is the "best"); yes, it's "small" and a bit "pricey", but all things considered it's a "neighborhood jewel."

Mozaic Mediterranean
26 | 19 | 22 | $56

Sarasota | 1377 Main St. (bet. Palm & Pineapple Aves.) | 941-951-6272 | www.mozaicsarasota.com

Moroccan chef Dylan Elhajoui "puts soul" into "every single piece of food" served at this "hospitable" Mediterranean "change of pace" for Sarasota that's notable for "melding distinctive flavors and influences"; the "bright" and "cheery" bi-level space is "small", and though the prices are not, most say it's "worth the cost."

Pané Rustica ☑ Italian
25 | 18 | 22 | $38

Tampa | 3225 S. MacDill Ave. (Bay to Bay Blvd.) | 813-902-8828 | www.panerusticabakery.com

"There's so much to choose from" that there's "no choice but to keep coming back" to this "friendly" South Tampa bakery/cafe/bar/restaurant with a "varied" menu of "well-executed" Italian-leaning fare that includes sandwiches, pastas, pizza, small plates, hearty entrees and baked goods; lunch is "fast paced" and "casual" with lots of orders to go, while dinner is more of a "dining experience" – but either way it can be "loud" in the "open", Tuscan-looking space centered on a large U-shaped bar.

The Refinery *American*

| 26 | 18 | 24 | $36 |

Tampa | 5137 N. Florida Ave. (Frierson Ave.) | 813-237-2000 | www.thetamparefinery.com

"Each visit provides a delicious, new dish to discover" thanks to the weekly changing American menu at this homey, "relaxed gem" in Tampa where a real "artist" of a chef is "continually inventive" with local, seasonal ingredients; add in an "informed", "über-courteous" staff, "awesome" craft beer and "top-notch" wine and most agree that "for the price, you can't beat it"; P.S. the "rooftop deck is great on cool nights."

Restaurant BT 🖂🅜 *French/Vietnamese*

| 28 | 22 | 22 | $66 |

Tampa | 2507 S. MacDill Ave. (Palmira Ave.) | 813-258-1916 | www.restaurantbt.com

"Spunky" chef-owner BT Nguyen is "a master" say fans of the "superb", "high-style" French-Vietnamese dishes that look like "works of art" at this Tampa retreat; "Zen-like" decor and attentive service abet the "relaxing" vibe, though diners may leave with "empty" wallets.

Selva *Peruvian*

| 26 | 23 | 23 | $55 |

Sarasota | 1345 Main St. (N. Palm Ave.) | 941-362-4427 | www.selvagrill.com

"Always terrific" Peruvian fare – including "super ceviche" – in "impressive" presentations "keeps you busy looking at every plate that goes by" at this "pricey" but popular Downtown Sarasota resto-lounge; there's "good people-watching" from the sidewalk tables, while the "trendy" neon-lit interior is a "cool, hip" spot to "relax", especially with the aid of "great" cocktails served by a "professional" staff.

SideBern's 🖂 *Mediterranean*

| 27 | 26 | 26 | $62 |

Tampa | 2208 W. Morrison Ave. (Howard Ave.) | 813-258-2233 | www.sideberns.com

"More adventurous" than big papa Bern's Steak House down the street (but "with the same well-trained staff" and similar high tabs), this Tampa eatery constantly "surprises" with its "creative", "quality" Mediterranean cuisine; it's "the place to be seen" for a "younger crowd" that is drawn to its "less stuffy yet refined" atmosphere and an "extensive" list of wines, most available at the attached wine shop.

Z Grille 🖂 *American*

| 24 | 20 | 20 | $45 |

St. Petersburg | 104 Second St. S. (bet. 1st Ave. & 2nd St.) | 727-822-9600 | www.zgrille.net

"On the cutting edge for St. Pete", this flashy Downtown New American from chef Zack Gross is a "must-try" on account of the "delicious", decadent comfort food's "interesting" flavor combos (Dr. Pepper ribs, cornflake-fried chicken); a "cool" "modern" setting with "on-par" service and an "excellent" wine and beer selection add to the "great atmosphere."

Washington, DC, Metro Area

Restaurant	Cuisine
28 Rasika	Indian
L'Auberge Chez François	French
Komi	American/Mediterranean
Marcel's	Belgian/French
Prime Rib	Steak
Corduroy	American
Minibar	Eclectic
Obelisk	Italian
Little Serow	Thai
Peking Duck	Chinese
27 CityZen	American
Restaurant Eve	American
Makoto	Japanese
Russia House	Russian
Palena	American
Ray's The Steaks	Steak
Blue Duck Tavern	American
Tosca	Italian
BlackSalt	American/Seafood
Fiola	Italian

OTHER NOTEWORTHY PLACES

Bourbon	Steak
Bread Line	Bakery/Sandwiches
Central Michel Richard	American/French
Clyde's	American
Cork	American
Five Guys	Burgers
Inn at Little Washington	American
Johnny's Half Shell	American/Seafood
Le Diplomate	French
Mintwood Place	American
NoPa Kitchen + Bar	American
Range	American
Ris	American
1789	American
Source	Asian
2941 Restaurant	American
2 Amys	Pizza
Vidalia	Southern
Volt	American
Zaytinya	Mediterranean/Mideastern

FOOD | DECOR | SERVICE | COST

BlackSalt *American/Seafood*

27 | 21 | 23 | $55

Palisades | 4883 MacArthur Blvd. NW (U St.) | 202-342-9101 |
www.blacksaltrestaurant.com

"Inventive, gorgeous and impeccably executed" New American seafood at "not-quite lobbyist prices" is served with "care" at the Black Restaurant Group's "popular" Palisades flagship; if the "decor is not up to the quality of the food", it's not apparent from the "sit-and-be-seen" hordes always packing the "fun bar", "lively" main dining room and somewhat more "intimate" and "elegant" back room; P.S. it's "hard to resist" the "terrific" on-site market for "fresh, fresh, fresh" fish "on your way out."

Blue Duck Tavern *American*

27 | 25 | 26 | $64

West End | Park Hyatt | 1201 24th St. NW (bet. M & N Sts.) |
202-419-6755 | www.blueducktavern.com

Birds of a feather are "wowed every time" by the elevated, "beautifully crafted" "comfort food" at this "elegant" West End New American; just as ducky: it's "high on style and low on pretension", with an "extremely gracious" staff that "knows how to show you a good time" in "modern", "Shaker-inspired" environs that are often graced by "famous" faces; P.S. should the bill "make you 'blue'", there are "lower prices" at lunch, and in the bar/lounge.

Bourbon Steak *Steak*

25 | 25 | 25 | $70

Georgetown | Four Seasons Hotel Washington DC | 2800 Pennsylvania Ave. NW (28th St.) | 202-944-2026 | www.bourbonsteakdc.com

"Of course the steaks are superb" at Michael Mina's DC chophouse, but "trust the chefs" to take you on an "amazing adventure" via the rest of the "inventive" New American menu at this "popular" Four Seasons venue – "the place to see, be seen and spend money in Georgetown"; "impeccable service" is de rigueur and "celebrity sightings" are common in the "modern and polished" dining room, as well as the bar that's "rife with power-sippers (and those looking to get attached to them)."

Bread Line 🗷 *Bakery/Sandwiches*

23 | 12 | 17 | $15

World Bank | 1751 Pennsylvania Ave. NW (bet. 17th & 18th Sts.) |
202-822-8900 | www.breadline.com

"It's the bread, stupid", say fans who find the way this gently priced bakery/cafe "down the block" from the White House and World Bank can "pack so many flavors and textures" into one "delicious" sandwich makes for an "unmatched" lunch; at midday, an "efficient" crew moves the "long" queue "fast", though many leave the "stark" industrial premises to sit outside or go "picnicking"; P.S. it's line-free at breakfast, or go for "fine pastry and coffee" in the afternoon.

Central Michel Richard 🗷 *American/French*

26 | 21 | 23 | $54

Penn Quarter | 1001 Pennsylvania Ave. NW (11th St.) | 202-626-0015 |
www.centralmichelrichard.com

"Proving Michel Richard doesn't need beaucoup bucks to be brilliant", his "high-energy brasserie" in Penn Quarter dazzles with its "outstanding" riffs on tradition that run from New American (fried chicken that "slaps the Colonel in the face") to French ("I'm going to marry their faux gras"); a "welcoming" staff and a "casual" vibe let ordinary folk feel like the "movers and shakers" that line the "striking" "modern" dining room and "hopping" bar – in short, a "winner."

CityZen ☒Ⓜ *American* 27 | 27 | 27 | $115

SW | Mandarin Oriental | 1330 Maryland Ave. SW (12th St.) |
202-787-6006 | www.mandarinoriental.com

Chef Eric Ziebold "delivers taste, imagination and fun" via a multicourse menu that adds up to a "fabulous meal full of pleasant surprises" at this "stunningly beautiful" "Nouvelle American" "destination" in the Mandarin Oriental; a "personal touch from the minute you walk in the door" enhances the experience, which leads flush foodies to exult "fine dining is still alive and worth every cent"; P.S. the "very hip" bar offers a "real-bargain" tasting menu.

Clyde's ❶ *American* 22 | 23 | 22 | $33

Chinatown | 707 Seventh St. NW (G St.) | 202-349-3700
Georgetown | Georgetown Park Mall | 3236 M St. NW (bet. Potomac St. & Wisconsin Ave.) | 202-333-9180
Chevy Chase | 5441 Wisconsin Ave. (Wisconsin Circle), MD | 301-951-9600
Rockville | 2 Preserve Pkwy. (bet. Tower Oaks Blvd. & Wootton Pkwy.), MD | 301-294-0200
Greater Alexandria | Mark Ctr. | 1700 N. Beauregard St. (Highview Ln.) | Alexandria, VA | 703-820-8300
Reston | Reston Town Ctr. | 11905 Market St. (bet. Library & Presidents Sts.), VA | 703-787-6601
Tysons Corner | 8332 Leesburg Pike (Pinnacle Dr.) | Vienna, VA | 703-734-1901
Broadlands | Willow Creek Farm | 42920 Broadlands Blvd. (Chickacoan Trail Dr.), VA | 571-209-1200
www.clydes.com

"Nostalgic" themes (old farmhouse, Adirondack lodge, the Golden Age of Travel) make each location of this homegrown American saloon feel like a "unique" "adventure", so it's no wonder they're "popular" stops for everyone from "kids" to "grandma" – indeed, they're Greater DC's Most Popular places to dine; "upbeat" service also plays a role, along with the fact that diners are sure to "get their money's worth" via a "value"-packed menu of "solidly appealing", "honest" eats.

Corduroy ☒ *American* 28 | 25 | 26 | $68

Mt. Vernon Square/Convention Center | 1122 Ninth St. NW (bet. L & M Sts.) | 202-589-0699 | www.corduroydc.com

"Every morsel from the kitchen is a thing of beauty", and matched by "excellent" wines, at Tom Power's "civilized" New American in a townhouse opposite the Convention Center; service that's "polished yet the antithesis of stuffy" and "clean-lined", "modern" decor both strike a balance between "elegant" and "casual", adding up to an "expensive-but-worth-it" experience; P.S. the "hideaway upstairs bar" offers what may be the "best" three-course "bar bargain" in town.

Cork Ⓜ *American* 25 | 22 | 23 | $44

Logan Circle | 1720 14th St. NW (bet. R & S Sts.) | 202-265-2675 | www.corkdc.com

At this über-trendy Logan Circle wine bar, "a huge array of wines by the glass without an outrageous markup" is paired with "delightful" New American small plates with an "extra edge of creativity"; the "well-informed" staff doubles as "eye candy" in the "stylish", brick-walled, "dimly lit" space that gets "loud" and "crowded" late, so best come "early."

Fiola ⊠ *Italian* | 27 | 25 | 26 | $68

Penn Quarter | 601 Pennsylvania Ave. NW (entrance on Indiana Ave. bet. 6th & 7th Sts.) | 202-628-2888 | www.fioladc.com

"Wow", Fabio Trabocchi's "sensational" Penn Quarter venue offers the "complete package" – "his elegant magic touch" with contemporary Italian cuisine, a "fabulous" (and "unstuffy") villalike ambiance plus "extremely engaging" help; aim for a table in the rear to "ogle" the objets d'art and the "lively crowd", and though it's not cheap, tabs are an "unbelievable" value given the "truly wonderful dining experience."

Five Guys *Burgers* | 24 | 14 | 21 | $12

Chinatown | 808 H St. NW (bet. 8th & 9th Sts.) | 202-393-2900
Georgetown | 1335 Wisconsin Ave. NW (Dumbarton St.) | 202-337-0400
Bethesda | 4829 Bethesda Ave. (Arlington Rd.), MD | 301-657-0007
Frederick | 1700 Kingfisher Dr. (Monocacy Blvd.), MD | 301-668-1500
Greater Alexandria | 4626 King St. (bet. Beauregard & 28th Sts.) | Alexandria, VA | 703-671-1606
Greater Alexandria | 7622 Richmond Hwy. (Outlet Rd.) | Alexandria, VA | 703-717-0090
Old Town | 107 N. Fayette St. (bet. Cameron & King Sts.) | Alexandria, VA | 703-549-7991
Herndon | Fox Mill Ctr. | 2521 John Milton Dr. (Fox Mill Rd.), VA | 703-860-9100
Springfield | 6541 Backlick Rd. (Springfield Blvd.), VA | 703-913-1337
Manassas | Manassas Corner | 9221 Sudley Rd. (Centerville Rd.), VA | 703-368-8080
www.fiveguys.com
Additional locations throughout the Washington, DC area

"Hot, juicy and smothered in whatever your heart desires", this is "the way a burger should be" say fans of these ubiquitous counters, rated the DC area's Most Popular chain; while the "sparse" white-and-red-tiled settings earn few raves, "who cares" when "the prices are right" and there are free peanuts to shell while you wait – which won't be long since the "hard-working" crews fill orders "fast."

Inn at Little Washington Restaurant *American* | 29 | 29 | 29 | $205

Washington | Inn at Little Washington | 309 Middle St. (Main St.) | 540-675-3800 | www.theinnatlittlewashington.com

"Simply the best", Patrick O'Connell's hunt-country New American "citadel" delivers a "life-altering experience" as guests get "pampered" in an "intimate", richly embroidered setting, where "revelatory" multicourse repasts are "prepared with extraordinary skill" and seasoned with a "touch of whimsy"; in short, it's "worth every penny . . . and that's a lot of pennies!"; P.S. "spend the night for the ultimate indulgence."

Johnny's Half Shell ⊠ *American/Seafood* | 21 | 20 | 20 | $47

Capitol Hill | 400 N. Capitol St. NW (Louisiana Ave.) | 202-737-0400 | www.johnnyshalfshell.net

Super-"fresh" seafood, seasoned with the "Congressional or Supreme Court gossip" that can be overheard at this Capitol Hill New American's "active bar" or in its "more reserved" dark-wood dining room, powers Ann Cashion and John Fulchino's "tightly run ship"; time-honored Gulf

FOOD | DECOR | SERVICE | COST

and Chesapeake recipes are "prepared with skill and served with speed", live jazz enlivens Saturdays and there's a contemporary look to its spacious courtyard terrace.

Komi ☒Ⓜ *American/Mediterranean* 28 | 22 | 28 | $176

Dupont Circle | 1509 17th St. NW (P St.) | 202-332-9200 | www.komirestaurant.com

Johnny Monis leads diners on a "gastro-adventure" at his Dupont Circle American-Med "temple" offering a "dazzling variety of dishes beautifully prepared and executed" in a "subdued", "understated" setting, made more "relaxing" by a staff that's "detail-oriented without being uptight"; "expect to spend the evening" as they "serve and serve and serve" a fixed-price "parade" of plates along with "witty wine pairings" – and while the "high price" and "hard-to-get reservations" give "mere eaters" pause, food fanatics chant "just go."

L'Auberge Chez François Ⓜ *French* 28 | 27 | 28 | $81

Great Falls | 332 Springvale Rd. (Beach Mill Rd.), VA | 703-759-3800

Jacques' Brasserie Ⓜ *French*

Great Falls | 332 Springvale Rd. (Beach Mill Rd.), VA | 703-759-3800 www.laubergechezfrancois.com

This "fairy-tale destination" in Great Falls, VA, is "like a fine wine that ages beautifully", eternally providing visitors with "wonderful", "gemütlich" Alsatian cuisine that's in perfect harmony with its "charming", "rustic" farmhouse setting; the "unstuffy" staff "pampers" diners during "long and leisurely" multicourse repasts, and though the air is "rarefied", the prix fixe menu means there's "no wincing" over surprises on the bill; P.S. thrifty types may prefer the more "casual ambiance" of the garden-level brasserie, whose à la carte menu has "less impact on your wallet."

Le Diplomate *French* - | - | - | M

Logan Circle | 1601 14th St. NW (Q St.) | 202-332-3333 | www.lediplomatedc.com

Trendy 14th Street NW feels a bit like the Champs-Élysées at Stephen Starr's movie set of a French brasserie, with its zinc bar, tile floors and vintage fittings plus a sidewalk cafe; a menu of Gallic classics completes the scene, along with cocktails, apéritifs, beer and wine, *bien sûr*; P.S. it's been a hit from the get-go, so reserve or go early to nab an outdoor seat.

Little Serow ☒Ⓜ *Thai* 28 | 19 | 27 | $60

Dupont Circle | 1511 17th St. NW (P St.) | www.littleserow.com

"Small in size but packed with flavor and flair", chef-owner Johnny Monis' Issan-style Thai in Dupont Circle "transports" taste buds with "intense and unusual", "kick-your-ass spicy" fare; it's "easier on the pocket" than his celebrated Komi (upstairs next door), and you should "check your control freak at the door" of this "super-dark" cave and let the "incredibly knowledgeable" staff guide you through the "delicious" set-menu journey.

Makoto Ⓜ *Japanese* 27 | 19 | 23 | $78

Palisades | 4822 MacArthur Blvd. NW (U St.) | 202-298-6866

"Leave your shoes – and your ego – at the door" of this tiny Palisades Japanese temple where the "exquisite jewel-box plates" on its multicourse omakase menu come to the table the "chef's way"; the setting is simple and traditional, with "hard" bench seating, but it's "unparalleled in DC" say those who "know the difference", so a little patience and a thick wallet will transport you "half a world away."

Marcel's *Belgian/French*
28 | 26 | 28 | $95

West End | 2401 Pennsylvania Ave. NW (24th St.) | 202-296-1166 | www.marcelsdc.com

"Build your own feast" at this "refined" West End modern French-Belgian by choosing from its "expansive" prix fixe menu selections, all of which showcase the "intricacy" and "subtlety" of Robert Wiedmaier's "brilliant" cuisine; factor in "pampering" service and an "elegant", "special-occasion" atmosphere and you get "full value" for the "expensive" tab – for a real deal, there's a pre-theater option that includes shuttle service to the Kennedy Center.

Minibar by José Andrés 🗷 🖂 *Eclectic*
28 | 21 | 27 | VE

Penn Quarter | 855 E St. NW (bet. 8th & 9th Sts.) | 202-393-0812 | www.minibarbyjoseandres.com

José Andrés' "rock-my-world" Eclectic "culinary adventure" is now firmly transplanted into svelte, modernist Penn Quarter digs, which are studded with playful Gaudí-esque touches (thus outdating the Decor rating); the "mind-bending" multicourse meals, prepared by "engaging" chefs, provide an "expensive" "treat of a lifetime", and though it now hosts a whopping 12 people per seating (double its old location), and has a lounge and bar area for dessert, it's still "nearly impossible" to score a reservation.

Mintwood Place 🖂 *American*
- | - | - | M

Adams Morgan | 1813 Columbia Rd. NW (Biltmore St.) | 202-234-6732 | www.mintwoodplace.com

There's a been-here-forever feel about this convivial, midpriced eatery in Adams Morgan, showcasing Cedric Maupillier's (ex Central Michel Richard) French-accented American cooking, much of it done in a wood-burning oven; the farmhouse-moderne look (pale wainscoting, antique implements) instills an easygoing ambiance, and there's a sidewalk patio for watching the neighborhood pass by.

NoPa Kitchen + Bar *American*
- | - | - | E

Penn Quarter | 800 F St. NW (bet. 8th & 9th Sts.) | 202-347-4667 | www.nopadc.com

Smart and sophisticated, this Penn Quarter American brasserie (from the owners of Rasika) boasts an airy, light-filled bar/lounge and chic dining rooms with whitewashed brick walls, which are conducive to casual, business and celebratory meals; the somewhat pricey menu offers a range of options (raw bar, fish, steaks, salads, sandwiches), and there are several private rooms suitable for large groups and events.

Obelisk 🗷 🖂 *Italian*
28 | 20 | 26 | $98

Dupont Circle | 2029 P St. NW (bet. 20th & 21st Sts.) | 202-872-1180
From the antipasto "spectrum of delights" to sweet endings, a "stellar" prix fixe dinner (no à la carte) at Peter Pastan's Dupont Circle Italian soars to "heights taller than the Washington Monument", DC's other obelisk; the "intimate", "informal" townhouse setting allows diners to focus on "what Italian cooking is really about": "simple but

	FOOD	DECOR	SERVICE	COST

expertly prepared food served by pros", which, along with "superb" wines, is "worth every euro."

Palena *American*

| 27 | 22 | 24 | $98 |

Cleveland Park | 3529 Connecticut Ave. NW (bet. Ordway & Porter Sts.) | 202-537-9250 | www.palenarestaurant.com

"Ambrosia fit for the gods" is on the menus at Frank Ruta's Cleveland Park New American, and fans swear the "quiet", "dimly lit" back room's prix fixe (no à la carte) is "worth" the "expense", while noting the "casual" front cafe is "one of the best bargains in town", with its "succulent" burgers, entrees and a bread basket "worth paying for" – and, indeed, they do charge; service matches the kitchen's "high competency", and a market annex sells "superb" desserts and savories.

Peking Duck Restaurant Ⓜ *Chinese*

| 28 | 18 | 23 | $35 |

Greater Alexandria | 7531 Richmond Hwy. (Woodlawn Trail) | Alexandria, VA | 703-768-2774 | www.pekingduck.com

No canard, "authentic barely begins to describe" this venerable but unassuming-looking Peking duck specialist "all the way out" near Fort Belvoir in Greater Alexandria, where the roasted fowl is sliced "in front of you" just "like in Peking" (er, Beijing); if that doesn't sound ducky, ask the "superb" staff for "suggestions" (hint: "delicious" soups), and have no fear of the bill – it won't bite.

Prime Rib Ⓩ *Steak*

| 28 | 26 | 28 | $71 |

Golden Triangle | 2020 K St. NW (bet. 20th & 21st Sts.) | 202-466-8811 | www.theprimerib.com

Do as they do in *"Mad Men"* – "dress up and have a martini" – at this "classic" Golden Triangle steakhouse that's operating at the "top of its game", delivering "fantastic" "slabs of meat" and "masterful seafood"; from the "1940s supper-club vibe" to the "sublime" tuxedoed service, it's a "perfect evening out"; P.S. business-casual dress is recommended.

Range ◗ *American*

| - | - | - | E |

Chevy Chase | Chevy Chase Pavilion | 5335 Wisconsin Ave. NW (Western Ave.) | 202-803-8020 | www.voltrange.com

Bryan Voltaggio (Frederick's Volt, etc.) is behind this sprawling Chevy Chase enterprise, where long marble bars, polished wood tables and informal groupings of low-backed booths provide a relaxed yet elegant backdrop for a contemporary American menu, which has a fittingly wide range of food choices and price points; there's also plenty to look at, what with multiple open kitchens and hearth stations – not to mention all the eye candy sipping state-of-the-art drinks at the bar.

Rasika Ⓩ *Indian*

| 28 | 25 | 26 | $51 |

Penn Quarter | 633 D St. NW (bet. 6th & 7th Sts.) | 202-637-1222
West End | 1190 New Hampshire Ave. NW (M St.) | 202-466-2500
www.rasikarestaurant.com

"Only superlatives" describe the "mind-blowing" "modern Indian" food that gives diners a "mouthgasm" at this "wildly popular", "classy" Penn Quarter destination (and its newer cosmopolitan West End sister) that has diners "salivating" for dishes like its crispy spinach; "luxurious" appointments, "knowledgeable" servers and a sommelier "savant" create a "sophisticated" environment that further makes it a "bargain for the quality" – translation: "plan early" for a reservation at Penn Quarter (West End is roomier) or "eat at the bar."

Ray's The Steaks *Steak*

27 | 18 | 22 | $46

Courthouse | Navy League Bldg. | 2300 Wilson Blvd. (Adams St.) | Arlington, VA | 703-841-7297 | www.raysthesteaks.com

"No-frills deliciousness" sums up Mike 'Ray' Landrum's Courthouse beefeteria that "rays-es the bar on great steaks" at "bargain-basement prices" – the "breathtaking" hunks are served with two sides along with "affordable" wines in "sparse" white surroundings by "knowl-edgeable", "efficient" servers; "why pay for decor and snootiness at 'fine' steakhouses?" ask acolytes who appreciate "not being nickeled, dimed and dollared", saying this may be the "best restaurant idea in history"; P.S. for those without reservations, there's an overflow space next door under the moniker Retro Ray's.

Restaurant Eve ⊠ Ⓜ *American*

27 | 25 | 26 | $86

Old Town | 110 S. Pitt St. (bet. King & Prince Sts.) | Alexandria, VA | 703-706-0450 | www.restauranteve.com

"You don't just dine" at Cathal Armstrong's "pitch-perfect" Old Town New American, you get a taste of "perfection" as you are "cosseted" in "plush" banquettes in the "romantic" tasting room, where "person-alized" multicourse menus evince the chef's "passion" and "attention to detail"; or head to the connecting bistro and bar to "savor the de-licious food" on the cheap – it offers à la carte choices and, at lunch, there's a two-course "bargain" prix fixe.

Ris *American*

25 | 22 | 24 | $57

West End | 2275 L St. NW (23rd St.) | 202-730-2500 | www.risdc.com

If only the "government was run as well as" Ris Lacoste's West End New American bistro sigh surveyors, citing "gold-star" service and a "polished kitchen" turning out "exciting" "market-fresh" dishes in a "sophisticated", "modern" setting; various deals offer a way around high prices, so whether headed for Kennedy Center, meeting "friends and family" or hanging at the bar, it suits the whole neighborhood.

Russia House Restaurant *Russian*

27 | 23 | 25 | $51

Herndon | 790 Station St. (bet. Elden St. & Park Ave.), VA | 703-787-8880 | www.russiahouserestaurant.com

"Someone in the kitchen truly knows how to cook" say fans of this high-end Herndon spot's "superb" French-influenced Russian special-ties that naturally don't come cheap; cocktails get a boost from the "welcoming" owners' "excellent stash of Russian vodka" ("flavored shots" work too), enhancing the "unique charm" of a "delightful" meal in formal surroundings.

1789 *American*

26 | 25 | 26 | $70

Georgetown | 1226 36th St. NW (Prospect St.) | 202-965-1789 | www.1789restaurant.com

"White gloves and pearls" might suit this "distinguished" Georgetown "classic" with a "refined", "historic" townhouse setting and "expertly prepared" "farm-to-table" New American cooking that together make it a "special place to impress or luxuriate"; politicians and parents vis-iting their kids at the university mean that the "people-watching" (and "eavesdropping") is as good as the food, while a "personable" staff makes diners feel so like "landed gentry" that it's "worth every penny" of its very contemporary prices.

The Source ☒ *Asian* — 27 | 24 | 24 | $68

Penn Quarter | Newseum | 575 Pennsylvania Ave. NW (6th St.) | 202-637-6100 | www.wolfgangpuck.com

"Brilliant East-meets-West fare" is the lead story (with a sidebar on "outstanding" bar bites) at this "hip" Wolfgang Puck destination adjacent to Penn Quarter's Newseum, sporting a "sleek" multilevel setting; "friendly but not intrusive" servers are another reason why subscribers place it in the "expensive-but-worth-it" column.

Tosca ☒ *Italian* — 27 | 24 | 26 | $68

Penn Quarter | 1112 F St. NW (bet. 11th & 12th Sts.) | 202-367-1990 | www.toscadc.com

"Fine dining gets no finer" say fans, than at this "sophisticated" Penn Quarter Italian where the "flawless", uniformed waiters deliver near-"perfect" food as "ex-senators and lobbyists swap business cards" in the "elegant" neutral-toned setting; it's a perfect place for observing "how Washington really works", and the relatively "affordable" pre-theater dinner menu is ideal "for those not on an expense account."

2941 Restaurant ☒ *American* — 27 | 27 | 26 | $70

Falls Church | 2941 Fairview Park Dr. (I-495), VA | 703-270-1500 | www.2941.com

This "French-meets-American" "oasis" "hidden" in a Falls Church office park boasts a "casually elegant" look (recently updated, possibly outdating its Decor rating) to match chef Bertrand Chemel's ambitious bistro menu, which includes a large number of offerings like small plates and pastas at "reasonable" prices; longtime loyalists say the "focused" staff and "stunning" setting – with floor-to-ceiling windows showcasing "beautifully landscaped" grounds – remain as some of the "2,941 reasons to love this place."

2 Amys *Pizza* — 25 | 17 | 20 | $25

Cleveland Park | 3715 Macomb St. NW (Wisconsin Ave.) | 202-885-5700 | www.2amyspizza.com

"Dough my god, the crust!" gush groupies wowed by the "ambrosial" DOC-certified Neapolitan pies at this "popular" Cleveland Park pizzeria (some tout the "exceptional" small plates too); the scene inside the "sunny", white-tiled premises can be "mayhem" – it's a "yuppies-with-kids" magnet – but once the "friendly" staff delivers the "excellent-for-the-price" food, most "everyone is happy" – especially after swigging one of the "treasures on tap" or something from the quieter wine bar's "adventurous selection."

Vidalia *Southern* — 26 | 24 | 25 | $63

Golden Triangle | 1990 M St. NW (bet. 19th & 20th Sts.) | 202-659-1990 | www.vidaliadc.com

"Southern roots" sprout "undeniably cosmopolitan" blossoms on the "inspired" New American menu at this fine-dining "favorite" in Golden Triangle, where the "impeccable" staff makes each meal "an event in itself"; hidden underground, the "comfortably" "elegant" setting is "just right" for "intimate moments" and "special events", with "witty" cocktails and happy-hour specials in the lounge; P.S. for around $20, the three-course lunch is a "fantastic deal."

Volt Ⓜ *American*   28 | 26 | 28 | $104

Frederick | Houck Mansion | 228 N. Market St. (bet. 2nd & 3rd Sts.), MD | 301-696-8658 | www.voltrestaurant.com

An "evening in foodie heaven" awaits at this true "dining destination" in a "beautiful", contemporized 1890s mansion in Frederick, where chef/co-owner Bryan Voltaggio "evokes a sense of wonder" with his "exotically scrumptious" New American meals based on seasonal ingredients; choose from several prix fixe options for dinner, including a "well-choreographed" 21-course "culinary adventure", then let the "incredibly friendly", "top-notch" servers take it from there; "is it expensive? yes – is it really worth it? yes."

Zaytinya *Mediterranean/Mideastern*   26 | 24 | 22 | $43

Penn Quarter | Pepco Bldg. | 701 Ninth St. NW (bet. G & H Sts.) | 202-638-0800 | www.zaytinya.com

"Who can resist" the "wonders" of chef José Andrés' "unbelievably tasty" Eastern Mediterranean meze, especially when paired with "phenomenal" regional wines in a "beautiful, light and airy" setting close to everything in the Penn Quarter; the city's "enduring" "love affair" with this "crazy, loud" stunner means reservations are "highly recommended", but once your "culinary tour" is booked, a "helpful staff" will be your "guide" – just beware: it's "hard to keep the bill down with so many tempting small plates."

Westchester/Hudson Valley

TOP FOOD RANKING

	Restaurant	Cuisine
28	Sushi Nanase	Japanese
	Xaviars at Piermont	American
	Il Cenàcolo	Italian
	Freelance Cafe & Wine Bar	American
27	Restaurant X & Bully Boy Bar	American
	Ocean House	Seafood
	Blue Hill at Stone Barns	American
	X2O Xaviars on the Hudson	American
26	Il Barilotto	Italian
	Restaurant North	American
	La Crémaillère	French
	La Panetière	French
25	No. 9	American
	Zephs'	American/Eclectic
	Union Restaurant & Bar Latino	American/Pan-Latin
	Hokkaido	Japanese
	Iron Horse Grill	American
	Aroma Osteria	Italian
	Ship Lantern Inn	American/Continental
	Crave	American

OTHER NOTEWORTHY PLACES

Restaurant	Cuisine
Arch	American/French
Bocuse	French
Caterina de Medici	Italian
Cookery	Italian
Crabtree's Kittle House	American
Elephant Tapas & Wine Bar	Spanish
Equus	American/French
42	American
Italian Kitchen	Italian
Le Petit Bistro	French
Mercato	Italian
Moderne Barn	American
MP Taverna	Greek
Mulino's	Italian
Polpettina	Italian
Serevan	Mediterranean
Sonora	Nuevo Latino
Sushi Mike's	Japanese
Tarry Lodge	Italian
Willett House	Steak

	FOOD	DECOR	SERVICE	COST

The Arch ⓜ *American/French*   24 | 23 | 23 | $69

Brewster | 1292 Rte. 22 (bet. Milltown & Old Milltown Rds.) |
845-279-5011 | www.archrestaurant.com

For "sophistication in a country setting", devotees turn to this "always-satisfying" Brewster French-American serving "classic" favorites "done to perfection" (including "to-die-for" soufflés) in a "traditional" space whose "old-world charm", "quiet elegance" and "inviting" fire-places provide an ideal backdrop for a "romantic" dinner; though "steep", the "prices are comparable to the excellence" of the cuisine and the "gracious" service from a "dedicated" team; P.S. jackets suggested at dinner.

Aroma Osteria ⓜ *Italian*   25 | 24 | 24 | $48

Wappingers Falls | 114 Old Post Rd. (Rte. 9) | 845-298-6790 |
www.aromaosteriarestaurant.com

"Step into Tuscany" at this "upscale" Wappingers Falls "favorite" where Eduardo Lauria turns out "decadent", "superbly prepared" "classic" Southern Italian plates backed by an "excellent" wine list and presented by an "alert staff" that's "always smiling"; if the "inviting" "traditional" interior is too "noisy" with the sound of diners "celebrating something special", summertime "date-night" duos may prefer the "enjoyable" outdoor terrace.

Blue Hill at Stone Barns ⓜ *American*   27 | 27 | 26 | $121

Pocantico Hills | Stone Barns Center for Food & Agriculture |
630 Bedford Rd. (Lake Rd.) | 914-366-9600 | www.bluehillfarm.com

This "premier" Pocantico Hills New American "encapsulates the best of farm-to-table" dining via Dan Barber's "inspired" prix fixe and tasting menus crafted with "the-ultimate-in-fresh ingredients" harvested from the "spectacular" bucolic grounds; "simple elegance" abounds inside the "beautiful farmhouse" where "service is orchestrated like a ballet", and though it's "not for the faint of wallet", it's "worth it" "for the grand occasion" – just "reserve well in advance", arrive "early to walk around" and be prepared for a "totally original experience" that lasts three to four hours; P.S. closed Monday and Tuesday; jackets and ties preferred.

Bocuse ⓜ *French*   - | - | - | E

Hyde Park | Culinary Institute of America | 1946 Campus Dr.
(Albany Post Rd.) | 845-471-6608 | www.ciarestaurants.com

Legendary French chef Paul Bocuse is the new namesake for this fresh concept in the longtime Escoffier space at Hyde Park's famed Culinary Institute of America, where students cook and serve fresh takes on French regional classics; diners can enjoy tableside preparations in the bright and airy contemporary dining room, but note that it will cost plenty of *sous* (though the three-course prix fixe Tuesday–Thursday is a relative deal).

Caterina de Medici ⓢ *Italian*   25 | 26 | 23 | $52

Hyde Park | Culinary Institute of America | 1946 Campus Dr.
(Albany Post Rd.) | 845-471-6608 | www.ciarestaurants.com

"They know exactly what they're doing" at this "sophisticated" student-staffed "gem" at the Hyde Park CIA where the "chefs of tomorrow" prepare and serve "marvelous" Italian fare in a "lovely", multilevel chandelier-bedecked space that "feels like you're in Tuscany"; a few fans note that staffers are "still learning", but conversing with them can make a meal "even more enjoyable"; P.S. closed weekends.

The Cookery ⓜ *Italian*   24 | 15 | 18 | $47

Dobbs Ferry | 39 Chestnut St. (bet. Main & Palisade Sts.) | 914-305-2336 | www.thecookeryrestaurant.com

A "dynamite take on Italian soul food" blends "rustic and refined flavors" at chef-owner Dave DiBari's "trendy" Dobbs Ferry destination where a "well-meaning" crew serves up "lovingly made" pastas and specials that "rock"; while the "tight quarters", limited reservations policy and often "ear-shattering noise" can sometimes "take away from the experience", most maintain dining in the "warm", "homey" space is "still a pleasure."

Crabtree's Kittle House *American*   24 | 23 | 23 | $65

Chappaqua | Crabtree's Kittle House Inn | 11 Kittle Rd. (Rte. 117) | 914-666-8044 | www.kittlehouse.com

This Chappaqua "château of culinary excellence" "sets the standard" for "civilized dining" with "inspired", albeit "expensive", New American meals (including a "spectacular" Sunday brunch) ferried by "impeccable" staffers who also help you navigate the "world-class" wine list; the "elegant" main dining room is "quiet" and "romantic", though some find the taproom "more relaxed" – either way it's the "perfect" backdrop for a "celebration."

Crave ⓜ *American*   25 | 19 | 22 | $47

Poughkeepsie | 129 Washington St. (bet. Orchard Pl. & Parker Ave.) | 845-452-3501 | www.craverestaurantandlounge.com

"Tucked under the Walkway Over the Hudson", this "lovely" Poughkeepsie New American makes the "perfect" "treat" after a river crossing thanks to "delicious" offerings from a "limited but well-chosen" seasonal menu crafted by chef-owner Edward Kowalski; few mind if it's "a bit pricey" after factoring in the "pleasantly intimate" setting with exposed-brick walls and a staff that "works hard to make you feel welcome."

Elephant Tapas & Wine Bar ⓈⓂ *Spanish*   25 | 18 | 17 | $38

Kingston | 310 Wall St. (bet. Front & John Sts.) | 845-339-9310 | www.elephantwinebar.com

Devotees advise "don't miss" this "lively" Spanish "hipster hangout" in Kingston where "half the fun" is "seeing what new twists" "creative" chef Rich Reeve puts on his minimalist (hot plate, microwave) open kitchen; since the "wonderful" cooking and "knowledgeable" service make it easy to overlook the "tiny", "spare" space, the only drawback is that "costs can mount", what with so many "delicious-sounding" selections.

Equus *American/French*   23 | 27 | 24 | $82

Tarrytown | Castle Hotel & Spa | 400 Benedict Ave. (Martling Ave.) | 914-631-3646 | www.castleonthehudson.com

"Arrive before sundown to take in the view" of the Hudson from this "enchanting" "old castle on the hills of Tarrytown" where "everything is excellent" – from the "superior" service to the "beautifully prepared", "delicious" French–New American fare; it tends to draw a "more sedate crowd" that doesn't mind paying "extraordi-

FOOD DECOR SERVICE COST

nary prices" for the "royal treatment", but the Sunday brunch lets you "save a little."

42 🗷 *American*

20 | 25 | 21 | $71

White Plains | Ritz-Carlton Westchester | 1 Renaissance Sq., 42nd fl. (Main St.) | 914-761-4242 | www.42therestaurant.com

Take "a trip up 42 flights to heaven" implore fans of this "glitzy" dining room in the White Plains Ritz-Carlton that "caters to the upscale, modern" foodie, offering chef Anthony Goncalves' "expertly prepared" New American fare with Iberian touches, enhanced by "gracious service" and "fantastic views"; if the less-wowed find the cuisine a "little too chichi", most feel it's worth "indulging" in – though it perhaps "tastes better on someone else's dime."

Freelance Cafe & Wine Bar Ⓜ *American*

28 | 20 | 25 | $56

Piermont | 506 Piermont Ave. (bet. Ash St. & Tate Ave.) | 845-365-3250 | www.xaviars.com

"Another fabulous dining experience" from Peter Kelly, this "informal brother" of Xaviars next door in Piermont is a "consistent winner" offering "clever", "expertly prepared" New American cooking at a more "reasonable price" than its sibling; sure, it's "tiny and tough to get into" (the "no-reservations policy can make waiting for a table hairy"), but with "so many terrific choices" and an "amiable" staff, fans swear it "always delivers."

Hokkaido *Japanese*

25 | 18 | 19 | $32

New Paltz | 18 Church St. (Front St.) | 845-256-0621 | www.hokkaidonewpaltz.com

"Top-notch quality" lures diners to this "tucked-away" New Paltz "favorite" serving "authentic" Japanese fare distinguished by some of the "freshest and most varied sushi north of New York City"; additional draws are moderate prices and a "low-key", "welcoming" space tended by a team that "wants to please."

Il Barilotto 🗷 *Italian*

26 | 22 | 24 | $48

Fishkill | 1113 Main St. (North St.) | 845-897-4300 | www.ilbarilottorestaurant.com

A sister to Aroma Osteria, this Fishkill "gem" showcases "sophisticated", "upscale" Italian fare "with personality" – including "mouthwatering pastas" and "always-appealing" specials – backed by an "impressive wine list", all served by a "warm", "knowledgeable" team; "from the moment you walk through the door" of this "attractive" restored 1800s carriage house "you feel like you are in Italy – and you can forget the rest of the world."

Il Cenàcolo *Italian*

28 | 22 | 24 | $58

Newburgh | 228 S. Plank Rd. (Gida Rd.) | 845-564-4494 | www.ilcenacolorestaurant.com

With an ambiance that conjures up "shades of Tuscany" as a backdrop for "superb" Northern Italian fare, including "to-die-for" daily specials "reeled off flawlessly" by "incredibly knowledgeable" servers, this "perennial favorite" in Newburgh may be "as close to Italy as you can get in the Hudson Valley"; if a few feel it's "not wallet-friendly", loyalists agree it "doesn't disappoint" for a "special occasion" with "all the bells and whistles."

	FOOD	DECOR	SERVICE	COST

Iron Horse Grill 🏠Ⓜ️ *American* | 25 | 19 | 24 | $63

Pleasantville | 20 Wheeler Ave. (bet. Bedford & Manville Rds.) | 914-741-0717 | www.ironhorsegrill.com
Champions "can't say enough" about this "charming" Pleasantville "destination" delivering "creative", "beautifully presented" New American plates and "interesting" wines "under the watchful eye" of "personable" chef-owner Philip McGrath; a "polished" team "makes up for the close quarters" inside a "transformed train station", and while the "top-of-the-class" fare may be "pricey", few seem to mind (and there are some "wonderful" prix fixe menu deals).

Italian Kitchen *Italian* | 23 | 14 | 20 | $49

Ardsley | 698 Saw Mill River Rd. (bet. Ashford Ave. & Colonial Ct.) | 914-693-5400 | www.ik-ny.com
"Don't be fooled by the pedestrian name" advise fans of this "upscale" yet rustic Ardsley eatery from Shea Gallante, where the "knowledge-able" crew presents an "ever-changing menu" that offers "a slice of Italian heaven" in the form of "rich, delicious" sauces and "freshly pre-pared" pastas; if some grumble about "tight quarters" and "loud" acous-tics, for most it's worth "planning ahead" to snag a "tough" reservation.

La Crémaillère Ⓜ️ *French* | 26 | 25 | 24 | $84

Bedford | 46 Bedford-Banksville Rd. (Round House Rd.) | 914-234-9647 | www.cremaillere.com
A Bedford "treasure" for many decades, this "class act" dispenses "sublime" French fare in a converted white-clapboard 18th-century farmhouse with "enchanting" "old-school elegant decor"; factor in a "gracious" staff both "unobtrusive" and "vigilant to your needs" and no one seems to mind paying "an arm and a leg" for a "true special-event experience"; P.S. jackets suggested.

La Panetière *French* | 26 | 25 | 26 | $82

Rye | 530 Milton Rd. (Oakland Beach Ave.) | 914-967-8140 | www.lapanetiere.com
"Outstanding, classic French" plates with an "original modern twist" are presented like "works of art" along with an "impressive" range of wines by a "refined" staff at this "dignified" Rye "grande dame"; the "flower-filled", Provence-style "country-house" setting makes it feel "like a trip to France", and even if it's "a bit *cher*", connoisseurs con-sider it a "lovely place to celebrate something"; P.S. jackets suggested.

Le Petit Bistro *French* | 24 | 18 | 22 | $50

Rhinebeck | 8 E. Market St. (Mill St.) | 845-876-7400 | www.lepetitbistro.com
"You get the feeling you're in Paris" at this "homey", "romantic" Rhinebeck bistro that has "stood the test of time" with a "classic" menu of "inspired", "authentic French" standards supplemented by "fabu-lous specials" and a "nice wine list"; true to its name, "it's a little tight" inside (reservations are a "must"), but the "sterling", "courteous" staff "makes you comfortable"; P.S. closed Tuesday and Wednesday.

Mercato Ⓜ️ *Italian* | 25 | 17 | 18 | $50

Red Hook | 61 E. Market St./Rte. 199 (Cherry St.) | 845-758-5879 | www.mercatoredhook.com
Fans from "far and wide make the trip" to this "friendly" Red Hook "standout" where Francesco Buitoni of the famed macaroni family

turns out "fabulous", "original" Italian plates complemented by "gently priced" wines; while some may quibble about the "noise level" and "close seating" in the renovated old house, porch tables in season help compensate, plus there's no denying the "perfection" of the pastas.

Moderne Barn American
19 | 23 | 18 | $53

Armonk | 430 Bedford Rd./ Rte. 22 (bet. Cox Ave. & Greenwich Rd.) | 914-730-0001 | www.modernebarn.com

A "broad and appealing" New American menu that has "something for everyone" keeps things "busy" at this "upscale yet relaxed" Armonk "hit" from the Livanos family (City Limits, NYC's Oceana, et al.); sure, the "stylish", "contemporary" space with its "soaring" ceilings can get "loud", especially "on weekends", but fans aren't deterred because it's "the closest you'll get to a NYC restaurant scene in Westchester."

MP Taverna Greek
22 | 21 | 21 | $49

Irvington | 1 Bridge St. (River St.) | 914-231-7854 | www.mptaverna.com

"A refreshing break from your father's taverna", this "lively", "handsome" Irvington spin-off of a Roslyn original set in a "reclaimed factory building by the Hudson" features upscale, "updated versions of Greek favorites" from chef-owner Michael Psilakis (NYC's Kefi) coupled with "extensive" wine and beer offerings; if a handful muse that the "original" fare "sometimes hits and sometimes misses", most deem it a "winner."

Mulino's of Westchester ●Ⓢ Italian
23 | 22 | 23 | $68

White Plains | 99 Court St. (Quarropas St.) | 914-761-1818 | www.mulinosny.com

"Local bigwigs" frequent this "classy" White Plains fixture for "real-deal" Italian eats starting with "out-of-this-world", "free" "Parmesan chunks" and ending with "heavenly" desserts, all delivered in a "formal", "old-school sophisticated" backdrop by a "gracious" staff; it's especially "wonderful" for special occasions or whenever you "don't mind dropping a little extra for a different dining experience."

No. 9 Ⓢ Ⓜ American
25 | 19 | 22 | $54

Millerton | Simmons' Way Village Inn | 53 Main St. (Dutchess Ave.) | 518-592-1299 | www.number9millerton.com

"A true fine-dining experience" in "quaint" Millerton, this "treasure" that's somewhat "hidden" inside the "charming" Simmons' Way Village Inn is "being increasingly discovered" thanks to chef Tim Cocheo's "inventive", "conscientiously prepared" New American cuisine with French and Austrian flourishes; the fare is "skillfully served" by "friendly" folks in a "cozy", "comfortable" setting, and "bargain" midweek prix fixe menus help lighten otherwise slightly "stiff" tabs.

Ocean House Ⓜ Seafood
27 | 17 | 24 | $48

Croton-on-Hudson | 49 N. Riverside Ave. (Farrington Rd.) | 914-271-0702 | oceanhouseoysterbar.com

"Superb seafood" reels in regulars to this "charming" Croton "favorite" set inside a "tiny" restored 1920s diner that feels like a "cross between a dining car and trailer", where an "always-attentive" crew serves up "delicately prepared" fish and some of the "freshest oysters around"; with already "fair prices" and a BYO policy to "keep the costs down", its "no-reservations policy" is the "only drawback."

	FOOD	DECOR	SERVICE	COST

Polpettina *Italian* | 24 | 12 | 18 | $32 |

Eastchester | 102 Fisher Ave. (Maple Ave.) | 914-961-0061 | www.polpettina.com

"A true find" in Eastchester, this "casual" Italian earns locals' "love" with "honest", "tasty" eats like its "excellent" signature meatballs (*polpettina*) and pizza, which are backed by a "grand" beer list; fans who "can't stop going back" almost "hate to tell others" because the "tiny" spot, wrapped with reclaimed wood and exposed bricks, is "already so crowded" at times; P.S. a Larchmont branch is slated to open in fall 2013.

Restaurant North 🈂️Ⓜ️ *American* | 26 | 22 | 23 | $62 |

Armonk | 386 Main St. (bet. Bedford Rd. & Elm St.) | 914-273-8686 | www.restaurantnorth.com

This "happening" Armonk "farm-to-table" "foodie find" earns accolades for its "imaginative", "thoughtfully prepared" New American fare, "smart" wine list and "sophisticated" staff that "makes each guest feel like a star"; "expensive" tabs and "hard-to-get" reservations come with the territory, as does a certain "noise level" – those who find the white-tablecloth main dining room a little too "lively" should "ask for the quieter room upstairs."

Restaurant X & Bully Boy Bar Ⓜ️ *American* | 27 | 24 | 26 | $64 |

Congers | 117 Rte. 303 N. (Lake Rd.) | 845-268-6555 | www.xaviars.com

"Everything sparkles" at Peter Kelly's (Xaviars, et al.) "rustic" Congers New American, from the "elegant", "creative" cooking to the "beautiful" yet "homey" setting that includes a "charming" bar room with a "roaring fire in cold weather"; for a more economical approach to generally "expensive" tabs, try the prix fixe lunch or let the "impeccable" staff present a "never-ending parade of decadent delights" during the "renowned" Sunday champagne brunch.

Serevan *Mediterranean* | 24 | 21 | 22 | $54 |

Amenia | 6 Autumn Ln. (Main St.) | 845-373-9800 | www.serevan.com

"Creative" chef-owner Serge Madikians "works miracles" in the kitchen at this "consistently excellent" Amenia "treasure" "nestled in the woods" where "top-of-the-line" local ingredients meet "heavenly" spices in "delicious" Mediterranean cuisine that's a "treat for the area"; "always-friendly" service and a "sophisticated" yet "homey" farmhouse setting are further reasons why it's "well worth the detour" and the expense.

Ship Lantern Inn Ⓜ️ *American/Continental* | 25 | 23 | 26 | $50 |

Milton | 1725 Rte. 9W (Old Indian Rd.) | 845-795-5400 | www.shiplanterninn.com

For a taste of "what fine dining used to be", boosters laud this "elegant", nautical-themed Milton "favorite" steered by a "jacketed" staff that "anticipates your needs" while performing "tableside food preparations" of "excellent" New American and Continental dishes; "old-world charm" abounds inside the "comfortable" Revolutionary War-era quarters where the "bargain" twilight menu (available 4-6 PM, Tuesday–Friday) offers another way to "feel like you're stepping back in time."

	FOOD	DECOR	SERVICE	COST

Sonora *Nuevo Latino*

| 23 | 19 | 20 | $53 |

Port Chester | 179 Rectory St. (bet. Locust & Willett Aves.) | 914-933-0200 | www.sonorarestaurant.net

"Awesome" chef-owner Rafael Palomino's "creatively prepared and presented" Nuevo Latino fare "never disappoints" at this "energetic" hangout "off the beaten track" in Port Chester where "seriously good" eats plus "powerful drinks" ensure that "you will leave happy"; it's a "little high priced" and the "colorful" confines "can get noisy", but the "caring" staff instills a "warm atmosphere" that makes it "a winner" overall.

Sushi Mike's *Japanese*

| 23 | 11 | 16 | $42 |

Dobbs Ferry | 146 Main St. (Cedar St.) | 914-591-0054 | www.sushimikes.com

"Good luck getting a table" at this "small", "funky" Dobbs Ferry Japanese with "lots of charisma" where owner Mike Suzuki's "hearty greeting" sets the stage for "exuberant" sushi including some of the "most creative rolls this side of Tokyo"; "cramped", "noisy" quarters and somewhat "rushed" service are products of its "popularity", but "takeout is always an option."

Sushi Nanase *Japanese*

| 28 | 17 | 17 | $73 |

White Plains | 522 Mamaroneck Ave. (bet. Bryant Ave. & Shapham Pl.) | 914-285-5351

"Always call for a reservation" before heading to this White Plains Japanese where "unsurpassed sushi" crafted from "perfect, fresh fish" by "hardworking" chef Yoshimichi Takeda earns it the No. 1 Food rating for Westchester/Hudson Valley; the traditional confines are "tiny" and the equally "small" menu is "pricey", but supporters vow that one bite of the "sublime", "artfully presented" fare will leave you "transported."

Tarry Lodge *Italian*

| 22 | 19 | 18 | $52 |

Port Chester | 18 Mill St. (bet. Abendroth Ave. & Main St.) | 914-939-3111 | www.tarrylodge.com

Mario Batali and Joe Bastianich are behind this "happening" Port Chester eatery dispensing "delicious Italian of every kind" from chef Andy Nusser including "outstanding", "fresh-made" pasta and "gourmet" pizza; a "professional" crew tends the "attractive", if "a bit noisy", surroundings, which have a "NYC feel" – and the "big prices" and "hard-to-get reservations" to match.

Union Restaurant & Bar Latino Ⓜ *American/Pan-Latin*

| 25 | 22 | 24 | $47 |

Haverstraw | 22-24 New Main St. (bet. B'way St. & Maple Ave.) | 845-429-4354 | www.unionrestaurant.net

A "fantastic gem" that's "unique for the area", this "comfortable" Haverstraw hacienda dishes up "inventive" New American dishes with a "Latin twist" that "always surprise"; add in "exemplary service", a "good bar crowd" and a "nice" patio, and it's no wonder that fans are unified in considering it an all-around "fun dining experience."

Willett House *Steak*

| 24 | 20 | 21 | $69 |

Port Chester | 20 Willett Ave. (Abendroth Ave.) | 914-939-7500 | www.thewilletthouse.com

This "traditional" Port Chester "standby" pleases carnivores with its "perfectly prepared", "succulent" steaks and "handsome", exposed-

	FOOD	DECOR	SERVICE	COST

brick and mahogany setting inside the turn-of-the-century former Westchester Grain Company building; while the "monstrous cuts" come with appropriately "huge prices", "attentive" service helps make it a "fabulous place for that special occasion" – plus the prix fixe menu is a "relative bargain."

Xaviars at Piermont ⓜ *American*　28 | 25 | 28 | $87

Piermont | 506 Piermont Ave. (bet. Ash St. & Tate Ave.) | 845-359-7007 | www.xaviars.com

"Special nights" start at this Piermont "icon" where Peter Kelly's "inspiring" New American "haute cuisine" is presented by an "incredible" staff (voted tops for Service in Westchester/Hudson Valley) alongside "fine wines" in a "sophisticated" yet "understated setting" that feels "like dining in someone's home"; prices are steep whether you opt for the "wonderful adventure" of a tasting menu or go à la carte, but if you "follow recommendations", it's an "exceptional" experience that's "as good as it gets"; P.S. closed Monday and Tuesday.

X2O Xaviars on the Hudson ⓜ *American*　27 | 27 | 26 | $69

Yonkers | Historic Yonkers Pier | 71 Water Grant St. (Main St.) | 914-965-1111 | www.xaviars.com

"Always an extraordinary experience", this "magnificent" New American – voted Westchester/Hudson Valley's Most Popular restaurant – boasts a "stunning setting" in a "glass-walled box" on the Yonkers pier ("even the ladies' room" has "breathtaking" Hudson River views) coupled with equally "gorgeous", "exciting" plates from the "unbelievably creative" chef-owner Peter Kelly, who "often makes the rounds at the tables"; the "first-class" package includes "meticulous" service and the "prices you'd expect", so for a real "bargain" try the prix fixe lunch and Sunday brunch.

Zephs' ⓜ *American/Eclectic*　25 | 18 | 23 | $56

Peekskill | 638 Central Ave. (Washington St.) | 914-736-2159 | www.zephsrestaurant.com

"Still one of Westchester's gems", chef Victoria Zeph's "unpretentious" Peekskill veteran "stays true to form" with an "ever-changing" New American–Eclectic menu featuring "wonderful, understated" fare "made with love" that's "like home cooking the way you wish it could be"; it's expensive and some find the "intimate" 19th-century mill building confines somewhat "sparse", but "attentive" service "earns respect and loyalty" from diners who've "been eating here for years"; P.S. closed Monday–Wednesday.

ALPHABETICAL
PAGE INDEX